Ius Gentium: Comparative Perspectives on Law and Justice

Volume 131

Ius Gentium is a book series which discusses the central questions of law and justice from a comparative perspective. The books in this series collect the contrasting and overlapping perspectives of lawyers, judges, philosophers and scholars of law from the world's many different jurisdictions for the purposes of comparison, harmonisation, and the progressive development of law and legal institutions. Each volume makes a new comparative study of an important area of law. This book series continues the work of the well-known journal of the same name and provides the basis for a better understanding of all areas of legal science.

The *Ius Gentium* series provides a valuable resource for lawyers, judges, legislators, scholars, and both graduate students and researchers in globalisation, comparative law, legal theory and legal practice. The series has a special focus on the development of international legal standards and transnational legal cooperation.

Doron Goldbarsht • Louis de Koker •
Jamie Ferrill
Editors

Combating Financial Crime

Intended and Unintended Consequences

Springer

Editors
Doron Goldbarsht
Macquarie University and Financial Integrity Hub (FIH)
Sydney, NSW, Australia

Louis de Koker
La Trobe University and Financial Integrity Hub (FIH)
Melbourne, VIC, Australia

Jamie Ferrill
Charles Sturt University and Financial Integrity Hub (FIH)
Canberra, ACT, Australia

ISSN 1534-6781 ISSN 2214-9902 (electronic)
Ius Gentium: Comparative Perspectives on Law and Justice
ISBN 978-3-032-06857-6 ISBN 978-3-032-06858-3 (eBook)
https://doi.org/10.1007/978-3-032-06858-3

This Springer imprint is published by the registered company Springer Nature Switzerland AG
The registered company address is: Gewerbestrasse 11, 6330 Cham, Switzerland

Acknowledgments

We thank the chapter contributors for their insightful work and collegiality throughout the project.

We are also grateful to the peer reviewers whose valuable feedback significantly enhanced the quality of this volume.

Finally, we thank our families for their unwavering support, encouragement, and patience.

Contents

Contributors

Sanaa Ahmed University of Calgary, Calgary, AB, Canada

Michael Brand RMIT School of Computing Technologies, Melbourne, VIC, Australia

Otzma Analytics, Melbourne, VIC, Australia

Derwent Coshott University of Sydney Law School, Financial Integrity Hub (FIH), Camperdown, NSW, Australia

Louis de Koker La Trobe University and Financial Integrity Hub (FIH), Melbourne, VIC, Australia

Jamie Ferrill Charles Sturt University and Financial Integrity Hub (FIH), Canberra, ACT, Australia

Michelle Gallant Faculty of Law, University of Manitoba, Winnipeg, MB, Canada

Doron Goldbarsht Macquarie University and Financial Integrity Hub (FIH), Sydney, NSW, Australia

Hannah Harris Macquarie Law School, Financial Integrity Hub (FIH), Asia Pacific Forest Crime Network (APFCN), Sydney, NSW, Australia

Carl Herse Kohei Consulting, Brisbane, QLD, Australia

Vivienne Lawack Academic at the University of the Western Cape, Cape Town, South Africa

Jeanne Nel Department of Business Law and Taxation, Monash Business School, Monash University and Financial Integrity Hub (FIH), Melbourne, VIC, Australia

Nic Ryder School of Law and Politics, Cardiff University, Cardiff, UK

Megan Styles Monash University, Melbourne, VIC, Australia

Yusuf Sulayman School of Law, University of Portsmouth, Portsmouth, UK

The Illusory Truth Effect and Financial Integrity Objectives and Consequences

Doron Goldbarsht, Louis de Koker, and Jamie Ferrill

> ... "No," said the man at the window, and he threw the book onto a small table and stood up. "You may not leave, you've been arrested." "So it seems," said K. "But why?" he asked, "We are not authorized to tell you. Go to your room and wait. Proceedings have already been initiated, and you will be told everything is due course. I'm doing more than I should by talking to you in such a friendly way. But I hope no one can hear except Franz, and he himself has defied regulations by being so friendly toward you. If you continue in the future to be as fortunate as you have been in you warders, you will have reason to be confident". K. wanted to sit down, but then saw that there was no seat in the entire room, except the chair by the window. "You'll come to realize the truth of all this", said Franz, as he walked toward him with the other man. Franz Kafka, 'The Trial' 1925

1 Introduction

Money laundering and the financing of terrorism and proliferation are widely recognised as posing severe and complex regulatory challenges that transcend international borders. What we know about these offences is, however, limited and it is unclear whether current crime combating measures have a sufficient impact on these crimes or what the current measures are aiming to achieve. While a global

D. Goldbarsht (✉)
Macquarie University and Financial Integrity Hub (FIH), Sydney, NSW, Australia
e-mail: doron.goldbarsht@mq.edu.au

L. de Koker
La Trobe University and Financial Integrity Hub (FIH), Melbourne, VIC, Australia
e-mail: l.dekoker@latrobe.edu.au

J. Ferrill
Charles Sturt University and Financial Integrity Hub (FIH), Canberra, ACT, Australia
e-mail: jferrill@csu.edu.au

D. Goldbarsht et al. (eds.), *Combating Financial Crime*, Ius Gentium: Comparative Perspectives on Law and Justice 131,
https://doi.org/10.1007/978-3-032-06858-3_1

approach of this nature will always have to contend with uncertainty and differences in views, the anti-money laundering and counter terrorist and proliferation (AML/CTF/CPF) venture, largely informed by the global standards of the intergovernmental Financial Action Task Force (FATF), is also challenged by the *illusory truth effect*—a repeated exposure to a claim increases its perceived accuracy, regardless of its empirical reliability.[1]

The FATF's *Methodology for Assessing Technical Compliance with the FATF Recommendations and the Effectiveness of AML/CFT Systems,*[2] first adopted in 2013, aims to achieve 'effective implementation' of AML/CTF measures. The effectiveness assessment, according to the report, "seeks to assess the adequacy of the implementation of the FATF Recommendations" and focuses on "the extent to which the legal and institutional framework is producing the expected results".[3] But what does that actually mean? The emphasis on effectiveness emerged over two decades after the FATF's establishment in 1989 and release of its first set of 40 Recommendations in 1990. This suggests a belated recognition that technical compliance alone was insufficient. Yet even with this shift towards outcomes-based assessment, we continue to construct our defences within a framework where the fundamental scope of the problem remains empirically unvalidated[4], raising profound questions about whether our measures of 'effectiveness' are themselves effective.

2 What Is the Volume of Money Laundering?

The challenges are perhaps best exemplified by AML measures, although the same questions arise in relation to terrorist and proliferation financing.

Since the 1980s, the scourge of money laundering has been recognised as a global phenomenon which undermines public perception of the financial system and dissuades international investment into domestic financial markets deemed to be 'high risk'.[5] Often-cited estimates of the global volume of money laundered annually range from US$800 billion to US$2.2 trillion—equivalent to approximately 2–5% of global GDP.[6] That GDP range is informed by the work done by Vito Tanzi since the late 1980s at the IMF.[7] Improved estimations have been

[1] Riesthuis and Woods (2024).

[2] FATF 2013; updated in 2022, 2023, and 2025.

[3] FATF 2013, p. 5.

[4] See also Ferrill et al. (2025).

[5] Albanese (2021), Naylor (2003), Hameiri (2020).

[6] United Nations Office on Drugs and Crime (2025), Europol (2025), Isolauri and Ameer (2022), Enderwick (2019), Levi and Soudijn (2020).

[7] Tanzi (1996), Ferrill et al. (2025), de Koker et al. (2025a).

made, for example, by Walker[8] and Walker and Unger.[9] The UNODC has made similar estimations on illicit financial flows resulting from drug trafficking and other transnational organised crimes, and the Australian Institute of Criminology's research on estimating the costs of serious and organised crime in Australia[10] provides a leading example of a jurisdiction-focused estimate that ranges broader than only proceeds of crime. Despite the availability of these studies and the potential to track changes in proceeds of crime, the oft-cited estimate of 2–5% of global GDP continues to feature in key communications.[11] Importantly, government appetites to update the estimates and track changes appear to remain low.

By its very nature, accurately estimating the quantum of money laundering activity occurring on a global scale is impossible, due to the obscure and secretive nature with which criminal enterprise occurs. As the end product of laundering illicit proceeds is to make it appear to have been legitimately generated, money laundering activities are typically only uncovered in connection with predicate offences. Indeed, according to Pol, the paucity of credible data as to the scale of money laundering activity as a corollary undermine the ability for regulators and academics to assess the efficacy of policies and processes designed to prevent laundering behaviour.[12] Specifically, to the extent to which money laundering activity is contingent on the commission of a predicate offence, the more offences which are captured by the concept of money laundering, the larger the scale of money laundering behaviour will be. Accuracy is, however, not necessarily required for sound policy purposes. Fair estimates may be sufficiently useful to track whether the necessary improvements are being achieved, at least in relation to priority predicate offences.

In recent years, the international scale of money laundering has been exacerbated by technological advancements, globalisation, and the development of novel financial structures and payment systems, such as cryptocurrencies, via the increased availability of anonymous, rapid, international capital movements.[13] In response, efforts to deter and undermine money laundering have largely focused on a multilateral approach towards preventing the entrance of criminal proceeds into the legitimate economy and preserving the integrity of the global financial system, as national or bilateral approaches have proved insufficient to address the transnational nature of laundering activities.[14] However, despite attracting increasing amounts of academic attention in recent decades, research into money laundering has continually been described as scarce, largely fragmented, and neglected, and has failed to result in a unified theoretical and practical understanding of money laundering in

---

[8] Walker (1999).

[9] Walker and Unger (2009). For an overview of key quantification papers, see Schmidt (2024).

[10] Smith (2024), UNODC (2011).

[11] E.g. Attorney General's Department (2024) first consultation paper, p. 17; Global Coalition to Fight Financial Crime (2024), United Nations Department of Economic and Social Affairs (2021).

[12] Pol (2019).

[13] Goldbarsht and de Koker (2022); Orchard (2024).

[14] Pavlidis (2023), Korejo, Rajamanickam and Said (2021), De Koker (2024).

terms of global scale.[15] This is, in part, due to the absence of a globally accepted definition as to the boundaries of what activities generate what qualifies as 'dirty money', further explored below.[16]

These ambiguities—in definitions, practice, research, and policy—are not merely academic concerns but reflect deeper geopolitical tensions within the global AML/CTF/CPF regime. Countries approach financial crime prevention through distinctly national lenses, shaped by economic, regulatory, and strategic interests and agendas. What may be legitimate financial innovation in one jurisdiction could be a vehicle for illicit flows in another. This paradox creates a complicated terrain where countries simultaneously (mostly) comply with—and cooperate within—the FATF framework while pursuing their own policies that may undermine collective effectiveness.[17] The result is a system where regulatory arbitrage becomes inevitable; jurisdictions will compete for financial flows by offering varying degrees of transparency, enforcement, and regulatory rigour, often through token or minimal compliance with the FATF standards. These conditions have been created by countries largely despite—and perhaps because of—their participation in the global regime. This, in turn, reveals an inherent tension between national interest and supranational coordination in financial crime control efforts.

Whilst the practice of money laundering, insofar as consisting of the acts and processes by which illicit funds are obscured so as to make them appear to have been generated via legitimate means, has been documented for many years, criminals continue to exploit incongruencies in regulatory and legislative structures via regulatory arbitrage so as to undermine the efficacy of global recourse.[18] Money laundering has recently been exacerbated by the adoption of novel laundering techniques via decentralised crypto assets, such as non-fungible tokens, channelled through tumblers using unhosted wallets, These activities further undermine the accuracy of attempts to estimate the global scope of money laundering activities as reflective of "known knowns".[19]

By way of example, as cryptocurrencies are increasingly recognised as vehicles for the placement and layering stages of money laundering, three interrelated issues raise significant legal and enforcement challenges: (a) the lack of a globally accepted scope of predicate offences, that is—the range of underlying crimes that give rise to laundered proceeds; (b) the inconsistent implementation of the FATF Recommendations as they apply to crypto-asset service providers; and (c) the absence of an agreed methodology to identify and assess the criminal abuse of crypto assets. These gaps raise serious concerns that current estimates of money laundering activity involving cryptocurrencies may be fundamentally flawed. Indeed, users that primarily use Bitcoin for illegal activity conduct annual

[15] Isolauri and Ameer (2022), Canhoto (2021), Van Duyne et al. (2018).

[16] De Koker and Goldbarsht (2024).

[17] See Ahmed (2025) in this book for further discussion.

[18] Isolauri and Ameer (2022), Albanese (2021).

[19] De Koker and Goldbarsht (2024), Orchard (2024).

transactions estimated at over US$76 billion,[20] comparable to the combined size of the illegal drug markets in the United States and Europe, while the total criminal abuse of all cryptocurrencies was estimated at US$51 billion in 2024.[21]

The inherently borderless and international nature of crypto assets significantly undermines the efficacy of efforts by individual states, as criminal agents are able to transfer assets to less-regulated jurisdictions with ease. This is increasingly relevant in circumstances where decentralised finance is increasingly becoming a strategic weapon in the arsenal of criminal enterprise.[22]

It is against the backdrop of this 'known unknown' that the efficacy of international efforts to combat money laundering cannot be meaningfully assessed. The central question remains: how can regulatory interventions be said to have a 'real' or 'balanced' impact in the absence of a reliable empirical understanding of the global scale of laundering behaviour? This uncertainty is compounded by the fact that such interventions often carry unintended consequences, both for regulated entities and broader financial and legal systems.

Within this highly fragmented and opaque environment, domestic legislators, and by extension, private sector entities, are expected to comply with what often appears to be a *Kafkaesque* system of regulatory norms set by the FATF: standards aim to mitigate the risks of money laundering, yet the actual scope and scale of the problem remain elusive. However, when risk-based approaches to new financial products, technologies, and business practices, including new delivery mechanisms, disproportionately impact emerging and low-capacity jurisdictions through significant unintended consequences,[23] there is cause for concern about whether such regulatory efforts are justified—particularly given that the global scale of laundering activities (and, as a corollary, the efficacy of such measures) remains increasingly opaque.

In turn, this tension between regulatory ambition and practical 'outcomes' illuminates the fundamental paradox herein: the measures designed at global, national, and local levels to combat illicit financial flows often generate new vulnerabilities and risks that may be as significant as those they seek to address. That is, regulatory innovations create both opportunities for enhanced detection and control *and* new avenues for exploitation. Technological advances for one may promise greater transparency while preserving privacy,[24] while at the same time enabling more sophisticated methods of concealment. At the same time, efforts to standardise global practices may inadvertently create regulatory gaps, leading to arbitrage opportunities for criminals. The paradox brings to light the idea that the unintended consequences of financial crime control and not just side effects but rather are systemic, structurally embedded functions of their own design. This dynamic is at the

[20] Leuprecht, Jenkins and Hamilton (2023).

[21] Chainalysis (2025).

[22] FATF (2024a).

[23] Goldbarsht and de Koker (2022).

[24] See Brand et al. (2025) in this book.

heart of this book; it suggests that financial crime prevention requires not only more thoughtful implementation of the frameworks we already have, but a reconsideration of how we conceptualise the relationship between AML/CTF/CPF regulations, crime, and how countries, institutions and criminals adapt. The FATF measures are expensive and indications that they are actually delivering crime combating value are limited.[25]

3 Defining Concepts

Definitional challenges in the AML/CTF/CPF context are often neglected, creating the "illusory truth" that there is consensus about the meaning of key concepts.

Such differences are, for example, built into the current FATF standards on the financing of weapons of mass destruction. The FATF adopted both a narrow definition (proliferation financing in breach of targeted financial sanctions of the United Nations Security Council) and a broader definition that covers what is generally understood as financing of weapons of mass destruction. FATF standards only apply to the narrow definition but countries were urged to consider the broader definition too. Some countries therefore adopted the narrow definition for purposes of their PF risk assessments and regimes while others adopt the broader definition or their own version of the broader definition.[26] Everyone can agree that steps are being taken to counter financing of weapons of mass destruction but countries are actually addressing very different aspects of the proliferation challenge.

The motivations behind money laundering activities are clear, being that they consist of processes by which criminal proceeds (or 'dirty money') are distanced from predicate offences so as to make them appear to have been generated via legitimate means in order for them to be re-invested into further criminal enterprise.[27] According to Horan, money laundering is defined as follows:

> … the process of creating the appearance that money, which was obtained from criminal conduct, originated from a legitimate source. It involves a practice of engaging in financial transactions to conceal the identity, source, or destination of the proceeds of crime, either to disguise the fact that the property is the proceeds of crime or to obscure the true beneficial owner of [it].[28]

The processes by which funds are laundered has been widely accepted as comprising the three-stage sequential process of 'placement', 'layering' and 'integration', by which funds are: (i) introduced into the financial system; (ii) obfuscated so as disguise their true origin; and (iii) integrated back into the economy so as to

[25] See Nazzari and Reuter (2025), Morris and De Koker (2025).

[26] De Koker (2024).

[27] Tiwari et al. (2023).

[28] Horan (2011) p. 23.01.

facilitate its reinvestment into further criminal enterprise, and has been adopted in global and domestic policy design and rhetoric, including by the FATF.[29]

However, the three-stage process has also been recognised in academic literature as outdated in light of the non-linear and contingent nature recent technological developments in the financial ecosystem, such as the proliferation of decentralised cryptocurrencies, which no longer rely on funds to be 'integrated' into the traditional financial system.[30] Accordingly, the recognition of the vulnerability of the cryptocurrency sector to criminal exploitation has resulted in the expansion of global, regional, and domestic policies to account for digital assets, with varying degrees of success.[31] Indeed, as the processes which criminals utilise to launder their illicit profits become progressively more globalised and sophisticated, the ability to assess the global scale of money laundering activity is increasingly reliant upon international cooperation, collaboration, and consistency, necessitating, as a starting point, a globally unified approach to the definition of 'money laundering' and 'dirty money'.

In 1988, the United Nations Convention against Illicit Traffic in Narcotic Drugs and Psychotropic Substances (Vienna Convention) was adopted. The Vienna Convention provided that each party to the convention shall establish as a criminal offence the conversion or transfer of property, knowing that such property is derived from an offence, for the purpose of concealing or disguising the illicit origin of the property or of assisting any person who is involved in the commission of such an offence or offences to evade the legal consequences of his action.

In 2000, the United National Convention against Transnational Organised Crime was adopted. The Palermo Convention defined money laundering as:

> the conversion or transfer of property, knowing that such property is the proceeds of crime, for the purpose of disguising the illicit origin of the property or of helping any person who is involved in the commission of the predicate offence to evade legal consequences of his/her action; the concealment or disguise of the true nature, source, location, disposition, movement or ownership of or rights with respect to property, knowing that such property is the proceeds of crime; the acquisition, possession or use of property, knowing at the time of receipt that such property is the proceeds of crime; participation in, association with or conspiracy to commit, attempt to commit and aiding and abetting, facilitating and counselling the commission of any of the offences established in accordance with this article.[32]

At the domestic level, in Australia for example, money laundering is regulated under the *Anti-Money Laundering and Counter-Terrorism Financing Act* 2006 (Cth) (AML/CTF Act), which defines money laundering as an offence against Division 400 of the *Criminal Code Act* 1995 (Cth), which provides that it is an offence to receive, possess, conceal, dispose, import, export or engage in a banking transaction

---

[29] Hopton (2009), Soudijn (2016), Goldbarsht (2022).

[30] Orchard (2024), Bakowski (2012). De Koker (2007) par 1.04 pointed out that the stages do not apply to many money laundering schemes in cash-based economies where money may be placed and spent rather than layered and integrated/

[31] Covolo (2020).

[32] Palermo Convention.

relating to, money or other property that either is, and the person believes it to be, proceeds of crime, or the person intends that the money or property will become an instrument of crime.[33] A person also commits an offence if they engage in conduct in relation to money or other property which is or is believed to be, or the person is reckless or negligent as to the fact that the money or property is, proceeds of crime and the conduct concealed or disguised any or all of the following: (i) the nature of the money or property; (ii) the value of the money or property; (iii) the source of the money or property; (iv) the location of the money or property; (v) any disposition of the money or property; (vi) any movement of the money; (vii) any rights in respect of the money or property; (viii) the identify of any person who has rights in respect of the money or property; and (ix) the identity of any person who has effective control of the money or property.

The FATF has adopted an expansive interpretation of money laundering. Its Recommendation 3 requires countries to criminalise money laundering on the basis of the Vienna Convention and the Palermo Convention, but adds: "Countries should apply the crime of money laundering to all serious offences, with a view to including the widest range of predicate offences".[34]

In addition to the core predicate offences envisaged in the two Conventions, countries bring different predicate offences into the scope of their money laundering offence, reflecting the unique money laundering risks they face.[35]

While it introduces important scope questions when cross-border laundering activities occur, the FATF's definitional approach helps to ensure a measure of strategic flexibility. Depending on national policy choices, money laundering offences can therefore extend to cybercrime, including the exploitation of technology for the purposes of committing or concealing a crime, as well as transferring criminal proceeds between accounts and across borders.

In this sense, technology has been recognised as attractive to criminal agents due to its immediacy and anonymity, allowing criminals to re-locate the fruits of their criminal enterprise to jurisdictions with lower levels of regulatory protection with minimal capital investment or specialised knowledge. In October 2018, the FATF expanded the scope of the Recommendations to apply to virtual assets (defined as a digital representation of value that can be digitally traded or transferred and can be used for payment or investment purposes) and virtual asset service providers. Further, in 2019, the FATF adopted an Interpretive Note to Recommendation 15 to confirm that countries should consider virtual assets as "property", "proceeds", "funds or other assets", or other "corresponding value". However, as of June 2024, the global implementation of the Recommendations in respect of virtual assets remains limited, with only one jurisdiction recorded as being fully compliant and 73% of jurisdictions not having conducted adequate risk assessments yet.[36]

---

[33] Criminal Code Act 1995 (Cth), s 400.2B(1).

[34] FATF (2025) Rec 3.

[35] Teichmann et al. (2020).

[36] FATF (2024a).

4 The Risk-Based Approach

As mentioned earlier, the FATF is the inter-governmental policy-making body responsible for setting the benchmark internal standards for legal, regulatory, and operational policies and procedures for combating money laundering and terrorism financing threats to the integrity of the international financial system.[37] A set of recommendations formulated in 1990 by the FATF firmed into a framework for the minimum regulatory standards required to be implemented across all domestic legal systems. This set of 40 non-binding standards (the FATF Recommendations), requires countries to subject financial institutions and designated non-financial institutions and professions to specified AML/CTF obligations, including Customer Due Diligence, transaction monitoring and reporting requirements.[38] Whilst technically 'soft law' and therefore non-binding, the Recommendations have attained normative character and have achieved near global implementation due to the self-interest of states, with over 200 jurisdictions committed to implementing the Recommendations into their domestic legal frameworks.[39]

Central to the Recommendations is the 'risk-based' approach, which requires individual countries to apply increasingly preventative measures in circumstances perceived to be of 'high risk', in contrast with the 'one-size-fits-all' approach.[40] Yet, despite calls for clear definitions,[41] the FATF for many years have been loath to define "risk", opting for a general statement that "risk can be seen as a function of three factors: threat, vulnerability and consequence".[42] In 2024, in its non-binding money laundering national risk assessment guidance, however, it adopted the following definition: "Risk occurs when a threat successfully takes advantage of a vulnerability to produce a consequence".[43] The difference is subtle but significant in terms of the risk assessment process. Does the new definition capture the "function" that FATF statement referenced? How important is likelihood in the assessment of this risk? Should this new definition now be applied to terrorist and proliferation financing assessments too?

However, in circumstances where risk assessments are judgment-based processes, the FATF has acknowledged that "[g]iven the challenges in determining or estimating the consequences of money laundering… it is accepted that incorporating consequences into risk assessments may not involve particularly sophisticated approaches…"[44] and, in relation to terrorist financing that countries may assume

[37] Goldbarsht (2017), De Koker (2022).

[38] Campbell-Verduyn (2018), De Koker, Ocal and Casanovas (2022), p. 152.

[39] Goldbarsht (2020a).

[40] De Koker and Goldbarsht (2024).

[41] E.g. De Koker (2011) par 3.5.

[42] See e.g. FATF (2013), par 10, FATF (2019) par 15, FATF (2021) par 20.

[43] FATF (2024b) p. 9.

[44] FATF (2013), par 10, now replaced by FATF (2024b).

that the consequences will be severe, unless they have data indicating the contrary.[45] Such assumptions undermine the rigour of the national risk assessment which, in turn, is supposed to inform institutional risk assessments. It also primes the national risk assessment to overestimate risks, especially terrorist financing risks. Its 2024 guidance on national risk assessments, however, the FATF took a different approach and recognised consequence and likelihood as key elements, stating that a country that fails to consider the likelihood and extent of the activity and the consequences will have a diminished ability to reach conclusions about their relative importance, severity and urgency. Despite this recognition the guidance still allows for a range of processes to identify consequences and determine likelihood: "Some countries may choose to employ more formal techniques such as surveys of experts or statistical analysis of the frequency of past ML risk related activity; others may choose to reflect on the conclusions of a group discussion or workshop to help develop this information."[46]

Combined with the use of questionable methodologies, national risk assessments may therefore not identify or assess the relevant risks appropriately. This in turn limits the chances of attaining intended policy objectives while increasing the chances of negative unintended consequences.

Developing countries tend not to use the full flexibility allowed by the FATF standards. According to research by the World Bank published in 2021, policy makers in developing countries were reluctant to implement simplified money laundering protections due to a fear of negative ratings in mutual evaluations. In such jurisdictions, the AML/CTF regulatory framework is more onerous than allowed by the FATF standards, for example in relation to customer identify verification or the application to low risk institutions that may qualify for an exemption from AML/CTF obligations.[47] Such a conclusion is consistent with findings of a 2018 report by the Inter-Governmental Action Group against Money Laundering in West Africa that financial service providers in West Africa do not take advantage of the risk based approach, such as exemptions from AML/CTF requirements in low-risk situations, and instead generally use traditional identification and verification processes.

Whilst the FATF has recognised that newly banked individuals and vulnerable groups generally pose lower risks to financial institutions, the impacts of financial exclusion can be exacerbated in circumstances where the risk-based approach is incorrectly applied so as to reduce access for these communities to regulated financial services such as bank accounts and credit facilities.[48] The above demonstrates a potentially problematic element inherent in the FATF's approach to the global regulation of money laundering, whereupon vague, non-scientific and judgment-based conceptualisations of 'risk' are coupled alongside subjective mutual assessments so as to impart damaging consequences on the financial health and stability of emerging

[45] See FATF (2019), par 15, FATF (2021) par 22.

[46] FATF (2024c), p. 34.

[47] Celik (2021).

[48] Pavlidis (2023), FATF (2021), De Koker & Casanovas (2024), Goldbarsht et al. (2025).

nations, in the absence of empirical assessment as to whether and the extent to which such efforts are having any impact on the global scale of laundering behaviour. In this regard, global regulatory efforts in response to money laundering concerns must be developed so as to promote financial inclusion and reduce unintended negative consequences on low-economic jurisdictions.

5 Black and Grey Listing

The FATF International Co-operation Review Group processes involve a continuous system of peer-reviewal by which a countries' level of technical compliance with each of the Recommendations is assessed as compliant, largely compliant, partially compliant or non-compliant.[49] Whilst the FATF has no formal powers to compel a country to improve its AML/CTF measures, countries are motivated to implement the Recommendations effectively into their domestic legal systems as those with 'strategic deficiencies', it may be placed on either the 'black' or 'grey' lists published by the FATF.

In the FATF's fourth round of mutual evaluations, conducting from 2013 to 2025, a jurisdiction would generally be placed on the 'grey list' and be subject to 'increased monitoring' when it was unable to demonstrate that it had an effective framework to protect the financial system from abuse, but was actively working with the FATF to address strategic deficiencies in its AML/CFT regimes, and was committed to swiftly resolve the identified strategic deficiencies within an agreed timeframe. Despite the clear indication that jurisdictions subject to increased monitoring have committed themselves politically to address the deficiencies identified by the FATF, and stating, since October 2019,[50] that the grey listing does not call for the application of engaged due diligence measures to be applied, the FATF simultaneously advised countries to take into account a countries' grey listing in their risk analysis.[51] Bar the changes for the fifth round of mutual evaluations discussed in Sect. 5.1 below, these communications still continue.

In 2016, the European Union adopted a list of AML and CTF related high-risk third countries which, in effect, adopts the FATF grey list unless such countries are members of the European economic area or if they satisfy the definition of "least-developed countries" that do not pose a threat to the EU financial system.[52] If countries are included on the EU list, they are subjected to mandatory enhanced due diligence measures based on the money laundering risks posed by those jurisdictions to the EU and the need for a consistent EU response.

---

[49] Goldbarsht (2020b).

[50] De Koker, Howell and Morris (2023), par. 2.2.

[51] De Koker (2024).

[52] De Koker and Goldbarsht (2024).

In contrast, jurisdictions will be placed on the 'blacklist' and subject to a 'Call to Action' if they are identified as having strategic deficiencies to counter money laundering, insofar as all member states are urged to apply 'countermeasures' in order to protect the international financial system from the money laundering, terrorist financing and proliferation financing risks emanating from the country.

In order for a country to be removed from FATF monitoring, it must address 'all or nearly all' of the actions agreed by the country and the FATF, which are sometimes vaguely defined, such as engaging national cooperation and coordination, sustaining an increase in money laundering investigations and prosecutions or enhance its understanding of money laundering risks and its regime for suspicious transaction reports. Countries that are listed spend on average 3 years on the list and vague actions that are open to interpretation by the FATF assessment team may lead to longer listing periods for some jurisdictions.

5.1 *Impact of Greylisting on Low-Capacity Jurisdictions*

Whilst technically soft law, jurisdictions are motivated to avoid being placed on either the black of grey list due to their self-interest and rationality.[53] This is increasingly relevant in circumstances where decisions by financial institutions to terminate or restrict business relationships with specific countries are, in large part, driven by risk perceptions and a desire to avoid increased compliance costs.[54] Whilst research has found that greylisted countries face "up to a 10 percent decline in cross border payments received from other jurisdictions",[55] and that the domestic currency of jurisdictions under increase monitoring depreciated during the review period,[56] research identifying weak to non-existent evidence that the FATF's mutual evaluative process is materially biased in racial terms is positive.[57] However, such research identified a strong bias against small island states, alongside a large and statistically significant bias in the FATF effectiveness assessments against black majority countries, relative to white majority countries.

Such biases are concerning in circumstances where research found that the net official development assistance, International Bank for Reconstruction and Development loans, and International Development Association credits seem to reduce during and after grey listing periods, which may disproportionality impact developing economies and their populations. Additional potential consequences include a decline in financial inclusion, international financial support, foreign direct investment, currency depreciation, and reduced capital inflows, which can

[53] Goldbarsht (2020b).

[54] Goldbarsht and Elizabeth (2024).

[55] Collin et al. (2016).

[56] Jayasekara (2021).

[57] Littrell (2024).

disproportionately impact financially isolated, low income and emerging market economies reliant upon foreign investment.[58]

For the new round of mutual evaluations, the FATF made a few changes that might ease the pressure on smaller jurisdictions and better advance the policy objectives of the FATF. The focus in the 5th round of mutual evaluations is, for example, more on larger economies and on the effectiveness of AML/CTF/CPF measures.[59] The FATF also amended the grey listing to ensure that it better targets the countries that pose the greatest risk to the international financial system and protects small lower risk economies from grey listing and accompanying negative economic impact.[60] These jurisdictions will be "pooled" rather than "greylisted". Whether that will shield them from harmful unintended consequences is unclear at this stage.

6 This Collection

The above demonstrates the 'Kafkaesque' paradox facing regulators and financial institutions alike, insofar as they are forced to comply with a vague system of compliance measures which have been found to impart significant unintended financial impacts on low-capacity jurisdictions without truly understanding the scope of money laundering activity globally, or risk significant consequences of non-compliance. As a starting point, a universally applied definition of money laundering needs to be properly developed so as to capture the extent of laundering activities utilising novel technologies, such as cryptocurrencies. Further, research should focus on what can be done to increase the flexibility of the risk-based approach as it is applied in low-capacity jurisdictions so as to limit its impact on financial exclusion.

The chapters in this collection explore the complex interrelationship between financial crime mitigation requirements and the unintended consequences of these measures on services and products, both globally and domestically. Each double-blind peer-reviewed contribution brings a distinct perspective to the effects of anti-financial crime efforts. Together, the chapters provide a nuanced examination of the various negative consequences that can arise in the process of addressing financial crime:

Michael Brand, Louis de Koker, and Carl Herse investigate in chapter "Privacy--Preserving Data Analytics: A Case Study in Anti-Money Laundering and Counter Terrorist and Proliferation Financing Innovation in Australia"[61] how privacy-preserving technologies can improve information sharing within Australia's AML/CTF framework. By focusing on FinTracer, a tool employing homomorphic

[58] De Koker, Howell and Morris (2023), World Bank (2015).

[59] Financial Action Task Force (2024c) par. 9.

[60] Financial Action Task Force (2024c) par. 154.

[61] Brand et al. (2025) in this book.

encryption, they highlight innovative ways to bridge intelligence gaps without compromising individual privacy.

Addressing the question of whether retail Central Bank Digital Currencies (CBDCs) can foster both financial inclusion and integrity, Vivienne Lawack's chapter "Central Bank Digital Currencies, Financial Inclusion and Financial Integrity: Trade-Off?"[62] draws upon international surveys and national case studies. The chapter critically examines motivations behind CBDC adoption, barriers to inclusion, and potential integrity risks, ultimately providing insights into how central banks may reconcile these sometimes-competing objectives.

Nic Ryder's chapter, "Coordinated Terrorist Financing: An Emerging Threat or a Glaring Omission? Time to Rethink the Financial War on Terrorism",[63] shines a spotlight on the underexplored phenomenon of coordinated terrorist financing. Through doctrinal analysis and illustrative case studies involving natural resources and cryptocurrencies, Ryder reveals growing collaboration among terrorist groups in fundraising and advocates for a revaluation of global CTF strategies.

In chapter "Re-evaluating Human Rights in Global Counter-Terrorism Financing: A Case for Preliminary Judicial Moderation", Yusuf Sulayman probes the delicate balance between national security and fundamental rights within global CTF regimes.[64] The chapter critiques post-9/11 legal frameworks that, despite enhancing enforcement, may jeopardise civil liberties through disproportionate or poorly substantiated actions. Sulayman proposes a judicial moderation approach based on evidentiality, effectiveness, and proportionality to better safeguard human rights alongside security objectives.

In chapter "Charities, Non-Profit Organisations and the FATF: Testing the Evidence Base and Proportionality of Risk-Based Counter-Terrorist-Financing Regulation", Jeanne Nel critically examines the influence of the FATF on the global regulation of charities and non-profit organisations.[65] Focusing on the Australian context, the chapter questions the evidence base underlying the FATF's long-standing framing of NPOs as particularly vulnerable to terrorist financing abuse. Nel explores how this framing led to disproportionate regulatory responses, often in the absence of jurisdiction-specific risk. The chapter argues that without robust empirical grounding, risk-based regulation risks becoming symbolic rather than proportionate, undermining both the FATF's legitimacy and the essential work of the non-profit sector.

Hannah Harris explores the intersection of environmental protection and financial crime enforcement in "Law Enforcement at the Forest-Finance Nexus in Papua New Guinea—Leveraging Tools Against Financial Crime in Defence of the Environment".[66] Through a Papua New Guinea case study, she demonstrates how

---

[62] Lawack (2025) in this book.

[63] Ryder (2025) in this book.

[64] Sulayman (2025) in this book.

[65] Nel (2025) in this book.

[66] Harris (2025) in this book.

financial crime mechanisms, including AML and proceeds of crime legislation, can be creatively applied to combat illegal logging, corruption, and related offenses. The chapter concludes by urging coordinated global action to strengthen accountability and defend the rights of forest-dependent communities.

Chapter "Surveilling the Citizen: Constitutional Tensions within the Canadian AML Regime", authored by Sanaa Ahmed, offers a critical analysis of Canada's AML laws through the prism of constitutional privacy protections.[67] Tracing the regime's legal architecture and alignment with global surveillance trends, the chapter argues that extensive data collection imposed on private actors circumvents state accountability, proposing reforms to strike a constitutional balance between enforcement efficacy and individual privacy.

Michelle Gallant's chapter, "New Zealand and Manitoba Unexplained Wealth Law: Surveying the Rights Landscape",[68] examines the emergence of unexplained wealth mechanisms as tools in the global financial crime war. Focusing on New Zealand and Manitoba, the discussion centres on how these laws alter traditional legal norms by reversing burdens of proof and imposing forfeiture risks under low evidentiary thresholds. Gallant interrogates their compatibility with rule of law principles and constitutional safeguards, illuminating key tensions between asset recovery efforts and individual rights.

The phenomenon of "de-banking"—financial institutions unilaterally terminating customer relationships—is the focus of Megan Styles's chapter "De-Banking 'Risky' Customers: Contractual Exclusion of Customers by Financial Institutions and AML/CTF Ramifications".[69] By examining case law from Australia, the UK, and New Zealand, Styles analyses how contractual rights intersect with regulatory and ethical considerations, questioning whether courts are moving towards recognizing duties of good faith. The chapter reflects on the adequacy of current legal frameworks in balancing customer rights with institutional risk management, highlighting potential needs for legislative reform.

In chapter "Challenging Risk: The Case of Maples Corporate Services v CIMA", Derwent Coshott explores the inherent tensions of the risk-based approach that underpins the international AML/CTF regime.[70] The chapter provides a detailed analysis of a landmark decision from the Grand Court of the Cayman Islands, where two Maples Group entities successfully contested regulatory findings related to customer due diligence. This case underscores the ongoing challenge of balancing business discretion in risk assessments with regulatory oversight.

Finally, in chapter "Intended and Unintended Consequences of the Combating of Financial Crime: A Research Agenda", Louis de Koker, Doron Goldbarsht, and Jamie Ferrill reflect on the broader impacts, both anticipated and unforeseen, of the

[67] Ahmed (2025) in this book.
[68] Gallant (2025) in this book.
[69] Styles (2025) in this book.
[70] Coshott (2025) in this book.

global AML/CTF regime.[71] While the FATF has long positioned its work as central to the integrity of the financial system and the pursuit of security and safety, the precise pathways through which these outcomes are achieved remain under-examined. This chapter revisits the FATF's original mandate and the evolution of its effectiveness framework to ask: what are the strategic objectives of global financial crime controls, and how can we evaluate their success?

Drawing on the volume's overarching themes, the chapter explores how efforts to protect the financial system from abuse can produce unintended effects, including financial exclusion, de-risking, and restrictions on civil society. The chapter outlines a future research agenda focused on measuring both the intended and unintended consequences of financial crime control. This includes a call for more nuanced analysis of how the FATF standards are implemented, how risks are managed, and how regulatory measures can better align with inclusive financial integrity.

References

Ahmed S (2025) Surveilling the citizen: constitutional tensions within the Canadian AML regime. In: Goldbarsht D, De Koker L, Ferrill J (eds) Combating financial crime: intended and unintended consequences. Springer, Cham

Albanese JS (2021) Organized crime as financial crime: the nature of organized crime as reflected in prosecutions and research. Vict Offender 16(3):431–443

Anti-Money Laundering and Counter-Terrorism Financing Act 2006 (AML/CTF Act) s 5

Attorney-General's Department (2024) Modernising Australia's anti-money laundering and counter-terrorism financing regime. first consultation paper. https://consultations.ag.gov.au/crime/aml-ctf/. Accessed 29 July 2025

Bakowski P (2012) Combatting money laundering: EU law in an international context. Library of the European Parliament https://www.europarl.europa.eu/thinktank/en/document/LDM_BRI(2012)120360. Accessed 29 July 2025

Brand M, De Koker L, Herse C (2025) Privacy-preserving data analytics: a case study in anti-money laundering and counter terrorist and proliferation financing innovation in Australia. In: Goldbarsht D, De Koker L, Ferrill J (eds) Combating financial crime: intended and unintended consequences. Springer, Cham

Canhoto AI (2021) Leveraging machine learning in the global fight against money laundering and terrorism financing: an affordances perspective. J Bus Res 131:441–452

Celik K (2021) Impact of the FATF recommendations and their implementation on financial inclusion: insights from mutual evaluation and national risk assessments. World Bank Reports

Chainalysis (2025) On-chain crime becomes increasingly diverse and professionalized. https://www.chainalysis.com/blog/2025-crypto-crime-report-introduction/

Collin M, Cook S, Soramaki K (2016) The impact of anti-money laundering regulation on payment flows: evidence from SWIFT data. Center for Global Development Working Paper No. 445. Centre for Global Development, Washington, DC

Coshott D (2025) Challenging risk: the case of maples corporate services V Cima. In: Goldbarsht D, De Koker L, Ferrill J (eds) Combating financial crime: intended and unintended consequences. Springer, Cham

[71] De Koker et al. (2025b) in this book.

Covolo V (2020) The EU response to criminal misuse of cryptocurrencies: the young, already outdated 5th anti-money laundering directive. Eur J Crime Crim Law Crim Justice 28(3):217–251
Criminal Code Act 1995 (Cth)
De Koker L (2007) South African money laundering and terrorist financing law. LexisNexis, Durban
De Koker L (2011) Aligning anti-money laundering, combating of financing of terror and financial inclusion: questions to consider when FATF standards are clarified. J Financ Crime 18:361–386. https://doi.org/10.1108/13590791111173704
De Koker L (2022) Regulatory impact assessment: towards a better approach for the FATF. J Money Laund Control 25:265–267
De Koker L (2024) The FATF's combating of financing of proliferation standards: private sector implementation challenges. In: Goldbarsht D, De Koker L (eds) Financial crime and the law. Springer, Cham, pp 99–116. https://doi.org/10.1007/978-3-031-59543-1_6
De Koker L, Casanovas P (2024) De-risking, de-banking and denials of bank services: an over-compliance dilemma? In: De Koker L, Goldbarsht D (eds) Financial crime, law and governance. Ius Gentium: comparative perspectives on law and justice, vol 115. Springer, Cham, pp 247–262
De Koker L, Goldbarsht D (2024) FATF's risk-based approach: has the pendulum swung too far? In: Goldbarsht D, De Koker L (eds) Financial crime and the law. Springer, Cham, pp 247–248
De Koker L, Ocal T, Casanovas P (2022) Where's Wally? FATF, virtual asset service providers, and the regulatory jurisdictional challenge. In: Goldbarsht D, De Koker L (eds) Financial integrity and the law. Ius Gentium: comparative perspectives on law and justice, vol 47. Springer, Cham, pp 151–183
De Koker L, Howell J, Morris N (2023) Economic consequences of greylisting by the financial action task force. Risks 11:81. https://doi.org/10.3390/risks11050081
De Koker L, Goldbarsht D, Ferrill J (2025a) Conclusions: the financial war on crime and terrorism: important research questions. In: Goldbarsht D, de Koker L, Ferrill J (eds) The financial war on crime and terrorism: opportunities and challenges. Springer
De Koker L, Goldbarsht D, Ferrill J (2025b) Intended and unintended consequences of the combating of financial crime: a research agenda. In: Goldbarsht D, De Koker L, Ferrill J (eds) Combating financial crime: intended and unintended consequences. Springer, Cham
Enderwick P (2019) Understanding cross-border crime: the value of international research. Crit Perspect Int Bus 15:119
Europol (2025) Money laundering. https://www.europol.europa.eu/crime-areas/economic-crime/money-laundering. Accessed 29 July 2025
Ferrill J, de Koker L, Goldbarsht D (2025) Financial crime prevention in an age of paradox. In: Goldbarsht D, de Koker L, Ferrill J (eds) The financial war on crime and terrorism: opportunities and challenges. Springer
Financial Action Task Force (2013) National money laundering and terrorist financing risk assessment. FATF, Paris. https://www.fatf-gafi.org/content/dam/fatf-gafi/reports/National_ML_TF_Risk_Assessment.pdf. Accessed 29 July 2025
Financial Action Task Force (FATF) (2019) Terrorist financing risk assessment guidance. FATF, Paris. https://www.fatf-gafi.org/publications/methodsandtrends/documents/Terrorist-Financing-Risk-Assessment-Guidance.html. Accessed 29 July 2025
Financial Action Task Force (2021) Guidance on proliferation financing risk assessment and mitigation. FATF, Paris. https://www.fatf-gafi.org/publications/financingofproliferation/documents/proliferation-financing-risk. Accessed 29 July 2025
Financial Action Task Force (2024a) Targeted update on implementation of the FATF standards on virtual assets and virtual asset service providers. https://www.fatf-gafi.org. Accessed 29 July 2025
Financial Action Task Force (2024b) Procedures for the FATF AML/CFT/CPF mutual evaluations, follow-up and ICRG updated October 2024. FATF, Paris. http://www.fatf-gafi.org/content/fatf-gafi/en/publications/mutualevaluations/Assessment-Follow-UpICRG-Procedures-2022.html. Accessed 29 July 2025

Financial Action Task Force (2024c) Money laundering national risk assessment guidance. FATF, Paris. https://www.fatf-gafi.org/en/publications/Methodsandtrends/Money-Laundering-National-Risk-Assessment-Guidance.html. Accessed 29 July 2025
Financial Action Task Force (FATF) (2025) Forty Recommendations. https://www.fatf-gafi.org/en/publications/Fatfrecommendations/Fatf-recommendations.html. Accessed 29 July 2025
Gallant M (2025) New Zealand and Manitoba unexplained wealth law: surveying the rights landscape. In: Goldbarsht D, De Koker L, Ferrill J (eds) Combating financial crime: intended and unintended consequences. Springer, Cham
Global Coalition to Fight Financial Crime (2024) Projects: coalition to fight financial crime. https://www.weforum.org/projects/coalition-to-fight-financial-crime. Accessed 29 July 2025
Goldbarsht D (2017) Who's the legislator anyway? How the FATF's global norms reshape Australian counter terrorist financing laws. Federal Law Rev 45:127–151
Goldbarsht D (2020a) New payment systems: potential counter-terrorist financing risks and the legal response in the United Kingdom. In: King et al (eds) Assets, crimes and the state: innovation in 21st century legal responses. Routledge, London, pp 125–139
Goldbarsht D (2020b) Global counter-terrorist financing and soft law: multi-layered approaches. Edward Elgar, Cheltenham
Goldbarsht D (2022) Virtual currencies as a quasi-payment tool: the case of frequent-flier programs and money laundering. J Money Laund Control 25:150–164
Goldbarsht D, de Koker L (2022) From paper money to digital assets: financial technology and the risks of criminal abuse. In: Financial technology and the law: combating financial crime. Springer, Cham, pp 1–15
Goldbarsht D, Elizabeth S (2024) Money laundering and the risk in the risk-based approach: the Australian context. Monash Univ Law Rev 50:31–60
Goldbarsht D, de Koker L, Ferrill J (2025) Intended and unintended consequences of the combating of financial crimen: a research agenda. In: Goldbarsht D, De Koker L, Ferrill J (eds) Combating financial crime: intended and unintended consequences. Springer, Cham
Hameiri S (2020) Institutionalism beyond methodological nationalism? The new interdependence approach and the limits of historical institutionalism. Rev Int Polit Econ 27:637–657
Harris H (2025) Law enforcement at the forest-finance nexus in Papua New Guinea – leveraging tools against financial crime in defence of the environment. In: Goldbarsht D, De Koker L, Ferrill J (eds) Combating financial crime: intended and unintended consequences. Springer, Cham
Horan S (2011) Corporate crime. Bloomsbury Professional
Hopton D (2009) Money Laundering: A Concise Guide for All Business (2nd ed.). Routledge
Isolauri EA, Ameer I (2022) Money laundering as a transnational business phenomenon: a systematic review and future agenda. Crit Perspect Int Bus 19:426–427
Jayasekara SD (2021) Deficient regimes of anti-money laundering and countering the financing of terrorism: agenda of digital banking and financial inclusion. J Money Laund Control 24:150–162
Korejo MS, Rajamanickam R, Said MHMD (2021) The concept of money laundering: a quest for legal definition. J Money Laundering Control 24:725–736
Lawack V (2025) Central Bank digital currencies, financial inclusion and financial integrity: trade-off? In: Goldbarsht D, De Koker L, Ferrill J (eds) Combating financial crime: intended and unintended consequences. Springer, Cham
Leuprecht J, Jenkins H, Hamilton J (2023) Virtual money laundering: policy implications of the proliferation in the illicit use of cryptocurrency. J Financ Crime 30:1036–1037
Levi M, Soudijn M (2020) Understanding the laundering of organised crime money. Crime Justice 49:579–631
Littrell C (2024) Economic and demographic biases in FATF mutual evaluation results. In: Goldbarsht D, De Koker L (eds) Financial crime and the law. Springer, Cham, pp 191–219
Morris N, De Koker L (2025) The impact of the Financial Action Task Force (FATF) standards and focus: from effectiveness to effect. In: Goldbarsht D, De Koker L, Ferrill J (eds) Combating financial crime: intended and unintended consequences. Springer, Cham

Naylor RT (2003) Towards a General Theory of Profit-Driven Crimes. The British Journal of Criminology, Vol. 43, Issue 1, pp. 81–101, Available at SSRN: https://ssrn.com/abstract=1160782 or http://dx.doi.org/10.1093/bjc/43.1.81
Nazzari M, Reuter P (2025) How well does the money laundering control system work? Crime Justice 54:000–000
Nel J (2025) Charities, non-profit organisations and the FATF: testing the evidence base and proportionality of risk-based counter-terrorist-financing regulation. In: Goldbarsht D, De Koker L, Ferrill J (eds) Combating financial crime: intended and unintended consequences. Springer, Cham
Orchard S (2024) Money laundering risks: the case of non-fungible tokens—key recommendations for Australia. In: Goldbarsht D, De Koker L (eds) Financial crime, law and governance. Ius Gentium: comparative perspectives on law and justice, vol 116. Springer, Cham
Pavlidis G (2023) The Dark Side of Anti-Money Laundering: Mitigating the Unintended Consequences of Financial Action Task Force Standards (September 1, 2023). Journal of Economic Criminology 2: 100040. https://doi.org/10.1016/j.jeconc.2023.100040. Available at SSRN: https://ssrn.com/abstract=4652143
Pol RF (2019) Anti-money laundering ratings: uncovering evidence hidden in plain sight. J Money Laund Control 22:836–857. https://doi.org/10.1108/JMLC-01-2019-0006
Riesthuis P, Woods J (2024) "That's just like, your opinion, man": the illusory truth effect on opinions. Psychol Res 88(1):284–306
Ryder N (2025) Coordinated terrorist financing—an emerging threat or a glaring omission? Time to rethink the financial war on terrorism. In: Goldbarsht D, De Koker L, Ferrill J (eds) Combating financial crime: intended and unintended consequences. Springer, Cham
Schmidt A (2024) Impacts of money laundering and terrorism financing: final report. Australian Institute of Criminology, Canberra. https://www.aic.gov.au/sites/default/files/2024-07/impacts_of_money_laundering_and_terrorism_financing.pdf
Smith R (2024) Estimating the costs of serious and organised crime in Australia, 2022–23. Stat Rep 50. https://doi.org/10.52922/sr77796
Soudijn MRJ (2016) Rethinking money laundering and drug trafficking. Journal of Money Laundering Control, Emerald Group Publishing Limited, vol. 19(3), pp. 298–310, July.
Styles M (2025) De-banking 'risky' customers: contractual exclusion of customers by financial institutions and AML/CTF ramifications. In: Goldbarsht D, De Koker L, Ferrill J (eds) Combating financial crime: intended and unintended consequences. Springer, Cham
Sulayman Y (2025) Re-evaluating human rights in global counter-terrorism financing: a case for preliminary judicial moderation. In: Goldbarsht D, De Koker L, Ferrill J (eds) Combating financial crime: intended and unintended consequences. Springer
Tanzi V (1996) Money laundering and the international financial system. IMF Working Paper WP/96/55. https://doi.org/10.5089/9781451847598.001
Teichmann FMJ, Falker M-C (2020) Money laundering through deposit boxes. J Money Laundering Control 23(4):805–818
Tiwari M, Ferrill J, Gepp A, Kumar K (2023) Factors influencing the choice of technique to launder funds: the APPT framework. J Econ Criminol 1:1–11
United Nations Convention against Transnational Organized Crime, opened for signature 15 November 2000, 2225 UNTS 209 (entered into force 29 September 2003) ('Palermo Convention')
United Nations Department of Economic and Social Affairs (2021) Tax abuse, money laundering and corruption plague global finance. https://www.un.org/en/desa/tax-abuse-money-laundering-and-corruption-plague-global-finance. Accessed 20 May 2025
United Nations Office on Drugs and Crime (2025). https://www.unodc.org/unodc/en/money-laundering/overview.html. Accessed 20 May 2025
UNODC (2011) Estimating illicit financial flows resulting from drug trafficking and other transnational organized crimes. Research report https://www.drugsandalcohol.ie/16151/1/Illicit_financial_flows_2011_web.pdf. Accessed 29 July 2025

Van Duyne PC, Harvey JH, Gelemerova LY (2018) The critical handbook of money laundering: policy, analysis and myths. Springer, London

Walker J (1999) How big is global money laundering? J Money Laund Control 3(1):25–37

Walker J, Unger B (2009) Measuring global money laundering: the Walker gravity model. Rev Law Econ 5(2):821–853

World Bank (2015) Withdrawal from correspondent banking: where, why and what to do about it. https://documents1.worldbank.org/curated/en/113021467990964789/pdf/101098-revised-PUBLIC-CBR-Report-November-2015.pdf. Accessed 29 July 2025

Doron Goldbarsht LLB LLM (HUJI) PHD (UNSW) is an Associate Professor at Macquarie Law School, the Director of the Financial Integrity Hub (FIH) and the Academic Head of the Graduate Certificate in Financial Integrity Law. With over 20 years of expertise in anti-money laundering and counterterrorist financing, he has co-edited several books on financial crime and compliance, including Financial Crime and the Law: Identifying and Mitigating Risks (Springer 2024) and Financial Technology and the Law: Combating Financial Crime (Springer, 2022). Certified as a lawyer in both Israel and Australia, Doron also provides expert opinions to government and private sector in litigation, advising on financial crime and regulatory matters.

Louis de Koker is a professor of law at La Trobe Law School (Australia), an advisory board member of the Financial Integrity Hub (FIH) and an extraordinary professor in the Department of Commercial and Labour Law of the University of the Western Cape (South Africa). A significant part of his financial crime research focuses on managing the relationship between financial inclusion and anti-money laundering and counter terrorist financing objectives. He has undertaken various university research engagements with the bodies such as the World Bank and the Asian Development Bank and has worked closely with the World Bank-housed Consultative Group to Assist the Poor (CGAP. This work extended to a range of developing countries including Ghana, Indonesia, Kenya, Kyrgyzstan, Malaysia, Namibia, Nigeria, Uganda, the Ukraine and Palau. His research has been cited in publications and research papers of international bodies such as the World Bank, the IMF, the Basel Committee on Banking Supervision, and the International Labour Organization. Louis has held visiting positions at a range of institutions including the Institute for Advanced Legal Studies (London) SOAS (London); Wolfson College (Oxford), the University of Florida (US) and the Autonomous University of Barcelona.

Dr Jamie Ferrill is a Senior Lecturer at the Australian Graduate School of Policing and Security, Charles Sturt University and a research fellow with the Financial Integrity Hub (FIH). Before transitioning to academia, she gained nearly a decade of experience in law enforcement, serving with the Canadian federal government. Jamie's research addresses threats to national and economic security, with a particular interest in the intersection of financial crime with border governance frameworks, international cooperation, and organizational effectiveness. Jamie has been a visiting fellow at the Academy of International Affairs NRW and the Border Policy Research Institute, and she is a fellow of the Financial Integrity Hub and the Institute of Intergovernmental Relations at Queen's University. Her latest book is titled Dirty Money: Financial Crime in Canada (McGill-Queen's University Press).

Privacy-Preserving Data Analytics: A Case Study in Anti-money Laundering and Counter Terrorist and Proliferation Financing Innovation in Australia

Michael Brand, Louis de Koker, and Carl Herse

Abstract In democracies, financial surveillance legislation attempts to balance the rights to privacy of customers, the strategic need to prevent the tipping-off of wrong-doers, and the policy objectives to ensure the integrity of the financial system.

The trade-offs in this regard in Australia's anti-money laundering and counter terrorist and proliferation financing (AML/CTF) regime limit the effectiveness of the AML/CTF measures. In practice, for example, privacy concerns resulted in limiting Australia's financial intelligence unit, AUSTRAC (2024) (the Australian Transaction Reports and Analysis Centre AUSTRAC), to receiving information that either relates to money entering or exiting the Australian financial system or around which prior suspicion already exists. They further limit the ability of financial institutions to share information between each other, even regarding suspicious matters that they are required to detect and report to AUSTRAC.

This chapter considers whether privacy-preserving data analytics can be used to close financial intelligence gaps while protecting the privacy of customers behaving lawfully. It focuses on initiatives in Australia to improve information-sharing among regulated institutions and between these institutions and AUSTRAC, which explore technological innovations that address the fundamental privacy constraints underlying the traditional AML/CTF model.

In particular, AUSTRAC supported the development of privacy-preserving analytical technologies that allow mass analysis of financial data without any data collection. The technology, FinTracer, applies homomorphic encryption to enable

M. Brand (✉)
RMIT School of Computing Technologies, Melbourne, VIC, Australia

Otzma Analytics, Melbourne, VIC, Australia
e-mail: michael.brand@rmit.edu.au

L. de Koker
La Trobe University and Financial Integrity Hub (FIH), Melbourne, VIC, Australia
e-mail: l.dekoker@latrobe.edu.au

C. Herse
Kohei Consulting, Brisbane, QLD, Australia

D. Goldbarsht et al. (eds.), *Combating Financial Crime*, Ius Gentium: Comparative Perspectives on Law and Justice 131,
https://doi.org/10.1007/978-3-032-06858-3_2

financial institutions to discover and to report to AUSTRAC suspicious actors in their data, even when this suspicion is based on behaviour of actors that spans multiple financial institutions of a kind that would have traditionally been impossible to detect without extensive information-sharing. AUSTRAC subsequently released the technology as open source, enabling further innovation.

This chapter considers the international, AUSTRAC and technological contexts within which FinTracer technologies were developed, describes the technology, and highlights how it navigates some of the pitfalls of applying privacy-preserving data analytical technologies in this space.

1 Introduction

Australia's statutory financial surveillance framework, primarily centred around the *Anti-Money Laundering and Counter-Terrorism Financing Act 2006* (Cth), attempts to balance the rights to privacy of customers,[1] the strategic need to prevent the tipping-off of wrongdoers, and the policy objective to ensure the integrity of Australia's financial system. Australia's framework in this regard mirrors aspects of the laws of more than 200 jurisdictions globally that are committed to ensuring that they meet the regulatory standards set by the Financial Action Task Force, the global standard-setter for anti-money laundering and counter terrorist and proliferation financing (AML/CTF/CPF).

The trade-offs in this regard in Australia's AML/CTF regime impact on the effectiveness of the relevant AML/CTF measures. In practice, for example, privacy concerns resulted in limiting Australia's financial intelligence unit (FIU), AUSTRAC (the Australian Transaction Reports and Analysis Centre (2024)), to receiving information that either relates to money entering or exiting the Australian financial system or around which prior suspicion already exists. They further limit the ability of financial institutions to share information between each other, even regarding suspicious matters that they are required to detect and report to AUSTRAC.

In 2024, amendments were made to the legislation to relax the information-sharing restrictions to some extent, for example modifying the prohibition on 'tipping off' customers to allow reporting entities to make disclosures to other reporting entities if the disclosure is made for the purpose of detecting, deterring, or disrupting money laundering, the financing of terrorism, proliferation financing, or other serious crimes and the conditions prescribed by the regulations are met.[2] While such amendments are welcome, restrictions and conditions still remain that will have to be navigated. In particular, the new regulation only impacts the distribution between

[1] The statutory framework in this regard includes privacy and data protection laws and standards, in particular the *Privacy Act 1988* (Cth) and its Australian Privacy Principles (APPs) as well as the official secrecy obligations that AUSTRAC and other public officials must observe. See in general Bennett Moses and De Koker (2017); Paterson (2024).

[2] S 123(5) of the Anti-Money Laundering and Counter-Terrorism Financing Act 2006.

reporting entities of information that would have a priori been reportable to AUSTRAC, and so do not expand AUSTRAC's surveillance capabilities.

Since 2017, Australia has been working on initiatives to improve information sharing among regulated institutions and between these institutions and AUSTRAC. These initiatives included the establishment of the Fintel Alliance as a public-private information-sharing partnership involving the large reporting institutions and government agencies; investigating options for law reform to support information sharing; and exploring technological innovation that alters the fundamental constraints underlying the traditional AML/CTF model. In particular, AUSTRAC supported the development of privacy-preserving analytical technologies that allow mass analysis of financial data without any data collection. The technology, FinTracer, is a means for financial institutions to discover, and to report to AUSTRAC, suspicious actors in their data, even when this suspicion is based on behaviour of actors that spans multiple financial institutions. This behaviour would have traditionally been impossible to detect without extensive information-sharing.

The core technology powering this novel process is homomorphic encryption, which allows oblivious computation: a form of computation in which the party performing the processing does not see the inputs or outputs of its own computation. Using oblivious computation, the financial institutions and AUSTRAC can jointly perform data analysis, while all information that would have otherwise required sharing is only shared in encrypted form, oblivious to the party it is shared with, and thus not running afoul of any information-sharing restrictions.

This chapter discusses the FinTracer case study. It considers the international, AUSTRAC-specific, and technological contexts within which it was developed, considers the context within which it was intended to function, describes the technology, and reflects on the potential impact, benefits, and risks relating to such technologies.

2 Information-Sharing Challenges and AML/CTF/CPF: Global Policy Background

The modern AML/CTF system requires effective information and data exchanges by public and private sector stakeholders to effectively counter criminal money flows. Initial design gaps and legal and operational barriers prevent effective information sharing.[3]

The AML/CTF regime is outlined in the non-binding standards of the Financial Action Task Force (FATF). First convened by the G7 plus 1 meeting in Paris in 1989 to advise the G7 on actions to be taken to protect their financial system from money laundering abuse, the task force's recommendations have since been amended, expanded, and hardened into global standards—the Forty Recommendations—that

[3] See Ahmed (2025) in this book for more on challenges to information sharing.

are endorsed and implemented by more than 200 jurisdictions. Technical compliance and effectiveness of implementation are reviewed by peers in a mutual evaluation program, and countries that are assessed as insufficiently compliant may be grey- or blacklisted.

The original recommendations were aimed at strengthening the measures agreed in the 1988 UN Convention on Drugs and Psychotropic Substances.[4] The latter, for example, required countries to criminalise drug-related money laundering.[5] The FATF's recommendations envisaged an expanded role for financial institutions that went beyond efforts to avoid committing a money laundering offence. The recommendations required countries to prohibit institutions from opening anonymous accounts or accounts in obviously fictitious names.[6] They also required institutions to identify and verify their customers.[7] Importantly, the recommendations also broke down the barriers formed by commercial "bank secrecy" by requiring countries to permit or compel institutions to report transactions suspected of involving funds stemming from criminal activity to competent authorities, now generally known as FIUs.[8]

The 1990 Recommendations addressed privacy in a number of ways. Firstly, they explicitly stated that financial institution secrecy laws should be conceived so as not to inhibit the implementation of the task force's recommendations.[9] Secondly, they required legal protection for institutions and their employees from criminal or civil liability for the breach of any restriction on disclosure of information imposed by contract or by any legislative, regulatory, or administrative provision when they report, in good faith, suspected criminal activity to competent authorities, regardless whether such activity actually occurred. Thirdly, they introduced an additional layer of confidentiality: financial institutions, their directors and their employees should not be allowed to warn their customers when information relating to them is being reported to the competent authorities.[10]

The Recommendations framework therefore created an information stream from individual regulated institutions to the FIU while also siloing those disclosures to prevent direct or indirect tipping off of the affected customers.

The initial framework viewed financial institutions as sufficiently informed to manage their compliance obligations and identify reportable transactions. The flow of information was uni-directional and siloed: institutions had to file reports with financial intelligence agencies but government agencies were not required to

[4] UN Convention against Illicit Traffic in Narcotic Drugs and Psychotropic Substances (1990).

[5] UN Convention against Illicit Traffic in Narcotic Drugs and Psychotropic Substances (1990), Art 3.

[6] Financial Action Task Force (1990), R 12.

[7] Financial Action Task Force (1990) R 12. R 13 required them to take reasonable measures to establish beneficial ownership.

[8] Financial Action Task Force (1990) R 16. The concept of a financial intelligence unit was only introduced into the 2003 revised Recommendations though more than 80 countries had established such specialised units by 1983. See International Monetary Fund (2004) 1.

[9] Financial Action Task Force (1990) R 2.

[10] Financial Action Task Force (1990) R 17.

provide any information to institutions.[11] Official secrecy obligations would generally prevent the sharing of meaningful information with the private sector, especially given the sensitivity of criminal intelligence.

These gaps and prohibitions remained in place as the FATF standards broadened to the proceeds of all serious offences (1996),[12] the financing of terrorists (2001),[13] and proliferation financing (2012).[14] However, the need for improved information-sharing increased when risk-based compliance measures were first allowed in 2003[15] and deepened when risk-based country and institutional responses became mandatory in 2012.[16] This has led to the emergence of national financial information-sharing initiatives such as the UK's Joint Money Laundering Intelligence Task Force, a partnership between law enforcement and the leading regulated institutions, intended for the sharing and analysis of information in order to prevent, detect and disrupt money laundering;[17] Transaction Monitoring Netherlands (TMNL), an initiative by five leading Dutch banks to combine their transaction data and enable the monitoring and analysis of transactions across different banks and financial institutions;[18] and, in Australia, the Fintel Alliance, discussed in Sect. 3 below.

These initiatives have however been hampered by legal barriers, especially by limited participation, mainly by large financial institutions and increasingly by privacy, data protection, and non-disclosure requirements.[19] Historically the FATF's privacy and data protection concerns were focused on these as barriers to law enforcement access to financial data but cybercrime has made it increasingly sensitive to the need to balance the access needs and privacy and data protection obligations.[20]

The past decade has also seen a rising interest in using technology to support more effective and efficient AML/CTF measures. Private sector AML/CTF compliance costs are estimated to amount to more than US $200 billion per year[21] and these costs form unintended barriers to financial inclusion. Responsible innovation can support improved AML/CTF measures while lowering the staggering private sector costs of the relevant AML/CTF compliance. Significant developments have

[11] De Koker and Turkington (2015), Chadderton and Norton (2019), Turkington (2019), Chadderton (2025).

[12] Financial Action Task Force (1996).

[13] Financial Action Task Force (2001).

[14] Financial Action Task Force (2012).

[15] Financial Action Task Force (2003).

[16] Financial Action Task Force (2012) R 1.

[17] Maxwell (2019).

[18] Siegers (2024). Note that they are amending their model to adapt to new EU AML regulations that provide a broad legal basis for inter-bank information-sharing cooperation and integration while also addressing relevant privacy and data protection. See Transactic Monitoring Nederland (2024).

[19] Chadderton (2025).

[20] Financial Action Task Force (2022).

[21] Lexis Nexis Risk Solutions (2023).

taken place in so-called RegTech, that could support improved legal compliance by institutions, and in SupTech, which would improve risk-based supervision by supervisory authorities.[22]

In 2017, the FATF adopted the so-called San Jose Principles to support responsible, risk-sensitive AML/CTF technology innovation.[23] In 2021, it endorsed a paper identifying innovative privacy-preserving technologies that enable robust AML/CTF information sharing and analysis while preserving privacy as one of a set of measures that may advance the San Jose Principles.[24] This endorsement was informed by a paper that considered a number of developments in privacy-preserving technology, including the project that is discussed in this paper.[25]

3 Australian Motivation to Develop New Technology

Australia has a robust regulatory framework, with AUSTRAC having a dual role as both the national FIU and as a regulator monitoring AML/CTF compliance in the financial system.

AUSTRAC operates under the *Anti-Money Laundering and Counter Terrorism Financing Act 2006*. The latter has been amended on several occasions, most recently to expand the list of reporting entities required to report suspicious transactions and to, inter alia, make it easier for reporting entities and AUSTRAC to take action without transgressing the otherwise strong prohibitions on infringing the 'tipping off' provisions in relation to reports made to AUSTRAC and AUSTRAC notices.

While simplifying some aspects, information-sharing restrictions remain. AUSTRAC was therefore motivated for some time to find technological solutions that allow near real time querying and analysis of data whilst adhering to the privacy protection regime.

3.1 Intelligence Gathering

As Australia's national FIU, AUSTRAC has the mandate to monitor suspicious financial activity, analyse transaction data, and collaborate with law enforcement agencies and international bodies in the investigation of criminal activity. As per other national FIUs globally, AUSTRAC's analysis of these reports is intended to help uncover trends, anomalies, and outliers indicative of financial crime.

---

[22] Financial Action Task Force (2017, 2021).

[23] Financial Action Task Force (2017, 2021).

[24] Financial Action Task Force (2021) 60.

[25] Maxwell (2020).

This intelligence helps identify potential illicit activity, which, in turn, assists law enforcement to target investigative efforts and build briefs of evidence that may result in prosecutions. As this description implies, AUSTRAC does not carry out criminal prosecutions itself, but has assisted in efforts to prosecute, for example, money laundering activities linked to international drug syndicates, tax evasion schemes and a range of other illegal activity.

Therefore the task for AUSTRAC as an FIU can be described as follows:

> Maximise the ability to detect signs/indications of wrongdoing ('first order' analysis);
>
> Carry out 'second order' (i.e. further targeted) analysis where warranted, taking into regard additional information; and
>
> Package that intelligence to be passed on or available to an appropriate authority, e.g., for it to build a brief of evidence aimed at a prosecution, or similar activity.

Advances in bulk data analytical capability and, latterly, the promise that artificial intelligence (AI) capabilities bring to enhanced analysis have increased the ability of entities like AUSTRAC to use algorithmic methods to detect suspicious patterns in financial flows. The more efficiently this can be done, the more likely that relatively scarce 'second order' analytical capabilities can be brought to bear on actual wrongdoing, thereby saving time and money and increasing the chances of success.

There are, perhaps, three broad categories of circumstances that motivate 'second order' analysis:

- Confirmation/enhancement of existing suspicion—FIU data holdings used to confirm and/or flesh out concerns generated externally (e.g., by law enforcement);
- Known typologies/patterns indicative of financial crime recognised by experienced FIU analysts or through automated means;
- Novel typologies/patterns of concern identified by FIU analysts or through automated means.

In each of these cases, whether performed by human analysts or technology, there is inherent bias in that the analysis in all these cases, to varying degrees, is influenced by the experience and knowledge of previous examples. To achieve the best outcomes an FIU needs access to the largest possible data set of historical financial transactions, ideally of the entire financial system. The danger of having only a very partial view of the data, such as the view that AUSTRAC has of suspicious transactions, is that this creates a significant learning bias: the examples visible are those of suspected bad actors working in known ways, creating a danger of the analysis being biased towards identifying similar actors and the same known methodologies. The ability to view the entire financial system, which AUSTRAC does not have due to privacy considerations, is therefore key to financial investigation, regulation and enforcement that are both more effective and more equitable.

3.2 *Navigating Privacy and Data Protection*

From the perspective of detecting patterns, indicators and typologies of concern, an FIU's most powerful data is contained in its indigenous data sets which are generated by information supplied by each reporting entity individually.

AUSTRAC functions within a privacy and data protection framework, formed in particular by the Privacy Act 1988 (Cth) and its Australian Privacy Principles (APPs). As a result, there are limitations to AUSTRAC's ability to 'see' the whole picture: when transactions are not considered a priori suspicious by AUSTRAC or by the reporting entity, the only reportable transactions are those that involve transfer of funds across Australia's borders and those involving cash deposits and withdrawals above threshold limits. In particular, without prior suspicion domestic transactions are not reportable at all.

The privacy protections also mean that individual financial institutions cannot freely share personal information about customers with each other. Prior to 2025 "tipping-off" provisions precluded any information-sharing with a body or person other than AUSTRAC to prevent alerting criminals that there might be or was an ongoing investigation of the suspicious activity. As discussed, the information-sharing measures introduced in 2024 lower some of the barriers under certain conditions but information-sharing remains restricted, also under the *Privacy Act 1988*.

This means that the decision regarding whether a customer acted suspiciously is formed by each institution based on that customer's transactions with it. Should a customer have bank accounts with three banks each bank would only report a transaction as suspicious if the customer's transactions with that bank appear suspicious. The full—and suspicious—patterns of interbank transactions might not be visible from the perspective of any individual bank, and hence it may not be reportable to AUSTRAC.

3.3 *Goals with FinTracer*

Given the above, when AUSTRAC considered its requirements in developing new technology, the effort which ultimately produced the technology that is the subject of this paper, its goals might have been said to be: avoiding the limitations in activity imposed by the privacy legislation, whilst infringing individual privacy to the minimum level possible; providing the ability to 'see' and analyse the entirety of the financial system and in a way that enabled algorithmic, user-friendly analysis; and maximising the ability to uncover patterns of concern associated with both known and novel techniques.

4 Privacy-Preserving Data Analytics

Privacy Enhancing Technologies (PETs) are a relatively new but rapidly evolving field. They include, for example,

1. *Zero Knowledge Proofs*[26] — A general method,[27] originating from the mathematical literature of Interactive Proof Systems,[28] that allows one party to prove a claim,[29] assert their knowledge of some secret,[30] or make a commitment,[31] all without revealing any additional information: the claim is proved to be true without the verifier gaining any information that would allow them to prove the claim or make the assertion themselves, and the commitment is made without the verifier gaining any information regarding what the party committed to. Such proofs, especially in their non-interactive forms,[32] are now in standard use in cryptocurrency blockchains in order to enable so-called "smart contracts".[33]
2. *Differential Privacy*[34] — An information-theoretic framework for adding noise into database query results in such a way that the querying party can learn aggregated statistical information about the contents of the data, but not gain knowledge about any specific data item within the database. This allows the release of statistical information such as from census data, without compromising the privacy of the individuals whose data is reported. Differential privacy is presently used in many organisations, including for official purposes, such as at the U.S. Census Bureau.[35]
3. *Pseudonymisation*[36] — This is one of the oldest and most ubiquitous PETs. It has been used to protect the privacy of individuals, for example, both in health data[37] and in processing personal information in educational institutions.[38] Use of it in designated contexts is now mandated both in the EU[39] and the USA.[40] Pseudonymisation consists of replacing identifying data by arbitrary data that

[26] Aad (2023).

[27] Ben-Or et al. (1990).

[28] Babai (1985), Goldwasser, Micali and Rackoff (1989).

[29] Blum (1986).

[30] Rackoff and Simon (1991).

[31] Jain et al. (2012).

[32] Blum, Feldman and Micali (1988), Wu and Wang (2014).

[33] Zhou et al. (2024).

[34] Dwork (2008).

[35] Abowd et al. (2022).

[36] Hintze and El Emam (2018).

[37] Tinabo, Mtenzi and O'Shea (2009).

[38] Limba and Šidlauskas (2020).

[39] European Union (2016).

[40] Centers for Medicare & Medicaid Services: The Health Insurance Portability and Accountability Act of 1996 (HIPAA).

consistently stands for it, in a way that preserves the logical structure of the information.

4. *Secure Multiparty Computation*[41] — This is a family of protocols that allow a set of participants to jointly compute a known function using inputs from all participants, in a way that the inputs of each individual participant remain private, and only the final result is revealed. The most commonly used protocol for this purpose is the Ben-Or–Goldwasser–Wigderson (BGW) algorithm,[42] which works over the Shamir secret sharing algorithm,[43] which is one of many known methods of how to divide a secret between multiple participants such that only a large enough coalition of the participants would be able to retrieve the secret.[44]

   Typically, as in the BGW algorithm, the coalition of participants can decide who they want to entrust the final computational result to, which may be, for example, one individual or all participants. These methods can be equipped with resilience against dishonest (or otherwise non-cooperative) participants, and their strength does not need to rely on cryptographic assurances. Secure Multiparty Computation is a general method, in the sense that any function of the inputs can be computed using it.

5. *Homomorphic Encryption*[45]— Stemming from public key cryptography,[46] homomorphic encryption is any encryption method that allows a party to perform arithmetic operations on encrypted data without decrypting it, a process known as "oblivious" computation. Early versions of it,[47] known as Partially Homomorphic Encryption methods, allowed one to compute only one arithmetic operation (typically addition) on the ciphertexts. Later, new algorithms were discovered that enabled both addition and multiplication (which, together, enable any function to be computed), but only a certain number of multiplications were allowed. These are known as Somewhat Homomorphic Encryption methods, or as Levelled Homomorphic Encryption because each multiplication conceptually happens on one of a predefined set of "levels".[48]

   Fully Homomorphic Encryption (FHE) was introduced in 2009 by Craig Gentry,[49] who devised a method, known as "bootstrapping", to allow to reset encryptions to their initial level, and by this to allow, theoretically, an unlimited number of multiplications and therefore the oblivious computation of general functions. In practice, bootstrapping was a very slow process, which was required

---

41 Cramer and Damgård (2015).

42 Ben-Or, Goldwasser, and Wigderson (2019).

43 Shamir (1979).

44 Krenn and Lorünser (2023).

45 Yi et al. (2014), Acar et al. (2018), Gentry (2010).

46 Rivest, Adleman and Dertouzos (1978).

47 E.g., Paillier (1999).

48 Boneh, Goh and Nissim (2005), Ishai and Paskin (2007).

49 Gentry (2009), Gentry and Halevi (2011).

very often, for which reason much research in FHE has since focused on speeding up this process. Bootstrapping can now be done in fractions of a second.[50]

Other recent advances in FHE include the ability to perform oblivious computation over floating-point numbers,[51] which has opened the door for the use of FHE in many new domains, such as machine learning. FHE algorithms are implemented in many commercial software libraries, such as HEAAN, SEAL, HElib and PALISADE, and are in practical use, for example in healthcare.[52]

As can be seen, each of these technologies solves a different type of privacy problem, and are appropriate in different situations. Each technology also has inherent drawbacks: Zero Knowledge Proofs and Homomorphic Encryption solutions are both typically very slow; Zero Knowledge Proofs and Secure Multiparty Computation both typically require orders of magnitude more communication than non-private computation of the same functions; differential privacy offers guarantees that erode with use; and pseudonymisation comes with no guarantees — indeed, many pseudonymisation attempts have failed because pseudonyms were identifiable from ostensibly non-identifying data.[53]

PETs of all types have been considered in the context of preventing financial crime. Secure Multiparty Computation has been considered, e.g., for the detection of fraud[54] and for anti-money laundering,[55] and FHE for anti-money laundering was analysed by Effendi and Chattopadhyay.[56]

In both approaches, the main problem is lack of speed, which prevents scalability. Considering two papers from 2024: in the Secure Multiparty Computation approach of Van Egmond et al.,[57] 3 hours were required to run one pass of the algorithm over only 200,000 accounts (which is far less than a full-scale deployment); in the FHE approach of Effendi and Chattopadhyay, the data was subsampled to only 9070 accounts and 5491 transactions in order to make the analysis feasible at all, and even so calculation of the basic features alone required 36 minutes.[58] This represents a slowdown compared to plaintext analysis by a factor of 90,000.

In addition to the slowdown (and associated blow-up in communication sizes), there are open questions regarding how solutions such as these address the larger context in which their algorithms are meant to operate. The FHE approach of Effendi and Chattopadhyay, for example, envisions financial crime investigation as proceeding as follows. First, all parties encrypt all of their data. They then give their encrypted data to a third party, which analyses all of it in one bucket in order to

[50] Chillotti et al. (2016).

[51] Cheon et al. (2017).

[52] Munjal and Bhatia (2022).

[53] See, e.g. Tudor, Almgren and Papatriantafilou (2015).

[54] Sangers et al. (2019).

[55] Van Egmond et al. (2024), Zand, Orwell, and Pfluegel (2020).

[56] Effendi and Chattopadhyay (2024).

[57] Van Egmond et al. (2024).

[58] Effendi and Chattopadhyay (2024).

derive a final result. This final result is then decrypted. It is not considered whether it is practicable for a bank to encrypt the entirety of all its data. It is not considered who would be suitable to be said third party, and who would be interested in taking on this task. Most problematically, it is never specified who holds the decryption key, though whoever does so would hold a great deal of power. Suppose, for example, that a government FIU is the party meant to ultimately see the final result, and therefore it owns the decryption key. All participants in the process, including all banks, must share their most sensitive data with a third party. Even though the data is encrypted and the third party cannot peek into it, the banks do still need to trust this party to not let the FIU peek into it. This requires substantially more trust than cryptographic algorithms typically allow.

The same FHE-based approach was also tried in the BIS Innovation Hub's first phase of Project Aurora,[59] but the approach was ultimately deemed "unfeasible due to the size of the encrypted financial transaction data".[60] As a result, fallbacks utilising other privacy-preserving methods, like differential privacy, were used instead.

By contrast to the above, a 2020 FFIS report[61] surveyed the state of privacy-preserving analysis for tackling financial crime in a practical setting. It included only 10 real-world examples, and they are characterised by using a mix of available technologies in order to address particular real-world scenarios.

One of the 10 examples cited in the FFIS report is the "Alerting Project" by the Australian Transaction Reports and Analysis Centre (AUSTRAC). This was the earlier name of FinTracer, which is discussed in this chapter.

FinTracer's core algorithm uses homomorphic encryption, but not FHE: partial homomorphic encryption is much faster and offers a practical alternative. It also does not use the typical homomorphic encryption paradigm in which computation is offloaded to a "third party". Instead, it plays to the strengths of the method by having the banks themselves perform computations obliviously, in a scenario where the secret being kept by the banks is the specifics of said computation.

Outside its core algorithm (and beyond the scope of this chapter), FinTracer also uses other PETs, such as differential privacy, where appropriate, mixing and matching techniques in order to create a desired outcome, both in terms of privacy preservation and in terms of computational capability.

5 FinTracer

In this section, we demonstrate how privacy-preserving data analytics can be used to close financial intelligence gaps created by Australia's financial integrity and privacy rules, while protecting the privacy of customers behaving lawfully.

---

[59] Bank for International Settlements (2023).

[60] Bank for International Settlements (2023), p. 49.

[61] Maxwell (2020).

Our case-in-point is FinTracer,[62] a name used to describe a suite of interrelated privacy-preserving algorithms that was initially conceived and developed as part of a project at AUSTRAC, and which AUSTRAC subsequently realised in software and released in open source under the name "FTILLite".[63]

5.1 When Privacy Is Not a Concern

If there had been no privacy or information-sharing restrictions or concern—a world where privacy-preserving technology would not have been needed—the most effective way to detect financial crime would have been to pool all available data from all institutions into a single database and query it.

Indeed, some countries, where such practices are not prohibited, do this already, embracing intrusion into privacy and the associated cybersecurity risks. Though many software tools exist that can be used to analyse such data, ultimately all rely on the underlying data being represented either directly in a graph database or otherwise in a way that allows it to be queried in much the same way as it would have been queried in a graph database.

Such graph databases allow users to define queries in some structured language (such as GQL, the ISO standard), [64] and these, ultimately, provide the user with programmatic control over what is queried. In the context of financial crime prevention, such programmatic control is essential, because financial crime is highly adaptive, and the effectiveness of any tool for detecting it hinges entirely on its versatility.

Notably, such querying, done over a consolidated, centralised dataset, is very different to what is typically done by private entities. An individual bank analysing its own data will typically query it using means such as those provided by traditional relational databases, with variants of SQL being their structured query language of choice. The difference is that while an individual bank has access to much information about individual accounts — not only their monetary inflows and outflows, but also significant amounts of Know Your Customer (KYC) data — it typically has no visibility of similar information relating to any counterparty accounts at other banks that any given account transacts with. A bank interested in analysing their own transactions, whether due to regulation or in order to manage their own financial risks, is therefore forced to do so using an account-centric method, where the risks and suspicions related to each of its accounts are determined independently of the attributes of the accounts they transact with at other institutions.

By contrast, when all data is pooled, this opens up much more effective ways to detect financial crime. Considered holistically, instances of financial crime are

[62] Brand, Ivey-Law, and Churchill (2023).

[63] AUSTRAC (2023a).

[64] Deutsch et al. (2022).

occurrences that often involve multiple accounts. Some of these may be victim accounts while others may belong to unknowing facilitators. Some are single-use accounts that have been set up by the criminals specifically for the perpetration of a particular crime, whereas others are accounts to which the ill-gotten funds are pooled, where they can be funnelled, laundered, and ultimately distributed. The full end-to-end unfolding of any given financial crime is a complex set of interactions between these various accounts. Different types of financial crime are characterised by distinct patterns of such interactions. We call such patterns *criminal typologies*.

The difference between relational databases (as are typically used by individual banks analysing their own data) and graph databases (as would be used to analyse nationally consolidated data) is that while the former is geared towards analysing the *properties* of individual accounts, the latter is naturally suited to describe *relationships* between them, including when these relationships are indirect: money may flow from one account to another, for example, across multiple intermediary accounts. This, it turns out, is the natural way to express criminal typologies.

The goal of the FinTracer algorithm suite is to provide financial investigators with querying capabilities analogous to those that would have been accessible to them through graph querying had all data been pooled together, but without this pooling and its associated risks, without prohibited private-to-private information exchange, and without intrusion into the privacy of uninvolved customers.

This allows criminal typologies to be defined as behavioural patterns, using a querying language that is as programmatically configurable, customisable and powerful as a graph database, and therefore delivering the effective financial oversight that historically would only have been possible through data pooling, but through means that are fully privacy-respecting.

5.2 A Practical Example

To explain how privacy and effective financial supervision are reconciled in the FinTracer methodology, let us introduce a very simple example that will serve as our motivating example and as a running example throughout. This example was chosen for its simplicity, and purposefully does not showcase FinTracer's more powerful and complex abilities. These will be discussed in later sections.

As our motivating example, we consider the practice of *layering*. Layering is when a criminal who introduced proceeds of crime into the financial system engages in different acts to move the money or value around the system to add layers of legitimacy to the funds and to make it harder to trace the proceeds back to its criminal origin.

Concretely, let us suppose that some account, *A*, in some bank, *AA Bank*, is a business account that receives some government assistance meant to facilitate the running of the business.[65]

If the money is received into account *A* and immediately transferred internationally, for example to a foreign account with known criminal ties, the account-based financial surveillance employed by *AA Bank* should be able to detect this, at which point the bank would be able to submit to AUSTRAC a Suspicious Matter Report (SMR). Consider how this situation can easily be characterised by a set of properties of the account, of a type that can easily be expressed in SQL. We are considering a situation in which an account

1. Receives significant amounts of government funding (which can be determined by considering the source account), and
2. Subsequently transfers a significant amount of funding internationally, to one of a list of accounts known to be suspicious.

In defining an actual typology, one may want to be more or less specific, for example in describing the actual amounts, the quantitative relationship between them, the time correspondence between inflow and outflow, the characterisation of source and destination accounts, etc. For our purpose, these specifics are immaterial. The main takeaway is only that account-centric monitoring can readily determine suspicion when faced with this behavioural pattern. It is not the case that such suspicion necessarily indicates wrongdoing, but it is enough to trigger a report to AUSTRAC, and to allow subsequent focused investigation, including one in which otherwise-private details may be revealed by the bank to AUSTRAC, in order to actually determine if any wrongdoing occurred.

Sophisticated criminals, knowing that this behavioural pattern is vulnerable to detection, can, however, complicate matters and avoid detection by a practice known as "layering": distancing the fund influx from its transfer out of the country. Suppose, for example, that the criminal organisation opens a new bank account, *B*, at a different bank, *BB Bank*, which it uses for the international transfer. Now, the behavioural pattern has changed: government funds enter account *A*, are funnelled through account *B*, and are only then transferred internationally.

Despite how small a distinction this is from a behaviour point of view, it is highly disruptive for account-centric surveillance. Consider what each party can observe. Bank *AA* sees the government funds coming in but cannot tell whether or not their transfer to *B* is done in the legitimate course of business of their customer. Bank *BB* sees the international transfer, but without visibility of the source of the funds, it would generally not be viewed as a suspicious transaction. AUSTRAC, at best, can see the first and last of the three transactions in the sequence. It has, however, no visibility of the connecting transfer from account *A* to account *B*. In short, despite the fact that this is suspicious behaviour involving only three transactions, and

[65] In Australia such business incentives are common. For example, at the time of writing, the Australian government is offering up to AU$25,000 in assistance to small businesses impacted by a severe weather event that occurred in Tasmania 4 months earlier.

despite the fact that there are AML programs in place that can observe any two of the three, no single organisation has visibility of the entire group of transactions, and therefore no organisation can identify the suspicious nature of the transactional activity.

In practice, if such behaviour is detected at all, this is done by means of a targeted search. For example, the Australian Federal Police (AFP) may be conducting a specific investigation against a particular organisation, it may then determine regarding specific individuals that they are in high likelihood participating in this type of fraud and may reach out to AUSTRAC for it to gather more information. AUSTRAC, in turn, may ask the banks to deliver to it all their information about the specific individuals' accounts. In the best-case scenario, both account *A* and account *B* will be among this list, providing AUSTRAC with all the information it needs. Less auspiciously, only one of the two accounts will be revealed to AUSTRAC, in which case this information will not be enough.

Let us say that only account *B* is in the suspicious list (and that AUSTRAC is only aware, a priori, of the single international transfer). As a last-resort option, if the AFP is convinced regarding *B* that it is involved in illicit behaviour, AUSTRAC may still be able to uncover the entire funnelling process by examining every one of *B*'s transactions, determining regarding each transaction and each counterparty account their likelihood of being part of an illicit scheme, and then approaching every other bank that transacted with *B* whose transactions are on AUSTRAC's suspicious list and require every one of the transactions of every one of the counterparty accounts to those transactions. Through such a massive blanket search, account A may be uncovered, but the cost of manual analyst labour, both at AUSTRAC and in the banks, will be substantial, the process itself may take weeks, and, most importantly for our present discussion, the cost to privacy will be highly significant, with the full information of hundreds of "innocent bystander" accounts being turned over to AUSTRAC despite no evidence of any wrongdoing.

If the criminal organisation distances the international transfer account even further from account *A* by introducing a few more intermediaries, discovery by such means as described becomes entirely unfeasible: the cost in time and labour becomes untenable, and the privacy implications grow exponentially with each added hop. The upshot is that even trivial amounts of layering defeat standard detection paradigms, and that only those criminal enterprises that are already well known and under heavy investigation can be brought to justice: the system is geared only towards confirming the guilt of already-targeted individuals, not towards the novel discovery of wrongdoing based on the available data.

This is as opposed to the type of graph-analytical, behaviour-based detection that can be done if one (somehow) has access to the entirety of the transaction data. In graph-query terminology, we are seeking to find two accounts, *A* and *B*, such that

1. *A* receives substantial amounts of funds from government assistance;
2. *B* transfers substantial amounts of funds internationally; and
3. There is a sequence of transactions of some small length through which *A* can transfer substantial amounts of funds to *B*, whether directly or indirectly.

A search for all accounts matching this criminal typology would have detected *A* and *B*, even when the two are significantly more separated from each other than in our original example.

Indeed, a recent study by the Bank for International Settlements[66] found that using behaviour-based analysis increases detection rates by a factor of 3.

As with account-centric queries, one can choose to make the criminal typology's behaviour-based definition broader or narrower. For our purpose, we will show how to discover a case where *A* transmits substantial funds to the international transfer account, *B*, while distancing itself from *B* by use of three separate intermediaries, none of which are previously known to investigators. However, even this example, which is far beyond the capabilities of normal financial investigation to uncover when respecting the privacy of individuals, should be understood to be merely a simple example in order to explain the workings of FinTracer. It is the tip of the iceberg of possible usages, and not, in any way, a demonstration of FinTracer's full capabilities.

5.2.1 The FinTracer Ecosystem

Before delving into the FinTracer algorithm, let us consider the organisational and technological framework within which it was developed to function.

FinTracer was designed to work with multiple parties, each party retaining full control and management of their own data, as well as sole visibility to it. In our purposefully minimalist example scenario, the parties are only those essential for the FinTracer suite: the banks and AUSTRAC itself. However, other parties may also participate. The FinTracer system is meant to allow one party (in the Australian case, AUSTRAC) to run queries on the system and receive the results of these queries.

The system runs over a set of cloud-connected computation nodes, which we refer to as "segment nodes". Each segment node may be, in practice, one or more computers. Each node is managed by one of the parties. In addition, there is one "compute node", which is the node managed by the query-runner. In practice, this means that each bank owns one segment node whereas AUSTRAC owns both a segment node and a compute node, but in our specific example we will not need AUSTRAC's segment node at all.

The segment nodes serve multiple functions:

1. They store data that the node owner decided to import into the FinTracer ecosystem. In AUSTRAC's FTILLite implementation, this data storage is in the form of a PostgreSQL database. This data is secret. It is not exposed to any of the other parties. However, for it to be used in FinTracer computations it must be laid out in a schema as instructed by or as agreed with the query-runner.

[66] Bank for International Settlements (2023).

2. They store data internal to the FinTracer system that is used as part of the system's computations. In the FTILLite implementation, this data is stored in Go variables and is not persistent. However, instructions from the segment node may cause all or parts of it to be saved to and loaded from a special schema in the PostgreSQL database.
3. They receive instructions from the compute node and perform them using their own data, returning results back to the compute node if needed. In the FTILLite implementation, basic data manipulation is done in Go, and compute-intensive cryptographic operations are performed on the node's GPU, in Nvidia CUDA, using a special library, "ftcrypto", also developed at AUSTRAC as part of the FinTracer project.[67]
4. When instructed by the compute node, segment nodes transmit and receive data between each other. Note, however, that FinTracer algorithms are designed in such a way that no secret data is ever revealed through such inter-node communication. In the FTILLite implementation, this communication is performed using https.

In FTILLite, the compute node itself runs Jupyter; user queries are written in Python and receive results via Python function calls. This is an environment that financial analysts are familiar and comfortable with. Communication between the compute node and the segment nodes is done via RabbitMQ. All FTILLite nodes are OCI instances that can be cloud-deployed using Docker.

Figure 1 demonstrates the overall FTILLite system architecture.

It should be noted that the data of banks is different between banks and also managed differently. It would not have been realistic to expect all banks to suddenly consolidate all their data management processes and upload all their data into their respective segment nodes. Instead, FinTracer only expects segment nodes to be populated when necessary for particular computations. In practice, AUSTRAC, managing the compute node, will inform the other parties when specific data should be uploaded, and its desired format.

However, there is one table that we expect almost all FinTracer queries to utilise, so this table can be assumed to be populated and kept updated at all times, without need for specific manual coordination. This is the transaction table. Each bank is expected to place on its respective segment node the basic information of all incoming and outgoing transactions: "from" account number, "to" account number, amount and date. Consolidating and importing this data into the segment node is the minimum requirement for a bank to participate in the FinTracer ecosystem. In tackling our running example, this will be the only table used.[68]

[67] AUSTRAC (2023b).

[68] Notably, there is no expectation for even this one table to be updated in real time. Even that would have been too large a burden placed on the participating banks, and for no good reason: FinTracer analysis is envisioned as forensic analysis, not real-time analysis. The expectation is for a reasonable update cadence to be agreed on. For example, it may be agreed that the transaction table should contain all transactions from the previous year, up to the first of 1 month prior to the current month.

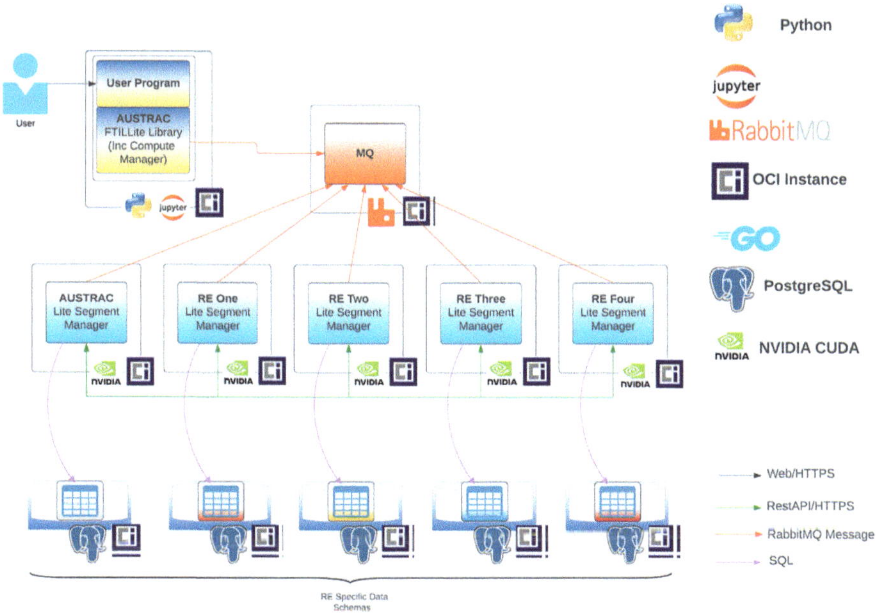

Fig. 1 High-level FTILLite architecture. (Image credit: David Spencer. Used with permission.)

5.2.2 How FinTracer Works

FinTracer is a suite of interconnected algorithms based around one core algorithm, but in order to tackle the criminal typology defined in our motivating example only the core algorithm is required. We will now walk through how this core algorithm functions, over the architecture described.

Consider Fig. 2, which depicts a (highly simplified) instance of the motivating example from which we started. Each of the four quadrants in the image represents one of Australia's four major banks. Letters in each quadrant represent individual accounts managed by each bank. Arrows between accounts indicate that a substantial sum of money was transferred between the accounts. We've highlighted two accounts in particular: account *E*, in green, is "Jim's Gym", a business account that has received government assistance; account *I*, in red, is an account known to transmit funds to foreign accounts with known criminal ties. The problem we will address—in itself, a highly simplified version of problems AUSTRAC needs to tackle—is determining whether account *E* is funnelling funds to account *I* via some intermediary accounts, making this a case of suspected layering.

In this specific instance, the correct answer would be that layering is, indeed, occurring: funds are transferred through the path marked in purple (*E* to *F* to *K* to *H* to *I*) as well as through a second path marked in blue (*E* to *F* to *G* to *L* to *I*). The question is how AUSTRAC can ascertain that such connections exist without gaining any information at all about any of the other transactions in the network, namely

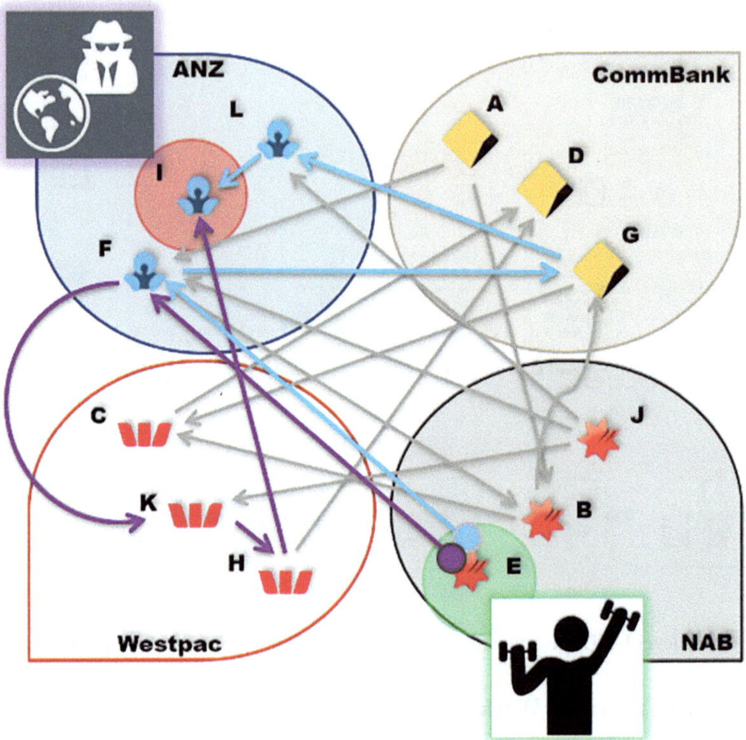

Fig. 2 A simple layering example. (Image credit: Dana Achrafi. Used with permission.)

those depicted in grey. Without FinTracer, following such a layering path through four separate transactions would have been entirely unfeasible, unless all relevant accounts have been previously flagged as suspicious.

For the purposes of our example, we will assume that AUSTRAC is interested in finding a layering connection specifically between E and I, as though these two accounts (but none of the others) have been previously flagged, but this is mainly in order to simplify the presentation. FinTracer would have been equally effective if the question had been, for example, regarding *any* account that received government assistance and *any* account with significant transfers to offshore accounts, without there having to be any prior suspicion regarding any of the participating accounts whatsoever.

The mechanism that powers FinTracer is the *FinTracer tag*. A FinTracer tag is a very small piece of information that each bank stores for each of the accounts it manages. Importantly, only the managing bank can see the tag related to each account. A FinTracer tag stores only a single bit of information, a 'yes' or a 'no'. The FinTracer algorithms use these tags as variables that can be manipulated, each variable representing a subset of all accounts (namely, those for which the bit is 'yes'). In our context, it is useful to think of a 'yes' as indicating 'interesting' (for the present query), but they can be used to mean anything at all, in the sense that they are manipulated completely programmatically.

A FinTracer tag stores its information in an encrypted form[69], for which only AUSTRAC has the key. The encrypted form is 128 bytes long (which is longer than 1 bit but still quite compact) and we guarantee by cryptographic means that it is impossible for an account's tag to store more than a single bit of information.

Figure 3 depicts the same transaction network as in Fig. 2, but rearranged for

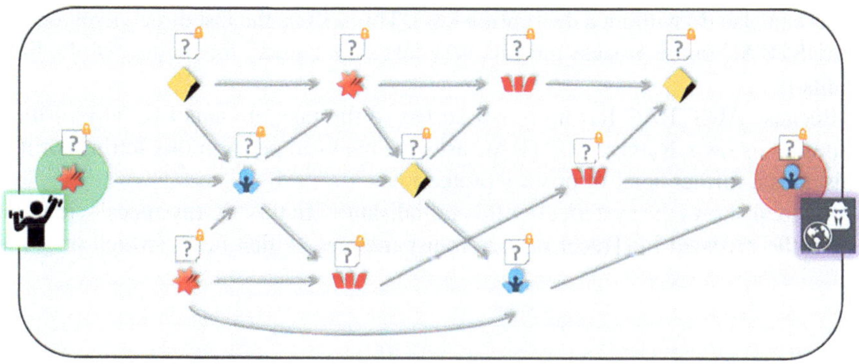

Fig. 3 The transaction network, with FinTracer tags. (Image credit: Dana Achrafi. Used with permission.)

visual clarity, and with a FinTracer tag represented for each account. The lock symbol next to each tag indicates that it is encrypted, and the question mark indicates that the bank managing the tag cannot read its value. This is because only AUSTRAC holds the encryption key.

What makes FinTracer tags so powerful is that no matter how they are manipulated or exchanged between the banks, no new information can be discovered by any party: the banks cannot divulge any information from the tags because they are encrypted, and AUSTRAC cannot glean any information because it has no visibility of the tag values; only the banks hold the tags and only AUSTRAC holds the key.[70] This arrangement provides us with ample flexibility to design algorithms that detect

[69] For those interested in the technical cryptographic details, FinTracer uses ElGamal encryption (ElGamal 1985; Menezes, Van Oorschot and Vanstone 2018 pp. 294-298) over the additive Curve25519 (Bernstein 2006) twisted Edwards elliptic curve group (Bernstein et al. 2008), storing curve points in their extended projective form (Hisil et al. 2008). This is the same curve as is used in the Ed25519 digital signature algorithm (Bernstein et al. 2011). It is a form optimised for speed, and is especially suited for GPU implementation, as was done in, e.g., Cui et al. 2014. FTILLite's own optimised GPU implementation of it, "libftcrypto", is based on the "libsodium" library (Bernstein and Denis 2019).

[70] For the benefit of cryptography experts, we add that tags are also "refreshed" prior to being communicated. This is yet another cryptographic protection meant to ensure that no unintended information reveal occurs.

desired typologies by a process of tag exchange, without this risking any information leakage (including the exposure of private information).

Although no party in the real world can see the values of the FinTracer tags, for the purpose of explaining the algorithm we will draw the tags with their values visible as if we have special powers to view information otherwise not visible, such as using "X-ray specs". In our specific example, the algorithm begins with AUSTRAC asking each bank to reset all of their tag values to 'no' (which banks can do, even without a decryption key). Following this, AUSTRAC asks the bank managing the account belonging to "Jim's Gym" to set that particular tag value to 'yes' (which the banks can also do without a decryption key). This will be the last direct involvement of AUSTRAC in the process until its very last step, namely the reading of the final results.

Because AUSTRAC has no direct access to the tags, it cannot set any of their values on its own. Rather, AUSTRAC asks the banks to perform this setting for it.[71] This adds a further layer of privacy protection.

Figure 4 shows the system after this initialisation. In this "X-ray specs" view, we depict the revealed FinTracer tags as transparencies. A tick mark (which only the

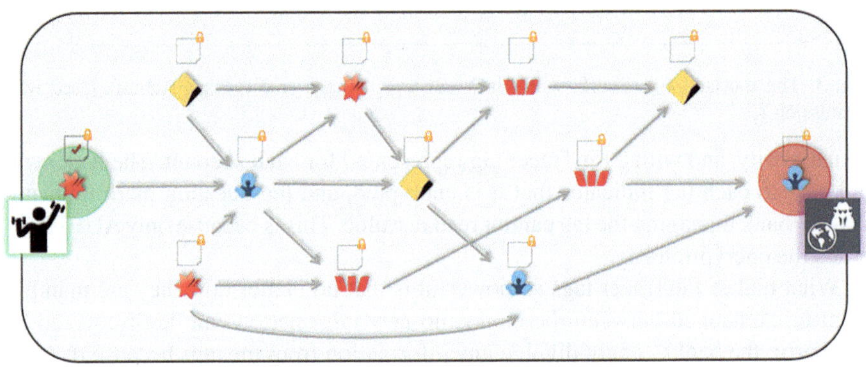

Fig. 4 Initial state of the FinTracer tags. (Image credit: Dana Achrafi. Used with permission.)

[71] Technically, in the FTILLite system, this would be the AUSTRAC compute node instructing the bank's segment node to set the tag value. If AUSTRAC knows the account number for "Jim's Gym", this can be done automatically, through purely programmatic means. However, the fact that it is the bank setting the value also allows for much flexibility, including flexibility that can only be attained through some manual intervention. For example, AUSTRAC may not know the account number for Jim's Gym, in which case it will ask the bank to upload this number into an agreed-upon new table in the bank's PostgreSQL database. This action does not reveal any new information to AUSTRAC, because it is done entirely in the bank's segment node. In the same way, AUSTRAC can ask the banks to tag all accounts belonging to, say, cash-heavy businesses that received government assistance, and the banks would be able to resolve this request manually, outside of the FinTracer system, based on their own KYC data and their own understanding of what "cash-heavy" means, and would then be able to upload this information to their segment node's PostgreSQL database, from which point all tagging can be done automatically. Even though potentially a great many accounts may get tagged in such a process, no new information is ever revealed through this to AUSTRAC or any other party.

tag relating to Jim's Gym possesses) indicates a 'yes', whereas an empty transparency (all other accounts) indicates a 'no'.

What follows now is an algorithmic step we refer to as "FinTracer tag propagation", which is the heart of the FinTracer algorithm. In this step, each bank transfers the tag value of each account along the propagation edges. Like other tag operations discussed, tag transfer is a process that can be done "obliviously", i.e., without either the sending bank or the receiving bank knowing what the tag value is.

Figure 5 depicts the state of the system after one tag propagation step. The tick mark from Jim's Gym has wandered to the account pointed to by the arrow from the gym's account. Importantly, however, all the tags without tick marks have also changed hands: the banks do not know, and don't need to know, what values their tags carry.

We note that in our specific example, the arrows represent "transactions of a substantial amount". In practice, different typologies require different propagation criteria. Just like we were able to filter from the graph of all transactions only those transmitting "a substantial amount" (where the term "substantial" can be used to mean different thresholds in different contexts, relevant to the finding of different typologies), it is also possible to filter by any other criterion, such as the transaction date, or the KYC properties of the sending and receiving accounts. For example, some accounts may be whitelisted altogether.[72] Moreover, in searching some typologies, one may not want to "follow the money" at all. It is often useful, for example, to propagate tags in a direction opposite to the money flow. As a concrete example, FinTracer may be used to determine whether the owners of two accounts had some dealings with each other, by observing that the two accounts had a direct transaction between them. In such a case, the direction of money flow in the transaction is immaterial to the detected connection.

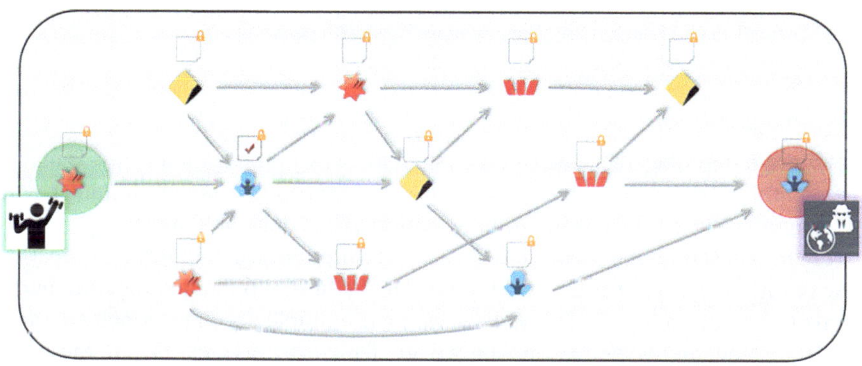

Fig. 5 After one propagation step. (Image credit: Dana Achrafi. Used with permission.)

[72] Though such filtering is always doable, the exact technicalities of how to do it properly are somewhat beyond the scope of the present description.

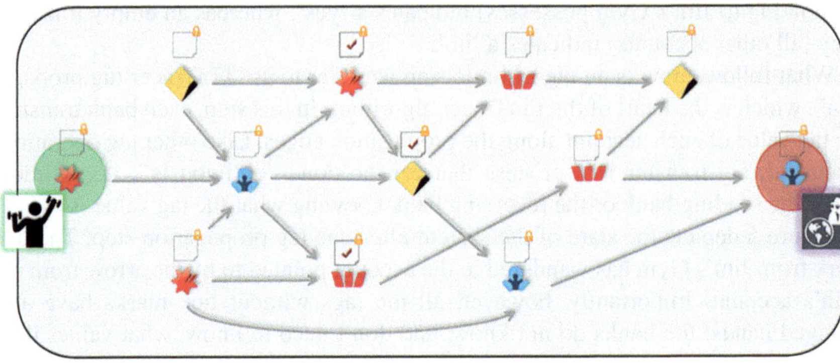

Fig. 6 After 2 steps. (Image credit: Dana Achrafi. Used with permission.)

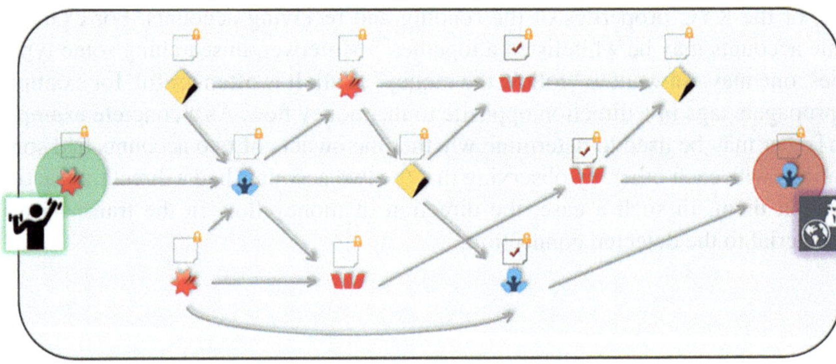

Fig. 7 After 3 steps. (Image credit: Dana Achrafi. Used with permission.)

Figure 6 describes the state of the system after two propagation steps. It makes the point that tags are not shared just with one connecting account but rather with all, simultaneously. This, again, is an operation that is done obliviously.

Figure 7 describes the state of the system after three propagation steps. Comparing it with Fig. 6, we see that the two top tick marks in Fig. 6 merged together into a single tick mark in Fig. 7. This is how we treat multiple accounts connecting to a single account, and is the reason why we are depicting FinTracer tags in these figures as transparencies: like transparencies layered on top of each other, it is enough for *any* of the original tags to be tick-marked, for the final result to carry a tick mark. Performing this consolidation of tag values obliviously, under encryption, requires a special type of encryption known as homomorphic encryption. The encryption type used in the project is homomorphic, and supports all other special properties that are required for the functioning of the algorithm, both from a functionality point of view and from a security one.

Assuming that we are interested in detecting cases of layering where the funds are funnelled through 4 "hops", we need to run 4 propagation steps of the FinTracer algorithm. The state of the system after the fourth and final propagation step is depicted in Fig. 8.

There may be many accounts tagged at this point, but the one important tag value for discovering our particular typology of interest is the tag value of the right-most account depicted, this being the account known to move money internationally, which is our suspected international transfer account for the illicit funds. In our example, this account is now tick-marked, and this indicates that the typology was detected: funds did flow from Jim's Gym to this destination account. We know this, because throughout the entire algorithm the tick marks followed the flow of the money. If the single tick mark that was initially seeded in the account belonging to Jim's Gym made it all the way to the jump-off account, it is because it travelled along the same path as funds that also made it from the former account to the latter. Conversely, if no such path had existed, the international transfer account would not have been tick-marked, leading the algorithm to conclude that these two accounts are not examples of the target typology.

This, however, is not the end of the algorithm. Recall from Fig. 3 that it is only due to our fictional "X-ray specs" that we can tell whether the final tag is tick-marked or not. In reality, no party in this algorithm is at this point aware of the tag's value.

In the actual FinTracer system, there are many different methods that can be used to read tag values, but in this particular instance the simplest method suffices: AUSTRAC (or, more specifically, the AUSTRAC compute node) may simply request from the relevant bank (which is to say, from its segment node) the value of this one tag. As previously discussed, we've made it impossible for a tag to store any more information than a single bit value. It is this bit value, namely the bit indicating whether the target typology was discovered or not, which is the final tag value

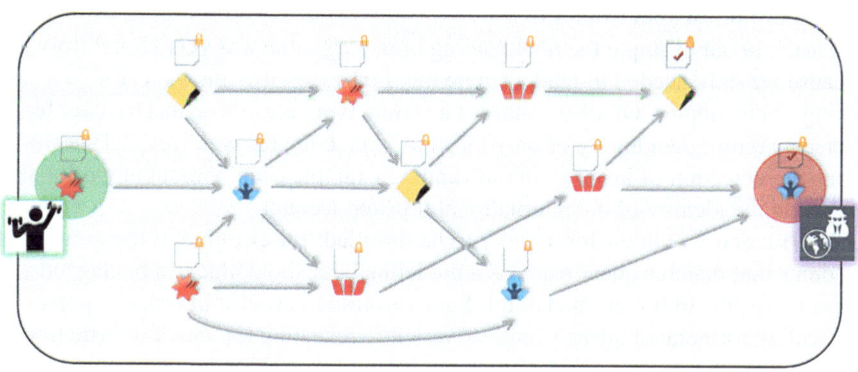

Fig. 8 After the final propagation step. (Image credit: Dana Achrafi. Used with permission.)

of the international transfer account, that the bank now transfers to AUSTRAC, in encrypted form. AUSTRAC can then decrypt it and discover the answer to whether the typology was found, without any other information being revealed to it or to any other party.

5.2.3 Handling More Complex Scenarios

The above example was chosen specifically to support a basic explanation of the technology, but FinTracer's capabilities extend far beyond this, and are limited only by what we choose to query. Similar, but slightly more complicated processes to what was demonstrated can be used in the FinTracer system to tackle more complex scenarios and more complex requirements.

For example, real world typologies are far more complicated than just a single link (even if indirect) between two accounts. Suppose, for example, we want to define a (still somewhat simplified) typology that would describe tender or procurement fraud. Such a typology may involve 3 entities, a government entity (G), an employee of said entity (E), and a tender applicant (A), and may be described by

1. G is a government entity,
2. G pays wages to E,
3. G pays substantial funds to A (presumably, upon winning the tender), and
4. A transfers funds (possibly indirectly) to E.

Furthermore, in a realistic formulation of such a typology, each of G, E and A would be represented by multiple accounts, and KYC information will be used to connect such accounts together, thus creating a typology involving many additional accounts and many additional connections.

FinTracer has the ability to join such conditions together, in order to find instances of G, E and A for which all the above conditions are simultaneously satisfied, and return only those as results.

FinTracer return values can also be arbitrarily complex. For example, instead of asking "Is there a connection from A to B?" we can ask "Which are the accounts along the shortest path from A to B?".

Lastly, in our example the final reading of the tag value was very straightforward because we only needed to read a single tag. FinTracer also allows reading tags by asking, for example, "Of all accounts of a certain type (e.g., those that transfer funds overseas) return the identity of only those for which the tag was 'yes'". This would allow the detection of layering in our running example even without any prior suspicion on the identity of the international transfer account.

FinTracer even allows for a query to be throttled: for example, if the number of accounts that match a query exceeds a predefined threshold, this can be flagged and allow no results to be returned at all. Such throttling is useful in order to prevent a too-widely formulated query from inadvertently revealing too much information.

There are many other variants that can be implemented using the same mechanisms. For example, in the AUSTRAC implementation, in order for the project to be appealing not just for AUSTRAC but also for AUSTRAC's Reporting Entities, it was agreed that that the Reporting Entities will always know exactly which queries are being run and will have visibility of the accounts matching the query before any results are communicated to AUSTRAC. Querying mechanisms working under other constraints would also have been possible.

In every case, FinTracer can return the correct answer, without revealing any additional information, and in all cases, FinTracer's searches, even when run on data as large as the entire Australian economy, can return their results within between minutes and hours, depending on the complexity of the query, replacing an otherwise long and arduous manual process entailing substantial intrusion into the privacy of uninvolved individuals.

5.2.4 Future Plans

The FTILLite implementation that currently exists in open-source was designed as a prototype. Although perfectly suitable for all examples described here, it does not implement some more advanced features that were initially envisioned for the project. As an example, perhaps the most important of the features still missing is that in the envisioned full solution Reporting Entities can meaningfully monitor and individually approve which queries they allow to be run on their segment nodes. Algorithmic solutions for all such more-nuanced requirements have already been devised (and are documented in the open-source documentation)[73] but additional work is needed to make these ideas into a reality.

Even without such additional complications, FinTracer is fully functional. We have demonstrated how it tackles layering and gave a high-level overview of what detecting tender fraud may look like, but the same principles apply if one searches for other financial crimes, including ones of corruption, fraud, and racketeering. Moreover, existing tools have difficulty integrating into their queries risk indicators such as whether a certain account belongs to a Politically Exposed Person (PEP) or whether a certain person has beneficial ownership over some trust fund. However, viewed as indicators that are a relationship between accounts, such indicators are straightforward to describe, and in FinTracer, they can easily be integrated into any query.

We hope soon more countries and stakeholders will consider the power of privacy preserving data analysis as illustrated by FinTracer, and will reap the benefits of better financial security at unprecedented levels of protection to the privacy of individuals.

[73] Brand (2023).

6 Reflection

The AML/CTF space can benefit greatly from analytical technologies that help stakeholders to navigate privacy and confidentiality rules. These rules are important to observe but they pose a range of challenges in relation to the sharing of crime-combating information.

Privacy-preserving data analytics appear to provide solutions, but attempts to apply it in the AML/CTF context have so far met with only limited success. The solutions were either too slow or too impractical to be employed successfully in practice. FinTracer, on the other hand, skirts those limitations.

It applies partial homomorphic encryption which is much faster than FHE and therefore offers a practical alternative. It also does not use the typical homomorphic encryption paradigm where computation is done by a third party. Instead, it leverages the strengths of the technology by having the banks themselves perform computations obliviously, in a scenario where the secret being kept by the banks is the specifics of said computation.

Outside its core algorithm (and beyond the scope of this chapter), FinTracer also uses other PETs, such as differential privacy, where appropriate, mixing and matching a variety of techniques in order to create a desired outcome, both in terms of protection of privacy and in terms of computational capability. FinTracer recognises that despite the wide array of available PETs, each designed to address a different situation, none of them was designed for the specific quirks of the privacy situation in financial analysis. Specifically, FinTracer capitalises on the fact that the details of every inter-bank transfer are known to both the payer's bank and the payee's bank. This is a fact not analysed in the standard PET literature, but which allows FinTracer to work orders of magnitude faster than other solutions, without any loss of privacy.

Furthermore, whereas many other attempts to use PETs at scale do so by restricting the system to essentially compute only one algorithm,[74] FinTracer's design recognises that financial crime is adaptive, and therefore only a highly flexible system can combat it. For this reason, FinTracer supports what amounts to general graph-database queries, as would normally be used by analysts in the non-privacy-preserving setting, where all information is pooled into a single data repository.

Lastly, FinTracer was designed with full consideration of the larger context, for example by providing incentives for each participating party: when running FinTracer, not only are detected criminal typologies reported to the FIU, but the portion of them that is relevant to each bank is also reported to the bank, thus providing for each bank tangible returns for their investment in the system. Again, while traditional PETs may consider different scenarios regarding who should be privy to the final results of the computation, the complexities of the partial reporting that are needed in the real-world situation, and which FinTracer was specifically built to account for, were never set as goals for any of the academic investigations into the topic.

---

[74] As in the case of Sangers et al. (2019).

Thus, while the FinTracer design represents a continuation of the existing literature on the topic, using only existing building blocks in its construction, the way these building blocks are put together is novel both in its aims and its accomplishments, and provides a new avenue for PETs in financial analysis that is specifically designed with practicality and real-world feasibility in mind.

The release of the technology as open source now provides an opportunity for AML/CTF stakeholders globally to consider the solution and to determine how best to use privacy-preserving data analytics to support effective, efficient, and responsible AML/CTF measures. This technology and approach can revolutionise the way in which not only AML/CTF but also related crime-combating measures, for example in relation to fraud and scams, has been approached since the 1990s. It can be an especially valuable tool for public-private and for private-private financial crime combating partnerships.

References

Aad I (2023) Zero-knowledge proof. In: Mulder V, Mermoud A, Lenders V, Tellenbach B (eds) Trends in data protection and encryption technologies. Springer, Cham, pp 25–30. https://doi.org/10.1007/978-3-031-33386-6_6

Abowd JM, Ashmead R, Cumings-Menon R, Garfinkel S, Heineck M, Heiss C, Johns R, Kifer D, Leclerc P, Machanavajjhala A, Moran B, Sexton W, Spence M, Zhuravlev P (2022) The 2020 census disclosure avoidance system TopDown algorithm. Harvard Data Sci Rev (Special Issue 2). https://doi.org/10.1162/99608f92.529e3cb9

Acar A, Aksu H, Uluagac AS, Conti M (2018) A survey on homomorphic encryption schemes: theory and implementation. ACM Comput Surv (Csur) 51(4):1–35

Ahmed S (2025) Surveilling the citizen: constitutional tensions within the Canadian AML regime. In: Goldbarsht D, de Koker L, Ferrill J (eds) Combating financial crime: intended and unintended consequences. Springer, Cham

AUSTRAC (2023a) FTILLite. https://github.com/AUSTRAC/ftillite. Accessed 29 July 2025

AUSTRAC (2023b) libftcrypto. https://github.com/AUSTRAC/libftcrypto. Accessed 29 July 2025

AUSTRAC (2024) About us. https://www.austrac.gov.au/about-us. Accessed 29 July 2025

Babai L (1985) Trading group theory for randomness. In: Proceedings of the seventeenth annual ACM symposium on theory of computing. ACM, New York, pp 421–429

Bank for International Settlements (2023) Project Aurora: the power of data, technology and collaboration to combat money laundering across institutions and borders. Basel. https://www.bis.org/publ/othp66.pdf. Accessed 29 July 2025

Bennett Moses L, De Koker L (2017) Open secrets: balancing operational secrecy and transparency in the collection and use of data by national security and law enforcement agencies. Melb Univ Law Rev 41(2):530–570

Ben-Or M, Goldreich O, Goldwasser S, Hastad J, Kilian J, Micali S, Rogaway P (1990) Everything provable is provable in zero-knowledge. In: Goldwasser S (ed) Advances in cryptology – CRYPTO '88, Lecture notes in computer science, vol 403. Springer, Berlin, pp 37–56

Ben-Or M, Goldwasser S, Wigderson A (2019) Completeness theorems for non-cryptographic fault-tolerant distributed computation. In: Goldreich O (ed) Providing sound foundations for cryptography: on the work of Shafi Goldwasser and Silvio Micali. ACM, New York, pp 351–371

Bernstein DJ (2006) Curve25519: new Diffie-Hellman speed records. In: Public key cryptography – PKC 2006: 9th international conference on theory and practice in public-key cryptography, New York, NY, USA, April 24–26, 2006, proceedings 9. Springer, Berlin, pp 207–228

Bernstein DJ, Denis F (2019) Libsodium – a modern, portable, easy to use crypto library. https://github.com/jedisct1/libsodium. Accessed 29 July 2025
Bernstein DJ, Birkner P, Joye M, Lange T, Peters C (2008) Twisted Edwards curves. In: International conference on cryptology in Africa. Springer, Berlin, pp 389–405
Bernstein DJ, Duif N, Lange T, Schwabe P, Yang BY (2011) High-speed high-security signatures. In: International workshop on cryptographic hardware and embedded systems. Springer, Berlin, pp 124–142
Blum M (1986) How to prove a theorem so no one else can claim it. In: ICM Proceedings, pp 1444–1451
Blum M, Feldman P, Micali S (1988) Non-interactive zero-knowledge and its applications. In: Proceedings of the twentieth annual ACM symposium on Theory of computing – STOC '88, pp 103–112
Boneh D, Goh EJ, Nissim K (2005) Evaluating 2-DNF formulas on ciphertexts. In: Theory of cryptography: second theory of cryptography conference, TCC 2005, Cambridge, MA, USA, February 10–12, 2005. Proceedings. Springer, Berlin, pp 325–341
Brand M (2023) The complete, authorised and definitive FinTracer compendium: a work in progress. https://github.com/AUSTRAC/ftillite/blob/main/Documentation/Purgles/ft_combined.pdf. Accessed 29 July 2025
Brand M, Ivey-Law H, Churchill T (2023) FinTracer: a privacy-preserving mechanism for tracing electronic money. https://eprint.iacr.org/2023/649. Accessed 29 July 2025
Chadderton P (2025) Take a look at what I just found! Anti-money laundering and public and private sector information and intelligence-sharing in Australia. PhD thesis, La Trobe University
Chadderton P, Norton S (2019) Public-private partnerships to disrupt financial crime: an exploratory study of Australia's Fintel Alliance (Swift Institute Working Paper 2017-003). https://www.swift.com/swift-resource/252230/download. Accessed 29 July 2025
Cheon JH, Kim A, Kim M, Song Y (2017) Homomorphic encryption for arithmetic of approximate numbers. In: Takagi T, Peyrin T (eds) Advances in cryptology – ASIACRYPT 2017. Lecture notes in computer science, vol 10624. Springer, Cham, pp 409–437
Chillotti I, Gama N, Georgieva M, Izabachene M (2016) Faster fully homomorphic encryption: bootstrapping in less than 0.1 seconds. In: Advances in cryptology – ASIACRYPT 2016: 22nd international conference on the theory and application of cryptology and information security, Hanoi, Vietnam, 4–8 December 2016, proceedings, part I. Springer, Berlin, pp 3–33
Cramer R, Damgård IB (2015) Secure multiparty computation. Cambridge University Press, Cambridge
Cui S, Großschädl J, Liu Z, Xu Q (2014) High-speed elliptic curve cryptography on the NVIDIA GT200 graphics processing unit. In: International conference on information security practice and experience. Springer, Cham, pp 202–216
De Koker L, Turkington M (2015) Anti-money laundering measures and the effectiveness question. In: Rider BAK (ed) Research handbook on international financial crime. Edward Elgar Publishing, Cheltenham, pp 520–531
Deutsch A, Francis N, Green A, Hare K, Li B, Libkin L, Zemke F (2022) Graph pattern matching in GQL and SQL/PGQ. In: Proceedings of the 2022 international conference on management of data, ACM, New York, pp 2246–2225
Dwork C (2008) Differential privacy: a survey of results. In: Agrawal M, Du D, Duan Z, Li A (eds) Theory and applications of models of computation, Lecture notes in computer science, vol 4978. Springer, Heidelberg, pp 1–19
Effendi F, Chattopadhyay A (2024) Privacy-preserving graph-based machine learning with fully homomorphic encryption for collaborative anti-money laundering. In: International conference on security, privacy, and applied cryptography engineering. Springer, Berlin, pp 80–105
ElGamal T (1985) A public key cryptosystem and a signature scheme based on discrete logarithms. IEEE Trans Inf Theory 31(4):469–472
European Union (2016) Regulation (EU) 2016/679 of the European Parliament and of the Council of 27 April 2016 on the protection of natural persons with regard to the processing of per-

sonal data and on the free movement of such data, and repealing Directive 95/46/EC (General Data Protection Regulation). https://eur-lex.europa.eu/eli/reg/2016/679/oj/eng. Accessed 4 October 2025

Financial Action Task Force (1990) The Forty Recommendations of the Financial Action Task Force on money laundering. FATF, Paris. https://www.fatf-gafi.org/content/dam/fatf-gafi/recommendations/FATF%20Recommendations%201990.pdf. Accessed 29 July 2025

Financial Action Task Force (1996) The Forty Recommendations. https://www.fatfgafi.org/en/publications/Fatfrecommendations/Review-and-history-of-fatf-standards.html. Accessed 29 July 2025

Financial Action Task Force (2001) FATF IX Special Recommendations. FATF, Paris. https://www.fatfgafi.org/en/publications/Fatfrecommendations/Ixspecialrecommendations.html. Accessed 29 July 2025

Financial Action Task Force (2003) The Forty Recommendations. https://www.fatf-gafi.org/content/dam/fatf-gafi/recommendations/FATF%20Recommendations%202003.pdf. Accessed 29 July 2025

Financial Action Task Force (2012–2025) International standards on combating money laundering and the financing of terrorism & proliferation: the FATF Recommendations. FATF, Paris. https://www.fatf-gafi.org/content/dam/fatfgafi/recommendations/FATF%20Recommendations%202012.pdf.coredownload.inline.pdf. Accessed 29 July 2025

Financial Action Task Force (2017) FATF FinTech and RegTech Forum. FATF, Paris. https://www.fatf-afi.org/en/publications/Fatfgeneral/Fatf-fintech-regtech-forum-may-2017.html. Accessed 29 July 2025

Financial Action Task Force (2021) Opportunities and challenges of new technologies for AML/CFT. FATF, Paris. https://www.fatf-gafi.org/publications/fatfrecommendations/documents/opportunities-challenges-newtechnologies-aml-cft.html. Accessed 29 July 2025

Financial Action Task Force (2022) Partnering in the fight against financial crime: data protection, technology and private sector information sharing. FATF, Paris. https://www.fatf-gafi.org/publications/digitaltransformation/documents/partnering-in-the-fightagainst-financial-crime.htm. Accessed 29 July 2025

Gentry C (2009) Fully homomorphic encryption using ideal lattices. In: Proceedings of the forty-first annual ACM symposium on Theory of Computing, ACM, New York, pp 169–178

Gentry C (2010) Computing arbitrary functions of encrypted data. Commun ACM 53(3):97–105

Gentry C, Halevi S (2011) Implementing Gentry's fully-homomorphic encryption scheme. In: Annual international conference on the theory and applications of cryptographic techniques. Springer, Heidelberg, pp 129–148

Goldwasser S, Micali S, Rackoff C (1989) The knowledge complexity of interactive proof systems. SIAM J Comput 18(1):186–208

Hintze M, El Emam K (2018) Comparing the benefits of pseudonymisation and anonymisation under the GDPR. J Data Protect Privacy 2(2):145–158

Hisil H, Wong KKH, Carter G, Dawson E (2008) Twisted Edwards curves revisited. In: International conference on the theory and application of cryptology and information security. Springer, Berlin, pp 326–343

International Monetary Fund (2004) Financial intelligence units – an overview. https://doi.org/10.5089/9781589063495.069

Ishai Y, Paskin A (2007) Evaluating branching programs on encrypted data. In: Theory of cryptography conference. Springer, Berlin, pp 575–594

Jain A, Krenn S, Pietrzak K, Tentes A (2012) Commitments and efficient zero-knowledge proofs from learning parity with noise. In: International conference on the theory and application of cryptology and information security. Springer, Berlin, pp 663–680

Krenn S, Lorünser T (2023) An introduction to secret sharing: a systematic overview and guide for protocol selection. Springer, Cham

Lexis Nexis Risk Solutions (2023) LexisNexis Risk Solutions study reveals global financial crime compliance costs for financial institutions totals more than U.S.$206 billion. https://risk.lexisnexis.com/global/en/about-us/press-room/press-release/20230926-global-financial-crime-compliance-costs. Accessed 29 July 2025

Limba T, Šidlauskas A (2020) Personal data processing in educational institutions: anonymisation and pseudonymisation. In: ICERI2020 proceedings. IATED, Valencia, pp. 9989–9997

Maxwell NJ (2019) Expanding the capability of financial information-sharing partnerships (RUSI Occasional Paper). https://static.rusi.org/20190320_expanding_the_capability_of_financial_information-sharing_partnerships_web.pdf. Accessed 29 July 2025

Maxwell NJ (2020) Innovation and discussion paper: Case studies of the use of privacy preserving analysis to tackle financial crime (RUSI FFIS Discussion Paper). https://www.gcffc.org/wp-content/uploads/2020/06/FFIS-Innovation-and-discussion-paper-Case-studies-of-the-use-of-privacy-preserving-analysis.pdf. Accessed 29 July 2025

Menezes AJ, Van Oorschot PC, Vanstone SA (2018) Handbook of applied cryptography. CRC Press, Boca Raton

Munjal K, Bhatia R (2022) A systematic review of homomorphic encryption and its contributions in healthcare industry. Complex Intell Syst 9(4):3759–3786

Paillier P (1999) Public-key cryptosystems based on composite degree residuosity classes. In: International conference on the theory and applications of cryptographic techniques. Springer, Berlin, pp 223–238

Paterson JM (2024) Know your customer in the digital age: challenges of privacy, data security and the speed of technological development. Univ Western Aust Law Rev 52:53–82

Rackoff C, Simon DR (1991) Non-interactive zero-knowledge proof of knowledge and chosen ciphertext attack. In: Annual international cryptology conference. Springer, Berlin, pp 433–444

Rivest RL, Adleman L, Dertouzos ML (1978) On data banks and privacy homomorphisms. Found Secure Comput 4(11):169–180

Sangers A, Heesch MV, Attema T, Veugen T, Wiggerman M, Veldsink J, Bloemen O, Worm D (2019) Secure multiparty PageRank algorithm for collaborative fraud detection. In: International conference on financial cryptography and data security. Springer, Cham, pp 605–623

Shamir A (1979) How to share a secret. Commun ACM 22(11):612–613

Siegers N (2024) Transaction monitoring Netherlands: fighting financial crime through data collaboration and advanced analytics. J Payments Strategy Syst 18(1):51–60

Tinabo R, Mtenzi F, O'Shea B (2009) Anonymisation vs. Pseudonymisation: which one is most useful for both privacy protection and usefulness of e-healthcare data? In: 2009 International Conference for Internet Technology and Secured Transactions (ICITST). IEEE, Piscataway, pp 1–6

Transactie Monitoring Nederland (2024) Collaborating towards effective transaction monitoring. https://tmnl.nl/en/. Accessed 4 October 2025.

Tudor V, Almgren M, Papatriantafilou M (2015) A study on data de-pseudonymization in the smart grid. In: Proceedings of the Eighth European Workshop on System Security, ACM, New York, pp. 1-6.

Turkington M (2019) The effectiveness of private sector engagement in international financial crime countermeasures. PhD thesis, La Trobe University

UN Convention against Illicit Traffic in Narcotic Drugs and Psychotropic Substances (opened for signature 20 December 1988, entered into force 11 November 1990) 1582 UNTS 95

Van Egmond MB, Dunning V, Van den Berg S, Rooijakkers T, Sangers A, Poppe T, Veldsink J (2024) Privacy-preserving anti-money laundering using secure multi-party computation. In: International conference on financial cryptography and data security. Springer, Berlin, pp 331–349

Wu H, Wang F (2014) A survey of noninteractive zero knowledge proof system and its applications. Sci World J 2014:560484

Yi X, Paulet R, Bertino E (2014) Homomorphic encryption. In: Homomorphic encryption and applications. SpringerBriefs in Computer Science. Springer, Cham. https://doi.org/10.1007/978-3-319-12229-8_. Accessed 29 July 2025

Zand A, Orwell J, Pfluegel E (2020) A secure framework for anti-money-laundering using machine learning and secret sharing. In: 2020 international conference on cyber security and protection of digital services (cyber security), IEEE, Piscataway, pp 1–7

Zhou L, Diro A, Saini A, Kaisar S, Hiep PC (2024) Leveraging zero knowledge proofs for blockchain-based identity sharing: a survey of advancements, challenges and opportunities. J Inf Secur Appl 80:103678

Michael Brand is an Adjunct Professor at the RMIT School of Computing Technologies. Previously, he was Associate Professor of Data Science and Artificial Intelligence at Monash University and director of the Monash Centre for Data Science. His publications range from fundamental number, graph and computation theory to highly practical statistical data analysis. Outside of academia, Michael has been a data scientist and an algorithm developer for the last 30 years, having held Chief Scientist or equivalent roles in multiple organisations worldwide, including as Chief Data Scientist of Telstra Corporation (at the time, the world's 14th largest telecom company by revenue). Since 2018, Michael has been the head and founder of Otzma Analytics (otzmaanalytics.com), a data science consultancy specialising in helping businesses maximise their value from data. As algorithm developer, Michael has developed novel privacy preservation technologies, as well as novel technologies for analysing speech, video and LIDAR data. Michael holds 19 patents and additional pending patents on topics ranging from Big Data analysis to information retrieval and from machine vision to speech analytics.

Louis de Koker is a professor of law at La Trobe Law School (Australia), an advisory board member of the Financial Integrity Hub (FIH) and an extraordinary professor in the Department of Commercial and Labour Law of the University of the Western Cape (South Africa). A significant part of his financial crime research focuses on managing the relationship between financial inclusion and anti-money laundering and counter terrorist financing objectives. He has undertaken various university research engagements with bodies such as the World Bank and the Asian Development Bank and has worked closely with the World Bank-housed Consultative Group to Assist the Poor (CGAP). This work extended to a range of developing countries including Ghana, Indonesia, Kenya, Kyrgyzstan, Malaysia, Namibia, Nigeria, Uganda, Ukraine and Palau. His research has been cited in publications and research papers of international bodies such as the World Bank, the IMF, the Basel Committee on Banking Supervision, and the International Labour Organization. Louis has held visiting positions at a range of institutions including the Institute for Advanced Legal Studies (London) SOAS (London), Wolfson College (Oxford), the University of Florida (US) and the Autonomous University of Barcelona.

Carl Herse After a 25-year career in Australia's Foreign Service, Carl served as the National Manager Intelligence Capabilities at AUSTRAC (Australia's Financial Intelligence Unit), where he led the development of the 'FIU of the Future' model. This emphasized advanced data analytics, cutting-edge analytical tools, and the delivery of actionable insights for AUSTRAC's key stakeholders in law enforcement, national security, and financial services. Since leaving AUSTRAC in late 2022 he has run his own consultancy which focuses on strategic advisory services in risk, data analysis and planning in Australia, PNG, the UAE and Japan.

Central Bank Digital Currencies, Financial Inclusion and Financial Integrity: Trade-Off?

Vivienne Lawack

Abstract Central Bank Digital Currency (CBDC) is a digital version of a country's fiat currency that is issued and backed by a country's central bank. The purpose of CBDCs is to provide a digital alternative to physical cash, which is becoming less popular due to the rise in usage of digital payments. This chapter examines the potential of retail CBDC to enhance financial inclusion in emerging markets and developing economies (EMDEs). To this end, the chapter examines the nature and characteristics of CBDC and the emergence of CBDC in EMDEs. The chapter highlights key considerations for financial inclusion and barriers pertaining to retail CBDC and how CBDC may address these barriers. It juxtaposes financial integrity by examining the financial integrity risks that may be introduced by CBDC, risks for central banks that may arise and how these may be mitigated. The chapter makes some observations on the trade-off between the competing interests of financial inclusion and financial integrity for retail CBDCs.

1 Introduction

Payment services are inextricably linked to the history of central banking. Ever since the inception of central banking, payment-related innovation has always been an integral part of central banking. Payments have evolved extensively over the years. For example, the arrival of financial technologies or 'fintech' has led to cryptocurrencies and now central bank digital currency (CBDC).[1] A CBDC represents

[1] On cryptocurrencies, Reddy and Lawack 2019, pp. 1–28; see also Deloitte 2021 https://www.deloitte.com/lu/en/Industries/banking-capital markets/research/central-bank-digitsl-currencies-money-tomorrow.html accessed on 5 February 2025 accessed on 3 May 2021.

V. Lawack (✉)
Academic at the University of the Western Cape, Cape Town, South Africa
e-mail: Vlawack@uwc.ac.za

D. Goldbarsht et al. (eds.), *Combating Financial Crime*, Ius Gentium: Comparative Perspectives on Law and Justice 131,
https://doi.org/10.1007/978-3-032-06858-3_3

another potential innovation in the area of an evolving branch of the law called 'fintech law'.

Central banks in emerging markets and developing economies (EMDEs) are increasingly considering central bank digital currencies (CBDCs) to enhance financial inclusion and support a digital economy. A Bank for International Settlements (BIS) survey of over 60 central banks found financial inclusion to be a primary motivation for pursuing CBDCs in EMDEs.[2] This was confirmed by an Alliance for Financial Inclusion (AFI) survey in 2021, where all participants cited financial inclusion as their main reason for developing CBDCs.[3]

This chapter examines retail CBDC as a vehicle for financial inclusion and juxtaposes this policy objective with financial integrity risks. The chapter explores the nature and characteristics of CBDC, some barriers to financial inclusion, financial integrity and potential risks that may arise should CBDCs be adopted. The author makes observations on whether a "trade-off" would be needed.

2 The Nature and Characteristics of Central Bank Digital Currency

There is no universal definition of CBDC as it can vary depending on the context and the design choices made by different central banks. For the purposes of this chapter, CBDC can best be described as a digital representation of cash or fiat currency. In other words, a CBDC is a digital payment instrument denominated in the local currency and is a direct liability of the central bank.[4] It can be either a balance in a central bank account or a digital equivalent of physical cash.

Two distinct types of CBDC exist, namely wholesale or retail forms. Wholesale CBDC supports large-scale payments in national systems such as real-time gross settlement systems (RTGS) and securities settlement.[5] Retail CBDC, similar to cash, is issued by the central bank and is directly usable by consumers for transactions or value storage via tokens or accounts.[6]

---

[2] Boar and Wehrli BIS Papers (2021), pp. 1–23.

[3] See the Alliance for Financial Inclusion Annual Report 2021 https://www.afi.global.org/publication/2021-afi-annual-report accessed on 23 January 2025.

[4] Bank of International Settlements 2020, pp. 1–118 https://www.bis.org/publ/arpdf/ar2021e.pdf accessed om 23 January 2025. See also Lawack (2022), pp. 118–134.

[5] Bech and Garratt, (2017), pp. 1–16.

[6] Kiff et al. 2020 IMF Working Paper No 2020/104 https://www.imf.org/en/Publications/WP/Issues/2020/06/26/A-Survey-of-Research-on-Retail-Central=Bank-Digital-Currency-49517 accessed on 24 January 2025. An account-based CBDC depends on the identity of a person. Identity is verified at the point of sale and it is the user who is verified. The identity of the account holder allows the holder to access the funds: 'I am therefore I own'. A token-based CBDC verifies the veracity of the token rather than the user. The physical possession of the banknotes and coins allows the holder to dispose of the funds: 'I possess therefore I own'. See Bossu et al. International Monetary Fund Working Paper (2020), p. 6. Box 4 in the appendix adds further clarity on this point. See also Auer et al. (2021) https://www.bis.org/publ/woek976.pdf accessed on 24 January 2025.

CBDC shares six key characteristics with a national currency as follows:

- Issued by a central bank: CBDC is created and regulated by a national monetary authority.
- Stored value: CBDC can preserve purchasing power over time.
- Unit of account: CBDC facilitates valuing goods and comparing prices.
- Fungible: CBDC is easily exchangeable, promoting inter-operability among payment systems.[7]
- Instant 24/7 settlement: CBDC allows for immediate and direct transfer of value.
- Peer-to-peer transactions: CBDC enables direct transactions between individuals.[8]

The digital nature of CBDC adds supplementary characteristics when compared to physical cash. Retail CBDC mirrors physical cash and adds two features. The first feature is programmability, in the sense that CBDC allows for automation. Second, CBDC offers transparency and traceability because it is electronic.[9]

CBDC is adaptable to various technologies, including centralised or distributed ledger technology (DLT) platforms, or even non-ledger systems.[10] Currently, DLT-based platforms are prominent in discussions about wholesale CBDC.[11] Central bank reserves, described as a 'wholesale form of CBDC', have existed for some time.[12]

It must be noted that retail CBDC is different from other retail digital payment instruments. Retail CBDC stands out as it is backed by the central bank and not a commercial entity. We now briefly examine the differences.

---

[7] An entity that provides services enabling funds to be deposited and withdrawn from an account; payment transactions involving transfers of funds; the issuance and/or acquisition of payment instruments such as cheques, e-money, credit cards and debit cards; and remittances and other services central to the transfer of funds. See Alliance for Financial Inclusion 2016 AFI Annual Report (2017), pp. 1–56.

[8] See Cooper et al. (2019), pp. 1–28 on the characteristics of retail CBDC.

[9] See also Cooper et al. (2019), pp. 1–28.

[10] For more detail on this terminology, see also Lawack (2022), pp. 118–134.

[11] Distributed ledger technology (DLT) is a consensus of replicated, shared and synchronised digital data geographically spread across multiple entities, sites, countries or institution. The updating mechanism for the ledger rests on a set of rules for network members that elicits the decentralised consensus on the unique, true history, without appeal to a trusted authority. Once consensus is reached, all network members then coordinate on using the unique, agreed version of the ledger. In this respect, decentralisation evens up the playing field and equalises the distribution of power. This differs from a centralised CBDC, where there is a centrally controlled database. For more detail see Auer et al. (2022), pp. 697–721.

[12] Mancini-Griffoli et al. (2018), https://www.imf.org/en/Publications/Staff-Discussion-Notes/Issues/2018/11/13/Casting-Light-on-Central-Bank-Digital-Currencies-46233 accessed on 23 January 2025.

While commercial retail instruments, EFT,[13] and e-money[14] share similarities with CBDC as electronic, fungible, and regulated forms of payment, the unique advantage of CBDC lies in its status as universally accepted legal tender, capable of storing value and serving as a unit of account.[15] Unlike e-money and EFT transfers, which are not central bank money,[16] CBDC is central bank money itself, enhancing its acceptability and trust.[17] Moreover, while commercial digital retail instruments clear instantly, they may not settle immediately, whereas retail CBDC settles instantaneously.[18]

Virtual assets, also known as crypto assets, represent digital value traded or transferred digitally, usable for payments or investments.[19] They share similarities with CBDC as they are fungible and electronic and offer programmability and instant settlement.[20] However, crypto assets are not universally accepted as a

---

[13] An electronic funds transfer (EFT) is a standard mechanism for electronically transmitting funds between two parties. See Bank of International Settlements BIS Quarterly Review 2001, pp. 1–74 https://www.bis.org/publ/r_qt0106.pdf accessed 23 January 2025.

[14] Electronic money (e-money) is considered as stored value held in the accounts of users, agents, and the provider of the e-money service. Typically, the total value of e-money is mirrored in (a) bank account(s), such that even if the provider of the e-money service were to fail, users could recover 100% of the value stored in their accounts, depending on the degree of protection afforded the e-money commercial deposit accounts against the creditors of the e-money service, or those of the bank which holds the liability for the deposit. That said, bank deposits can earn interest, while e-money in most instances cannot. See GSMA Annual Report (2010), https://www.gsma.com/solutions-and-impact/connectivity-for-good/mobile-for-development/wp-content/uploads/2012/03/annualreport2010.pdf accessed on 30 January 2025.

[15] Conventus Law (2021) https://conventuslaw.com/report/fintech-non-fungible-tokens-whats-all-the-fuss/; Scott (2014) https://papers.ssrn.com/sol3/papers.cfm?abstract_id=2539150 accessed on 30 January 2025.

[16] Technically, e-money and commercial money are not claims against the central bank, but central bank money is used as a mechanism to transfer liabilities across institutions at par value. E-money is a claim on a commercial money deposit, which is then also a claim on the commercial bank itself. It is only when either an e-money or EFT transaction results in a movement between commercial banks that it becomes necessary to swop one commercial instrument for another. The movement of central bank money is required for finality in extinguishing the liability and risk attached to one commercial instrument, and to replace it with a similar claim upon another commercial institution at par value. The central bank currency represents the single consistent measure of value in a jurisdiction. The reasoning behind this is that commercial instruments are priced in terms of the risk or valuation of the commercial entity itself, and hence the value of the EFT claim would in reality fluctuate perpetually. Using central bank money establishes finality in terms of price and risk as the liability is transferred to another commercial institution.

[17] Kalogirou (2022), https://www.iflr.com/article/2a647e1ubbp4genwpw2yo/authorities-explore-how-to-design-central-bank-digital-currencies accessed on 24 January 2025.

[18] Central Bank of the Bahamas (2020), https://www.cemla.org/actividades/2020-final/2020-09-i-meeting-market-infrastructures/2020-09-i-meeting-market-infrastructures-2.pdf accessed on 20 January 2025.

[19] Financial Action Task Force (2019), https://www.fatf-gafi.org/en/publications/Fatfrecommendations/Guidance-rba-virtual-assets.html; IFWG (2021) at https://www.treasury.gov.za/comm_media/press/2021/IFWG_CAR%20WG_Position%20paper%20on%20crypto%20assets_Final.pdf accessed on 30 January 2025.

[20] For more detail on bitcoin and beyond see the book by Campbell-Verduyn, M (2018).

medium of exchange or unit of account in most jurisdictions, limiting their transaction utility.[21] Unlike private crypto assets, CBDC offers trust and security as it is a liability against the central bank, reducing risks for consumers. If a country excludes the liability of the central bank, it would not be a true CBDC.[22] Another important difference is that private crypto assets, depending on their structure, have either no supporting liability or liabilities based upon a claim against a physical store of assets or a derivative asset-based security. Very few private crypto assets are prudentially-regulated and cross-border jurisdictional contexts can be complex, while CBDC has very clear liabilities against a central bank and in terms of original statute-derived powers of the central bank.

Stablecoins, a type of crypto asset, are designed to maintain a stable value by being pegged to an underlying asset, frequently a fiat currency, and are typically backed by reserves held by the issuer.[23] Typically issued by private entities, they operate on public blockchain ledgers. Stability hinges on their stabilisation mechanism and their ability to maintain the peg to the underlying asset.[24] As they lack central bank backing, the risk of issuer insolvency is higher, potentially undermining user trust.[25] Additionally, diverse jurisdictional blockchain holdings may create regulatory oversight gaps.[26]

It can be argued that retail CBDCs, whether account or token-based, are more likely to directly enhance financial inclusion, compared to wholesale CBDCs. Individuals and merchants can access and use retail CBDCs as alternatives to traditional banking services, storing and transacting value, while pricing goods. Unlike other digital payment methods, retail CBDCs are sovereign legal tender, backed and supervised by central banks, universally accepted,[27] and exchangeable without additional payment instruments such as e-money. Furthermore, retail CBDCs offer

---

[21] Bartrem et al. (2017), https://www.studocu.com/row/document/jamaa%D8%A9-aleskndry%D8%A9/financial-decission-making/9-2017-aep-risks-and-vulnerabilities-of-virtual-currency/4190686 accessed on 30 January 2025.

[22] The development and implementation of stablecoins is nascent to date, with very few developing and emerging countries such as Thailand and Singapore having begun to look into its feasibility. See I de Bode et al. (2021), https://www.mckinsey.com/industries/financial-services/our-insights/cbdc-and-stablecoins-early-coexistence-on-an-uncertain-road accessed on 29 January 2025; Freeman Law (2021), at https://freemanlaw.com/cryptocurrency/tanzania/accessed on 29 January 2025.

[23] De Bode et al. (2021), https://www.mckinsey.com/industries/financial/services/our-insights/cbdc-and-stablecoins"accessed accessed on 29 January 2025.

[24] Most stablecoins rely on the backing collateral to maintain the peg, but there are also stablecoins that rely on algorithmic stabilisation mechanisms to off-load the stablecoin's price volatility to investment token holders. See Catalini et al. (2021), https://papers.ssrn.com/sol3/papers.cfm?abstract_id=3986192 accessed on 20 January 2025.

[25] World Economic Forum (2021b), https://www3.weforum.org/docs/WEF_Digital_Currency_Consumer_Protection_2021.pdf accessed on 23 January 2025.

[26] Smialek (2021), https://www.nytimes.com/2021/09/17/business/economy/federal-reserve-virtual-currency-stablecoin.html accessed on 5 February 2025..

[27] Subject to electronic devices and systems being available to both the payer and payee.

instant settlement and potential programmability. Fintechs[28] can also use retail CBDCs instead of indirect access to central bank accounts, as there is technically no difference between the value and effect of different forms of sovereign currency. This can create the potential for diversification of financial services, particularly where CBDC is used as a value transfer or immediate settlement mechanism. Fintech services operating in CBDC have the potential to offer the same or lower risk profiles than conventional commercial banks.

3 Barriers to Financial Inclusion

Financial inclusion can be described as providing access to an adequate range of safe, convenient, and affordable financial services to vulnerable groups who are underserved or excluded, in a fair and transparent manner. Whilst this definition derived from the Financial Action Task Force (FATF) Supplement to the 2013 FATF Guidance on AML/CTF Measures and financial inclusion focuses on access, FATF is considering broadening its definition to usage of financial products. Financial inclusion for the purpose of this chapter includes not only access and usage but also access of providers to the CBDC ecosystem. It is, therefore, important to understand the barriers to financial inclusion.

Various barriers to financial inclusion exist, both from the demand side and the supply side. Demand-side barriers are those factors hindering financial inclusion and affecting the demand by users of CBDCs. On the demand side, barriers include gender inequalities, lack of trust, higher sensitivity to fees, merchant acceptance, low digital literacy, lack of identity documentation, and the inability to provide instant payments. Text Box 1 provides a summary of these barriers.[29] Supply-side barriers are those factors that are obstacles to the supply of CBDCs by providers. On the supply side, barriers include provider interoperability, prevalence of third-party intermediaries, cash management, low connectivity, high operational costs, and unreliable connectivity. Text Box 2 provides a summary of the supply-side barriers.[30] While these barriers apply to digital financial services (DFS), the barriers would apply equally to CBDCs.

[28] This refers to Fintech firms.

[29] GSMA (2020), at https://www.gsma.com/solutions-and-impact/connectivity-for-good/mobile-for-development/wp-content/uploads/2020/05/GSMA-The-Mobile-Gender-Gap-Report-2020.pdf accessed on 5 February 2025. Alliance for Financial Inclusion (2021), https://www.afi-global.org/wp-content/uploads/2021/02/AFI_IGF_disaster-resilience_AW_1304.21_digital.pdf accessed on 24 January 2025. insight2impact (i2i) (2017), https://issuu.com/i2i-insight2impact/docs/i2i_mfw_note_3_-_financial_services accessed on 24 January 2025; CGAP (2018), https://www.cgap.org/blog/balancing-economics-of-interoperability-in-digital-finance accessed on 24 January 2025; McKinsey (2020), https://www.mckinsey.com/~/media/mckinsey/industries/financial%20services/our%20insights/the%20next%20frontier%20in%20asia%20payments/the-future-of-payments-in-asia-vf.pdf accessed on 24 January 2025.

[30] See Arabehety et al. CGAP (2016), https://www.cgap.org/sites/default/files/researches/documents/interoperability.pdf accessed on 24 January 2025; Gray J (2021), https://cenfri.org/articles/

Text Box 1: Demand-Side Barriers

Gender inequalities: This remains an overarching challenge across the demand side. Many of the demand-side barriers identified below are often exacerbated by a number of additional contextual factors that tend to be felt more severely by women across EMDEs.

Lack of trust: Trust is essential for individuals' engagement with any digital new financial service (DFS). It is influenced by experiences such as service efficiency, user satisfaction and external factors. Barriers such as high fees, lack of interoperability, and service complexity undermine this trust.

Higher sensitivity to fees: A key demand-side barrier to adopting new DFS is the perception of high fees. Consumers, especially low-income individuals, feel they do not earn enough to justify opening a financial account, leading them to prefer cash.

Merchant acceptance: Merchants prefer cash because it is universally accepted. A major challenge for digital payments is the need for merchants to maintain multiple POS terminals and e-money accounts to cater for customers' demands.

Low digital literacy: Low-income, potential first-time users of formal financial services often lack awareness and the skills needed to use these services responsibly. This lack of knowledge hampers their adoption of financial products. For P2P and P2B transactions, insufficient financial numeracy skills, such as navigating e-money menus or reading financial texts, make it hard for consumers to use these channels and expose them to fraud risks.

Lack of identity documentation: In P2B cases, businesses without proper KYC documentation, such as formal registration or trading licences, cannot access new DFS. Many merchants choose to remain anonymous to avoid privacy and compliance issues, so new DFS such as CBDCs must offer significant value to encourage their participation. This identification gap is more pronounced among women, migrants, and rural residents. Women, especially, face cultural and legal barriers to obtaining national identification, which hinders their access to DFS. Despite progress, legal obstacles for women obtaining IDs persist.

Inability to provide instant payments: Existing e-money and banking systems are not inclusive of all providers and often rely on non-instant payments, failing to meet the growing demand for instant transactions. This inability to provide instant clearing makes digital payments less attractive compared to cash, which transfers value immediately in face-to-face settings. This issue affects various use cases, including P2P and merchant payments, as merchants need proof of fund transfers to complete transactions and provide goods or services.

---

interoperability-of-data-the-next-paradigm-shift-for-financial-markets-in-the-development-world/ accessed on 25 January 2025; Klapper and Singer (2017), http://documents.worldbank.org/curated/en/403611493134249446/Financial-inclusion-and-inclusive-growth-a-review-of-recent-

Text Box 2: Supply-Side Barriers

Provider interoperability: Bilateral agreements add costs and complexity in facilitating non-interoperable payments: In a 2016 study by Arabehety et al. CGAP) covering 20 EMDEs, the Consultative Group to Assist the Poor (CGAP) found that while some level of interoperability existed in each market, bilateral arrangements or third-party/aggregator systems were the most common types. Even in cases with multilateral agreements, some providers still relied on bilateral agreements, which are unique to each pair and costly to maintain. This inefficiency and costliness hinder innovation and competition by allowing monopolies to thrive on network effects gained from closed-loop systems (Arabehety et al. CGAP (2016), https://www.cgap.org/sites/default/files/researches/documents/interoperability.pdf accessed on 24 January 2025.

Prevalence of third-party intermediaries: E-money instant clearing faces challenges due to back-end inefficiencies like the requirement for a one-to-one matching value between trust and settlement accounts to mitigate risks. However, this ties up funds that could otherwise be invested. Transactions between two providers require settlement, leading to complexity and slower settlement speeds due to interoperable e-money switches and third-party intermediaries.

Cash management: High liquidity costs inhibit the ability of providers to reach vulnerable groups. Payment service providers (PSPs) with brick-and-mortar operations struggle to extend cash-in, cash-out points to remote areas, due to weak business cases and high liquidity costs. Agents without bank-linked mobile wallets must physically rebalance their float, discouraging deployment in remote areas lacking nearby bank branches.

Low connectivity: Traditional payment providers struggle to meet the payment needs of customers and merchants in areas with low connectivity. Reliable electricity and basic mobile telephony infrastructure are essential prerequisites for providers to consider launching basic DFS in an area. However, the lack of digital infrastructure in some EMDEs poses a supply-side barrier. Poor connectivity makes it challenging for traditional providers to justify investing in point-of-sale (POS) terminals, e-money agents, physical branches, or automated teller machines (ATMs), as the business case is weak in such environments.

High operational costs and lack of customer understanding: Providing financial services in underserved areas can be costly due to factors such as infrastructure limitations, low population density and lack of economies of scale. These high operational costs can deter financial institutions from extending their services to these areas. In addition, financial institutions may have limited understanding of the specific needs and preferences of underserved populations. This can result in a mismatch between the products and services offered and the actual requirements of these individuals, leading to limited uptake and use.

Unreliable connectivity: In sub-Saharan Africa, only 46% of the population subscribes to mobile services, compared to 69% in Latin America and 58% in the Asia Pacific region. Additionally, unreliable electricity connectivity in sub-Saharan Africa hinders the digital payments ecosystem. Limited access to electricity (46.75%) affects the ability to charge digital devices, creating a significant barrier to mobile P2P payments. This unreliability discourages merchants from investing in digital payment infrastructure and makes customers less likely to use digital payment methods.

The above text boxes highlight the most pertinent barriers that may impact the demand by users of CBDCs, namely gender inequalities, lack of trust, higher sensitivity to fees, merchant acceptance, low digital literacy, lack of identity documentation, and the inability to provide instant payments. These barriers apply to new digital financial services and may equally apply should CBDCs be introduced without being cognisant of these barriers. Similarly, barriers impacting the supply of CBDCs may include provider interoperability, prevalence of third-party intermediaries, cash management, low connectivity, high operational costs, and unreliable connectivity.

In addition to the above barriers to financial inclusion, a significant proportion of the populations in EMDEs cannot interact with internet-intensive DFS. Internet access is limited across the developing world: 29% in sub-Saharan Africa, 35% in South Asia, 69% in Latin America, and 70% in East Asia and the Pacific. Reliability and quality of internet access are crucial for secure connectivity to DFS. Many people in developing countries lack smartphones and rely on 2G connectivity, using Unstructured Supplementary Service Data (USSD). USSD is a Global System for Mobile Communication (GSM) that is used to send text messages. USSD is similar to Short Message Service (SMS) and uses codes made up of characters that are available on mobile phones, USSD methods are vital for financial service accessibility, as seen in sub-Saharan Africa, where most e-money transactions use USSD.[31] These issues are more pronounced for women, vulnerable groups and rural populations. The gender digital divide is significant, especially in the least developed countries, where 50% of women use the internet compared to 57% of men.

Depending on the design of CBDCs, CBDCs can enhance consumer trust in digital payments by addressing key factors that influence trust. They can ensure reliable and instantaneous payments with high finality and irrevocability, supported by the

empirical-evidence accessed on 25 January 2025; Perez HS et al. (2019), https://www.imf.org/en/Publications/WP/Issues/2019/08/16/The-Impact-of-Remittances-on-Economic-Activity-The-Importance-of-Sectoral-Linkages-47091 accessed on 25 January 2025; World Bank (2020), https://socialprotection.org/es/g2p-payments-covid-19-context-key-areas-action-and-experiences-country-emergency-actions accessed on 26 January 2025.

[31] Sofrecom (2019), https://www.sofrecom.com/en/news-insights/traditional-mobile-money-assets-weakened-by-new-models.html accessed on 26 January 2025.

central bank. CBDCs can also minimise service downtime by using decentralised systems with multiple servers, reducing the risk of total system failure. Additionally, technologies in centralised systems can distribute processing loads across multiple nodes, enabling both online and offline capabilities.

Some of the key design features that can alleviate some of the barriers are:

- *Offline/online capabilities*: CBDC can be designed to work both online and offline. This can happen through Near Field Communication and Bluetooth technology, which can facilitate offline payments between two mobile or payment devices.[32]
- *24/7/365 availability*: a key design feature of decentralised CBDC is continuous availability. Multiple servers allow for CBDC to continue operating if one server goes down. The recent outage experienced by the Eastern Caribbean Central Bank's (ECCB) DCash underlined the importance of putting in place mechanisms to mitigate against the possibility of downtime,[33] including having robust protocols in place in the case of an outage and ensuring proper and timely renewal of expired certificates and system updates (as was the case with the DCash outage).[34]
- *Assured irrevocability*: CBDC can further enable trust in digital payments by promising a high level of finality and irrevocability. This is assured because of

[32] The level of offline functionality is dependent on a number of factors, including the overall scheme cryptography and design, instrument design and protocols, wallet and wallet class structure specifications, and the specific and proportionate mitigation measures required for the CBDC system as specified, to operate in the national context. It should be noted that offline transactions are not a given, and without finding a secure solution, CBDCs could open themselves up to digital counterfeiting. One proposal to negate this risk includes the creation of a secure payment system protocol that can allow a user to make a digital payment in CBDC while both the sender and receiver are temporarily offline. See Visa 'Reports fiscal fourth quarter and full-year 2021 results' (2021) https://s1.q4cdn.com/050606653/files/doc_financials/2021/q4/Visa-Inc.-Fourth-Quarter-and-Full-Year-2021-Financial-Results.pdf. Moreover, 'double-spending' attacks, a form of counterfeiting where the CBDC is spent multiple times illegitimately, given undeveloped encryption protocols, can be mitigated by imposing spending limits and transaction frequency when the CBDC user is offline. Further, once a device that is conducting transactions comes back online, the transaction offline history is uploaded as part of the instrument and/or wallet sync, in systems designed to operate offline. In other system designs with offline features, compliance software could sync with any transactions that have concurred during the offline period. See World Economic Forum 'Shared principles for an inclusive financial system' (2021) https://www3.weforum.org/docs/WEF_Shared_Principles_for_an_Inclusive_Financial_System_2021.pdf.

[33] The problem was related to an expiring certificate on the version of the Hyperledger Fabric that hosts the DCash ledger, which forced the bank to roll out updates. Not only can expired certificates cause unplanned system or service outages, but they can also provide an entrance through which malicious actors can find entry into a CBDC's operating platform. Proper and timely renewal of expired certificates is key to mitigating man-in-the-middle attacks See Security Boulevard 'Cyberattacks 2022: Phishing, ransomware and data breach statistics' (2023) https://securityboulevard.com/2023/04/cyberattacks-2022-phishing-ransomware-data-breach-statistics/.

[34] Eastern Caribbean Central Bank 'Annual economic and financial review' (2022) https://www.eccb-centralbank.org/publications/economic-and-financial-review.

settlement being guaranteed by the central bank.[35] As with cash, the transaction between two parties using central bank money ensures immediate settlement, without the counterparty risk that occurs with commercial payment instruments. This means that the risk of failed transactions and fraud is significantly reduced.

- *CBDC Interoperability*: Retail CBDC can enable full network and channel interoperability, simplifying and reducing fees in the payment process. Unlike current systems that require stepwise clearing and settlement between different schemes, CBDC can serve as a universal digital instrument integrated through secure open APIs for all licensed providers.[36] This creates a ubiquitous clearing channel, eliminating the need for bilateral integration or multiple external switches. As a sovereign currency with legal tender status, CBDC can universally integrate and interoperate with any local digital currency scheme. This reduces payment frictions and enhances ease and convenience for consumers. For instance, the Bahamas' Sand Dollar allows all payment service firms to use the Sand Dollar network for settling retail Bahamian dollar payments, ensuring interoperability between various payment channels.[37]
- *Costs*: A fully interoperable CBDC can eliminate unnecessary third parties and streamline the settlement process, enabling direct P2P transactions and reducing costs for PSPs.[38] If these cost reductions are passed on to consumers, they can benefit from more affordable payment services. Real-world applications, such as Ghana's e-Cedi, aim to lower cost and fee barriers for merchant payments.[39] Additionally, CBDCs can operate on mobile-based USSD wallets with SIM encryption, requiring minimal investment for basic phone users. CBDCs could also include contactless hard wallets and near field communication wearables for in-store and transit payments, as seen with the digital Yuan.[40]

[35] Bank of International Settlements 'Annual economic report' (note XX).

[36] An API allows one software program to 'talk' to another. APIs enable a wide range of innovative products and services that millions of people use every day. For instance, APIs are what make it possible for ride-hailing apps to leverage other companies' mapping and payments systems. Sometimes companies create an API for a single or small number of partners. When a financial services provider 'opens' its APIs, it makes them widely available for other companies to consume. For example, a digital payments provider could open APIs to enable a whole range of e-commerce companies to plug seamlessly into its payments system. If operated correctly, open APIs generate revenue for the provider and accelerate innovation in the marketplace. See CGAP 'Annual Report 2021' (2021) https://www.cgap.org/story/annualreport2021.

[37] Central Bank of the Bahamas 'Annual Report & Statement of Accounts for the year ended December 31, 2022' (2022) https://www.centralbankbahamas.com/viewPDF/documents/2023-05-09-12-27-39 2022 CBOB Annual-Report-and-FS.pdf.

[38] See Cooper et al. 'The use cases' (note XX).

[39] Bank of Ghana '2022 Annual Report and financial statements of the Bank of Ghana' (2022) https://www.bog.gov.gh/news/2022-annual-report-financial-statements-of-the-bank-of-ghana/.

[40] Equally CBDC instruments that can be accommodated on chip cards would not be dependent on mobile phone ownership, which can reduce the wallet roll-out cost to the similar cost of a chip and PIN NFC debit card per citizen not using a mobile phone. Tap on phone, PIN on glass NFC technology can convert smart phones into POS devices, with the potential to create near ubiquitous

It is evident from the above that CBDC may enhance financial inclusion provided that the barriers are sufficiently overcome.[41] However, financial inclusion needs to be carefully balanced with financial integrity by applying a risk-based approach. As will be evident below, it is ironic that the very design features of CBDCs that may enhance financial inclusion, could introduce financial integrity threats. The following section deals with these risks.[42]

4 Financial Integrity Risks of CBDC

4.1 Financial Integrity Risks

CBDCs could have both a positive and negative impact on financial integrity. First, CBDCs would constitute a new means of payment, which presents some challenges. Similar to older forms of payments that brought about challenges, older forms of payment also brought opportunities to collect financial intelligence. For example, contrary to cash, older payment methods such as prepaid cards, mobile and electronic money provided additional leads for LEA through the generation of an electronic record, which LEAs could use to track transactions.[43] CBDCs may create financial integrity threats, similar to cryptocurrencies. For example, China's eYuan has been used to launder oversees fraud proceeds and conduct other crimes. Similarly, the International Monetary Fund (IMF) has highlighted Nigeria's e-Naira as a potential terrorist financing or corruption channel.[44]

The threat posed by CBDCs depends on the design features chosen for the CBDC and how CBDCs are implemented within the current AML/CTF/CPF framework of a particular country. It goes without saying that where CBDCs can be used in cross-border transactions, criminals may be able to exploit arbitrage opportunities in legal

---

merchant and P2P CBDC acceptance. See also 'Payments, Cards and Mobile' www.paymentscardsandmobile.com.

[41] Lannquist et al. (2023), at https://www.imf.org/en/Publications/fintech-notes/Issues/2023/09/22/Central-Bank-Digital-Currency-s-Role-in-Promoting-Financial-Inclusion-538728 accessed on 30 January 2025.

[42] See also Styles (De-banking 'risky' customers: Contractual exclusion of customers by financial institutions and AML/CTF ramifications) for example would be a good one and Coshott (2025) in this book.

[43] Financial Action Task Force (FATF) (2010), https://www.fatf-gafi.org/media/fatf/documents/reports/ML%20using%20New%20Payment%20Methods.pdf accessed on 23 January 2025.

[44] Bloomberg (2021), https://www.bloomberg.com/news/articles/2021-11-17/chinese-police-makes-arrest-over-digital-yuan-scam accessed on 24 January 2025. See also International Monetary Fund (2022), Nigeria: 2021, Article IV Consultation-Press Release https://www.imf.org.en/Publications/CR/Issues/2022/02.09/Nigeria-2021-Article-IV-Consultation-Press-Release-Staff-Report-Staff-Statement-and-512944 accessed on 24 January 2025..

frameworks or take advantage of differences in enforcement capacity in the respective jurisdictions.[45]

As mentioned above, CBDCs can be either account-based or token-based and be issued directly by the central bank or via intermediaries. CBDCs could also be a hybrid, combining account-based and token-based design features. Some observations are worth mentioning in this regard.

First, an intermediated CBDC design does not of itself present a systemically significant shift from the status quo. If accountable institutions hold accounts or wallets, they also remain the main vehicle for onboarding clients and performing customer due diligence (CDD) procedures. This would especially be the case if payment access and processes for retail CBDC occur through the traditional vehicle of financial institutions. During the introductory phase central banks would have to evaluate the trends in shifts from the use of cash, especially if the CBDC is introduced alongside a slowdown in the issuance of cash by the central bank. Organised crime and money laundering networks may begin to retain cash to build up reserves or move their transactions into underground or informal transfer systems if the CBDC comes with more stringent transaction monitoring capability.[46]

Second, it is prudent to understand how tokenisation leads to changes in available data, considering that the level of programmability may be high. As the goal for CBDC is for CBDC payment to take place in real-time, commercial banks may need to prepare their capacity to assess much higher volumes and rates of payments. Real-time payment may undermine the ability of banks to prevent payment fraud, thus creating vulnerability.[47] This means that central banks may have to share the responsibility for assessing transaction trails and share a data exchange system with financial intelligence centres (FICs), law enforcement agencies (LEAs), and other public authorities. At the moment, efficiently tracing cryptoassets remains a challenge, because cryptoassets are privately issued. By combining similar tokens and a possible exchangeable CBDC that can perform many nearly simultaneous transactions at real time, one may create the equivalent of "virtual asset tumblers". Virtual asset tumblers mix identifiable or tainted cryptoassets with others. This enhances the privacy of cryptoassets by hiding their origins and destinations.[48] Investigation of one required years of investigation and the active coordination of seven public agencies.[49]

Third, the off-line availability of CBDCs can pose a risk. Off-line availability potentially creates significant financial integrity risks in various ways. If the CBDC

---

[45] Many of which are highlighter in Ryder (2025) in this book.

[46] See the Financial Intelligence of Latvia (2023), https://www.fid.gov/uploads/files/2023/cbdc/CBDC Digital Euro Risk Final.pdf accessed on 23 January 2025.

[47] See https://www.bankingriskandregulation.com/banks-slow-down-payments-in-response-to-new-uk-fraud-rules/ accessed on 7 June 2025.

[48] For more on "mixers" and "tumblers", see Reddy and Minnaar (2018), pp. 77–78.

[49] See Financial Crimes Enforcement Network "(2020), https://www.fincen.gov/news/news-releases/first-bitcoin-mixer-penalized-fincen-violations-anti-moneylaundering-laws accessed on 24 January 2025.

allows for interchangeability of off-line and online payments at will, this may create an information gap in the access to payment records, changing the digital forensics necessary to trace financial flows. If these payments are unrecorded, it means that it may be necessary to place limits on the amount of transactable off-line and on-line CBDC and the number of wallets that can be transmitted. Furthermore, depending on the size if these limits, off-line payments may make cross-border movement of monetary value easier. Bearing in mind the ability to exchange currency held within smartphone digital wallets for cash at will, there may be a variety of ways to exploit the fungibility of cash and CBDC.[50] It is unclear how financial intelligence should use gaps in the audit trail based on anonymous off-line transactions. Since the off-line mode of payment of CBDC can be enabled with the specific purpose of allowing untraceability because of cash, it further remains unclear how intermediaries/accountable institutions performing examinations or public authorities conducting investigations should account for the utilised sums. A high level of anonymity and privacy protection, especially if a CBDC is used off-line, would increase the level of financial integrity threats. It is for this reason that aligned to FATF Standards, the AML/CTF/CPF proposed by the European Commission in July 2021 extended the ban on anonymous accounts and wallets. It is submitted that this was a prudent step.[51] The question is whether governments can be trusted to not use the information at their disposal.

Fourth, another privacy-related risk arises related to the design of the CBDC. A token-based CBDC enables the use of cryptographic and institutional arrangements to enable a higher degree of privacy. Users may be able to select the extent to which data is shared with different entities at the digital wallet level, which may not be accessible to financial intermediaries banking the client. This raises concerns about who has access to the data and the ability of supervisory authorities to perform compliance functions and access the full transaction history of the clients. The same risk applies in relation to secondary access to this data by FICs, LEAs, and other authorities.[52] Novel data analytics tools such as indirect analyses and Artificial Intelligence (AI) may help mitigate the lack of access to certain information. However, these possibilities need to be carefully managed against other regulatory limitations, e.g., be privacy-preserving and minimise profiling of individuals.[53] One such privacy-preserving tool is discussed by Brand et al. in a previous chapter in this book.[54]

---

[50] Auer and Bőhme (2020), https://papers.ssrn.com/abstract=3561198 accessed on 23 January 2025.

[51] European Banking Authority (2021), https://www.eba.europa.edu/sites/default/documents/files/document-library/Publications/Opinion%20on%20MLTF%20risks.pdf accessed on 23 January 2025.

[52] For human rights concerns, see also Sulayman (2025) in this book.

[53] See an interesting article of Soana and de Arruda (2024), pp. 467–486.

[54] See Brand, Herse and De Koker (2025) in this book. See also SAS KPMG "Global AML Research: The road to Integration—The state of AI and machine learning adoption in anti-money laundering compliance at https://www.sas.com/content/dam/sasdam/documents/20250124/global-aml-research-the-road-to-integration-114143.pdf. There are many other crypto forensics being

Fifth, unfettered programmability in a CBDC may lead to a variety of new money laundering typologies and exploitation schemes. Programmability can be enabled through a smart contract functionality allowing for payment interface providers to build software services that interact directly with the digital wallet of the retail customer. With a real-time CBDC payment system programmability can be made to perform currency swaps instantaneously, automatically and via micropayments.[55] Such schemes would be exploited for layering stage activities by concealing the criminal origin of proceeds, by creating a "clean" digital paper trail for money that has travelled through many CBDC wallets. Upon integration, these digital funds may appear to be legitimate. These criminal proceeds can then be used for personal benefit once they appear to be legitimate. Similarly, a criminal may use the digital cash for direct consumption or for purchasing other investments. This can be done through trading of underground networks such as non-compliant Dark Net crypto exchanges through a virtual money-mule system, where wallets and programmes replace the currency mule. Criminal entities can also tumble money through various wallets automatically, creating distance between themselves and the illicit source of funds. Retail merchants who agree to be fronts can also move funds, co-mingling funds through a high volume of business transactions to conceal illicit proceeds. Through smart contracts, trade-based transactions can conceal illicit proceeds by falsifying invoices for virtual systems and creating a system of money mules with fictitious clients and supply chains that interact instantly across the Web. In addition, programmability may also contribute to the growth of economies by utilising the hawala schemes to move money internationally through ledger-based systems that visibly changes location in the CBDC account. Hawala schemes involve the payment of money to an agent who then instructs an associate in the relevant country to pay the final recipient. The transaction would then take place through bargaining with services, goods or cash assets outside of the digital network, allowing cross-border informal transfer of value without transfer of actual funds. Enabling such smart contracts would be difficult to extract and intertwine with a money laundering network without having access to an insider.[56]

developed to detect and trace suspicious transactions, e.g. Elliptic, a blockchain analytics for financial crime, risk management and regulatory compliance in crypto company at https://www.elliptic.co/ accessed on 7 June 2025.

[55] See Reiners (2021), https://sites.duke.edu/thefinregblog/2021/09/21/cbdc-how-dangerous-is-programmability accessed on 24 January 2025.

[56] Fanusie (2023), https://www.fid.gov/uploads/files/2023/cbdc/CBDC Digital Euro Risk Final.pdf accessed on 23 January 2025, Gao et al. (2020) at https://doi.org/10.1145/3428335 accessed on 23 January 2025.

4.2 CBDC and Identity Gaps

CBDC can cater for, and ease, the severity of identity gaps. The lack of universal access to identity is a major challenge for payments. According to Cooper et al. (2021),[57] CBDC can address this identity gap using four approaches:

The first avenue may arguably be the simplest, as pairing a CBDC rollout with a digital identity initiative means that standard identification processes can be performed. As people sign up for their CBDC wallet, they can concurrently be enrolled in the digital identity scheme.

Second, CBDC may be issued subject to use limitations on the strength of limited identity verification. Close monitoring of transactional activity may over time strengthen the assurance that the person provided their correct identify details and may allow higher transactional limits to be considered. CBDC could, therefore, be used to verify a person's identity on an ongoing basis, rather than once-off in order to create more robust identity profiles, especially for individuals without IDs.

Third, CBDC could draw on various types of ID proxies (such as phone numbers, biometrics or email addresses) currently held at government entities. It could achieve this by drawing on each of these unique identifiers to create digital identity proxy stacks. These stacks could in turn act as a unique ID for individuals without any form of ID, as well as be used to enhance the robustness of identities for those that already have some form of ID. This may therefore give individuals a convenient and verifiable form of identification that can be used in the place of paper-based documents to access services digitally.[58]

Fourth, CBDC can be designed to manage identification risk. CBDCs can enhance identification processes by using identification proxies or stacks, combined with multiple wallet classes to manage risks for those with less robust digital identities. This approach could reduce the risk of improper CDD compared to traditional in-person verification, which relies on physical documents that can be forged. Digital systems can more effectively validate documents using technology, rather than subjective in-person assessments. While CBDC alone cannot solve identification issues, it can significantly improve the identification process.[59]

5 Analysis: A Trade-Off?

CBDCs may require changes in the governance, accounting, and financial reporting standards to recognise their unique functionalities. This means that there should be clear standards on how CBDCs are issued and a governance structure that specifies

[57] Cooper et al. (2021), https://intarch.ac.uk/journal/issue56/18/ia.56.18.pdf accessed on 23 January 2025.

[58] Cooper et al. Ibid.

[59] Cooper et al. Ibid. See also Ahmed (2025) in this book.

the central banks', any intermediaries, and payment system providers' roles and accountability for privacy, errors, loss etc. Similarly, the accounting and financial reporting standards should consider the unique functionalities of CBDCs. The broader infrastructural systems underpinning CBDCs may also impact on interoperability of multiple authorities that depend on existing frameworks to fulfil their financial integrity. Central banks, prudential authorities, market conduct regulators, financial intelligence centres, law enforcement agencies, amd taxation and capital markets authorities are among the affected stakeholders.

Cyber fraud may increase when a token-based CBDC is initially released. This can include counterfeiting, hacking, or exploits that can potentially double spend by digitally creating currency without legal authorisation or hackers can create self-executing smart contracts that exchange the digital currency automatically. It is unclear how AML/CTF/CPF compliance duties and financial intelligence would be performed where parties use programmability design features that obscures traceability after counterfeiting, hacking or other forms of cyber fraud.

An equivalent compliance system must enable accountable institutions to analyse CBDC networks and flows to perform their CDD compliance duties. If a bank is dealing with a hosted wallet, it should be able to analyse transactions in real-time to ensure that payments only travel through other trusted wallets. Similarly, it is unclear how financial intelligence centres, LEAs, and other supervisory authorities would access the data associated with programmable money flows. Cross-border CBDCs would require intense cooperation between these stakeholders. It is submitted that interoperability and cooperation between agencies could enhance the view of money flows.

It is evident from the above that it is important to demarcate the lines of privacy, programmability design and availability as these present challenges and interdependencies. It is ironically the very same design features which may enhance financial inclusion that may exacerbate financial integrity risks. It is submitted that a trade-off may be necessary if CBDCs are issued to strike a balance between the policy objectives of financial inclusion and financial integrity.

In 2021, the FATF issued updated recommendations for member countries in its report, 'Updated Guidance for a Risk-Based Approach for Virtual Assets and Virtual Asset Service Providers (VASPS)'. According to the FATF Updated Guidance Report, countries are required to assess and mitigate their risks associated with virtual assets and virtual asset activities and VASPS. VASPS are subject to the same relevant FATF measures that apply to financial institutions. The 2021 Guidance included updates in six key areas, namely clarification of the definitions of virtual assets and VASPs, guidance on how the FATF Standard apply to stablecoins and additional guidance on the risks and tools available to countries to address financial integrity risks for P2P transactions. Additionally, the Guidance included updated guidance on the licensing and registration of VASPs, additional guidance for the public and private sectors on the implementation of the "travel rules" and principles of information-sharing among VASP Supervisors.[60] It is imperative that a risk assessment be conducted involving multiple stakeholders as alluded to above. This needs to be considered not only from a technology perspective, but also from a financial regulatory perspective. It is important to consider the regulation of business analytics to ensure that there is sufficient commitment to fraud detection and fraud resolution in the use of CBDC.[61]

CBDCs have the potential to enhance financial inclusion by reducing resistance to digital payments, especially in developing and emerging countries. However, their implementation carries risks and potential unintended consequences for central banks, consumers and PSPs. These risks arise if CBDCs are not appropriately tailored to the specific context and needs of a financial system and broader economy. A discussion of these risks falls outside of the scope of this chapter. It is however, necessary to understand the risks and responsibilities of central banks.

Implementing a CBDC can pose significant financial stability risks for central banks, including the potential disintermediation of banks. However, the greatest risk may be the central bank's responsibility for introducing new payment instruments and technologies. If technical failures occur and consumers cannot access their income, central banks will most likely be blamed, potentially damaging their reputation and consumer trust. For example, as mentioned above, the Nigerian eNaira faced criticism from the IMF for inadequate money laundering and terrorist financing risk assessments, highlighting potential reputational damage. Additionally, poorly designed CBDCs that are not user-friendly can exacerbate issues in developing and emerging countries with low financial and digital literacy. If consumers avoid using CBDC, this could result in wasted taxpayer money and further erode trust in the central bank's capabilities.

Two main cybersecurity risks are associated with the design and implementation of a retail CBDC. The first cybersecurity risk concerns end users, where compromised CBDC wallets could result from system or infrastructure vulnerabilities.[62] Banks and PSPs must manage this risk, which increases with CBDC introduction, especially in EMDEs with lower digital and financial literacy rates. The second risk relates to the CBDC system itself. While many CBDCs may use DLT, centralisation by central banks introduces vulnerability. Any attack on this system could disrupt large populations and make the central bank and its CBDC system attractive targets

---

[60] https://www.fatf-gafi.org/en/publications/Fatfrecommendations/Guidance-rba-virtual-assets-2021.html accessed on 7 June 2025. See also the 2025 FATF Recommendations International Standards on Combating Money Laundering and the Financing of Terrorism & Proliferation as amended in February 2025 at and the FATF Money Laundering National Risk Assessment Guidance issued on 7 November 2024 at https://www.fatf-gafi.org/content/fatf-gafi/en/publications/Farfrecommendations/Fatf-recommendations.html accessed 7 June 2025 and https://www.fatf-gafi.org/en/publications/Methodsandtrends/Money-Laundering-National-Risk-Assessment-Guidance.html accessed 7 June 2025.

[61] Cooper et al. (2021), https://cenfri.org/wp-content/uploads/2019/06/CBDC-and-financial-inclusion_A-case-for-mobile-money.pdf accessed on 15 June 2021.

[62] Deloitte (2021) https://www2.deloitte.com/cn/en/pages/human-capital/articles/global-human-capital-trends-2020.html accessed on 5 February 2025.

for sophisticated cyberattacks, similar to past incidents involving large databases like Equifax or SolarWinds.[63]

Central banks must prioritise designing CBDCs to meet domestic needs, encouraging adoption by businesses and individuals. However, there is a risk of designing CBDCs solely based on current needs, overlooking evolving trends in the digital and payment landscape. Additionally, a narrow focus on domestic needs might negatively impact on future cross-border CBDC payments.

Lastly, central banks must critically evaluate whether a retail CBDC is the most effective tool for advancing financial inclusion, compared to other digital payment interventions. While CBDCs can address many barriers associated with financial inclusion, their key distinction—being issued by the central bank—does not inherently make them superior to other digital payment instruments for addressing use case barriers. For instance, interoperability and affordability, key CBDC design features, are also crucial for all digital payment instruments. It is submitted that introducing CBDCs alone will not solve these challenges and could add complexity to systems that need to be simple and efficient for financial inclusion. However, this does not mean that central banks should completely avoid CBDCs.

Issuing CBDCs is a complex project that would have to involve multiple stakeholders beyond its traditional central bank counterparts. The issuance of a CBDC therefore requires carefully reviewing the legal, technical, and institutional preconditions to ensure that it does not jeopardise financial integrity goals. It is evident that there are myriad risk areas which need to be considered and reflected in an AML/CTF/CFP risk framework.

Furthermore, a range of institutional interactions between multiple public agencies need to occur before a CBDC can be issued. These include financial intelligence centres, tax agencies, capital market and statistical agencies, supervisors of consumer protection and other market conduct authorities, and private sector stakeholders, including merchants and users that will be impacted by the introduction of a CBDC.

Central banks who are considering issuing a CBDC may consider establishing national consultative committees of stakeholders to facilitate communication among these stakeholders, possibly also via surveys and focus group discussions. It is submitted that clear mandates and effective collaboration would be key to help prioritise tasks, scope of development of the CBDC and maximise resource effectiveness and efficiency. In addition, regions could explore seamless cross-border monitoring through shared platforms and countries can work together to establish common rules for combating illicit activities through CBDCs. It is hoped that the establishment of the South African Development Community Fintech Workgroup under the auspices of the SADC Committee of Central Bank Governors would explore the possibilities of regional integration and cooperation.

[63] https://preventionweb.net/news/preparing-next-pandemic-early-lessons-covid-19accessed on 5 February 2025.

A lot of progress has been made in many countries who are in pilot, design, or research phase with their CBDC projects. However, the success of CBDCs may be hampered by corruption of central bank officials, such as was the case in China and Nigeria where specific technology service providers were used to benefit the central bank official financially. In the case of Nigeria, the central bank official watched as riots occurred amidst the shortage of cash, driving an adoption rate of 0.5 percent to 6 percent and holding a large number of off-shore accounts.[64] In the case of Jamaica, the take-up of the Jam-Dex CBDC is slow because of an uncompetitive banking system, high charges, inability to fulfil KYC and AML requirements, and lingering distrust of authority. This is a good example that simply offering a CBDC as an equivalent to cash without dealing with the underlying barriers to financial inclusion does not work.[65]

AI tools are on the rise to assist LEAs and other supervisory bodies to improve the detection, surveillance, and monitoring of financial integrity risks through flagging patterns such as unusually large transactions or frequent transfers to high-risk areas. Transaction limits can also be introduced, as can risk scoring, where every transaction is scored based on how risky it looks, enabling the stopping of suspicious transactions before they are completed.[66]

One can only speculate what impact the President of the United States of America's 2025 Executive Order to ban the "digital dollar" and cancelling the USA CBDC work that has already been undertaken would have on the global adoption and development of CBDC. This may open the door for China and Europe's CBDCs to make their already advanced prototypes into global trendsetters. This is a development that warrants further research on the impact especially on EMDEs, especially African countries, if any.[67]

6 Concluding Remarks

Central banks in EMDEs have long viewed financial inclusion as a primary goal for implementing CBDCs. This commitment is evident from central bank surveys and discussions in financial inclusion networks. However, despite the widespread belief in the potential of CBDCs to promote financial inclusion, significant questions

[64] Seehttps://hrf.org/latest/corruption-trails-cbdc-projects-in-china-nigeria-and-lebanon/ accessed on 7 June 2025.

[65] See the discussion by Kevin Dowd "So far, Central Bank Digital Currencies have failed" at see https://hrf.org/latest/corruption-trails-cbdc-projects-in-china-nigeria-and-lebanon/ accessed on 7 June 2025.

[66] See https://www.chaintech.network/blog/money-laundering-challenges/challenges can cbdcs-be-the-solution/#:~:text=CBDCs%20don't%20just%20work,making%20it20hard%20to%to%20-track accessed on 24 February 2025.

[67] See the interesting article by Jones (2025), https://www.reuters.com/markets/currencies/trumps-digital-dollar-ban-gives-china-europes-cbdcs-free-rein-2025-01-28 accessed on 24 February 2025.

remain unanswered, and evidence gaps persist. This is especially relevant in developing countries, where digital poverty is a significant barrier to engaging in DFS.[68] Without addressing these evidence gaps, it is unclear whether CBDCs can truly address the financial needs of citizens or if they might inadvertently reinforce existing exclusionary factors affecting vulnerable populations like the elderly, rural households, SMMEs, displaced individuals and women, among others.

The objective of this chapter was to examine the potential of retail CBDC in accelerating financial inclusion in developing and emerging economies, particularly for vulnerable populations. While CBDC can address some barriers, it cannot resolve all of them. CBDCs' greatest contribution to financial inclusion lies in enhancing convenience, affordability, and security, thus fostering consumer demand. This chapter argued that there may very well be a trade-off between the policy objectives of financial inclusion and financial integrity with the introduction of a retail CBDC, as the very same features which may enhance financial inclusion may pose financial integrity risks. Further, the responsibilities of central banks and that coordination would be paramount with other supervisory authorities, FICs, LEAs and government authorities before a retail CBDC is launched. It is submitted that this chapter is the tip of the iceberg and that more research is needed on CBDCs and financial integrity, especially on the data analytics and AI tools that can enhance tracking of CBDC financial flows, whilst preserving the privacy of individuals.

References

Ahmed S (2025) Surveilling the citizen: constitutional tensions within the Canadian AML regime. In: Goldbarsht D, de Koker L, Ferrill J (eds) Combating financial crime: intended and unintended consequences. Springer, Cham

Alliance for Financial Inclusion (2017) 2016 AFI annual report: making financial services more accessible to the world's unbanked 1–56. https://www.afi-global.org/publication/2016-afi-annual report. Accessed 23 Jan 2025

Alliance for Financial Inclusion (2021) Disaster resilience through financial inclusion: the role of financial regulators in disaster risk reduction https://www.afi-global.org/wp-content/uploads/2021/02/AFI_IGF_disaster-resilience_AW_1304.21_digital.pdf. Accessed 24 Jan 2025

Alliance for Financial Inclusion Annual Report (2021). https://www.afi.global.org/publication/2021-afi-annual-report/. Accessed 23 Jan 2025

Arabehety PG, Chen G, Cook W, McKay C (2016) Digital finance interoperability and financial inclusion: a 20-country scan. CGAP https://www.cgap.org/sites/default/files/researches/documents/interoperability.pdf. Accessed 24 Jan 2025

Auer R, Bőhme R (2020) The technology of retail Central Bank currency SSRN paper. https://papers.ssrn.com/abstract=3561198. Accessed 23 Jan 2025

Auer R, Frost J, Gambacorta L, Monnet C, Rice T, Shin HS (2021) BIS Working Papers No 976 Central bank digital currencies, motives, economic implications and the research frontier. https://www.bis.org/publ/woek976.pdf. Accessed 24 Jan 2025

[68] UNCTAD Annual report 2019 (2020), at https://unctad.org/annualreport/2019/Pages/index.html accessed on 24 February 2025.

Auer R, Frost J, Gambacorta L, Monnet C, Rice T, Shin HS (2022) Central bank digital currencies: motives, economic implications, and the research frontier. Ann Rev Econ 14:697–721
Bank of International Settlements (2020) Annual economic report: promoting global monetary and financial stability. https://www.bis.org/publ/arpdf/ar2021e.pdf. Accessed 23 Jan 2025
Bartrem K, Curtis J, Dorosz J (2017) Risks and vulnerabilities of virtual currency: cryptocurrency as a payment method. https://www.studocu.com/row/document/jamaa%D8%A9-aleskndry%D8%A9/financial-decission-making/9-2017-aep-risks-and-vulnerabilities-of-virtual-currency/4190686. Accessed 25 Jan 2025
Bech ML, Garratt R (2017) Central bank crypto assets. BIS Quarterly Review 1–16. https://www.bis.org/publ/qtrpdf/r_1709f.pdf. Accessed 23 Jan 2025
Bloomberg (2021) Chinese police makes arrest over digital yuan scam. https://www.bloomberg.com/news/articles/2021-11-17/chinese-police-makes-arrest-over-digital-yuan-scam. Accessed 24 Jan 2025
Boar C, Wehrli A (2021) Ready, steady, go? Results of the third BIS survey on central bank digital currency. BIS Papers. https://www.bis.org/publ/bppdf/bispap114.htm. Accessed 23 Jan 2025
Bossu W, Itatani M, Margulis C, Rossi ADP, Weenink H, Yoshinaga A (2020) Legal aspects of central bank digital currency: Central bank and monetary law considerations. International Monetary Fund Working Paper WP/20/254. https://www.imf.org/en/Publications/WP/Issues/2020/11/20/Legal-Aspects-of-Central-Bank-Digital-Currency-Central-Bank-and-Monetary-Law-Considerations-49827. Accessed 23 Jan 2025
Brand M, de Koker L, Herse C (2025) Privacy-preserving data analytics: a case study in anti-money laundering and counter terrorist and proliferation financing innovation in Australia. In: Goldbarsht D, de Koker L, Ferrill J (eds) Combating financial crime: intended and unintended consequences. Springer, Cham
Campbell-Verduyn M (2018) Bitcoin and beyond: crypto assets, blockchains, and global governance. Routledge, Oxon/New York
Catalini C, Li W, de Gortari A (2021) From stablecoins to CBDCs: the public benefits of a public-private partnership. https://papers.ssrn.com/sol3/papers.cfm?abstract_id=3986192. Accessed 24 Jan 2025
Central Bank of the Bahamas (2020) Driving financial inclusion and fintech innovation in the midst of COVID-19. https://www.cemla.org/actividades/2020-final/2020-09-i-meeting-market-infrastructures/2020-09-i-meeting-market-infrastructures-2.pdf. Accessed 25 Jan 2025
CGAP (2018) Balancing the economics of interoperability in digital finance https://www.cgap.org/blog/balancing-economics-of-interoperability-in-digital-finance. Accessed 24 Jan 2025
Conventus Law (2021) Fintech: Non-fungible tokens: what's all the fuss? https://conventuslaw.com/report/fintech-non-fungible-tokens-whats-all-the-fuss/. Accessed 24 Feb 2025
Cooper B, Esser A, Allen M (2019) The use cases of central bank digital currency for financial inclusion: A case for mobile money. https://cenfri.org/wp-content/uploads/2019/06/CBDC-and-financial-inclusion_A-case-for-mobile-money.pdf. Accessed 23 Jan 2025
Cooper C, Hadley D, Empsall J, Wallace J, Bax N, Fleetwood D (2021) Digital heritage and public engagement: reflections on the challenges of co-production. Int Archaeol 56:1–29. https://intarch.ac.uk/journal/issue56/18/ia.56.18.pdf. Accessed 23 Jan 2025
Coshott D (2025) Challenging risk: the case of maples corporate services V CIMA. In: Goldbarsht D, de Koker L, Ferrill J (eds) Combating financial crime: intended and unintended consequences. Springer, Cham
De Bode I, Higginson M, Niedekorn M (2021) CBDC and stablecoins: early coexistence on an uncertain road. https://www.mckinsey.com/industries/financial-services/our-insights/cbdc-and-stablecoins-early-coexistence-on-an-uncertain-road. Accessed 24 Jan 2025
Deloitte (2021) Are Central Bank Digital Currencies (CBDCs) the money of tomorrow? https://www.deloitte.com/lu/en/Industries/banking-capitalmarkets/research/central-bank-digitsl-currencies-money-tomorrow.html. Accessed 5 Feb 2025
European Banking Authority (2021) Opinion of the European banking authority on the risks of money laundering and terrorist financing affecting the European Union's financial sector.

https://www.eba.europa.edu/sites/default/documents/files/document-library/Publications/Opinion%20on%20MLTF%20risks.pdf. Accessed 23 Jan 2025
Fanusie Y J (2023) Central bank digital currencies: The threat from moneylaunders and how to stop them. https://www.fid.gov/uploads/files/2023/cbdc/CBDC%20Digital%20Euro%20Risk%20Final.pdf. Accessed 23 Jan 2025
Financial Action Task Force (2010) Money laundering using new payment methods. https://www.fatf-gafi.org/media/fatf/documents/reports/ML%20using%20New%20Payment%20Methods.pdf. Accessed 23 Jan 2025
Financial Action Task Force (2019) Guidance for a risk-based approach to virtual assets and virtual asset service providers. https://www.fatf-gafi.org/en/publications/Fatfrecommendations/Guidance-rba-virtual-assets.html. Accessed 25 Jan 2025
Financial Crimes Enforcement Network (2020) First Bitcoin 'Mixer' penalized by FINCEN for violating anti-moneylaundering laws. https://www.fincen.gov/news/news-releases/first-bitcoin-mixer-penalized-fincen-violations-anti-moneylaundering-laws. Accessed 24 Jan 2025
Financial Intelligence of Latvia (2023) The AML/CFT implications of central bank digital currency and the digital euro. https://www.fid.gov/uploads/files/2023/cbdc/CBDC%20Digital%20Euro%20Risk%20Final.pdf. Accessed 23 Jan 2025
Freeman Law (2021) Tanzania and cryptocurrency: blockchain and cryptocurrency laws and regulations. https://freemanlaw.com/cryptocurrency/tanzania/. Accessed 24 Feb 2025
Gao B, Wang H, Xia P, Wu S, Zhou Y, Luo X, Tyson G (2020) Tracking counterfeit cryptocurrency end-to-end. at https://arxiv.org/pdf/2011.02673 (accessed 23 Jan 2025)
Gray J (2021) Interoperability of data: The next paradigm shift for financial markets in the development world CENFRI. https://cenfri.org/articles/interoperability-of-data-the-next-paradigm-shift-for-financial-markets-in-the-development-world/. Accessed 25 Jan 2025
GSMA (2010) Mobile money for the unbanked: annual report 2010. https://www.gsma.com/solutions-and-impact/connectivity-for-good/mobile-for-development/wp-content/uploads/2012/03/annualreport2010.pdf. Accessed 23 Jan 2025
GSMA (2020) Connected women: the mobile gender gap report 2020. https://www.gsma.com/solutions-and-impact/connectivity-for-good/mobile-for-development/wp-content/uploads/2020/05/GSMA-The-Mobile-Gender-Gap-Report-2020.pdf. Accessed 24 Jan 2025
insight2impact (i2i) (2017) Framework note 3—Financial services usage: a conceptual model. https://issuu.com/i2i-insight2impact/docs/i2i_mfw_note_3_-_financial_services. Accessed 24 Jan 2025
Intergovernmental Fintech Work Group (2021) Crypto Assets Regulatory Working Group Position paper on crypto assets. https://www.treasury.gov.za/comm_media/press/2021/IFWG_CAR%20WG_Position%20paper%20on%20crypto%20assets_Final.pdf. Accessed 25 Jan 2025
International Monetary Fund Nigeria (2022) Article IV consultation-press release of 9 February 2022. https://www.imf.org.en/Publications/CR/Issues/2022/02.09/Nigeria-2021-Article-IV-Consultation-Press-Release-Staff-Report-Staff-Statement-and-512944. Accessed 24 Jan 2025
Jones M (2025) Trumps digital dollar ban gives China and Europe's CBDCs free rein. https://www.reuters.com/markets/currencies/trumps-digital-dollar-ban-gives-china-europes-cbdcs-free-rein-2025-01-28. Accessed 24 Feb 2025
Kalogirou X (2022) Authorities explore how to design central bank digital currencies. https://www.iflr.com/article/2a647e1ubbp4genwpw2yo/authorities-explore-how-to-design-central-bank-digital-currencies. Accessed 24 Jan 2025
Kiff J, Alwazir J, Davidovic S, Farias A, Khan A, Khiaonarong T, Majid M, H Monroe K, Sugimoto N, Tourpe H, Zhoi P (2020) IMF working paper no 2020/104 a survey of research on retail central Bank digital currency. https://www.imf.org/en/Publications/WP/Issues/2020/06/26/A--Survey-of-Research-on-Retail-Central=Bank-Digital-Currency-49517. Accessed 24 Jan 2025
Klapper L, Singer D (2017) Financial inclusion and inclusive growth: a review of recent empirical evidence. Policy research working paper WPS 8040. http://documents.worldbank.org/curated/

en/403611493134249446/Financial-inclusion-and-inclusive-growth-a-review-of-recent-empirical-evidence. Accessed 25 Jan 2025
Lannquist A, Tan B (2023) Central Bank digital currency's role in promoting financial inclusion IMF Fintech Notes No 2023/011. https://www.imf.org/en/Publications/fintech-notes/Issues/2023/09/22/Central-Bank-Digital-Currency-s-Role-in-Promoting-Financial%2D%2DInclusion-538728. Accessed 24 Feb 2025
Lawack V (2022) An exploratory analysis of central bank digital currencies: some considerations. South Afr Mercantile Law J 34(1):118–134
Mancini-Griffoli T, Peria MSM, Agur MI (2018) Casting light on central bank digital currency. International Monetary Fund Staff Discussion Note. https://www.imf.org/en/Publications/Staff-Discussion-Notes/Issues/2018/11/13/Casting-Light-on-Central-Bank-Digital-Currencies-46233. Accessed 23 Jan 2025
McKinsey (2020) Global banking practice: the future of payments in Asia. https://www.mckinsey.com/~/media/mckinsey/industries/financial%20services/our%20insights/the%20next%20frontier%20in%20asia%20payments/the-future-of-payments-in-asia-vf.pdf. Accessed 24 Jan 2025
Perez HS, Dridi J, Gursoy T, Bari M (2019) The impact of remittances on economic activity: the importance of sectoral linkages. IMF Working Papers https://www.imf.org/en/Publications/WP/Issues/2019/08/16/The-Impact-of-Remittances-on-Economic-Activity-The-Importance-of-Sectoral-Linkages-47091. Accessed 25 Jan 2025
Reddy E, Lawack V (2019) An overview of the regulatory developments in South Africa regarding the use of cryptocurrencies. South Afr Mercantile Law J 31:1–28
Reddy E, Minnaar A (2018) Cryptocurrency: a tool and target for cybercrime. Acta Crim South Afr J Criminol 31(3):71
Reiners L (2021) CBDC – how dangerous is programmability? The FinReg Blog (blog). https://sites.duke.edu/thefinregblog/2021/09/21/cbdc-how-dangerous-is-programmability. Accessed 24 Jan 2025
Ryder N (2025) Coordinated terrorist financing – an emerging threat or a glaring omission? Time to rethink the financial war on terrorism. In: Goldbarsht D, de Koker L, Ferrill J (eds) Combating financial crime: intended and unintended consequences. Springer, Cham
Scott HS (2014) The importance of the retail payment system. https://papers.ssrn.com/sol3/papers.cfm?abstract_id=2539150. Accessed 24 Jan 2025
Smialek J (2021) Why Washington worries about stablecoins. https://www.nytimes.com/2021/09/17/business/economy/federal-reserve-virtual-currency-stablecoin.html. Accessed 21 Feb 2025
Soana G, de Arruda T (2024) Central Bank digital currencies and financial integrity: finding a trade-off between privacy and traceability within a changing financial architecture. J Bank Regul 25:467–486
Sofrecom (2019) Traditional mobile assets weakened by new models 2019. https://www.sofrecom.com/en/news-insights/traditional-mobile-money-assets-weakened-by-new-models.html. Accessed 26 Jan 2025
Sulayman Y (2025) Re-evaluating human rights in a global counter-terrorism financing: a case for preliminary judicial moderation. In: Goldbarsht D, de Koker L, Ferrill J (eds) Combating financial crime: intended and unintended consequences. Springer, Cham
UNCTAD (2019) Annual report, 2020. https://unctad.org/annualreport/2019/Pages/index.html. Accessed 24 Feb 2025
World Bank (2020) G2P Payments in COVID-19 context: key areas of action and experiences from country emergency actions. https://socialprotection.org/es/g2p-payments-covid-19-context-key-areas-action-and-experiences-country-emergency-actions. Accessed 26 Jan 2025
World Economic Forum (2021a) Digital currency consumer protection risk mapping. https://www3.weforum.org/docs/WEF_Digital_Currency_Consumer_Protection_2021.pdf. Accessed 24 Jan 2025
World Economic Forum (2021b) https://www3.weforum.org/docs/WEF_Digital_Currency_Consumer_Protection_2021.pdf. Accessed 23 Jan 2025

Professor Vivienne A Lawack is the Deputy Vice-Chancellor: Academic at the University of the Western Cape since 1 April 2015 and Acting Director: Centre for African Fintech, Innovation and Law at the Faculty of Law at the UWC. She is also a Professor of Law in the Department of Mercantile and Labour Law in the Faculty of Law at UWC. She serves on a number of boards and councils, including being a member of the Cenfri board, member of the South African Judicial Education Institute Council and a member of the Kepler Institute Board and Kepler College Board (Rwanda). Professor Lawack holds a B. Juris (cum laude), an LLB (cum laude) and an LLM from Nelson Mandela University in Port Elizabeth. She also holds an LLD from UNISA. She is an admitted, non-practicing advocate of the High Court of South Africa.

Coordinated Terrorist Financing: An Emerging Threat or a Glaring Omission? Time to Rethink the Financial War on Terrorism

Nic Ryder

Abstract This chapter examines the effectiveness of the Financial War on Terrorism in light of identifying an emerging terrorist financing typology—coordinated terrorist financing. The chapter begins by undertaking a doctrinal analysis of the international, regional, and domestic counterterrorist financing laws and identifying emerging related typologies. The chapter then moves onto define the Financial War on Terrorism and by using a case study approach illustrates how terrorist organisations are using similar funding methods and, in some instances, using a coordinated approach to raising funds. The case studies focus on natural resources, cryptocurrencies, and coordination between terrorist organisations. The chapter concludes with an assessment of the Financial War on Terrorism in light of the new terrorism financing typology and offers an updated interpretation.

1 Introduction

Terrorist financing has been defined by the World Bank as "providing the financial support, in any form, of terrorism or of those who encourage, plan, or engage in it".[1] It has also been referred to as 'reverse money laundering', a practice whereby 'clean' or 'legitimate' money is acquired and then funnelled to support acts of terrorism.[2] As detailed elsewhere, money laundering involves the conversion of 'dirty' or 'illegal' money into clean money via its laundering through several phases.[3]

[1] World Bank (2006), p. 19.

[2] Cassella (2003), p. 92.

[3] Levi and Reuter (2006), p. 289.

N. Ryder (✉)
School of Law and Politics, Cardiff University, Cardiff, UK
e-mail: RyderN@cardiff.ac.uk

D. Goldbarsht et al. (eds.), *Combating Financial Crime*, Ius Gentium: Comparative Perspectives on Law and Justice 131,
https://doi.org/10.1007/978-3-032-06858-3_4

However, this description and process has been challenged with the advancement of electronic money flows and the evolution of the global banking system.[4]

Prior to the al Qaeda terrorist attacks in the United States of America (US) on September 11, 2001 (9/11), the international community's efforts towards tackling financial crime focused on the prevention of money laundering and the related illegal drugs trade.[5] A consequence of 9/11 was a fundamental change in attitudes towards implementing counter-terrorist financing (CTF) laws. However, the legislative response by the United Nations (UN), the Financial Action Task Force (FATF) and the European Union (EU) was incorrectly based on the global anti-money laundering (AML) strategy which focused on targeting the proceeds of crime.[6] The global AML strategy targets mechanisms used by money launderers to conceal the profits of crime that contribute towards a so called 'champagne lifestyle'.[7] As Alldridge noted "clean money is worth more than dirty money".[8] However, terrorists tend not to generate profits to facilitate a 'champagne lifestyle', and their financing typologies often differ from money launderers.[9] The terrorist attacks in 2001 resulted in terrorist financing being propelled from political anonymity to the top of the international political agenda. Consequently, the international community, led by the US, instigated the Financial War on Terrorism. On September 24, 2001, President George Bush declared "we will starve terrorists of funding, turn them against each other, rout them out of their safe hiding places".[10] This announcement was followed by declarations of the freezing of the assets of terrorists and their supporters.[11] These declarations have been referred to as the 'Rose Garden Strategy', which laid the foundations for the Financial War on Terrorism.[12] The Financial War on Terrorism could be defined as "attacking, by criminalisation, confiscation, forfeiture, freezing, or sanctioning, the financial assets of known or suspected terrorists. Furthermore … [it] … also contains the use of preventative methods that have previously been used for money laundering and the collection of financial intelligence from suspicious activity reports".[13] This resulted in a seismic alteration in the financial crime strategies of the international community and nation states.

Prior to 9/11, terrorists relied on two forms of financial support—state sponsorship and donations from private individuals.[14] State-sponsorship of terrorism is where national governments provide support to terrorist organisations. It is impos-

---

[4] Koningsveld (2013).

[5] Ryder (2012), pp. 8–39.

[6] Ryder (2018a).

[7] National Audit Office (2007).

[8] Alldridge (2003), p. 1.

[9] Irwin et al. (2012).

[10] White House (2001).

[11] United States State Department (2001).

[12] Suskind (2006), p. 142.

[13] Ryder (2015), p. 11.

[14] Chase (2004).

sible to provide an accurate statistical figure for the amount of funding that terrorists receive from nation states, but it has been and still is considerable. For example, Richard took the view that "in the 1970s and 1980s, the majority of terrorist groups were sponsored by sympathetic governments".[15] Since 9/11 there has been a steady decline in the availability of this funding stream and terrorists are more likely to receive funding from private sponsors or donors.[16] However, Hardouin warned that "state sponsorship has been decreasing but not disappearing".[17] Several factors have contributed toward the decline in state sponsored terrorism—a smaller number of states are supporting terrorists;[18] the development of 'global terrorist networks',[19] a closer relationship between terrorist financiers and organised crime;[20] the end of the Cold War,[21] and the emergence of new terrorist financing typologies.[22] Whilst the role of state sponsored terrorism has been recognised, and at the time of writing the US has identified four state sponsors of terrorism: Cuba, Iran, North Korea and Syria.[23] Therefore, the decline in state-sponsored terrorism has forced terrorist organisations to diversify their funding activities and, in effect, become self-sustainable and rely on private benefactors.

The use of private financial benefactors was highlighted by the US Department of Treasury, which conducted an analysis of terrorist financing cases and prosecutions between 2001 and 2014. The study concluded that approximately one-third of the cases involved financial support from private donors.[24] Therefore, the FATF concluded that, "wealthy private donors can be an important source of income for some terrorist groups".[25] In order to understand and identify common and emerging terrorist financing mechanisms, the international community have used typologies. The FATF stated that "these typologies provide a contemporary snapshot of the ways in which terrorists raise, move and use funds".[26] Some of the most frequently used terrorist financing methods include the proceeds of drug trafficking,[27]

[15] Richard (2005), p. 6.

[16] Acharya (2009), p. 7.

[17] Hardouin (2009), p. 205.

[18] Richard (2005), p. 6.

[19] Ibid.

[20] Hutchinson and O'malley (2007).

[21] Acharya (2009), p. 7.

[22] Ryder (2020).

[23] United States Department of State (2025).

[24] United States Department of Treasury (2015).

[25] Financial Action Task Force (2015), p. 13.

[26] Ibid, p. 5.

[27] Federal Research Division Library of Congress (2002).

kidnapping for ransom,[28] counterfeit currencies,[29] oil refining,[30] natural resources,[31] piracy,[32] Hawala,[33] private donations, and extortion.[34] The Financial War on Terrorism has been able to limit some of these funding avenues and as a result terrorist financiers have turned towards alternative sources.[35] Therefore, we have seen the emergence of new terrorism funding typologies. For example, 'low cost' terrorism has become a prominent typology as illustrated by the terrorist attacks in Madrid,[36] London,[37] London,[38] Paris,[39] London,[40] Manchester,[41] London,[42] London [43] and London.[44] Other emerging terrorist financing typologies include fraud.[45] Here, terrorists have obtained funding via passport fraud, immigration fraud, identity fraud, financial fraud, online fraud, public funding and grant fraud, benefit fraud, student loan fraud, non-profit organisation fraud, tax fraud, counterfeiting, insurance fraud, mortgage fraud and trade-based fraud.[46] Furthermore, terrorists have been able to obtain funding from cryptocurrencies and social networking platforms.[47] The anonymity and speed provided by the internet is an appealing tool for terrorists to solicit financial donors. There is evidence that terrorist financiers have established relationships with organised criminal gangs (OCGs). This association has been described as the 'crime terror nexus'.[48] Here, terrorist financiers have exploited the OCGs infrastructure to raise funds via sexual and gender-based,[49] human trafficking [50] and drug trafficking.[51] Finally, the unprecedented scale of

[28] Financial Action Task Force (2015), p. 18.
[29] Financial Action Task Force (2012).
[30] Financial Action Task Force (2015).
[31] Ibid, pp. 39–42.
[32] Financial Action Task Force (2011).
[33] Financial Action Task Force (2013).
[34] Financial Action Task Force (2015).
[35] Gurulé (2008).
[36] Nepoleoni (2007).
[37] HM Government (2005), p. 23.
[38] BBC News (2014).
[39] CNN (2015).
[40] BBC News (2017).
[41] Ryder et al. (2023).
[42] Ryder (2020).
[43] BBC News (2017).
[44] Ryder (2020).
[45] Ryder (2024).
[46] Ibid.
[47] Choo (2015), Wang and Zhu (2021) and Wagman (2022).
[48] Hutchinson and O'malley (2007), Basra and Neumann (2016).
[49] Kenny and Malik (2019).
[50] Coonan and Thompson (2005).
[51] Williams (2007) and Clarke (2016).

Islamic State of Iraq and Levante's (ISIL) finances illustrated 'corporate' or 'hierarchical' typology.[52] This can also be referred to as 'economy based' terrorist financing.[53] The unprecedented scale of ISIL's finances has been underscored by the development of its own currency: an unparalleled development in the financing of terrorism.

Therefore, the chapter focuses on 'coordinated terrorist financing' and illustrates via the use of a doctrinal analysis of the Financial War on Terrorism and case studies that terrorists are using not only similar funding mechanisms but also cooperating to obtain funding. The 'coordinated terrorist financing' typology is largely under-researched and has received little academic attention, with existing literature focusing on the legal response to terrorist financing;[54] the evolution of terrorist financing;[55] how terrorists are funded,[56] and the response to terrorist financing in emerging economies.[57] Several scholars have focused on how terrorist organisations from co-operative relationships, but with little discussion on terrorist financing.[58]

Building on this theoretical basis, the chapter adopts a doctrinal analysis of the 'Financial War on Terrorism' and the case study methodology to define and identify 'coordinated terrorist financing'. A doctrinal analysis helps us towards offering a new definition of the 'Financial War on Terrorism' and illustrate loopholes that are exploited by this new typology, thus supporting policy and legislative recommendations. A case study has been defined as 'an intensive study of a single unit with an aim to generalise across a larger set of units'.[59] This approach is "particularly well suited to new research areas or research areas for which existing theory seems inadequate".[60] This chapter identifies a new typology which increases our understanding of terrorist financing, it provides a unique illustration of the shortcomings of the Financial War on Terrorism, and it divided into three parts. The first part defines the Financial War on Terrorism and identifies the legal mechanisms used to address terrorist financing since 9/11. The second part adopts a case study methodology that identifies a new terrorist financing typology—'coordinated terrorist financing'. The final part of the chapter critically appraises the impact of the Financial War on Terrorism on coordinated terrorist financing.

---

[52] Ryder (2018b).

[53] Brisard and Martinez (2014).

[54] Gurule (2008) and Donohue (2008).

[55] Vittori (2011).

[56] Freeman (2011).

[57] Azinge-Egbri (2021).

[58] Karmon (2005), Byman (2012), Moghadam (2017), Phillips (2018) and Cengiz and Karademir (2020).

[59] Gerring (2004), p. 342.

[60] Eisenhardt (1989), pp. 548–549.

2 The Financial War on Terrorism

Prior to 9/11, the international community's attempts to tackle financial crime were directed towards the prevention of money laundering.[61] The ineffectiveness of this approach was illustrated by loopholes exploited by the financiers of 9/11 who funded the terrorist attack by wire transfers: the physical transport of cash or traveler's cheques and the accessing of funds held in foreign financial institutions by debit or credit cards.[62] The Financial Recordkeeping and Reporting of Currency and Foreign Transactions Act, or Bank Secrecy Act (1970) imposes a legal obligation on US deposit taking institutions to complete and submit a Currency Transaction Report (CTR) to the Financial Crimes Enforcement Network (FinCEN) for all financial transactions of $10,000 or more. The terrorists received monies from financial facilitators via bank-to-bank transfers and wire transfers from Dubai via SunTrust Bank worth $10,000, $9500, $20,000, and $70,000.[63] The terrorists used "other banks including Bank of America, Hudson United Bank, and Dime Savings Bank. Here, no financial institution filed a Suspicious Activity Report in connection with *any* [author's emphasis] transaction of any of the 19 hijackers before 9/11".[64] The Bank Secrecy Act was not aimed at tackling terrorist financing, it was aimed at organised crime, financial crime, and deterring and preventing the use of secret foreign bank accounts for tax fraud.[65] US efforts to tackle terrorist financing before 9/11 focused on money laundering, fraud, and corruption. The CTF efforts were limited to mechanisms within the Trading with the Enemy Act (1917), International Emergency Economic Powers Act (1977), Anti-terrorism and Effective Death Penalty Act (1996) and Presidential Executive Orders 12,947 and 13,099. Therefore, the US was ill-prepared to tackle terrorist financing. These terrorist attacks set in motion a new, inventive and intensive legislative approach towards attacking the sources of terrorist funding.[66] The response from the international community was instantaneous and severe.

Terrorist financing was pushed to the summit of the international communities' counter-terrorist agenda. The UN called for "states to work together … to bring to justice the perpetrators, organizers and sponsors of these terrorist attacks".[67] The UN Security Council acted under Chapter VII of the UN Charter, to compel all nation states to implement mechanisms to counteract terrorist attacks.[68] Consequently, UN Security Council Resolution 1373 included four CTF provisions. Firstly, nation states are expected to "prevent and suppress the financing of terrorist

[61] Allen (2003), p. 306.

[62] National Commission on Terrorist Attacks Upon the United States (2004a), p. 13.

[63] National Commission on Terrorist Attacks Upon the United States (2004b).

[64] Ibid, p. 140.

[65] Bourton (2024), p. 182.

[66] Walker (2014), p. 229.

[67] United Nations (2001).

[68] United Nations (n.d.).

acts".[69] Secondly, members are expected to "criminalize the wilful provision or collection, by any means, directly or indirectly, of funds by their nationals or in their territories with the intention that the funds should be used, or in the knowledge that they are to be used, in order to carry out terrorist acts".[70] Thirdly, nation states were obliged to "freeze without delay funds and other financial assets or economic resources of persons who commit, or attempt to commit, terrorist acts".[71] Finally, states are obliged to "prohibit their nationals or any persons and entities within their territories from making any funds, financial assets or economic resources or financial or other related services available, directly or indirectly, for the benefit of persons who commit or attempt to commit or facilitate or participate in the commission of terrorist acts".[72] Additionally, the Counter-Terrorism Committee, which is assisted by the Counter-Terrorism Committee Executive Directorate, was created to observe compliance with UN Security Council Resolution 1373. Similarly, the EU implemented a series of CTF measures following the terrorist attacks. In December 2001, the European Council published its Common Position,[73] which provides that the EU will use financial sanctions to ensure that funds, financial assets, and economic resources are unavailable to designated terrorists. Furthermore, the EU published a Council Regulation with "[s]pecific restrictive measures directed against certain persons and entities with a view to combating terrorism".[74] This requires the "freezing of funds, other financial assets, and economic resources belonging to, owned, or held by individuals, groups, or entities".[75] This was followed by the adoption of a Council Framework Decision that combats terrorism which includes all terrorist offences prepared or committed in the EU (2002). The FATF published its 'Special Recommendations' that were aimed at tackling terrorist financing.[76] The Special Recommendations included ratifying and implementing relevant UN Security Council Resolutions, criminalising terrorist financing, permitting nation states to freeze and confiscate terrorist assets, reporting suspicious transactions that relate to terrorism, the promotion of international co-operation to tackle terrorist financing, alternative remittance systems, wire transfers, and non-profit organisations.[77] A ninth Special Recommendation was added in October 2004.[78]

[69] United Nations (2001).

[70] Ibid.

[71] Ibid.

[72] Ibid.

[73] [2001] OJ L344/93.

[74] (2002).

[75] Ibid.

[76] Financial Action Task Force (2001).

[77] Ibid.

[78] Financial Action Task Force (2004).

The Recommendations are not legally binding,[79] are viewed as international best practice,[80] but have been criticised.[81] In February 2012, the FATF published its amended set of Recommendations which "fully integrate counter-terrorist financing measures with anti-money laundering controls".[82] However, the Financial War on Terrorism has become stagnant, and it is no longer fit to tackle modern terrorist financing typologies. As illustrated in the next section, terrorist financing typologies continue to evolve, and coordinated terrorist financing represents an unprecedented threat not seen since the adoption of the 'corporate or hierarchical' typology.

3 Coordinated Terrorist Financing

This part identifies a new terrorist financing typology that involves terrorists and terrorist organisations using similar funding mechanisms but also coordinating their funding activities. Coordinated terrorist financing is defined as organised efforts by individuals, groups, or networks to fund terrorist activities. This involves pooling resources, collaborating across borders, and using various methods to move and conceal funds. The first of three cases studies focuses on the link between natural resources, terrorist financing, the Taliban, and al Qaeda.

3.1 Case Study 1: Natural Resources and Terrorist Financing—The Taliban and al Qaeda

The link between natural resources and terrorist financing has been described as an "emerging terrorist financing risk".[83] Terrorist financiers have abused natural resources and committed environmental crime because it is low-risk and it has the potential to be a profitable source of revenue.[84] This has been referred to as 'transnational economic crime'.[85] Terrorists are able to obtain funding via natural resources such as illegal mining, charcoal and timber trafficking, oil and gas smuggling, and wildlife trafficking. These resources are either sold directly or taxed at various points (production, transport, export), generating revenue for terrorists.[86] Once the funds have been raised, they can move through informal value transfer

[79] Turner (2014).

[80] Gardner (2007).

[81] de Koker et al. (2023).

[82] Financial Action Task Force (2012).

[83] Financial Action Task Force (2015).

[84] Wang and Tian (2024), p. 213.

[85] Elliott (2012), p. 87.

[86] Shelley (2020).

systems,[87] companies,[88] non-profit organisations,[89] converted into cryptocurrencies.[90] or high-value goods to hide their true origin.[91] The funds are then distributed to operatives or terrorist cells via cash couriers, bank transfers of cryptocurrencies and are used to purchase weapons, pay salaries, or support logistics.[92] Furthermore, the funds could be invested into local economies to either gain influence or legitimacy.[93] This process is difficult to disrupt because it often involves legitimate supply chains, cross-border smuggling, and jurisdictional loopholes.

The natural resources sector in mineral rich countries is susceptible to abuse by terrorist organisations due to weak political infrastructure where corruption is widespread.[94] The related illicit financial flows are facilitated by the lack of regulation or institutional capacity,[95] or enforcement of any relevant regulation in many resources rich countries.[96] These conditions have become a focal point for terrorist financing.[97] Natural resources terrorist financing is a complex and multi-faceted issue [98] and terrorist organisations "have deep operational, logistical and financial links with the production and trade of natural resources".[99] Natural resources are often traded by terrorists for gold, diamonds, and oil, as well as minerals integral to supply chains such as marble, chromite, tin, and talc.[100] The OECD explains that "terrorist organisations occupying large areas may seize the state-owned financial assets and natural resources within the territory under their control … non-cash assets and resources … must then be monetised … those black markets may operate largely outside of the territories or countries where the terrorists are located".[101] This illustrates a complex network that transcends borders, in which terrorists can exploit natural resources.[102] There is ample evidence of the link between natural resources and terrorist financing. For example, the sale of conflict diamonds has provided a funding source for terrorists [103] and untraceable precious stones and metals make it

87 Raphaeli (2003).
88 Jacobson (2010).
89 Romaniuk and Keatinge (2018).
90 Ryder (2020).
91 Ryder (2018b)
92 Davis (2021).
93 Omelicheva and Markowitz (2021).
94 Bhattacharyya and Hodler (2010).
95 Financial Action Task Force (2015).
96 Global Financial Integrity (2022).
97 Organisation for Economic Co-operation and Development (2015).
98 Financial Action Task Force (2015).
99 Organisation for Economic Co-operation and Development (2017), p. 4.
100 Ibid, p. 4.
101 Organisation for Economic Co-operation and Development (2019), p. 23.
102 Bannon and Collier (2003).
103 Financial Action Task Force (2009).

easy for terrorists to use these commodities.[104] Other commodities include oil, charcoal, diamonds, and coal.[105] Oil as a natural resources terrorist financing source,[106] as illustrated by ISIL when it gained control of several oil fields.[107] Furthermore, charcoal has become an important revenue for Al-Shabaab's terrorist activities.[108]

Now that the link between natural resources and terrorist financing has been established, this section of the case study illustrates how the Taliban and al Qaeda have established a coordinated relationship to collectively raise funds. In August 2021, following the capturing of several supply roads and border crossings, the Taliban took control of Kabul, announcing the creation of an interim government.[109] The collapse of the Afghanistan government prompted a humanitarian crisis that resulted in thousands of people escaping to Pakistan and the Islamic Republic of Iran.[110] The Australian Department of Foreign Affairs and Trade noted that "Afghanistan continues to face substantial humanitarian and economic challenges, compounded by natural disasters".[111] Furthermore, the United Nations High Commissioner for Refugees reported that there are 6.4 million Afghan refugees and approximately 10.9 million Afghans remain displaced.[112] This has resulted in a renewed focus on the extensive natural resources in Afghanistan which are estimated to be worth USD$1 trillion.[113] The then Afghanistan Ministry of Mines and Petroleum estimated that the country holds "more than 2.2 billion tonnes of iron ore, 1.3 billion tonnes of marble and 1.4 million tonnes of rare earth mineral".[114] As a result, "the export of and custom duties from coal have become a key source of revenue for the Taliban".[115] However, Global Witness warned that the ability of the Taliban to extract the unmined minerals is limited by corruption.[116]

The FATF determined that the "opiate trade in Afghanistan found that the multi-million-dollar profits of drug trafficking networks have leaked into the funds of terrorist organisations".[117] The Taliban has been described as the 'driving force' behind the poppy farming in Afghanistan.[118] Wang and Tian went further and stated that al Qaeda and the Taliban consider the illegal drugs trade to be their largest

---

[104] Aufhauser (2003), p. 301.

[105] Interpol (n.d.).

[106] Lee (2018).

[107] Financial Action Task Force (2015).

[108] Petrich (2022).

[109] BBC News (2021a).

[110] Horowitz (2021).

[111] Australian Department of Foreign Affairs and Trade (n.d.).

[112] United Nations High Commissioner for Refugees (2024), p. 9.

[113] Hussein and Haddad (2021).

[114] Ibid.

[115] Siddique (2022).

[116] Global Witness (2017), p. 1.

[117] Financial Action Task Force (2015).

[118] Ibid.

source of funds.[119] The UN Security Council estimated that one third of the Taliban budget in 2011/2012 was solicited from the poppy trade.[120] The World Bank noted that "the Taliban and Al-Qaeda produced thousands of metric tons of opium each year in 18 of the 31 Afghan provinces … the Taliban also taxed heroin laboratories and heroin and opium convoys passing through Taliban checkpoints, charging producers and smugglers 10–20 percent of the total value of the wholesale opium".[121] The association between the Taliban and al Qaeda is well documented. For instance, the Taliban harboured and provided sanctuary for al Qaeda and Osama Bin Laden in the 1990s and early 2000s,[122] allowing them to operate from Afghanistan during the late 1990s and early 2000s. This alliance was most notably highlighted when the Taliban sheltered Osama bin Laden, the leader of al Qaeda, after the 9/11 attacks.[123]

The Taliban, an Islamist militant group that developed in Afghanistan in the 1970s,[124] is based on a strict interpretation of Islamic law and has focused on administering Afghanistan.[125] Therefore, it has been described as a national movement.[126] Conversely, al Qaeda is a militant Islamic fundamentalist group that has the objective of establishing 'one or more states ruled by its own favoured version of Islam'.[127] Despite these differences, there have been instances of collaboration when their interests and financial networks align. For example, as highlighted, the Taliban and al Qaeda have strong links to the manufacturing, distribution and sale of narcotic substances. The Taliban have profited from Afghanistan's opium trade, which has represented a portion of global opium production. Additionally, the Taliban has taxed opium farmers,[128] managed smuggling routes [129] and even operated drug labs.[130] Similarly, al Qaeda has also been implicated in drug trafficking, often collaborating with other groups to exploit the trade.[131] The Taliban and al Qaeda continue to have a close relationship,[132] as confirmed by the National Terrorist Financing Risk Assessment,[133] they have similar financing methods and coordinated their funding activities.

[119] Wang and Tian (2024).

[120] United Nations Security Council (2012).

[121] Bannon and Collier (2003), p. 205.

[122] National Commission on Terrorist Attacks (2004a), p. 66.

[123] Ibid.

[124] Johnson (2022), p. 1350

[125] Misra (2002).

[126] Raqib and Barreto (2014).

[127] Sedgwick (2004), p. 811.

[128] Peters (2009).

[129] Sinaee and Khatibi (2023).

[130] Nasab et al. (2020).

[131] National Commission on Terrorist Attacks Upon the Unites States (2004b), pp. 22–23.

[132] United Nations (2022).

[133] United States Department of Treasury (2024), p. 10.

This case study has illustrated the link between natural resources and terrorist financing, especially in the case of the Taliban and al Qaeda, who have relied on Afghanistan's natural resources. These organisations have maintained a co-operative relationship which has allowed them to coordinate control over rich natural resource areas in Afghanistan, where state regulation is weak. These areas are abundant in natural resources which are illegally extracted and taxed or directly controlled by the Taliban and al Qaeda. The opium trade in Afghanistan is an important revenue stream for both the Taliban and al Qaeda. The Taliban has taxed poppy cultivation and protected the drug trafficking supply chains, whilst al Qaeda has leveraged its transnational networks to facilitate distribution and laundering of profits. This collaboration has allowed for a shared logistical infrastructure, making the drug trade more efficient and profitable. The co-operation between the Taliban and al Qaeda has turned Afghanistan's natural resources into an integral asset for financing terrorism, blending local control with a global network.

3.2 *Case Study 2: Cryptocurrencies and Terrorist Financing—The Islamic Republic of Iran and Hamas*

The second case study focuses on the link between cryptocurrencies, terrorist financing, and the sponsorship of Hamas by the Islamic Republic of Iran. The association between cryptocurrencies and money laundering,[134] fraud,[135] market manipulation, and other associated crimes is well established.[136] However, the link between cryptocurrencies and terrorism financing is less established. Therefore, it is necessary to illustrate how terrorist financiers have used cryptocurrencies, the process involved and how transactions are anonymised and the challenges in tracking them. Terrorist groups have used social media platforms, to solicit donations in Bitcoin and other cryptocurrencies,[137] which include wallet addresses that allows supporters to directly send funds.[138] Cryptocurrencies allow peer-to-peer transfers that enable terrorist financiers to direct transfers without involving a financial intermediary, thus making easier to avoid the CTF reporting mechanisms.[139] The next stage of the process is the conversion of the cryptocurrency into a usable asset. Here, the cryptocurrency could be converted in a fiat currency or good such as gift cards or prepaid cards. These transactions are difficult to detect and despite being recorded on the public blockchain, the user is only identified by the wallet address, not by name,

[134] Hillman (2024).

[135] Trozze et al. (2022).

[136] Kethineni and Cao (2019).

[137] Ryder (2020).

[138] FATF (2023).

[139] Carlisle (2017).

thus making is difficult to establish any illegal activity.[140] Furthermore, decentralised exchanges do not require identity verification, allowing anonymous trading and the conversion of funds.[141] The inconsistent global, national, and regional regulation of cryptocurrencies has also contributed towards difficulties in detecting terrorist financing.[142] Finally, the evolution of privacy focused cryptocurrencies and mixing services make it even more difficult to trace funds intended for terrorism financing.[143]

Nonetheless, the Indonesian Financial Transaction Reports and Analysis Centre reported that ISIL had used Bitcoin for terrorist financing purposes.[144] Furthermore, in August 2015, a computer hacker demanded a ransom of two Bitcoins from a retailer in exchange for removing bugs from their computer system. The hacker was able to use the extracted data from the server to create a 'kill list' of over 1300 names of US government and military personnel that was provided to ISIL.[145] Another example was Ali Shukri Amin, who was convicted and sentenced to 11 years and 4 months imprisonment for using the "internet to provide material support and resources" to ISIL.[146] Amin pleaded guilty and admitted to using his Twitter handle '@Amreekiwitness' to "provide instruction [to ISIL] on how to use Bitcoin … to mask the provision of funds to ISIL".[147] This case demonstrates that terrorism financiers are using cryptocurrencies and social media to provide support and resources to ISIL.

The anonymity and speed provided by the internet is an appealing tool for terrorists to solicit financial donors. In evidence presented to the House Foreign Affairs Committee (Subcommittee on Terrorism, Non-proliferation, and Trade Subcommittee on the Middle East and North Africa), the Washington Institute for Near East Policy stated that some of terrorism fundraising was carried out in plain sight on online social media platforms.[148] The evidence referred to a video uploaded to YouTube in October 2016 by Abd Allah al-Muhaysini who "thanked Gulf donors for supporting jihadists in Syria … as for the businessmen, and I will mention some of them, the ones who prepared these hundred rockets, may Allah reward them … I tell all the businessmen of the Muslims, this is your money now, fighting in the path of Allah".[149] Further evidence of the association is illustrated by the US Department of the Treasury, which imposed sanctions on three terrorism financiers for "fundraising appeals on social media".[150] Here, the US Department of the Treasury stated

---

140 Ibid.

141 Dion-Schwarz et al. (2019).

142 Ibid.

143 Ibid.

144 Indonesian Financial Transaction Reports and Analysis Centre (2015), pp. 15–17.

145 Centre for New American Security (2017), p. 12.

146 United States Department of Justice (2015).

147 Ibid.

148 Blumenstein-Katz (2018).

149 Ibid.

150 United States Department of Treasury (2014).

that "Al-Ajmi operates regular social media campaigns seeking donations for Syrian fighters and is one of the most active Kuwaiti fundraisers for Al-Nusra Front. In July 2014, Al-Ajmi publicly admitted that he collected money under the auspices of charity and delivered the funds in person".[151] Further sanctions were imposed on Abdul Mohsen Abdullah Ibrahim al-Sharikh, who "is a senior ANF leader and al-Qaida facilitator based in Syria … in this role, al-Sharikh has used social media posts to demonstrate his aspiration to target Americans and US interests".[152] In 2015, Mohamed Elshinawy was convicted for "conspiracy to provide material support to ISIL, providing and attempting to provide material support to ISIS; terrorism financing; and making false statements in connection with a terrorism matter".[153] Elshinawy admitted his role in a conspiracy to provide funding for ISIL via a variety of mechanisms including PayPal and Western Union, totalling $8700.[154] In March 2019, Gregory Lepsky was sentenced to 16 years' imprisonment after pleading guilty to attempting to provide material support to a designated foreign terrorist organisation. Here, law enforcement authorities were able to determine that Lepsky had used several social media platforms to plan his terrorist attack.[155] In September 2019, the US Department of Treasury stated that "HAMAS solicit[ed] Bitcoin donations via social media, using two Bitcoin addressed. As of late March 2019, those two known addressed had received at least $5,000 worth of Bitcoin".[156] Another example of terrorism financiers exploiting cryptocurrencies was Zoobia Shahnaz, who was arrested by the FBI after attempting to transfer $62,000 worth of Bitcoin. The Department of Justice stated that Shahnaz had entered into a number of financial transactions designed to circumvent the transaction reporting obligations imposed by the Currency and Foreign Transactions Reporting Act. In November 2018, Shahnaz pleaded guilty to providing material support to ISIL and was sentenced to 13 years imprisonment.[157] Therefore, terrorists are "creating safe havens to raise funds hiding in the shadows of the dark net … using cryptocurrencies such as Bitcoin to generate funds".[158] The Jackson Society noted that an al Qaeda-linked entity, al-Sadaqah, used a public channel on Telegram to campaign for Bitcoin funding.[159] Clearly, then, modern forms of technology, especially social media platforms, are used by terrorism financiers. More often than not, the payments made over the internet, the Dark Web, or social media platforms involve small amounts of funding which do not raise suspicion. In 2021, Hisham Chaudary was convicted of several offences under the Terrorism Act 2000 and sentenced to

[151] Ibid.

[152] United States Department of Treasury (2014).

[153] United States Department of Justice (2018).

[154] Ibid.

[155] United States Department of Justice (2019).

[156] United States Department of Treasury (2019).

[157] United States Department of Justice (2020).

[158] Townsend (2018).

[159] The Jackson Society (2018), p. 425.

12 years imprisonment.[160] Chaudary had converted £52,000 into cryptocurrency to support ISIL, which he claimed was used for funding an 'humanitarian purpose'.[161] The US Treasury Department concluded "at least part of the ISIL attack on the Crocus Hall in Moscow was funded using virtual assets that transferred through various ISIS entities, including ISIL Core and al-Siddiq Office. ISIS Khorasan reportedly transferred at least $2,000 in virtual assets to the Crocus Hall attackers, showing a direct link between ISIL's use of virtual assets and external operations".[162]

In February 2024, Victoria Jacobs was convicted of soliciting or providing support for an act of terrorism after using cryptocurrency to provide financial support terrorist groups operating in Syria.[163] Jacobs had provided $6000 to the terrorist training group 'Malhama Tactical' and laundered $12,000 on behalf of this group by receiving cryptocurrency that was sent to Bitcoin wallets controlled by 'Malhama Tactical'.[164] In December 2024, Mohammed Azharuddin Chhipa was convicted of providing material support to Islamic State of Iraq and al-Sham.[165] Over a 3-year period, Chhipa accumulated and distributed money to ISIS members in Syria fighters via social media. Chhipa would convert the money to cryptocurrency and send it to Türkiye, where it was smuggled to ISIS members in Syria. In December 2024, Amin Rahman pleased to guilty to terrorist funding after he sent over £16,000 of cryptocurrency to ISIL.[166] Rahman admitted to funding the Afghanistan-based IS franchise Islamic State Khorasan Province. Now that the link between cryptocurrencies and terrorist financing has been established this part of the case study focuses on the funding relationship between the Islamic Republic of Iran and Hamas.

Hamas, like the other terrorist organisations discussed in this chapter, receives funding from a wide range of different sources, legal and illegal. The Islamic Republic of Iran is the prominent financial and military supporter of Hamas, which like ISIL has a very sophisticated terrorist financing operation including cryptocurrencies which has been used to hide transactions.[167] Hamas has used cryptocurrencies to raised funds since 2019[168] and it has been described as the most "successful initiators of cryptoasset-based fundraising to date in terms of amount raised".[169] In March 2023, the US Department of Justice announced that it has dismantled "three terrorist financing cyber-enabled campaigns, involving the al-Qassam Brigades, Hamas's military wing, al-Qaeda, and Islamic State of Iraq and the Levant". The DoJ started how the terrorists "have *similarly adapted* (authors emphasis) their ter-

[160] BBC News (2021b).

[161] Ibid.

[162] United States Department of Treasury (2024), p. 2.

[163] Manhattan District Attorney's Office (2024).

[164] Ibid.

[165] United States Department of Justice (2024).

[166] BBC News (2024).

[167] Vidino and Altuna (2023).

[168] Wagman (2022).

[169] Glover et al. (2023).

ror finance activities to the cyber age. Each group used cryptocurrency and social media to garner attention and raise funds for their terror campaigns".[170] Furthermore, in March 2025 the Department of Justice revealed it had seized 'approximately $201,400 in cryptocurrency held in wallets and accounts intended to benefit Harakat al-Muqawama al-Islamiyya (Hamas). The seized funds were traced from fundraising addresses purportedly controlled by Hamas that were used to launder more than $1.5 million in virtual currency since October 2024'.[171] Following the terrorist attacks on Israel in October 2023, US law makers wrote to the Department of Treasury citing a report by the Wall Street Journal [172] asserting that "in the months leading up to their brutal and horrific October 7th attack on Israel, Hamas and Palestinian Islamic Jihad (PIJ) raised millions of dollars in crypto – evading US sanctions and funding their operations. Indeed, between August 2021 and June 2023, the two groups raised over $130 million in crypto".[173] However, it has been suggested that "there is no evidence to suggest that crypto fundraising has raised anything close to this amount, and data provided … has been misinterpreted".[174] However, in July 2023, the Israeli National Bureau for Counter Terror Financing announced it had seized "seized millions of dollars' worth of cryptocurrency belonging to the Lebanese terrorist group Hezbollah and Iran's Islamic Revolutionary Guard".[175] This seizure represented "Israel's largest terrorism related cryptocurrency seizure and the first that targets Hezbollah and its primary backer, the Islamic Revolutionary Guard".[176] Further evidence of the Islamic Republic of Iran providing funding for Hamas via cryptocurrencies is illustrated by the announcement of sanctions on key personnel in the Hamas financial network. The UK, US, and Australia sanctioned Zuheir Shamlakh who "exploited digital currencies and existing systems of informal money transfers to move large sums of money from Iran to Hamas ahead of the 7 October attacks. This underground financial network uses legitimate businesses as a front to conceal the flow of terrorist funding".[177]

Cryptocurrencies have been used to fund terrorism and this typology has been used by several terrorist organisations, thus it is a common funding method. However, this typology accounts for only a very small part of terrorist financing. As noted above, the appeal for Hamas and is supporters is the apparent anonymity and ease of cross-border transactions. Hamas has cryptocurrencies solicit donations and transfer funds from the Islamic Republic of Iran. The link between cryptocurrencies and terrorist financing is complex and the co-operation between the Islamic Republic of Iran and Hamas illustrates how digital assets can be used to fund acts of

[170] Ibid.

[171] United Sates Department of Justice (2025).

[172] Berwick and Talley (2023).

[173] Warren (2023).

[174] Elliptic (2023).

[175] TRM (2023).

[176] Ibid.

[177] Foreign, Commonwealth and Development Office (2024).

terrorism. Hamas has adopted cryptocurrencies as a mechanism of seeking donations and secretly moving funds. Wallets linked to Hamas have received millions of dollars in cryptocurrencies via public fundraising campaigns on social media or encrypted messaging platforms. Some of these wallets are connected to Iranian financial networks, suggesting there is a coordinated effort to move funds using decentralised financial systems.

3.3 *Case Study 3: Allegiance and Committee—Boko Harem, Al-Shaabab, al Qaeda and ISIL*

The final case study focuses on the terrorist financing links between Boko Haram, al Qaeda, ISIL, and Al-Shabaab. Boko Haram, a Nigerian based terrorist group, was established in 2002.[178] The US House of Representatives Committee on Homeland Security Subcommittee on Counterterrorism stated that "the group was not founded as a violent insurgency bent on overthrowing the Nigerian government ... [they call themselves] the Nigerian Taliban ... and have established a camp in a remote area of northeast Nigeria".[179] According to the FATF there was an increase in the number of terrorist attacks in Africa which can be attributed to Boko Haram who "conducted 136 attacks in 2011 — up from 31 in 2010. In 2012, Boko Haram conducted 364 terrorist attacks, which killed 1,132 people".[180] The increased terrorist activity of Boko Haram was also recognised by the US Department of State who noted "Boko Haram maintained a high operational tempo ... [who have] carried out kidnappings, killings, bombings, and attacks on civilian and military targets in northern Nigeria". The Department of State added that they were concerned with the increasing levels of sophistication from Boko Haram and that this terrorist group has been able to effortlessly conduct terrorist attacks in Cameroon, Chad, and Niger.[181]

A direct comparison exists between the funding of Boko Haram and ISIL. For example, Boko Haram has multiple avenues of funding that include "the sale of goods, extracting the profits of supportive businesses, child beggars which are also used as spies for the organisation, extorting local traders and cross-border smuggling of arms and cash".[182] Furthermore, Boko Haram, like ISIS, has received funding from private benefactors.[183] The Inter-governmental Action Group Against Money Laundering in West Africa concluded that the "level of [private] donations

[178] Financial Action Task Force (2016), p. 43.

[179] US House of Representatives Committee on Homeland Security Subcommittee on Counterterrorism and Intelligence (2011), p. 6.

[180] Financial Action Task Force (2016), p. 5.

[181] Ibid.

[182] Institute for Economics and Peace (2014), p. 53.

[183] Ibid.

could be relatively easily maintained".[184] The FATF provided several examples of how Boko Haram acquires its financing. This includes the sale of goods and other lucrative activities, business profits/logistical support, contributions (collections) from members of a terrorist group, begging (alms collection) by vulnerable persons, extortion of civilians by means of intimidation, arms smuggling at the Nigerian border, women cash couriers and arms smugglers in Nigeria, cash couriers and arms smugglers, and financial contributions of political leaders.[185] Another funding opportunity that has been used by Boko Haram is armed robberies and the theft of oil, and that these are their "primary means of funding".[186] Interestingly, "al-Qaeda is now involved in contributing funds supporting [Boko Haram] … in August of 2011 Boko Haram leadership travelled to Saudi Arabia to discuss financial and logistical operations with al-Qaeda leaders. The financial alliance between the two groups as well as the recent transnational UN building target may be enough evidence to support the theory of Boko Haram's shift from a strictly Nigerian based anti-government sect to an international terrorist organization".[187] The funding was provided to Boko Haram through an al Qaeda affiliate, al Qaeda in the Islamic Maghreb. The co-operation between Boko Harem and al Qaeda is illustrated by training exchanges and ideological mentorship. For example, Boko Haram's founder, Muhammad Yusuf, respected al Qaeda's ideology and sent members to train with al Qaeda in the early 2000s.[188] Additionally, the co-ordination between the two terrorist groups was logistical and financial, which contributed to Boko Haram becoming a more structured and organised terrorist group.[189] Therefore, once again, there is a clear link between Boko Haram and other terrorist groups.[190] Al-Shabaab is closely affiliated to al Qaeda, in fact the terrorist organisation pledged allegiance to al Qaeda in 2012. Onat et al. stated that "the leaders of Al-Shabaab swore allegiance to al-Qaeda under the leadership of Usama bin Laden, but its pledge was formally accepted by Ayman Al-Zawahiri, the successor of bin Laden, in 2012".[191] The Wilson Centre reported that the Al-Shabaab "has stepped up attacks … Al-Shabaab killed one US servicemember and two US contractors in an attack on a Kenyan military base in January 2020".[192]

ISIL was once described as one of the wealthiest terrorist organisations,[193] and it was able to exploit numerous funding streams, thus making it very difficult for the

[184] Inter-governmental Action Group Against Money Laundering in West Africa (2010), p. 94.

[185] Financial Action Task Force (2016).

[186] US House of Representatives Committee on Homeland Security Subcommittee on Counterterrorism and Intelligence above (2011), p. 18.

[187] Connell (2012), p. 82.

[188] Zenn (2017).

[189] Comolli (2016).

[190] United States Department of State (2014), p. 40.

[191] Onat et al. (2021), p. 284.

[192] The Wilson Centre (2021).

[193] Lander (2014).

'Financial War on Terrorism' to limit the finances of this terrorist groups. However, it is "a mischaracterisation to describe ISIL as the world's richest terrorist organisation".[194]

One such funding stream is, for example, the sale of oil,[195] that would generate 'between $1m to $3m per day'.[196] This view is supported by Jonsson who noted that "whereas difficult to substantiate with certainty, it is also plausible that ISIS continued to benefit from thefts and corruption within the Iraqi oil industry, as it had done in 2006-2010".[197] Another funding source for ISIL is through foreign investors and private benefactors from several countries including Kuwait.[198] Supporters in Jordan, Syria, and Saudi Arabia have provided Islamic State with financial support.[199] Therefore, comparisons can be drawn with the other two case studies. Other mechanisms included criminal activities such as looting, kidnapping and extortion.[200] Indeed, it has been suggested that kidnapping has become a major source of income for Islamic State with "tens of millions of dollars paid by some European governments and wealthy relatives of the kidnap victims over the past 2 ears. The low end of the estimate range is well above $25m".[201] Therefore, the funding activities of ISIL are like those of al Qaeda, Hamas and the Irish Republican Army.[202]

Despite its territorial defeat in 2019, which has limited its ability to raise funds, ISIL is "still able to raise and receive funds, through legal and illegal sources, and maintains roughly USD$25-50 million in reserves. These funds help the group to sustain some activities and to seek a potential resurgence".[203] ISIL, like other terrorist organisations, have a large number of affiliates in different parts of the world. For example, the US Department of Treasury stated that ISIL have connected in "across Central, Eastern, and Southern Africa" including "affiliates in the Democratic Republic of the Congo (DRC), Mozambique, Somalia, and ISIS cells in South Africa".[204] Furthermore, ISIL has affiliates in Afghanistan, Iraq, Syria, Mali, Burkina Faso, and the Niger.[205] However, ISIL's presence in Africa remains 'small' but the Crisis Group described the terrorist organisations as an "important part of the jihadist group's worldwide network".[206] Yet, ISIL in Africa has become an "important logistical and financial hub for Islamic State's African and global

194 House of Commons Foreign Affairs Committee (2016), p. 5.

195 Hawramy et al. (2014).

196 Institute for Economics and Peace (2014), p. 51.

197 Jonsson (2014), p. 11.

198 Ibid.

199 Laub (2014).

200 Institute for Economics and Peace (2014), p. 51.

201 NBC News (2014).

202 Carey (2014).

203 Financial Action Task Force (2021).

204 US Department of Treasury (2024).

205 Loft and Brooke-Holland (2025).

206 The Crisis Group (2024).

network".[207] ISIL has been able to collaborate with other terrorist organisations in numerous ways including funding arrangements. For example, this included funding activities including oil smuggling, extortion and taxation.[208] Furthermore, ISIL and al Qaeda have collaborated with each other by direct financial transfers. These partnerships can be opportunistic, driven by shared goals or mutual benefits in specific regions. Their funding methods are diverse and adaptable, which has allowed them to sustain operations.

The final case study has demonstrated that while these four terrorist groups operate in different parts of the world, pursuing distinctive agendas, there is evidence of intermittent coordination in terrorist financing strategies. For example, each of these terrorist groups shares common financing mechanisms including kidnapping for ransom, smuggling and trafficking, extortion and taxation, and natural resource exploitation. These groups use informal money transfer networks which creates overlapping financial corridors that can facilitate indirect cooperation. Furthermore, they have been involved in training exchanges and ideological mentorship. For example, Boko Haram's early leadership received training from al Qaeda affiliate; Al-Shabaab is an affiliate of al Qaeda affiliate and it has received funding and strategic guidance from them. All four groups have used online platforms for fundraising and there have been instances of shared media strategies and the use of similar cryptocurrency tactics to solicit donations. Therefore, these terrorist groups have indirectly coordinated through shared tactics, overlapping networks, and mutual ideological goals. Their financing efforts reflect an adaptive ecosystem, where best practices in terror finance are learned, copied, and sometimes shared.

4 Recommendations

To counter the threat of terrorists co-ordinating their funding efforts, there are a number of improvements that could be made to the 'Financial War on Terrorism.' For example, developments could be made to enhancing international cooperation, improved data sharing, and stricter global regulation of cryptocurrencies. Enhanced international cooperation between countries and financial institutions is crucial for data sharing and co-ordinating efforts to identify and disrupt terrorist financing. Real-time data sharing and joint analysis could help detect complex, cross-border funding networks more effectively. The use of the collection of financial intelligence from suspicious activity reports in the Financial War on Terrorism could be extended to include 'pre' and 'post' data sharing to the collection and exchange of financial intelligence related to suspicious activity, including data shared prior to the submission of a SAR (such as internal alerts, risk indicators, and typologies), and information disseminated or received after submission (such as feedback from

[207] Loft and Brooke-Holland (2025), p. 5.

[208] Al-Khatteeb and Gordts (2014).

authorities, inter-institutional collaboration, and follow-up investigations). This would align with the FATFs emphasis on dynamic information sharing to tackle terrorist financing which supports the development of common standards for collecting and sharing data to improve efforts to identify the financial patterns and trends when terrorist groups operate across borders. Improved information sharing between the public and private sectors in neighbouring countries would enhance the detection of suspicious transactions and activities associated to this typology.

The second case study has illustrated how the terrorist financing via cryptocurrencies has become an established terrorist financing typology. Therefore, given the increasing use of cryptocurrencies by terrorists, the FATF Recommendations have focused on addressing the anonymity they provide and ensuring that these transactions can be traced. Consequently, the definition of the Financial War on Terrorism could be extended to include 'and the monitoring of emerging technologies such as cryptocurrencies that may facilitate anonymous or cross-border terrorist financing'. The case studies have illustrated the problems of cross border terrorist financing and CTF measures to the specific risks of each jurisdiction would be more effective and efficient that a one-size-fits-all approach. The definition of the Financial War on Terrorism includes the risk-based approach which allows competent authorities to focus their CTF efforts where the threat is greatest, rather than applying uniform measures. The risk-based approach is crucial to the FATFs Recommendations, which encourages both public and private sectors to tailor their CTF strategies to specific vulnerabilities. The inclusion of the risk-based approach could be enhanced by referring to mutual legal assistance mechanisms that reflect how it enables countries to request and provide evidence, enforce asset freezes, and pursue prosecutions across borders, a necessity where terrorist financing spans multiple jurisdictions. Therefore, the updated definition of the Financial War on Terrorism is:

> Attacking, by criminalisation, confiscation, forfeiture, freezing, or sanctioning, the financial assets of known or suspected terrorists, guided by a risk-based approach that prioritises resources and measures according to the assessed level of terrorist financing threat. It includes the facilitation of cross-jurisdictional investigations and prosecutions through formal and informal legal assistance frameworks. Furthermore, the use of preventative methods that have previously been used for money laundering, the collection and exchange of financial intelligence related to suspicious activity, including data shared prior to the submission of a SAR (such as internal alerts, risk indicators, and typologies), and information disseminated or received after submission (such as feedback from authorities, inter-institutional collaboration, and follow-up investigations).

5 Conclusions

The Financial War on Terrorism was swift and represented the most coordinated action by the international community to address the threat of terrorist financing. Initially, the CTF mechanisms were able to limit some of the common sources of terrorism finance, and terrorist financiers were forced to adapt their funding strategies and seek new funding mechanisms. Therefore, we have witnessed the development of new terrorist financing typologies including low-cost terrorism, fraud, cryptocurrencies, natural resources, and the corporate funding model. Some parts of the Financial War on Terrorism have been extended to address these new terrorism financing typologies, such as the extension of the FATF Recommendations to cryptocurrencies. The Financial War on Terrorism has remained static, with no new CTF mechanisms to address the threat of these typologies. This chapter has identified a new terrorist financing typology, coordinated terrorist financing which is defined as "organised efforts by individuals, groups, or networks to fund terrorist activities. This involves pooling resources, collaborating across borders, and using various methods to move and conceal funds".

The objective of the Financial War on Terrorism was to increase the levels of co-operation and coordination amongst the international community to address the threat presented by terrorist financing. In doing so, it has resulted in increasing the levels of co-operation and coordination between terrorist financiers and terrorist organisations. The wealth of terrorist groups is impossible to determine, but the case studies illustrate that several of the groups are well funded. Indeed, ISIL was a well-funded terrorist group that which reminiscent of al Qaeda in its pomp, belittles their achievements and those of other terrorist groups. Assessing the wealth of publicly traded companies is extremely difficult, as evidenced in the 2007/2008 global financial crisis, and so it is no surprise that evaluating the wealth of illicit organisations relies at best on educated guesswork. Therefore, from a financial perspective, those terrorist groups that use the new typology have the financial capability to operate for many years. This financial resilience has come about because of the global financial infrastructure that now exist, on a more advanced level than we have seen before. The Financial War on Terrorism is redundant and is not fit for purpose. The definition needs to be extended to include new mechanisms to address the threat of this new typology. Not only do all financial institutions need to redouble their efforts to avoid being conduits for this new typology, the regulatory regimes that oversee them also need to be better monitored to ensure the consistency and efficiency of their CTF measures. Even with more consistent implementation of CTF measures the fact remains that this typology has proved to be extremely flexible, adaptable and it has become a benchmark for other terrorist groups to follow.

References

Acharya A (2009) Targeting terrorist financing—international cooperation and new regimes. Routledge, London

Al-Khatteeb L, Gordts E (2014) How ISIS uses oil to fund terror, 27 September. Available from How ISIS Uses Oil to Fund Terror. Accessed 13 Apr 2025

Alldridge P (2003) Money laundering law: forfeiture, confiscation, civil recovery, criminal laundering and taxation of the proceeds of crime. Bloomsbury, London

Allen W (2003) The war against terrorism financing. J Money Laundering Control 6(4):306–310

Aufhauser D (2003) Terrorist financing: foxes run to ground. J Money Laundering 6(4):310–305

Australian Department of Foreign Affairs and Trade (n.d.) Afghanistan. Available from Afghanistan, Australian Government Department of Foreign Affairs and Trade. Accessed 21 Jan 2025
Azinge-Egbri V (2021) Regulating and combating money laundering and terrorist financing: the law in emerging economies. Routledge, London
Bannon I, Collier P (2003) Natural resources and violent conflict options and actions. World Bank, Washington DC
Basra R, Neumann PR (2016) Criminal pasts, terrorist futures: European jihadists and the new crime-terror nexus. Perspect Terror 10(6):25–40
BBC News (2014) Lee Rigby murder: Adebolajo and Adebowale jailed, 26 February. Available from http://www.bbc.co.uk/news/uk-26357007. Accessed 28 July 2025
BBC News (2017) London attack: who was Khalid Masood? 26 March. Available from https://www.bbc.co.uk/news/uk-39377645. Accessed 14 Feb 2025
BBC News (2021a) Afghanistan: Taliban flag raised above border crossing with Pakistan, 14 July. Available from https://www.bbc.com/news/world-asia-57812647. Accessed 13 Apr 2025
BBC News (2021b) Hisham Chaudhary: Oadby terrorist who funded IS with Bitcoin jailed, 3 September. Available from https://www.bbc.com/news/uk-england-leicestershire-58411297. Accessed 13 Apr 2025
BBC News (2024) Cryptocurrency sent to Islamic State Group by Luton man, 20 December. Available from https://www.bbc.com/news/uk-england-beds-bucks-herts-68137751. Accessed 14 Apr 2025
Berwick A, Talley I (2023) Hamas militants behind Israel attack raised by millions in crypto, 10 October. Available from Hamas Militants Behind Israel Attack Raised Millions in Crypto – WSJ. Accessed 13 Apr 2025
Bhattacharyya S, Hodler R (2010) Natural resources, democracy and corruption. Eur Econ Rev 54(45):608–621
Blumenstein-Katz K (2018) The Washington Institute for Near East Policy 'Grading counterterrorism co-operation with GCC states' — Testimony submitted to the House Foreign Affairs Committee Subcommittee on Terrorism, Non-proliferation, and Trade Subcommittee on the Middle East and North Africa, 26 April. Available from http://www.washingtoninstitute.org/uploads/Documents/testimony/BauerTestimony20180426.pdf. Accessed 18 Mar 2024
Bourton S (2024) Tax evasion and the law: a comparative analysis of the UK and USA. Routledge
Brisard J, Martinez D (2014) Islamic state: the economy-based terrorist funding. Thomson Reuters:3
Byman D (2012) Breaking the bonds between Al-qa'ida and its affiliate organizations. The Saban Centre for Middle East Policy at Brookings 27:30–54
Carey G (2014) Financing jihad: why ISIL is a lot richer than al-Qaeda, 26 June. Available from http://www.bloomberg.com/news/2014-06-26/looted-banks-fund-iraq-fighters-eyeing-wealth-al-qaeda-never-had.html. Accessed 16 Sept 2014
Carlisle D (2017) Cryptocurrencies and terrorist financing: a risk, but hold the panic, 2 March. Available from https://www.rusi.org/explore-our-research/publications/commentary/cryptocurrencies-and-terrorist-financing-risk-hold-panic. Accessed 18 June 2025
Cassella S (2003) Reverse money laundering. J Money Laundering Control 7(1):92–94
Cengiz M, Karademir K (2020) Why salafi-jihadist terrorist organizations pledge allegiance to Al Qaeda or Isis. Int J Criminol 7:7–29
Centre for New American Security (2017) Terrorist use of virtual currencies — containing the potential threat. Centre for New American Security
Chase A (2004) Legal mechanisms of the international community and the United States concerning state sponsored terrorism. Virgina J Int Law 4:41–138
Choo K (2015) Cryptocurrency and virtual currency: corruption and money laundering/terrorism financing risks? In: Handbook of digital currency. Academic Press, pp 283–307
Clarke CP (2016) Drugs & thugs: funding terrorism through narcotics trafficking. J Strateg Secur 9(3):1–15

CNN (2015) A timeline of the Charlie Hebdo terror attack, January 10 2015. Available from http://edition.cnn.com/2015/01/08/europe/charlie-hebdo-attack-timeline/. Accessed 10 Aug 2015
Comolli V (2016) Boko haram and Islamic state. In: Staffell S, Awan A (eds) Jihadism transformed: Al-Qaeda and Islamic State's Global Battle of Ideas, Oxford
Connell S (2012) To be or not to be: is Boko Haram a foreign terrorist organisation? Global Secur Stud Summer 3(3):87–93
Coonan T, Thompson R (2005) Ancient evil, modern face: the fighting against human trafficking. Georgetown J Int Aff 6:43–52
Davis J (2021) Illicit money: financing terrorism in the twenty-first century. Lynne Rienner Publishers
de Koker L, Howell J, Morris N (2023) Economic consequences of grey listing by the financial action task force. Risks 11(5):81
Dion-Schwarz C, Manheim D, Johnston PB (2019) Terrorist use of cryptocurrencies: technical and organizational barriers and future threats. Rand Corporation
Donohue L (2008) The cost of counterterrorism – powers, politics and liberty. Cambridge University Press
Eisenhardt K (1989) Building theories from case study research. Acad Manag Rev 14:532
Elliott L (2012) Fighting transnational environmental crime. J Int Aff 66(1):87–104
Elliptic (2023) Setting the record straight on crypto crowdfunding by Hamas. October 25 2023. Available from Setting the record straight on crypto crowdfunding by Hamas. Accessed 11 Apr 2025
Federal Research Division Library of Congress (2002) A global overview of narcotics-funded terrorist and other extremist groups. Library of Congress
Financial Action Task Force (2001) FATF IX special recommendations. Financial Action Task Force, Paris
Financial Action Task Force (2004) FATF 40 recommendations. Financial Action Task Force, Paris
Financial Action Task Force (2009) Terrorist financing. Financial Action Task Force
Financial Action Task Force (2011) Organised maritime piracy and related kidnapping for ransom. Financial Action Task Force
Financial Action Task Force (2012) FATF steps up the fight against money laundering and terrorist financing, 16 February 2012. Available from http://www.fatf-gafi.org/topics/fatfrecommendations/documents/fatfstepsupthefightagainstmoneylaunderingandterroristfinancing.html. Accessed 19 Sept 2014
Financial Action Task Force (2013) The role of Hawala and other similar service providers in money laundering and terrorist financing. Financial Action Task Force
Financial Action Task Force (2015) FATF report: emerging terrorist financing risk. Paris, October 2015
Financial Action Task Force (2016) Terrorist Financing in West and Central Africa. Financial Action Task Force
Financial Action Task Force (2021) FATF Public Statement on the Financing of ISIL, Al Qaeda and Affiliates, 21 Oct 2021. Available from FATF Public Statement on the Financing of ISIL, Al Qaeda and Affiliates. Accessed 13 Apr 2025
Financial Action Task Force (2023) Crowdfunding for terrorism financing. Financial Action Task Force
Foreign, Commonwealth and Development Office (2024) UK, US and Australia sanction key figures in Hamas's financial network, 22 January 2024. Available from UK, US and Australia sanction key figures in Hamas's financial network – GOV.UK. Accessed 11 Apr 2024
Freeman M (2011) The sources of terrorist financing: theory and typology. Stud Conflict Terrorism 34(6):461–475
Gardner KL (2007) Fighting terrorism the FATF way. Glob Gov 13:325–345
Gerring J (2004) What is a case study and what is it good for? Am Polit Sci Rev 98:341, 342
Global Financial Integrity (2022) Why are natural resources at risk of illicit financial flows? https://gfintegrity.org/issue/natural-resources/. Accessed 2 Dec 2022

Global Witness (2017) Extractives, corruption, and conflict in Afghanistan: avoiding the resource curse. Global Witness, at 1

Glover S, Devine C, Puy Kamp M, Bronstein S (2023) They're opportunistic and adaptive: how Hamas is using cryptocurrency to raise funds, 12 October 2023. Available from 'They're opportunistic and adaptive': how Hamas is using cryptocurrency to raise funds | CNN. Accessed 13 Apr 2024

Gurule J (2008) Unfunding terror – the legal response to the financing of global terrorism. Edward Elgar, Cheltenham

Hardouin P (2009) Banks governance and public-private partnership in preventing and confronting organized crime, corruption and terrorism financing. J Financ Crime 16(3):199–209

Hawramy F, Mohammed S, Harding L (2014) Inside Islamic state's oil empire: how captured oilfields fuel Isis insurgency, 19 November 2014. Available from http://www.theguardian.com/world/2014/nov/19/-sp-islamic-state-oil-empire-iraq-isis. Accessed 19 Nov 2014

Hillman H (2024) Pass or play: should regulators address money laundering risks increasingly posed by cryptocurrencies themselves of await legislative reform. J Bus Law 4:301–328

HM Government (2005) House of commons report of the official account of the bombings in London on 7th July 2005. House of Commons, London

Horowitz J (2021) The Taliban are sitting on $1 trillion worth of minerals the world desperately needs, 19 August 2021. Available from The Taliban are sitting on $1 trillion worth of minerals the world desperately needs | CNN Business. Accessed 17 Jan 2025

House of Commons Foreign Affairs Committee (2016) The UK's role in the economic war against ISIL First Report of Session 2016–17. House of Commons Foreign Affairs Committee

Hussein M, Haddad M (2021) Mapping Afghanistan's untapped natural resources, September 24 2021. Available from Mapping Afghanistan's untapped natural resources | Infographic News | Al Jazeera

Hutchinson S, O'malley P (2007) A crime–terror nexus? Thinking on some of the links between terrorism and criminality. Stud Conflict Terror 30(12):1095–1107

Indonesian Financial Transaction Reports and Analysis Centre (2015) Indonesia National Risk Assessment. Indonesian Financial Transaction Reports and Analysis Centre

Institute for Economics and Peace (2014) Global Terrorism Index. Institute for Economics and Peace, New York

Inter-governmental Action Group Against Money Laundering in West Africa (2010) Threat assessment of money laundering and terrorist financing in West Africa. Inter-governmental Action Group Against Money Laundering in West Africa

Interpol (n.d.) Tracing terrorist finances n.d. Available from https://www.interpol.int/en/Crimes/Terrorism/Tracing-terrorist-finances. Accessed 20 Dec 2024

Irwin S, Kim-Kwang A, Choo R, Liu L (2012) Modelling of money laundering and terrorism financing typologies. J Money Laundering Control 15(3):316–335

Jackson Society (2018) Terror in the dark: how terrorists use encryption, the darknet and cryptocurrencies. Jackson Society

Jacobson M (2010) Terrorist financing and the internet. Stud Conflict Terrorism 33(4):353–363

Johnson R (2022) The Taliban and the modern history of Afghanistan. In: Sheehan M, Marquardt E, Collins L (eds) Routledge handbook of US counterterrorism and irregular warfare operations. Routledge, pp 134–147

Jonsson M (2014) Following the money: financing the territorial expansion of Islamist insurgents in Syria. FOI Memom

Karmon E (2005) Coalitions between terrorist organizations: revolutionaries, nationalists and islamists. Brill

Kenny C, Malik N (2019) Trafficking terror and sexual violence: accountability for human trafficking and sexual and gender-based violence by terrorist groups under the Rome Statute. Vanderbilt J Trans Law 52:43

Kethineni S, Cao Y (2019) The rise in popularity of cryptocurrency and associated criminal activity. Int Crim Justice Rev 30(3):325–344

Koningsveld J (2013) Money laundering – you don't see it until you understand it: rethinking the stages of money laundering process to make enforcement more effective. In: Unger B, Linde D (eds) Research handbook on money laundering. Edward Elgar

Lander M (2014) In U.N. Speech, Obama vows to fight ISIS network of death, 24 Sept 2014. Available from http://www.nytimes.com/2014/09/25/world/middleeast/obama-syria-un-isis.html?_r=0. Accessed 19 Nov 2014

Laub Z (2014) Islamic state in Iraq and Syria, 8 Aug 2014. Available from http://www.cfr.org/iraq/islamic-state-iraq-syria/p14811. Accessed 22 Sept 2014

Lee CY (2018) Oil and terrorism. J Confl Resolut 62(5):903–928

Levi M, Reuter P (2006) Money laundering. Crime Justice 34(1):289–375

Loft P, Brooke-Holland L (2025) Countering Islamic State/Daesh in Africa, Syria and Iraq 2025. House of Commons Library

Manhattan District Attorney's Office (2024) Victoria Jacobs sentenced to 18 years in prison for using cryptocurrency to fund Syrian-based terrorist groups, April 30 2024. Available from D.A. Bragg: Victoria Jacobs sentenced to 18 years in prison for using cryptocurrency to fund Syrian-Based Terrorist Groups; Launder Supporters' Contributions—Manhattan District Attorney's Office. Accessed 13 Apr 13 2025

Misra A (2002) The Taliban, Radical Islam and Afghanistan. Third World Q 23(3):577–589

Moghadam A (2017) Nexus of global jihad: understanding cooperation among terrorist actors. Columbia University Press, New York

Nasab AM, Shafiee N, Shafiee H, Babri Qonbad S (2020) The role of the Taliban in drug production and trafficking in Afghanistan. J Polit Strategy 4(14):57–75

National Audit Office (2007) The asset recovery agency. National Audit Office

National Commission on Terrorist Attacks Upon the United States (2004a) The 9/11 commission report: final report of the national commission on terrorist attacks upon the United States. National Commission on Terrorist Attacks Upon, Washington DC

National Commission on Terrorist Attacks Upon the United States (2004b) Monograph on terrorist financing. National Commission on Terrorist Attacks Upon, Washington DC

NBC News (2014) ISIS Terror, n.d. Available from http://www.nbcnews.com/storyline/isis-terror/deep-pockets-dark-goals-how-will-isis-keep-funding-terror-n187296. Accessed 22 Sept 2014

Nepoleoni L (2007) Terrorism financing in Europe. In: Trinkunas H, Giraldo J (eds) Terrorism financing and state responses. Stanford University Press

Omelicheva M, Markowitz L (2021) Rethinking intersections of crime and terrorism: insights from political economies of violence. Int Stud Rev 23(4):1541–1565

Onat O, Guler A, Hsu H, Reyes J (2021) A VAR analysis of the effects of Al-Shabaab's pledge to Al-Qaeda on bombings and fatalities. J Policing Intell Counter Terror 16(3):283–301

Organisation for Economic Co-operation and Development (2015) Illicit financial flows from developing countries: measuring OECD responses. Organisation for Economic Co-operation and Development

Organisation for Economic Co-operation and Development (2017) Terrorism corruption and the criminal exploitation of natural resources. Organisation for Economic Co-operation and Development

Organisation for Economic Co-operation and Development (2019) Money laundering and terrorist financing awareness handbook for tax examiners and tax auditors. Organisation for Economic Co-operation and Development

Peters G (2009) How opium profits the Taliban. United States Inst Peace 31:19–62

Petrich K (2022) Cows, charcoal and cocaine: Al Shabaab's criminal activities in the horn of Africa. Stud Conflict Terror 45:479–500

Phillips BJ (2018) Terrorist group rivalries and alliances: testing competing explanations. Stud Conflict Terror 42:1–23

Raphaeli N (2003) Financing of terrorism: sources, methods, and channels. Terror Polit Violence 15(4):59–82

Raqib M, Barreto AA (2014) The Taliban, religious revival and innovation in afghan nationalism. Nat Identities 16(1):15–30

Richard A (2005) Fighting terrorist financing: transatlantic co-operation and international institutions. Centre for Transatlantic Relations: John Hopkins University

Romaniuk P, Keatinge T (2018) Protecting charities from terrorists... and counterterrorists: FATF and the global effort to prevent terrorist financing through the non-profit sector. Crime Law Soc Change 69:265–282

Ryder N (2012) Money laundering an endless cycle? A comparative analysis of the anti-money laundering policies in the USA, UK, Australia and Canada. Routledge

Ryder N (2015) The financial war on terror: a review of counter-terrorist financing strategies since 2001. Routledge

Ryder N (2018a) Is it time to reform the counter-terrorist financing reporting obligations? A critical and comparative assessment of the counter-terrorist financing reporting obligations in the European Union and the United Kingdom. German Law Rev 19(5):1169–1190

Ryder N (2018b) Out with the old and ... in with the old? A critical review of the financial war on terrorism on the Islamic state of Iraq and Levant. Stud Confl Terror 41(2):79–95

Ryder N (2020) Cryptoassets, social media platforms and defence against terrorism financing suspicious activity reports: a step into the regulatory unknown. J Bus Law 8:668–693

Ryder N (2024) To report or not to report? An analysis of the relationship between defence against terrorism financing suspicious activity reports and fraud in the United Kingdom. In: de Koker L, Goldbarsht D (eds) Financial crime, law and governance – navigating challenges in different contexts. Springer, pp 169–202

Ryder N, Bourton S, Hall D, Hillman H (2023) Higher education institutions and the anti-money laundering and counter-terrorism financing regulations. Crim Law Rev 9:560–580

Sedgwick M (2004) Al-Qaeda and the Nature of Religious Terrorism. Terror Polit Violence 16(4):795–814

Shelley L (2020) Illicit trade and terrorism. Perspect Terror 14(4):7–20

Siddique A (2022) Cash-strapped Taliban 'Exploiting' Afghanistan's natural resources to boost revenue, July 15. Available from Cash-Strapped Taliban 'Exploiting' Afghanistan's Natural Resources To Boost Revenue. Accessed 17 Jan 2025

Sinaee V, Khatibi A (2023) Taliban political economy (2001-1996). Central Eurasia Studies 16(1):223–248

Suskind R (2006) The one percent doctrine. Simon & Schuster, New York

The Crisis Group (2024) The Islamic State in Somalia: responding to an evolving threat. Crisis Group Africa Briefing

Townsend M (2018) Terrorists 'plot in shadows of the dark net', report warns (8 April), The Guardian. https://www.theguardian.com/uk-news/2018/apr/08/terrorists-plot-shadows-dark-net-report. Accessed 18 Sept 2020

TRM (2023) In Wake of Attack on Israel, Understanding How Hamas Uses Crypto, 10 October. Available from In Wake of Attack on Israel, Understanding How Hamas Uses Crypto | TRM Blog. Accessed 11 Apr 2024

Trozze A, Kamps J, Akartuna E, Hetzel F, Kleinberg B, Davies T, Johnson S (2022) Cryptocurrencies and future financial crime. Crime Sci 11:1–35

Turner NW (2014) The financial action task force: international regulatory convergence through soft law. New York Law Sch Law Rev 59:547–560

UN Security Council Resolution 1368 (2001) Adopted by the Security Council at its 4370th meeting, on 12 September 2001

United Nations (2001) United Nations Security Council Resolution 1373, 28 Sept 2001. Available from http://www.un.org/en/sc/ctc/specialmeetings/2012/docs/United%20Nations%20Security%20Council%20Resolution%201373%20(2001).pdf. Accessed 23 Nov 2014

United Nations (2012) First report of the analytical Support and Sanctions Implementation Monitoring Team submitted pursuant to resolution 1988 (2011) concerning the Taliban and

associated individuals and entities, S/2012/683, 5 September 2012, United Nations Security Council, New York, United States. www.un.org/Docs/journal/asp/ws.asp?m=S/2012/683
United Nations (2022) Thirteenth report of the Analytical Support and Sanctions Monitoring Team submitted pursuant to resolution 2611 (2021) concerning the Taliban and other associated individuals and entities constituting a threat to the peace stability and security of Afghanistan. Available from Document Viewer. Accessed 13 Apr 2024
United Nations (n.d.) Chapter VII: Action with respect to threats to the peace, breaches of the peace, and acts of aggression, n.d. Available from http://www.un.org/en/documents/charter/chapter7.shtml. Accessed 21 Oct 2014
United Nations High Commissioners for Refugees (2024) Global trends force displacement in 2023. United National High Commissioner for Refugees
United States Department of Justice (2015) Virgina man sentenced to more than 11 years for providing material support to ISIL. 28 August 2015. https://www.justice.gov/opa/pr/virginia-man-sentenced-more-11-years-providing-material-support-isil. Accessed 18 Sept 2020
United States Department of Justice (2018) Maryland man sentenced to 20 years in prison for providing material support to ISIS and terrorism financing. 30 March 2018. https://www.justice.gov/opa/pr/maryland-man-sentenced-20-years-prison-providing-material-support-isis-and-terrorism. Accessed 18 Sept 2020
United States Department of Justice (2019) New Jersey man sentenced to 16 years in prison for attempting to provide material support to ISIS. 1 March 2019. https://www.justice.gov/opa/pr/new-jersey-man-sentenced-16-years-prison-attempting-provide-material-support-isis. Accessed 18 Sept 2020
United States Department of Justice (2020) Long Island Woman Sentenced to 13 Years' Imprisonment for Providing Material Support to ISIS, 13 March 2020. Available from Office of Public Affairs | Long Island Woman Sentenced to 13 Years' Imprisonment for Providing Material Support to ISIS | United States Department of Justice. Accessed 8 Apr 2025
United States Department of Justice (2024) Virginia man convicted for crypto financing scheme to ISIS, 16 December 2024. Available from Office of Public Affairs | Virginia Man Convicted for Crypto Financing Scheme to ISIS | United States Department of Justice., Aaccessed 13 April 13 2025
United States Department of Justice (2025) Justice Department Disrupts Hamas Terrorist Financing Scheme Through Seizure of Cryptocurrency, 27 Mar 2025. Available from Office of Public Affairs | Justice Department Disrupts Hamas Terrorist Financing Scheme Through Seizure of Cryptocurrency | United States Department of Justice. Accessed 14 Apr 2025
United States Department of State (2001) Executive Order 13,224, 23 September 2001. Available from Executive Order 13224 – United States Department of State. Accessed 9 Jan 2025
United States Department of State (2014) Country Reports on terrorism 2013. Department of State, Washington DC
United States Department of State (n.d.) State sponsors of terrorism, n.d., available from State Sponsors of Terrorism – United States Department of State. Accessed 20 Apr 2025
United States Department of the Treasury (2014) Treasury designates three key supporters of terrorists in Syria and Iraq. 6 August 2014. https://www.treasury.gov/press-center/press-releases/Pages/jl2605.aspx. Accessed 18 Sept 2020
United States Department of Treasury (2015) National Terrorist Financing Risk Assessment 2015. United States Department of Treasury
United States Department of Treasury (2019) Under Secretary Mandelker remarks at the 19th Annual International Conference on Counterterrorism. 11 September 2019. https://home.treasury.gov/news/press-releases/sm773. Accessed 18 Sept 2020
United States Department of Treasury (2024) 2024 National Terrorist Financing Risk Assessment. United States Department of Treasury
United States House of Representatives Committee on Homeland Security Subcommittee on Counterterrorism and Intelligence Boko Haram Emerging Threat to the U.S. (2011)

Homeland U.S. House of Representatives Committee on Homeland Security Subcommittee on Counterterrorism and Intelligence
Vidino L, Altuna S (2023) Tackling Hamas funding in the west. The George Washington Univeristy
Vittori J (2011) Terrorist financing and resourcing. Palgrave Macmillan, London
Wagman S (2022) Cryptocurrencies and national security: the case of money laundering and terrorism financing. Harvard Nat Secur J 14:87–101
Walker C (2014) Terrorism financing and the policing of charities: who pays the price? In: King C, Walker C (eds) Dirty assets – emerging issues in the regulation of criminal and terrorist assets. Ashgate
Wang S, Tian Z (2024) New challenges in financial supervision: environmental crime terrorism financing. Trends Organized Crime 27(2):212–228
Wang S, Zhu X (2021) Evaluation of potential cryptocurrency development ability in terrorist financing. Policing: J Policy Pract 15(4):2329–2340
Warren E (2023) Letter to United States Treasury Department and White House, 17 October. Available from 2023.10.17 Letter to Treasury and White House re Hamas crypto security.pdf. Accessed April 14 2025
White House (2001) Fact sheet on terrorist financing executive order, 24 September. Available from Fact Sheet on Terrorist Financing Executive Order. Accessed 9 Jan 2025
Williams P (2007) Terrorist financing and organized crime: nexus, appropriation, or transformation? In: Bierskeker T, Eckert S (eds) Countering the financing of terrorism. Routledge, pp 142–165
Wilson Centre (2021) US Report: ISIS and Al Qaeda Threats, December 16 2021. Available from US Report: ISIS and Al Qaeda Threats | Wilson Center. Accessed 11 Apr 2024
World Bank (2006) Reference guide to anti-money laundering and combating the financing of terrorism. World Bank, Washington DC
Zenn J (2017) Demystifying al-Qaida in Nigeria: cases from Boko Haram's Founding, Launch of Jihad and Suicide Bombings. Perspect Terror 11(6):173–189

Nic Ryder has played advisory roles both nationally (Home Affairs Select Committee, Home Office, National Crime Agency, Law Commission, the Nationwide, Transparency International, Synalogik and the Foreign and Commonwealth Office) and internationally (NATO, United Nations, Cepol, Europol, EUROMED Police, the Dutch Police, the France Telecom Group, the Law Reform Commission of Ireland). Between 2023 and 2024 Nic acted as a 'Special Advisor' for the Home Affairs Select Committee for the duration of its investigation into fraud. His research has attracted funding (£2.1 m) from the Joffe Trust, StopScams, Economic and Social Research Council (ESRC), LexisNexis Risk Solutions, the City of London Police Force, the Royal United Services Limited, The Alan Turing Institute, ICT Wilmington Risk & Compliance, the France Telecom Group and the European Social Fund. Professor Ryder created, and edits Routledge's Law of Financial Crime Series and he is the co-editor in chief of the Journal of Economic Criminology. Collectively, he has published 5 monographs, edited books and over 50 articles in internationally recognised journals including the Criminal Law Review, Legal Studies, the Cambridge Law Journal, the Journal of Business Law, Studies in Conflict and Terrorism and Contemporary Issues in Law. Beyond academia, he has delivered numerous counter-terrorism financing training seminars for multiple financial crime stakeholders including Cepol, Europol, EUROMED Police, NATO and several multinational telecommunication and financial services companies.

Re-evaluating Human Rights in Global Counter-Terrorism Financing: A Case for Preliminary Judicial Moderation

Yusuf Sulayman

Abstract This chapter discusses the balance between enforcing Counter-Terrorism Financing (CTF) programs and protecting civil liberties and human rights. In light of escalating threats to world peace, countering and suppressing the financing of terrorism is a desideratum to delegitimising terrorism and protecting citizens and the financial system. At the heart of this are measures such as terrorist finance tracking program, data mining, immediate seizure of assets, and economic sanctions based on suspicion of terrorism that raise the question of priority between national security and human rights. The chapter critically examines the fundamental rights and freedoms implications of the current CTF measures against the three-pronged test of credible evidence, effectiveness, and proportionality. The findings suggest many CTF measures can defeat decades of human rights gains if not properly contextualised. The study concludes that CTF measures must be coordinated within a judicially-moderated framework to balance enforcing security and safeguarding fundamental rights and freedoms effectively.

1 Introduction

Even in the face of the threat of international terrorism, the safety of the people is not the supreme law. We must be just as careful to guard against unrestrained encroachments on personal liberty.[1]

International law considers the security of people's lives and property an important objective. One of the United Nations' (UN) cardinal objectives is to take

[1] Lord Hope in *HM Treasury v Ahmed* [2010] UKSC 2 para 6.

Y. Sulayman (✉)
School of Law, University of Portsmouth, Portsmouth, UK
e-mail: yusuf.sulayman@port.ac.uk

D. Goldbarsht et al. (eds.), *Combating Financial Crime*, Ius Gentium: Comparative Perspectives on Law and Justice 131,
https://doi.org/10.1007/978-3-032-06858-3_5

effective steps to prevent and reduce threats to peace and other acts of aggression.[2] Since the 9/11 attacks on the United States (US), however, the threat to both international and national security has been on the increase. This event, and other 'trigger' attacks such as the 7/7 attacks on the United Kingdom (UK) and the Independence Day bombing in Nigeria, marked "a giant escalation of an evolving threat", and provided the context for the current global counter–terrorism (CT) regime.[3] These events have been tagged as terrorist acts or terrorism because they entail the use of violence against noncombatants for political ends, or to put the public in fear,[4] thus posing a serious challenge for modern democracies worldwide. Terrorism, it must be said, is an age-long problem, but new scales of violence that threaten not just individual nations but the stability of the entire international state system reinforce the need for a more coordinated response.[5] It takes different dimensions, including domestic and international, state and nonstate, and spreads across almost all sectors of life in the form of both physical terrorism and cyberterrorism.[6]

There have, therefore, been growing national and international efforts to counter state and nonstate terrorism and other uses of violence to reassure citizens of the government's commitment to their security against threats posed by enemies. These involve organisational and programmatic responses in the form of targeted laws, diplomacy, and physical countermeasures aimed at aggressively countering the indiscriminate use of violence by organisations, political parties, nationalist groups, religious groups, revolutionaries, and governments in pursuit (or in support) of their agendas.[7] Prior to the 9/11 attacks, efforts to combat financial crime in the US were primarily anchored in anti-money laundering (AML) frameworks, such as the *Bank Secrecy Act of 1970* and the *Money Laundering Control Act of 1986*, which criminalised the act of knowingly engaging in financial transactions involving proceeds of unlawful activity. These laws were largely geared toward tackling organised crime, drug trafficking, and financial fraud, with terrorism financing receiving comparatively limited attention. However, after the 9/11, the US enacted the *Uniting and Strengthening America by Providing Appropriate Tools Required to Intercept and Obstruct Terrorism (USA PATRIOT) Act of 2001* (*Patriot Act*), being the first major legislative response among several other measures activated by the US to establish bureaucratic procedures that enhanced intelligence gathering, inter-agency coordination, and financial surveillance.[8] It significantly expanded the scope of pre-existing AML measures by embedding counter-terrorism financing (CTF) as a

---

[2] Charter of the United Nations (UN Charter) 1945, art 1. See also Constitution of the Federal Republic of Nigeria (CFRN) 1999 (as amended), s 14 (2)(b).

[3] Howard and Sawyer (2002) cited in Kraft and Marks, (2011), p. 15.

[4] Stone (2008), p. 227.

[5] Kraft and Marks (2011), p. 3.

[6] Nathalie Rébé, Counter-Terrorism Financing: International Best Practices and the Law (BRILL 2019) 8.

[7] Kraft and Marks (2011) 4–6.

[8] Kraft and Marks (2011) 15.

national security imperative. This singular measure triggered a cascading effect, paving the way for the adoption of similar measures both within the US and on a global scale. CT and national security issues have become a 'whole of government' affair requiring an integrated government agency enlisting and cooperation between global states.[9] Issues of defence, diplomacy, and development were now to be considered as interconnected objectives of every government and its units.[10] The UK's response was the enactment of the *Anti-Terrorism, Crime and Security Act (ATCSA) 2001*, which effectively redirected the country's preference from one reliant on prosecution to one that now validates indefinite detentions without charge or trial.[11] These merely represent a global general pattern that was ushered in by the events of 9/11.

While CT measures and strategies had been managed globally before these trigger events, they started attracting governments' priority attention and a greater scale of funding afterward. The emerging dimensions of state and nonstate terrorism have seemingly provided justification for governments to legitimise previously controversial and highly contentious ambitions of states.[12] CTF measures have progressively normalised governmental powers and activities that were once regarded as extraordinary and draconian, integrating them into standard legal and policy frameworks without significant objections.[13]

At the core of this CT campaign are CTF programs designed to disrupt the misuse of financial systems for advancing terrorist objectives. While these programs primarily target terrorism, they also encompass broader efforts to address organised crime and grand corruption, all of which depend on financial resources. Consequently, AML policies are closely integrated with CTF initiatives. For this chapter, therefore, while the primary focus remains on TF and CTF, the programs will be considered together as illicit financing. The integrity and stability of international financial systems and national economies rely on the effective implementation of AML and CTF measures. However, these national and international measures often pose significant challenges to the fundamental rights and freedoms (FRF) of the very populations they aim to protect. A critical issue, therefore, is the development of solutions that are not only sufficient but also holistically suitable and effective for combating illicit financing.[14]

This chapter discusses the tensions arising from the intersection of FRF and national security initiatives, particularly in the context of CTF efforts by governments worldwide. The integration of illicit financing into ostensibly legitimate industries, such as crowdfunding, arms trade, cryptocurrency, art and antique

[9] The term 'whole-of-government' within national security framework was first adopted in the US National Security Strategy 2010. The original known use of the idea was credited to the UK Treasury Department in 1998. See Kraft and Marks (2011), p. 17.

[10] Kraft and Marks (2011) 17.

[11] See pt 4 cl 21-32 of the Act.

[12] Hamilton (2019), p. 5.

[13] Hamilton (2019), pp. 6–7.

[14] Rébé (2019), p. 1.

markets, international politics, religion, and global trade, exposes lawful activities to significant risks of abuse. Furthermore, when 'hasty' actions are taken against suspected individuals or entities without sufficient evidence or due process, the ripple effects on their dependents, including families, business partners, and employees can be devastating. While countering illicit financing through AML and CTF initiatives is germane, existing frameworks remain ambitious but inconsistently aligned with FRF principles. Despite the nominal recognition of FRF concerns, there is a pressing need to strengthen the alignment between security measures and FRF protections to ensure their practical and holistic realisation. Misuse of AML/CTF measures frequently impact non-terrorists and human rights defenders, raising critical concerns about the "holistic suitability and effectiveness" of such efforts within global CT frameworks.[15]

To address these challenges, the chapter emphasises the importance of a measured and proactive approach to countering illicit financing, including the introduction of a 'cooling-off' period to ensure that actions meet established standards of evidence, effectiveness, and proportionality. The chapter evaluates the global AML/CTF strategies, critically assessing their suitability and effectiveness. It proposes a three-pronged test to be incorporated into international frameworks as a prerequisite for adopting national or global AML/CTF measures, ensuring that such initiatives balance security concerns with the protection of FRF and legitimate interests.

2 Combating the Financing of Terrorism: An Overview of Global Strategies

The protection of lives, properties, and the rights and freedoms of citizens is undoubtedly a fundamental obligation of government.[16] States are required to take positive measures to safeguard FRF against all threats and to bring perpetrators to justice under the rule of law. One of the primary challenges facing modern democracies, however, is the persistent threat of terrorism. Governments have, therefore, adopted significant countermeasures to mitigate this threat, particularly focusing on disrupting the financial networks that sustain terrorist operations. CTF has emerged as a critical component of these efforts, with international legal instruments playing a central role in fostering global cooperation. Following the statement by President Bush that every nation must choose between aligning with the US or with terrorists, the global CT agenda was firmly set in motion, including initiatives targeting illicit financing.[17] Key conventions such as the *International Convention for the*

[15] UN General Assembly Seventy-Seventh Session, 'Activities of the UN System in Implementing the UN Global Counter-Terrorism Strategy' Report of the Secretary General, para 61.

[16] Office of the United Nations High Commissioner for Human Rights, Palais des Nations, Geneva (n.d.), p.1.

[17] Address to a Joint Session of Congress and the American People (2001). See also: Boyle (2008), pp. 191, 191.

Suppression of the Financing of Terrorism (1999), the *International Convention for the Suppression of Terrorist Bombings* (1997), and the *Convention for the Suppression of Unlawful Seizure of Aircraft* (1970) highlight the importance of international commitments to combating illicit financing.

In the aftermath of the 9/11 attacks, the international community witnessed a significant progressive shift in the willingness of states to ratify and implement CT treaties, particularly those addressing financial networks used by terrorist organisations. These treaties have served as the basis for national legislation aimed at identifying, disrupting, and prosecuting terrorist financing activities[18].

2.1 *The Global Strategy*

International terrorism requires structure alongside funding to perpetuate. The strategy of 'choking off' terrorist financing and 'following the money trail' is often regarded as one of the most effective methods for curbing their capacity to orchestrate and execute aggressive attacks.[19] Disrupting terrorists' financial channels is pivotal not only for undermining their operational capabilities but also for impeding their ability to organise, recruit, and disseminate their ideologies.[20] Consequently, AML/CTF efforts focus on dismantling these financial networks as an integral component of the broader strategy to combat terrorism.

The UN plays a leading role in maintaining international peace and security. According to its mandate under the Charter of the United Nations (UN Charter), it seeks to address conditions conducive to the spread of terrorism, including the financing of such activities through its international conventions and resolutions. A significant aspect of the UN's role in AML/CTF lies in its collaborative efforts with specialised agencies. The United Nations Office on Drugs and Crime (UNODC) addresses, among other concerns, terrorism and its financing.[21] The International Monetary Fund (IMF) helps to ensure financial integrity, shape global AML/CTF policies and provide states with technical assistance,[22] while the World Bank supports states' capacity to detect and trace illicit financing happening within the global financial system.[23] Additionally, the International Criminal Police Organization (INTERPOL) strategically cooperates with relevant bodies, such as the Financial

---

[18] For more on the post-9/11 Financial War on Terrorism, see Ryder (2025) in this book.

[19] Realuyo (2011), p. 109. See also Roth et al. (2004), p. 1 cited in Kraft and Marks (2011), p. 91.

[20] Kraft and Marks (2011), p. 89.

[21] United Nations Office on Drug and Crimes (UNODC), 'About Us' https://www.unodc.org/unodc/en/about-unodc/index.html accessed 28 June 2025.

[22] International Monetary Fund (IMF), 'Anti-Money Laundering and Combating the Financing of Terrorism (AML/CFT)' https://www.imf.org/en/Topics/Financial-Integrity/amlcft assessed 26 December 2024.

[23] World Bank Group, 'Financial Integrity' https://www.worldbank.org/en/topic/financialmarketintegrity accessed 28 June 2025.

Action Task Force (FATF), to provide and act on critical intelligence to combat terrorism financing,[24] cooperate with states, and ensure that its capabilities are available whenever needed.[25] It also shares intelligence on transnational terrorist networks to understand their methods, motives and financing, and to ultimately identify and arrest suspects.[26] Although efforts to achieve consensus on the *Comprehensive Convention on International Terrorism* (CCIT), which aims, among other objectives, to deny terrorists access to financial resources,[27] are ongoing, the UN's CTF framework primarily operates under the *International Convention for the Suppression of the Financing of Terrorism* (ICFST) (1999). This convention explicitly defines and criminalises the financing of terrorism by any means and urges states to enact measures establishing jurisdiction over such offences.[28]

In 2017, the UN further reinforced its counter–terrorism efforts by establishing the Office of Counter–Terrorism. This office incorporates the Counter-Terrorism Implementation Task Force Office and the United Nations Counter-Terrorism Centre, providing a unified mechanism to support member states in implementing the Global Counter-Terrorism Strategy and enhancing the effectiveness of CTF measures.[29] By adopting the Global Counter-Terrorism Strategy (UN Strategy) in 2006, the UN established a consensus among member states on a unified strategic and operational framework for combating terrorism.[30] This strategy is implemented through the cooperation of member states to ensure that member states retain the primary responsibility of implementing the UN Strategy in preventing and countering terrorism and its funding.[31]

The UN Strategy is structured around four key pillars: (i) addressing conditions conducive to the spread of terrorism, (ii) preventing and combating terrorism, (iii) building state capacity and strengthening the UN's role, and (iv) ensuring the respect for human rights and the rule of law as integral components of CT efforts. The UN Strategy, therefore, operates to harmonise global CT measures by fostering

---

[24] The United Nations Global Counter-Terrorism Strategy: Eight Review, A/RES/77/298, para 30.

[25] INTERPOL, 'Tracing Terrorist Finances' https://www.interpol.int/Crimes/Terrorism/Tracing-terrorist-finances#:~:text=We%20maintain%20relationships%20with%20a%20number%20of,money%20laundering%20and%20the%20financing%20of%20terrorism;&text=We%20also%20advise%20our%20member%20countries%20on,all%20INTERPOL's%20capabilities%20are%20used%20when%20appropriate. accessed 28 June 2025.

[26] INTERPOL, 'Terrorism' https://www.interpol.int/Crimes/Terrorism accessed 28 June 2025.

[27] Draft Comprehensive Convention on International Terrorism, A/C.6/55/1 (United Nations Digital Library, 28 August 2000). See also: The United Nations Global Counter-Terrorism Strategy: Eight Review (A/RES/77/298), para 5.

[28] Arts 1, 2 & 7 Convention for the Suppression of the Financing of Terrorism (ICFST) 1999.

[29] The UN General Assembly Resolution (A/RES/71/291), paras 1 & 2.

[30] United Nations Office of Counter-Terrorism, 'United Nations Global Counter-Terrorism Strategy' https://www.un.org/counterterrorism/un-global-counter-terrorism-strategy accessed 28 June 2025.

[31] United Nations Office of Counter-Terrorism, 'United Nations Global Counter-Terrorism Strategy' https://www.un.org/counterterrorism/un-global-counter-terrorism-strategy accessed 28 June 2025.

cooperation among member states while promoting adherence to international legal standards. Last reviewed in 2023, the UN Strategy emphasises the critical need for states to implement robust measures to prevent and suppress the financing of terrorism.[32] It advocates for actions such as the rapid freezing of assets and the imposition of arms trade embargoes on individuals or entities suspected of links to terrorist organisations.[33]

The coordination of AML/CTF strategies has been the primary function of the FATF since its establishment in 1989 under a time-bound mandate.[34] Initially focused on combating money laundering (ML), the FATF's mandate was expanded in 2001 to include terrorist financing (TF).[35] Following three decades of operation, the FATF was granted an 'open-ended mandate' in 2019, reinforcing its role in coordinating global CTF efforts and enhancing the integrity of the international financial system.[36] In addition to its coordination role, the FATF conducts research into emerging trends and methods of terrorism financing, equipping countries to better identify and mitigate money laundering and terrorist financing risks. Recent analyses by the FATF have highlighted how terrorists exploit contemporary mechanisms such as crowdfunding on social media platforms, ransomware attacks, and the art and antiquities market to secure funding for their operations.[37] This ongoing research ensures that AML/CTF strategies remain adaptive and responsive to evolving financial threats. The US, as the world's largest economy, and the UK, as the leading global provider of financial services, have both been active members of the FATF since 1990. While Nigeria, as a leading economy in Africa with its terrorism concerns, is not yet a direct member of the FATF, it maintains membership in the FATF-style Intergovernmental Action Group against Money Laundering in West Africa (GIABA). Nigeria adheres to FATF recommendations through this affiliation, aligning its AML/CTF frameworks with international standards.[38]

[32] The United Nations Global Counter-Terrorism Strategy: Eight Review, A/RES/77/298, paras 58–61.

[33] Security Council Resolution 2368 (S/RES/2368), para 1. See also: Art 8 Convention for the Suppression of the Financing of Terrorism (ICFST) 1999.

[34] Rébé (2019), p. 16.

[35] FATF, 'History of the FATF' https://www.fatf-gafi.org/en/the-fatf/history-of-the-fatf.html accessed 26 December 2024.

[36] FATF, 'Mandate of the Financial Action Task Force' https://www.fatf-gafi.org/en/the-fatf/mandate-of-the-fatf.html#accordion-ffd0cfcabc-item-a5fb5ae357 accessed 26 December 2024.

[37] FATF, 'Methods and Trends' https://www.fatf-gafi.org/en/topics/methods-and-trends.html accessed 26 December 2024.

[38] Para 30 (1)(b) Central Bank of Nigeria (Anti-Money Laundering, Combatting the Financing of Terrorism and Countering Proliferation Financing of Weapons of Mass Destruction in Financial Institutions) Regulations 2022.

2.2 *The United States (US)*

The US has positioned itself as the de facto leader in the global war on terror, with its enactment of significant national security legislation since 2001 catalysing similar actions by other nations. Among the most notable legislative measures with extreme FRF implications are the *Patriot Act* (2001) and the amendments to the *Foreign Intelligence Surveillance Act* (FISA) in 2008. These statutes have not only redefined the domestic CT framework within the US but have also influenced international approaches to CT, particularly in the areas of intelligence gathering and financial surveillance.

2.2.1 The Patriot Act[39]

The *Patriot Act* was enacted to deter and punish terrorist acts within the US and globally, as well as to enhance law enforcement investigative capabilities.[40] It introduced significant amendments to several existing national security laws, including the *FISA, Electronic Communications Privacy Act, Computer Fraud and Abuse Act, Right to Financial Privacy Act*, and the *Immigration and Nationality Act*, among others.

In 2011, the *PATRIOT Sunset Extension Act* extended three key provisions for an additional 4 years.[41] These provisions included: (i) roving wiretaps, which authorise the surveillance of additional suspects without requiring new orders; (ii) searches of business records, permitting access to a broad range of personal records for investigative purposes; and (iii) surveillance of lone wolves, allowing monitoring of individuals not affiliated with terrorist groups or foreign powers.[42] Additionally, the Act expanded law enforcement's ability to obtain information from communication providers. Under the voluntary disclosure provisions, providers may share customer records and communications if they reasonably believe an emergency involving imminent danger of death or serious physical injury justifies the disclosure.[43] It also broadened the scope of subpoenas issued to internet service providers, requiring them to divulge information such as service types and durations, communication device addresses, and payment details, including bank account and credit card numbers.[44] These measures collectively enhanced the investigative reach of law enforcement agencies, while raising critical discussions about privacy and civil liberties.

[39] USA PATRIOT Act is derived from the following initials: Uniting and Strengthening America by Providing Appropriate Tools Required to Intercept and Obstruct Terrorism Act of 2001.

[40] See the preamble to the Act.

[41] Mascaro (2011).

[42] See sections 206–209, USA PATRIOT Act (U.S H.R 3162, Public Law 107-56) Title II.

[43] USA PATRIOT, s 212.

[44] USA PATRIOT, s 210.

Under the enhanced surveillance provisions of the *Patriot Act*, the use of 'sneak and peek' warrants is authorised, allowing law enforcement to conduct clandestine physical entry and searches of private premises without the knowledge or consent of the owner or occupant.[45] This investigative tool is intended to facilitate evidence gathering in sensitive cases without alerting the subject of the investigation. The Act also introduced measures to enhance security in the issuance of US visas. It empowered the National Institute for Standards and Technology (NIST) to establish technology standards for conducting background checks, which have evolved to include fingerprint identification systems and detailed information searches on visa applicants.[46] The miscellaneous national security authorities provisions of the Act authorised the Federal Bureau of Investigation (FBI), alongside agencies such as the Central Intelligence Agency (CIA) and the Department of Defense (DoD), to obtain sensitive information through National Security Letters (NSLs). These demand letters enable the collection of an individual's complete web browsing history, IP addresses, correspondence records, site location data, and online purchase histories from the preceding 180 days.[47] NSLs are accompanied by gag orders, preventing the recipient from disclosing the issuance of the letter. Furthermore, under the provisions related to educational records, the Attorney General or an Assistant Attorney General can demand, obtain, and retain educational records relevant to the investigation or prosecution of federal terrorism-related crimes. Educational institutions are legally obligated to comply and are granted immunity from liability for producing such records.[48]

Several provisions of the *Patriot Act* explicitly target financial institutions to strengthen AML/CTF measures. These provisions include enhanced due diligence requirements for politically exposed persons engaged in private or correspondent banking which applies to, for instance, FATF non-cooperative countries such as Nigeria.[49] Additionally, special measures authorise the Secretary of the Treasury to access and retain records and information from financial institutions' users if "reasonable grounds" exist to justify such actions.[50]

Although several provisions of the *Patriot Act* expired in 2015, they were largely reinstated through the *USA Freedom Act of 2015*, extending their application until 2019, and later to 2023. However, some provisions have faced judicial scrutiny and have been declared unconstitutional, particularly for violating the Fourth Amendment, which prohibits unreasonable searches and seizures. These rulings underscore the ongoing tension between national security imperatives and the

45 USA PATRIOT, s 213.

46 USA PATRIOT, Title IV s 403.

47 USA PATRIOT, Title V, s 505.

48 USA PATRIOT, s 507.

49 USA PATRIOT, Title III, ss 312-319.

50 USA PATRIOT, Title III, s 311.

protection of civil liberties within the legal framework of the US.[51] The Act remained expired as from 2020.

2.2.2 The Foreign Intelligence Surveillance Act[52]

The *FISA* of 1978 is a legislative framework that authorises electronic surveillance to collect foreign intelligence information critical to national security. With the amendments introduced in 2008, the Act established a streamlined procedure for authorising specific acquisitions of foreign intelligence.[53] Under the FISA, upon a formal declaration of war, the government is empowered to conduct electronic surveillance and physical searches without obtaining a court order.[54] It also permits the use of pen registers, trap-and-trace devices, and access to certain business records for foreign intelligence investigations.[55]

A key provision of the Act allows for the targeting of non-U.S. persons reasonably believed to be located outside the US.[56] This authority has served as the legal foundation for mass surveillance programs within the US, including the monitoring of electronic communications involving foreigners abroad. Initially scheduled to expire in 2012, the provisions of FISA were extended by Congress, first to December 31, 2017, and subsequently to December 31, 2023.

2.3 *The United Kingdom (UK)*

The UK, as a leading global financial centre, manages substantial volumes of financial transactions, rendering its financial sector particularly vulnerable to the risks associated with terrorism financing.[57] While the UK had initiated CT measures prior to 9/11, primarily in response to Irish-related terrorism and political violence in its former colonies,[58] the trigger events largely influenced the adoption of more com-

---

[51] For instance, the 'sneak and peek' provision was declared inconsistent with the US Constitution by Judge Ann Aiken in 2007 after a Portland Attorney, Brandon Mayfield was wrongly jailed as a result of the searches. See also the case of *Doe v. Ashcroft,* 334 F. Supp. 2d 471 (S.D.N.Y. 2004) where the provisions of USA PATRIOT Act (U.S H.R 3162, Public Law 107-56) Title V, s 507 was declared unconstitutional.

[52] FISA 1978 Amendments Act of 2008.

[53] See Preamble to the Acts of 1978 and Amendment of 2008.

[54] See ss 1821 & 1813 of the Act.

[55] FISA, s 1844.

[56] FISA, s 702.

[57] FATF, 'The United Kingdom's Measures to Combat Money Laundering and Terrorist Financing' https://fatf-gafi.org/en/publications/Mutualevaluations/Mer-united-kingdom-2018.html accessed 26 December 2024

[58] Hamilton (2019) 16.

prehensive legislative frameworks, closely aligning with the US approach. Among the most significant legislative enactments with profound implications for FRF are the *Terrorism Act 2000*, the *Anti-Terrorism, Crime and Security Act 2001*, the *Terrorism Prevention and Investigation Measures Act 2011,* and *the Economic Crime (Transparency and Enforcement) Act 2022.*

2.3.1 The Terrorism Act[59]

The *Terrorism Act 2000* serves as a foundational legislative framework for the UK's national security approach to CT-. Subsequently modified by the *Terrorism Act 2000* (Remedial) Order 2011 (S.I. 2011/631) and further amended by the *Terrorism Act 2006*, the Act criminalises the provision or receipt of money and other assets likely to be used for terrorism-related purposes, including fundraising, financial arrangements, insurance, and money laundering.[60] It also establishes measures aimed at preserving peace and maintaining public order in the context of CT efforts.

Under the Act, the Secretary of State is empowered to maintain a list of proscribed organisations deemed to be engaged in or associated with terrorism.[61] Membership in or active support of such organisations is criminalised, extending the scope of liability to individuals who provide material or symbolic support.[62]

The Act significantly broadens police powers, allowing constables to arrest and detain individuals 'reasonably suspected' of engaging in terrorism without a warrant,[63] search premises for evidence of terrorism-related activities,[64] stop and search a person reasonably suspected to be a terrorist,[65] and seize items believed to be intended for terrorist use.[66] It also permits the detention and questioning of individuals who may not be directly involved in a terrorist act but are suspected of possessing relevant information.[67] Additionally, the Act amended the *Anti-Terrorism, Crime and Security Act 2001* to authorise applications for the detention of seized funds to be conducted *ex parte*, allowing hearings in the absence of the affected individuals or their representatives.[68]

---

[59] FISA 1978 Amendments Act of 2008.

[60] Terrorism Act 2000, pt III.

[61] Terrorism Act 2000, s 3.

[62] Stone (2008) 229.

[63] Terrorism Act 2000, s 41.

[64] Terrorism Act 2000, s 42(1).

[65] Terrorism Act 2000, s 43-44.

[66] Terrorism Act 2000, s 43E.

[67] Stone (2008) 235.

[68] Terrorism Act 2006, s 35.

2.3.2 The Anti-terrorism, Crime and Security Act[69]

The *Anti-Terrorism, Crime and Security Act 2001* grants the Treasury significant discretionary authority to issue freezing orders without judicial oversight. These orders prohibit the provision of funds to individuals or entities reasonably believed to act in ways detrimental to the UK's economy or that pose threats to lives and property.[70] The Act further authorises the seizure of funds by authorised officers upon the establishment of 'reasonable grounds' to suspect that such monies are associated with terrorist activities.[71] This framework reflects the UK's stringent approach to disrupting financial networks that support terrorism.

2.3.3 The Terrorism Prevention and Investigation Measures Act[72]

The *Terrorism Prevention and Investigation Measures Act 2011* grants the Secretary of State authority to impose a range of restrictive measures aimed at mitigating terrorism-related risks. These measures include house arrest, restrictions on travel and movement, and limitations on access to property and financial services.[73] Such financial restrictions may curtail an individual's ability to access or utilise their assets, funds, or financial services, thereby disrupting potential avenues for supporting or engaging in terrorism-related activities.

2.3.4 The Economic Crime (Transparency and Enforcement) Act 2022

The *Economic Crime (Transparency and Enforcement) Act 2022* was enacted in the wake of the 2022 invasion of Ukraine by Russia to set up a register of overseas entities, make provisions about unexplained wealth orders, and provide for sanctions in that regard.[74] It empowers the Secretary of State to impose financial penalties,[75] empowers imposition of monetary penalties for breaching financial sanctions,[76] amends the *Proceeds of Crime Act 2002* to shift the burden of proof by requiring

---

[69] The Economic Crime and Corporate Transparency Act 2023 (ECCTA) amended Schedule 1 to ATCSA 2001 to extend the existing regimes for law enforcement to seize, detain, apply to freeze, and forfeit terrorist assets to include terrorist crypto assets, following an increase in their use in both criminal and terrorism investigations.

[70] Anti-Terrorism, Crime and Security Act 2001, s 4.

[71] Anti-Terrorism, Crime and Security Act 2001, sch 1 pt 2 para 2.

[72] This Act was preserved through the enactment of the *Terrorism Prevention and Investigation Measures Act 2011 (Continuation) Order 2021*, extending its validity until December 13, 2026, to ensure its continued application in counter-terrorism efforts.

[73] Terrorism Prevention and Investigation Measures Act 2011, sch 1 pt 1.

[74] Economic Crime (Transparency and Enforcement) Act 2022, introductory text.

[75] Economic Crime (Transparency and Enforcement) Act 2022, s 39.

[76] Economic Crime (Transparency and Enforcement) Act 2022, s 54.

individuals subject to unexplained wealth orders or sanctions to prove the legitimacy of assets,[77] requires beneficial owners of UK property to disclose personal information,[78] and empowers the Secretary of State to permit the disclosure of protected information.[79]

2.4 *Nigeria*

Nigeria has experienced significant impacts from the global rise in terrorism, being home to some of the world's most violent terrorist organisations, such as Boko Haram, which maintains active collaborations with foreign groups like the Islamic State of the West African Province (ISWAP). Stemming the flow of financial resources to these entities remains a critical national security priority.

Nigeria's CT framework is centralised and primarily governed by the *Terrorism (Prevention and Prohibition) Act 2022*. This legislation provides a comprehensive framework for addressing offenses related to acts of terrorism and associated purposes. Complementing this Act, the *Central Bank of Nigeria (Anti-Money Laundering, Combatting the Financing of Terrorism, and Countering Proliferation Financing of Weapons of Mass Destruction in Financial Institutions) Regulations 2022* was issued, reinforcing efforts to disrupt the financial networks that enable terrorism and associated illicit activities.

2.4.1 The Terrorism (Prevention and Prohibition) Act 2022[80]

The *Terrorism (Prevention and Prohibition) Act 2022* establishes comprehensive provisions for detecting, preventing, and managing terrorism and its financing in Nigeria. The Act criminalises the knowing participation in, support for, and financing of terrorist activities.[81] It grants the Attorney-General the authority to apply *ex parte* to the court for the proscription of individuals, associations, or entities that promote or encourage terrorism.[82] Furthermore, the Attorney-General may also declare any person or group of persons 'suspected' to have connections with terrorism or terrorism financing as an international terrorist or international terrorist

[77] Economic Crime (Transparency and Enforcement) Act 2022, pt 2.

[78] Economic Crime (Transparency and Enforcement) Act 2022, ss 3 – 6, 12 – 15.

[79] Economic Crime (Transparency and Enforcement) Act 2022, s 23. It is imperative to note that s 26 of the Act mandates compliance with the Data Protection Act 2018.

[80] The legislation was originally introduced as the Terrorism (Prevention) Act 2011, subsequently amended in 2013, and later consolidated and expanded under the Terrorism (Prevention and Prohibition) Act 2022.

[81] Terrorism (Prevention and Prohibition) Act 2022, ss 11-23.

[82] Terrorism (Prevention and Prohibition) Act 2022, s 48.

group or terrorist financier, and where the person so declared is a Nigerian citizen other than by birth, he may be deprived of his citizenship.[83]

The Act also mandates the 'immediate' freezing of funds, assets, or other economic resources suspected to belong to designated individuals or organisations or intended for use in terrorism-related activities.[84] It empowers Nigerian law enforcement agencies to conduct searches without warrant and seizures of properties when obtaining a warrant is deemed prejudicial to the maintenance of peace and order.[85] These activities are only required to subsequently be reported to the Attorney-General, along with justifications for the urgency. Additionally, the Act permits courts, on an *ex parte* application, to authorise the interception of communications.[86] Such authorisations include the installation of interception and retention devices on premises, covert surveillance operations, and the acquisition of communications data through service providers.

Under the provisions of the *Terrorism (Prevention and Prohibition) Act 2022*, individuals arrested on reasonable suspicion of involvement in terrorism-related offenses may be subjected to administrative detention for up to 48 hours without access to any person or a legal counsel of their choice.[87] Furthermore, the Act permits the detention of such individuals for a period of up to 60 days upon an *ex parte* application to the court.[88]

3 Human Rights Implications of the AML/CTF Regime

The Russo-Ukrainian war, which began full-scale in February 2022, was met with immediate condemnation from the UN, which characterised Russia's actions as an 'invasion' of Ukraine.[89] The European Parliament, on its part, passed a resolution to label Russia a state sponsor of terrorism, and called on the European Union and its members to isolate and implement significant restrictive measures against Russia internationally.[90] While there has not been an official declaration of Russia as a state sponsor of terrorism, there have been positive steps to suggest such a status, and

[83] Terrorism (Prevention and Prohibition) Act 2022, ss 49-51.

[84] Terrorism (Prevention and Prohibition) Act 2022, s 54.

[85] Terrorism (Prevention and Prohibition) Act 2022, s 64.

[86] Terrorism (Prevention and Prohibition) Act 2022, s 68.

[87] Terrorism (Prevention and Prohibition) Act 2022, s 67.

[88] Terrorism (Prevention and Prohibition) Act 2022, s 66.

[89] United Nations, 'General Assembly Overwhelmingly Adopts Resolution Demanding Russian Federation Immediately End Illegal Use of Force in Ukraine, Withdraw All Troops' (*United Nations, 2 March 2022)* https://press.un.org/en/2022/ga12407.doc.htm accessed 31 December 2024.

[90] Press Release, 'European Parliament Declares Russia to be a State Sponsor of Terrorism' (*European Parliament,* 23 November 2022) https://www.europarl.europa.eu/news/en/press-room/20221118IPR55707/european-parliament-declares-russia-to-be-a-state-sponsor-of-terrorism accessed 29 June 2025.

clear efforts have been made to choke off its funding sources. Echoing the European Parliament's sentiments, the North Atlantic Treaty Organization (NATO) described Russia's role as the 'gravest threat to Euro-Atlantic security in decades', asserting that the conflict shattered peace and posed significant challenges to global security.[91] NATO further urged its members and allies to support Ukraine's resistance against Russia's 'aggression' through the imposition of extensive sanctions and diplomatic measures aimed at isolating the Kremlin.

As a founding NATO member, the UK played a prominent role in these efforts. On March 10, 2022, it announced sanctions against seven Russian oligarchs allegedly linked to the Kremlin and implicated in supporting Russia's aggression against Ukraine.[92] The sanctions were designed to ensure Putin's 'invasion' of Ukraine fails by 'crippling Russia's economy supporting his war machine'.[93] Among those sanctioned was Roman Abramovich, the then-owner of Chelsea Football Club, whose steel company was suspected to have been a Russian military supplier.[94] As part of the sanctions, Abramovich's assets, including Chelsea FC, were frozen, effectively blocking the club's funding sources. Abramovich was compelled to relinquish ownership of the club, which marked a significant intervention by the UK government. However, this decision lacked substantiated evidence of Abramovich's direct financial involvement in supporting Russia's war efforts in Ukraine and the effectiveness of the effort in crippling Russia's effort was never established. More importantly, the move was not sanctioned by any judicial or quasi-judicial authority. While Abramovich may not necessarily be widely impacted by these measures and Russia remains relentless, Chelsea FC reported a financial loss of approximately £121 million, which it attributed to the government-imposed sanctions.[95]

This raises critical questions about the proportionality and fairness of AML/CTF measures, particularly when their FRF implications are overlooked. For instance, if investigations ultimately conclude that Abramovich's finances were unrelated to Russia's military activities, it remains unclear how he could be recompensed for the significant financial and reputational damage caused by years of sanctions. While delisting procedures allow designated persons or entities to have their names removed and assets unfrozen under the legal regime set out by the sanctioning

---

[91] NATO, 'Statement by NATO Heads of State and Government' (*NATO*, 24 March 2022) https://nato.int/cps/ge/natohq/official_texts_193719.htm accessed 31 December 2024.

[92] Press Release, 'Abramovich and Deripaska among 7 Oligarchs Targeted in Estimated £15 Billion Sanction Hit' (*GOV.UK*, 10 March 2022), https://www.gov.uk/government/news/abramovich-and-deripaska-among-seven-oligarchs-targeted-in-estimated-15bn-sanction-hit > accessed 31 December 2024.

[93] Press Release, 'Abramovich and Deripaska among 7 Oligarchs Targeted in Estimated £15 Billion Sanction Hit' (*GOV.UK*, 10 March 2022), https://www.gov.uk/government/news/abramovich-and-deripaska-among-seven-oligarchs-targeted-in-estimated-15bn-sanction-hit > accessed 31 December 2024.

[94] Allegretti and Jolly, (2022).

[95] PA Media 'Chelsea Claim Roman Abramovich Sanctions a Factor in £121 m Losses' (*The Guardian,* 27 March 2023), https://www.theguardian.com/football/2023/mar/27/chelsea-claim-abramovich-sanctions-a-factor-in-121m-losses-for-last-season accessed 31 December 2024.

country,[96] it is arguable whether such remedies exist to return them to *status quo,* especially in reputation terms. Furthermore, the sanctions inadvertently penalised individuals and entities with no connection to Russia's actions, including Chelsea FC's fans, staff, and other beneficiaries, who were impacted by the financial and operational disruptions. This case, like many others, opens up the profound and far-reaching consequences of AML/CTF measures when FRF concerns are not incorporated as a fundamental component of its delivery.

The threats and effects of terrorist acts are real and extremely difficult to address, the temptation to seriously confront and address them usually leads to measures that significantly restrict FRF.[97] Terrorism, as we know, and to a large extent, attracts desperate responses by governments which in itself pose more threat than what they seek to address. It has direct and indirect consequences on the enjoyment of FRF; particularly the rights to privacy, liberty, and the dignity of the human person.[98] It is a basic challenge that national security responses by states equally erode the fundamental rights which they seek to protect.[99]

The existential concern on human rights in AML/CTF is twofold: (i) ML/TF is integrated into legitimate business and (ii) states pursue AML/CTF in a self-defeating approach by playing into the terrorist's grand plan.

3.1 The Integration Strategy

The nature of the terrorist threat, including its financing mechanisms, has undergone a marked evolution, shifting from traditionally hierarchical structures to more diffuse, decentralised, and networked formations that are strategically designed to circumvent and adapt to CTF measures.[100] Terrorist financing involves soliciting, collecting, or providing funds to support terrorist acts, but in most cases, they are not all the time tied to huge amounts or illicit businesses.[101] For example, while the 9/11 attacks were estimated to have cost between $400,000 and $500,000, the 7/7 London bombings was estimated to have cost less than £8000, with overseas trips, bomb making equipment, rent, car hire, and UK travel constituting the main cost elements.[102] A significant emerging trend for raising and transferring funds for ter-

[96] FATF, (Recommendation 6) (2013), p. 12.

[97] Stone (2008), p. 225.

[98] Stone (2008), p. 225.

[99] Stone (2008), p. 225.

[100] Department of Treasury, '2024 National Terrorist Financing Risk Assessment' p. 27 https://home.treasury.gov/system/files/136/2024-National-Terrorist-Financing-Risk-Assessment.pdf. accessed 30 June 2025.

[101] Rébé (2019), p. 13; For a counterargument, see Goldbarsht (2020).

[102] Report of the Official Account of the Bombings in London on 7th July 2005, para 63 https://assets.publishing.service.gov.uk/media/5a7c7bc840f0b626628ac62e/1087.pdf accessed 30 June 2025.

rorism lies in the effective organisation and concealment of activities, often through legitimate businesses that mask their illicit purposes.[103]

These businesses may include cryptocurrency trading, social media platforms, crowdfunding initiatives, citizenship and residency-by-investment programs, electronic commerce, arts and antiquities, mineral and natural resource trading, and even the exploitation of ethnicity and religion.[104] While there are ongoing efforts to safeguard legitimate interests from unintended consequences and the risk of overregulation,[105] distinguishing between preventing the exploitation of these ventures for terrorist ends and disrupting legitimate businesses remains a considerable challenge. A pertinent example is the directive issued by the Central Bank of Nigeria (CBN) in February 2021, requiring financial institutions to close all accounts associated with virtual currencies and to identify users of such accounts.[106] This measure was motivated by ML/TF risks linked to cryptocurrency transactions. However, the blanket ban disrupted legitimate users until its lifting in December 2023, resulting in significant economic repercussions without a justifiable public account of the effectiveness of the initial measure.

The strategy of integration employed by terrorists poses significant challenges to AML/CTF measures, as they risk inadvertently causing substantial harm to the broader population. While AML/CTF initiatives are often ambitious in their scope and intent, their potential overreaching effects, however, necessitate refinement to strike a balance between achieving security objectives and minimising collateral societal and economic impacts.

3.2 *Playing into the Terrorists' Game*

Terrorist activities usually impact the norms and ideals of human rights, democracy, and the rule of law, it attacks the values established and enshrined under the UN Charter and other international and domestic instruments on the respect of FRF of all persons across the globe.[107] AML/CTF has indisputably become a central component of the global security strategy, aimed at disrupting the financial lifelines that sustain terrorist operations. While essential, they have often been implemented in ways that undermine FRF. In the wake of the 9/11 attacks, the US spearheaded the global campaign against terrorism, with a strong emphasis on countering terrorism financing. However, this campaign has often prioritised aggressive national security

[103] National Crime Agency (n d)

[104] FATF, 'Methods and Trends' https://www.fatf-gafi.org/en/topics/methods-and-trends.html accessed 30 June 2025.

[105] FATF, 'Mitigating Unintended Consequences' https://www.fatf-gafi.org/en/publications/Financialinclusionandnpoissues/Unintended-consequences-project.html accessed 29 June 2025.

[106] Bakare (2021), p. 2.

[107] Office of the United Nations' High Commissioner for Human Rights, Palais des Nations, Geneva, 'Human Rights, Terrorism and Counter-terrorism, Fact Sheet No. 32', p. 7.

measures at the expense of FRF. For instance, over 40 US charity groups with religious ties have, since 2001, had their assets frozen for providing material support to terrorism, without any evidence or even prosecution, while the UK and Canada have equally launched aggressive campaigns that unduly targets charity organisation for fear that charity funds might end up in support of terrorism.[108] The introduction of stringent CTF frameworks has, at times, as recalled by the Office of UN High Commissioner for Human Rights recalled, disregarded the rights of those affected, including non-terrorist individuals and organisations inadvertently caught in the expansive scope of financial monitoring and sanctions.[109] The internet, for instance, now 'listens' in a way that compromises users' data privacy. A vast amount of data on people's profiles that goes beyond what they choose to share, to those tracked from their engagement with the digital world, is reported to be collected, aggregated, and sold in ways that compromise details about their lives and behaviour.[110] This is evident from the targeted online advertisements that commonly appear to internet users following private discussions they have had or their previous search history. These actions have raised significant concerns regarding their proportionality and compliance with international legal obligations.

Despite the consensus that terrorist financing is a menace that must be contained and the ambitious nature of AML/CTF frameworks across jurisdictions, certain patterns are disturbingly recurring. Central issues of FRF across the frameworks include: (i) following the money trail and (ii) *ex parte* hearings.

3.2.1 Following the Money Trail

Following the 9/11 attacks, the US Department of the Treasury launched the Terrorist Finance Tracking Program (TFTP) as a strategic initiative to 'identify, track, and pursue terrorists and their networks,' with a particular focus on monitoring financial flows.[111] The program enables US authorities to access cross-border financial transaction data through the database of the Society for Worldwide Interbank Financial Telecommunication (SWIFT). In August 2010, the US formalised a cooperative framework with the European Union (EU) to ensure continued access to financial transaction data, following the relocation of SWIFT's data storage to the EU. The transition placed such data outside the scope of US

[108] UN General Assembly, Promotion and Protection of All Human Rights, Civil, Political, Economic, Social and Cultural Rights, including the Right to Development: Report of the Special Rapporteur on the Promotion of Human Rights and Fundamental Freedoms while Countering Terrorism, Martin Scheinin, A/HRC/6/17, paras 42–45.

[109] Office of the United Nations' High Commissioner for Human Rights, Palais des Nations, Geneva, 'Human Rights, Terrorism and Counter-terrorism, Fact Sheet No. 32', p. 9.

[110] Amnesty International (2019).

[111] US Department of Treasury, 'Terrorist Finance Tracking Program (TFTP)' https://home.treasury.gov/policy-issues/terrorism-and-illicit-finance/terrorist-finance-tracking-program-tftp accessed 1 January 2025.

administrative subpoenas, necessitating collaboration to maintain the effectiveness of the program.

Furthermore, PRISM, a code name for a classified program was initiated in 2007 to enable the US National Security Agency (NSA) to access stored internet communications that align with its search criteria. This access is granted under Section 702 of the *FISA Amendments Act of 2008* and involves major US-based internet companies such as Google and Yahoo. The program operates on a demand basis, allowing the NSA to collect data directly from these companies.

Since its inception, PRISM has been central to the NSA's surveillance activities, accounting for approximately 91% of the agency's yearly internet communications acquisitions under Section 702 of FISA.[112] Given that most of the global internet infrastructure and leading technology corporations including Google, Yahoo, Microsoft, Facebook, YouTube, AOL, Skype, and Apple are headquartered in the US, a significant portion of the world's electronic communications traverse its networks. This dominance in internet traffic flow has facilitated the interception and collection of vast amounts of electronic data through PRISM, raising critical privacy concerns.[113]

Every individual possesses an inherent right to privacy, encompassing their homes, correspondence, and all forms of communication.[114] Consequently, individuals are safeguarded against unnecessary, unwarranted, and arbitrary intrusions into their privacy, dignity, and privileges. However, in pursuing national security in the manner they do, states have increasingly adopted practices that encroach upon personal privacy. These include financial tracing, surveillance of residences, localisation of mobile devices, wiretapping, tracking technologies, computerised profiling, and enhanced security screenings. It is widely recognised that any measure infringing upon individual privacy must be lawful, explicitly authorised by legal frameworks, and must avoid arbitrariness.[115] Furthermore, personal information obtained through lawful means must be protected against unauthorised access, disclosure, or misuse.[116]

Despite these principles, the contemporary emphasis on national security has seen routine misuse of these measures. Notably, mechanisms intended for CT are frequently exploited to target political and economic adversaries, unjustifiably labelling them as terrorists.[117] This practice restricts their access to financial

---

[112] Donohue (2015), p. 120.

[113] Mark Memmott, 'Report: NSA Has Broken Into Google And Yahoo Data Centers' (*NPR*, 30 October 2013) https://www.npr.org/sections/thetwo-way/2013/10/30/241855353/report-nsa-has-broken-into-google-and-yahoo-data-centers accessed 12 January 2025.

[114] UDHR 1948, art 12; International Covenant on Civil and Political Rights, art 17.

[115] Office of the United Nations' High Commissioner for Human Rights, Palais des Nations, Geneva, 'Human Rights, Terrorism and Counter-terrorism, Fact Sheet No. 32', p.38.

[116] The Human Rights Committee General Comment No. 16 (1998).

[117] General Assembly, 'Activities of the United Nations system in implementing the United Nations Global Counter-Terrorism Strategy: Report of the Secretary-General' Seventy-Seventh Session (A/77/718), para 61.

resources and imposes disproportionate reporting obligations, exceeding the bounds of reasonableness and undermining the fundamental right to privacy.

While the underlying objective of the PRISM surveillance program and TFTP are commendable; which it claims is to facilitate 'targeted searches' within a narrowly defined subset of records rather than an indiscriminate data sweep and purportedly adhering to data privacy standards, the program remains vulnerable to potential misuse or exploitation. In the absence of a robust framework that integrates stringent FRF compliance safeguards, there is a risk of its deployment for purposes such as unauthorised data mining or other unjustifiable activities, undermining its legitimacy and public trust.

National security and CT measures, including CTF, require a careful balance between effectiveness and adherence to human rights principles. Governments must ensure that their actions align with international legal standards and incorporate robust safeguards to prevent abuses.[118] By adopting transparent and proportionate AML/CTF measures, states can more effectively combat terrorism while maintaining their commitment to protecting FRF and upholding the rule of law.

3.2.2 Ex Parte Hearings

A prominent method employed by states such as the US and UK to combat terrorism financing within the framework of AML/CTF measures is the proscription of organisations linked to terrorism. This approach criminalises belonging to or actively supporting such organisations upon the determination of relevant authorities. The UK Home Secretary is empowered under Section 3 of the *Terrorism Act 2000* to unilaterally proscribe organisations 'believed' to be involved in terrorism. This includes acts such as committing or participating in terrorism, preparing for such acts, or promoting and encouraging terrorism. Similarly, in the US, the Secretary of State is empowered to designate organisations as Foreign Terrorist Organizations (FTOs) under Section 219 of the *Immigration and Nationality Act (INA)*.[119] While these decisions are required to be proportionate and may be subject to appeal or judicial review, with potential compensation available under provisions like the *Criminal Justice Act* (Compensation for Miscarriage of Justice),[120] the exclusive reliance on executive discretion, without representation or prior consultation with affected entities, introduces risks of overreach and misuse.

As of April 2024, 81 international organisations had been proscribed under the Terrorism Act 2000.[121] While several of these organisations, such as Al-Qaeda and Boko Haram, have been widely regarded as justifiable inclusions, especially because

---

[118] Maogoto (2004–05), p. 45.

[119] U.S. Department of State (n.d.).

[120] Terrorism Act 2000, ss 3-7.

[121] Home Office, 'Policy Paper: Proscribed Terrorist Groups or Organisations', https://www.gov.uk/government/publications/proscribed-terror-groups-or-organisations%2D%2D2/proscribed-terrorist-groups-or-organisations-accessible-version#deproscription accessed 3 January 2025.

they operate in hiding, there are notable instances where proscription decisions have been reversed. For example, the International Sikh Youth Federation (ISYF) was deproscribed following a successful appeal, and Mujaheddin e Khalq (MeK) was removed after judicial review.[122] Given the severity of penalties associated with proscription, ranging from financial restrictions to reputational damage, it is evident that errors in the initial designation process can cause irreparable harm. There have also been questions around its suitability and compliance with the rule of law, especially for its perpetual application.[123] This highlights the necessity for greater substantive and procedural safeguards, ensuring that such significant decisions are subjected to thorough scrutiny and fair trial protections from the outset.

A follow-up to this is the 'immediate' freezing of assets belonging to individuals or entities suspected of terrorism. This action is often undertaken either as an administrative decision or with judicial approval, frequently without the prior knowledge or representation of the affected parties. Such practices raise significant concerns, as they are fundamentally inconsistent with Pillar IV of the UN Global Counter-Terrorism Strategy, which emphasises respect for human rights and the rule of law as foundational principles in the fight against terrorism. The absence of procedural safeguards and transparency in these asset-freezing measures raises the tension between CT objectives and the protection of fundamental rights.[124] By imposing restrictions on these groups' operations and financial activities, proscription serves as a vital mechanism for curbing the flow of funds to terrorism. However, such measures must be carefully balanced with due process and FRF considerations to prevent their misuse or overreach.

Every individual has the right to a fair hearing and trial in the determination of issues that affect their interests.[125] A fair hearing is synonymous with a fair trial, as both require adherence to the fundamental principles of *audi alteram partem* (hear the other side) and *nemo judex in causa sua* (no one should be a judge in their own case). These principles emphasise that all parties must be given an opportunity to present their case, and impartiality must be maintained throughout the decision-making process. Additionally, the right to a fair hearing encompasses related rights such as the presumption of innocence until proven guilty,[126] the right to adequate guarantees to prepare a defence,[127] and the right to self-representation or legal representation conducive to a fair trial.[128]

---

[122] Home Office, 'Policy Paper: Proscribed Terrorist Groups or Organisations', https://www.gov.uk/government/publications/proscribed-terror-groups-or-organisations%2D%2D2/proscribed-terrorist-groups-or-organisations-accessible-version#deproscription accessed 3 January 2025.

[123] Dawson (2025), p. 9.

[124] Terrorism Act 2006, s 35.

[125] UDHR 1948, art 10.

[126] UDHR 1948, art 11(1).

[127] UDHR 1948, art 11(1).

[128] In the matter of an application by Kevin Maguire for Judicial Review (Northern Ireland) [2018] UKSC 17.

In practice, however, certain AML/CTF measures such as the proscription of organisations based solely on executive discretion, effectively making the government a judge in its own case, and the immediate freezing of assets without prior notification or representation, undermine the essence of fair hearing and consequently conflict with these long-established and democratically-cherished ideals.

To align with the principles of fairness, the standards required to ensure a fair hearing, as articulated in various international and municipal human rights frameworks, must include the right of individuals and entities to be promptly informed of measures taken against them and to know the case against them to the greatest extent possible.[129] This transparency should occur without undermining the objectives of the sanctions regimes. By balancing the requirements of due process with the imperatives of security, such standards serve to uphold the rule of law while mitigating the risk of arbitrariness and overreach in AML/CTF measures.

4 Balancing AML/CTF Ambitions and Human Rights: A Rethink

The implementation of CT measures aimed at ensuring national security presents significant challenges for states, particularly in reconciling these measures with their obligations to uphold and guarantee FRF.[130] The effectiveness of AML/CTF initiatives is inherently flawed if they undermine decades of progress in human rights protection. To achieve a balance between the imperatives of security and the protection of human rights, it is essential to critically examine how the AML/CTF framework can be pursued without infringing on fundamental freedoms. This inquiry is crucial for preserving the integrity of established international and domestic human rights frameworks in the face of contemporary terrorism trends. The lifeline of terrorist activities—access to funding—must be severed through AML/CTF measures, but this must be done in a manner that avoids eroding the foundational values of human rights.

AML/CTF frameworks should transcend the perception of opportunistic state power expansion and instead be carefully adapted to align with national contexts.[131] These frameworks must be designed to incorporate pragmatic mechanisms that effectively balance the competing imperatives of national security and the protection of individual freedoms, ensuring that CT measures operate within a just and rights-respecting framework.[132] It can be contended that the UN's role, through its specialised agencies and Special Rapporteurs on Human Rights, has done

[129] Office of the United Nations' High Commissioner for Human Rights, Palais des Nations, Geneva, 'Human Rights, Terrorism and Counter-terrorism, Fact Sheet No. 32', p. 38.

[130] Stone (2008), p. 84.

[131] Woods (2005), p. 37.

[132] Limbach, (2009), p. 22.

significant work in this regards, and the FATF, for instance, need not duplicate these efforts. This chapter, however, argues that the UN has equally done tremendous work in setting standards for CTF. If it is deemed appropriate to reaffirm the normative and operational frameworks surrounding CTF, then, by the same logic, it would also be fitting to reassert the importance and inviolability of FRF. By addressing the procedural and substantive aspects of AML/CTF measures, states can ensure that CT efforts do not diminish the value of human rights protections but instead operate within a framework that respects and reinforces these rights.

4.1 The Current Order: Why Is It Self-Defeating?

The inherent tension between respecting FRF norms and pursuing national security objectives is rooted in the costs and benefits that states assess in their quest for security, often at the expense of fundamental rights. This conflict is particularly pronounced in the implementation of AML/CTF measures, where states face challenges in balancing legal compliance with the perceived necessity of robust security actions.

The legal tradition plays a crucial role in shaping the planning and execution of national security measures by emphasising long-term stability, evaluating the costs and benefits of compliance versus violation of human rights norms, and considering a spectrum of international conflict management options.[133] However, within the global AML/CTF regime, and as will be explored in this section, this balance is often neglected. This has led to the proliferation of measures that prioritise expedient security objectives over the protection of human rights. In the words of a former UN Secretary-General Kofi Annan, this trend poses a significant challenge to the international security system founded on the UN Charter, which remains the sole universally accepted legal framework for the use of force.[134] The unchecked implementation of AML/CTF measures under this framework risks undermining the rule of law and eroding the sanctity of international human rights protections.

Due to the overlapping legal norms and systems that constitute the CT arena, the UN mandates all measures to fully comply with human rights treaty obligations and customary obligations in their design, implementation, and assessment strategies.[135] The FATF, as the leader of global AML/CTF action, is mandated to set international standards, monitor their implementation, and hold countries accountable for

[133] Moore (1973), pp. 413–416.

[134] Report of the Secretary General on the Work of the Organization, UN GOAR, 54th sess, Supp No.1, para 66, UN DOC A/54/1/1999, cited in Maogoto (n 117), p. 42.

[135] United Nations Human Rights Office of the High Commissioner, 'International Standards on the Promotion and Protection of Human Rights and Fundamental Freedoms while Countering Terrorism: Special Rapporteur on counter-terrorism and human rights' https://ohchr.org/en/special-procedures/sr-terrorism/international-standards-promotion-and-protection-human-rights-and-fundamental-freedoms-while accessed 5 January 2025.

non-compliance.[136] However, a significant disconnect exists between the global AML/CTF framework and FRF considerations, which originates from the leadership approach adopted by the FATF itself in contradiction of the UN's directive.

While the UN, in addition to general human rights instruments, specifically integrates FRF and the rule of law as a core pillar of its Global Counter-Terrorism Strategy (Pillar IV), the FATF does not explicitly prioritise or incorporate such safeguards within its objectives or operational functions. The FATF's mandate technically consists of one overarching objective and ten functions, yet none of these addresses the need for FRF safeguards in the pursuit of AML/CTF measures. Consequently, FRF considerations do not form part of the FATF's monitored standards or accountability mechanisms. As earlier argued, if the FATF is justified in dedicating substantial resources to developing specific standards for CTF, notwithstanding potential overlaps with the mandates of the UN's specialised agencies, because it offers a focused approach distinct from broader CT efforts, then a parallel rationale supports the incorporation of FRF within these CTF standards as a complementary and connected normative objective. This omission has implications for both the FATF's role and states' practices it influences, such as the US, the UK, and Nigeria, as it perpetuates a lack of emphasis on reconciling security imperatives with fundamental rights within the global AML/CTF regime.

The US national AML/CTF strategy is structured around three goals and four priorities, none of which attempts to incorporate FRF protections within its framework. Although *Supporting Action 1* under *Priority 1* mentions data protection and compliance, this appears more as a cursory mention than a substantive commitment to FRF.[137] Notably, the 2024 strategy is entirely silent on these issues when reporting progress on priorities and supporting actions from the 2022 strategy.[138] Even if *Supporting Action 1* genuinely reflected a commitment to data protection, it would still fall short of ensuring comprehensive compliance with international human rights. Similarly, the UK's AML/CTF action plan centres on three priorities, predominantly emphasising the expansion of aggressive legal powers, yet it does not embed FRF safeguards within its strategy.[139]

Following the precedent set by the FATF, both the US and the UK have neither an expressed intent to address AML/CTF threats in adherence to human rights nor any concrete prioritisation of such protections within their strategic agendas. In contrast, Nigeria's national security strategy includes a presidential directive that ostensibly calls for preserving FRF while addressing AML/CTF threats.[140] However, this ambition fails to permeate the core agenda, as none of its five work streams

[136] FATF, 'Mandate of the Financial Action Task Force' https://www.fatf-gafi.org/en/the-fatf/mandate-of-the-fatf.html#accordion-ffd0cfcabc-item-a5fb5ae357 accessed 26 December 2024.

[137] US Department of Treasury, '2024 National Strategy for Combating Terrorism and Other Illicit Financing' (*Department of Treasury,* 2024) 9.

[138] US Department of Treasury (2024), p. 40.

[139] Home Office (2016).

[140] Office of the National Security Adviser (ONSA), Federal Republic of Nigeria, 'The National Counter Terrorism Strategy (NACTEST)' (Rev., ONSA, 2016).

explicitly incorporates this directive. Nigeria's action plan for countering violent extremism adopts a more commendable approach, identifying respect for FRF as a priority component.[141] This distinction likely arises because the framework for countering violent extremism is guided by the UN's framework, which emphasises FRF protections, rather than the FATF's standards.

The absence of a mandate for human rights protection within the FATF's global AML/CTF framework represents a fundamental flaw. It overlooks article 17 of the *International Convention for the Suppression of the Financing of Terrorism*, which expressly requires that CTF measures respect FRF. It also disregards pillar IV of the UN Global Counter-Terrorism Strategy on the imperative of ensuring respect for human rights and the rule of law as integral components of all CT efforts. By failing to prioritise (or even draw attention to) FRF observance, the FATF has perpetuated a model that allows national strategies to neglect essential FRF safeguards. FRF protection within the AML/CTF framework cannot receive the necessary attention and enforcement if states are either encouraged to deprioritise or not held accountable for equitably balancing their commitment to FRF with their focus on combating terrorism and its financing. The absence of a mandated parity between these objectives perpetuates a disproportionate emphasis on security measures, often at the expense of fundamental rights, thereby undermining the broader legitimacy and effectiveness of global AML/CTF efforts.

The current AML/CTF regime is, therefore, structurally deficient in enforcing measures that uphold FRF for two critical reasons. First, as influenced by the FATF, states often fail to incorporate FRF considerations at the inception of their AML/CTF strategies. Although the United Nations Special Rapporteur (UNSR) on the promotion and protection of human rights and fundamental freedoms is mandated to identify, exchange, and promote best practices for CT measures that respect FRF,[142] this mandate has yet to be effectively realised within the AML/CTF domain. It is particularly concerning that despite the mandate of the Special Rapporteur on CT and human rights extending to the promotion of rights-compliant CT policies through the provision of expertise and technical assistance to the relevant stakeholders,[143] there is no tangible evidence that this mandate has influenced FATF's standards. The UNSR's activities appear to be confined largely to coordination within UN bodies, particularly the Human Rights Council, rather than

[141] Federal Republic of Nigeria, 'Policy Framework and National Action Plan for Preventing and Countering Violent Extremism: Partnering for Safer and Resilient Communities' (2017).

[142] United Nations General Assembly, 'Protection of Human Rights and Fundamental Freedoms While Countering Terrorism: Mandate of the Special Rapporteur on the Promotion and Protection of Human Rights and Fundamental Freedoms While Countering Terrorism' (A/HRC/RES/15/15) Resolution adopted by the Human Rights Council 15/15, para 2 (a)&(d).

[143] Special Rapporteur on Counter-Terrorism and Human Rights, 'About the Mandate of the Special Rapporteur on Terrorism' https://www.ohchr.org/en/special-procedures/sr-terrorism/about-mandate-special-rapporteur-terrorism accessed 30 June 2025.

extending to non-UN entities such as the FATF.[144] Enhanced collaboration between the UNSR and the FATF is essential to ensuring that FRF considerations are integrated into the FATF's mandate and its oversight of state AML/CTF measures.

Second, where specific AML/CTF measures reference FRF standards, such references are often corrective (rather than preventive) and tied to implementing authorities, as exemplified by the proportionality requirement in the UK's proscription measures. This reactive approach permits potential breaches of FRF to occur before individuals can seek redress through judicial mechanisms. Consequently, the system fails to provide pre-emptive safeguards, leaving FRF vulnerable to infringement during the execution of AML/CTF measures. The necessary legislative framework for the protection of FRF is only the first step in equipping states to pursue a national security agenda; the will and political commitment to uphold the instruments is a more important desire.

4.2 The Alternative: Towards a Rights-Friendly Regime

The imperative for national security measures to respect and uphold FRF is not a novel concept; there have long been calls for a balanced approach that aligns security objectives with the preservation of human rights, particularly in the context of combating terrorism. As reiterated by the UNSR, states must fulfil their obligations in a manner consistent with their international human rights commitments.[145] While AML/CTF efforts, primarily led by the FATF, have yet to incorporate this principle, other initiatives such as the UN Global Counter-Terrorism Strategy and the Draft United Nations Cybercrime Convention have commendably affirmed the necessity of balancing security with human rights.[146]

This chapter aims to address two interconnected objectives. First, it explores the necessity for a AML/CTF framework that is substantively aligned with FRF principles. Second, it suggests an operational mechanism required to implement such a framework effectively, emphasising the importance of embedding human rights safeguards into both the design and execution of AML/CTF measures. The preceding section discussed the first leg, and this section will deliver on the second.

[144] See United Nations General Assembly, 'Protection of Human Rights and Fundamental Freedoms While Countering Terrorism: Mandate of the Special Rapporteur on the Promotion and Protection of Human Rights and Fundamental Freedoms While Countering Terrorism' (A/HRC/RES/15/15) Resolution adopted by the Human Rights Council 15/15, para 2 (e) & (f).

[145] United Nations Human Rights Special Procedures, 'Human Rights Assessment of the Draft United Nations Cybercrime Convention: Statement by the United Nations Special Rapporteur on the Promotion and Protection of Human Rights While Countering Terrorism, Ben Saul' 25 July 2024.

[146] See the UN Global Counter-Terrorism Strategy, Pillar IV, and the Draft United Nations Cybercrime Convention, art 6.

4.2.1 Legislative Framework for AML/CTF: Proposing a Three-Pronged Suitability Test

To achieve a rights-friendly AML/CTF regime, the pillars and mandates of the regime must fully prioritise FRF concerns as a complementary objective alongside its aim of blocking illicit financing. To avoid replicating the errors observed during the prosecution of Red Army Faction terrorists in Germany, it is imperative to avoid reliance on symbolic policies that undermine core democratic values.[147] States must be actively encouraged to uphold their foundational principles, ensuring that judicial actors remain unwavering in their commitment to fundamental rights and the rule of law.[148]

One pathway to achieving this objective is to institutionalise the integration of international human rights standards into the routine implementation of national security measures.[149] By embedding these norms into the operational framework of security policies, states can fortify their national security apparatus while simultaneously upholding both international and domestic human rights protections. While this largely remains a soft law as it is not readily binding, the FATF already operates a robust compliance framework that could be leveraged to institutionalise binding FRF norms championed by the UN.[150]

The critical question that follows is: what standards should be incorporated to ensure AML/CTF measures align with FRF? At present, there is no established legal framework providing a definitive benchmark for validating AML/CTF actions. This chapter seeks to address this gap by proposing a clear yardstick for assessing AML/CTF measures and urging the FATF to integrate specific FRF standards as prerequisites for sanctioning such actions.

Previous scholarly contributions have outlined potential evaluative frameworks for CT measures. Limbach suggests that these measures must be scrutinised against three critical questions: (i) are they genuinely effective in combating terrorism; (ii) is the resulting loss of freedom proportionate to the severity of the intervention; and (iii) could the measures lead to unintended and undesirable consequences?[151] Similarly, Moore emphasises that national security decisions should consider: (i) what are the specific national security goals; (ii) are these goals realisable within the contextual constraints of their pursuit; (iii) are they achievable at a cost-benefit ratio that aligns with the national interest; (iv) are there preferable alternatives with more favourable outcomes; and (v) how can the chosen policies be most effectively implemented and justified?[152] There is also the three-part test developed by the

[147] According to Limbach, at that time, the measures against the terrorism of the Red Army were passed at breakneck speed which chiefly signalled the activity and was persistent, but hardly tackled the problem.

[148] Limbach (2009), p. 26.

[149] Moore (1973), p. 421.

[150] Goldbarsht (2020), p. 13.

[151] Limbach (2009), p. 23.

[152] Moore (1973), p. 409.

European Court of Human Rights as a framework to assess the legitimacy of limitations imposed on FRF.[153] According to this framework, any interference must: (i) be prescribed by law, meaning it must have a clear and accessible legal basis that enables individuals to foresee the consequences of their actions; (ii) pursue a legitimate aim, such as the prevention of crime or the protection of national security, as recognised under the Convention; and (iii) be necessary in a democratic society, implying a pressing social need and proportionality between the means employed and the aim pursued. Furthermore, the measure adopted must represent the least restrictive means of achieving the objective, so as not to impair the essence of the right.

Building on these scholarly perspectives, this chapter formulates a three-pronged evaluative framework grounded in the principles of (i) verifiable evidence, (ii) effectiveness, and (iii) proportionality. Conjunctively, this framework serves as a standard for assessing the validity and appropriateness of national security measures before they are implemented. By integrating these elements, the framework seeks to strike a critical balance between the imperatives of national security and the safeguarding of FRF. It provides a structured basis for the comprehensive assessment and implementation of AML/CTF measures, ensuring alignment with both security objectives and human rights norms.

4.2.1.1 Evidence-Based

A significant concern regarding FRF within the current AML/CTF regime is the considerable discretion granted to implementing bodies. Such discretion often results in decisions that infringe upon the rights of the individuals or entities involved, whether justified or not. Assets and financial resources serve as critical lifelines not only for terrorists but also for innocent individuals. Any unwarranted disruption to these resources can result in severe and far-reaching consequences for the affected individuals and their families.[154] Given the profound implications of AML/CTF measures, anchoring such actions exclusively on the 'reasonable suspicion' of the executives, without prior review and determination by an impartial arbiter, fundamentally undermines both the sanctity of FRF and the legitimacy of these measures. Allowing the executives to act as both the prosecutor and the judge in matters that critically affect FRF is antithetical to the principles of justice, accountability, and the rule of law. The reliability of initial assessments by security operatives has frequently proven fallible, underscoring the necessity for neutral and impartial scrutiny before the imposition of far-reaching AML/CTF measures. For instance, in the UK, as of December 31, 2023, judicial reviews revealed that 16% of

---

[153] See: *Sunday Times v United Kingdom* (No. 1) (1979) 2 EHRR 245, para 49; *Handyside v United Kingdom* (1976) 1 EHRR 737, paras 48–50.

[154] HM Treasury v Ahmed [2010] UKSC 2 para 4.

charges initially classified as terrorism-related were ultimately found not to be so.[155] By contrast, only 3.5% of cases initially upheld as terrorism-related by courts failed to result in a conviction, highlighting the critical importance of independent oversight in preserving FRF while ensuring effective AML/CTF enforcement.

The evidence-based principle, as suggested here, is rooted in the associated framework of epistemic modality, emphasising the necessity for the claimant to ground their inferences in concrete and verifiable evidence that allows the prediction of the probability.[156] This requirement ensures that any suspicion against an individual or entity is substantiated to the extent that it demonstrates the existence of a prima facie case warranting the measure sought to be activated. In the absence of a clearly embedded requirement within frameworks such as AML/CTF regimes to ensure that suspicion is grounded in credible and verifiable evidence, government measures risk perpetuating practices that lack procedural rigour. Such deficiencies not only undermine the legitimacy and effectiveness of enforcement efforts but, as prior experiences have shown, may ultimately prove counterproductive.[157] While disrupting terrorist financial flows is vital to combating terrorism, ensuring that such suspicion is substantiated by compelling evidence through judicial oversight is not merely a procedural formality; it is a foundational requirement for aligning CT efforts with principles of justice and accountability. In essence, the foundational question is whether the suspicion or allegation is grounded in verifiable evidence, ensuring that AML/CTF measures do not compromise FRF without due justification.

4.2.1.2 Effectiveness

Another important aspect of this concern is whether the measures are clearly thought out as the most effective way to combat the suspected ML/TF threat. It can hardly be disputed that the AML/CTF is generally successful in reducing the capacity of terrorists to carry out coordinated attacks. While terrorism continues to pose a dynamic and evolving threat globally, the capacity of states to prevent and disrupt terrorist attacks has also significantly improved. Within the European Union, for example, official data indicate that of the six terrorist attacks recorded in 2022, four (approximately 67%) were successfully thwarted. In 2023, 14 attacks were reported, with nine (64%) foiled, while in 2024, 24 incidents were identified, 18 of which

[155] Home Office, 'Transparency Data: Counter-Terrorism Disruptive Powers Report 2023' (*GOV. UK*, 2024).

[156] Ayoun et al. (2018), pp. 146–7.

[157] UN General Assembly, Promotion and Protection of All Human Rights, Civil, Political, Economic, Social and Cultural Rights, including the Right to Development: Report of the Special Rapporteur on the Promotion of Human Rights and Fundamental Freedoms while Countering Terrorism, Martin Scheinin, A/HRC/6/17, paras 46.

(75%) were prevented.[158] Notably, the completed attacks in 2024 were perpetrated by lone attackers targeting mass events, without sophisticated weapons, and with no established connections to terrorist groups.[159] At the global level, whilst the number of deaths from terrorism increased by 22% as of 2023, the number of recorded terrorist incidents declined by around 22%–23%.[160] In the same vein, the rate of misses has also been phenomenal, especially in terms of unintended consequences and gaps in the effective implementation of FATF standards.[161]

In light of the sanctity of FRF, the few unintended consequences can quickly overwhelm the successes of the entire AML/CTF regime. As stated earlier, for instance, the Central Bank of Nigeria (CBN) in 2021 imposed restrictions on cryptocurrency operations, citing risks associated with ML and TF. However, after over 2 years, the CBN reversed its position, acknowledging that regulating cryptocurrency activities would better mitigate their misuse for illicit financing than outright restrictions.[162] During the same period, the CBN implemented a controversial currency redesign policy aimed, among other objectives, at 'supporting security agencies in combating banditry and ransom-taking in Nigeria'.[163] Despite the profound implications of these measures on FRF and the rights of citizens, their tangible benefits were negligible. Nigeria's ML/TF risk index score remained at approximately 6.9 points, indicating no significant improvement and retaining Nigeria's record as one of the countries most vulnerable to terrorism.[164]

The implications of AML/CTF measures extend far beyond the immediate targets, often causing disproportionate harm to third-party interests, including businesses, families, and broader economic systems.[165] Such collateral impacts highlight the profound costs of operating within a 'trial-and-error' framework. It is therefore imperative that AML/CTF measures are demonstrably the most effective means of achieving their intended security objectives, accompanied by compelling evidence that no viable alternatives exist that would yield equivalent results with reduced implications for FRF.

[158] EUROPOL, *European Union Terrorism Situation and Trend Report 2025* (European Union Agency for Law Enforcement Cooperation, 2025) 25.

[159] EUROPOL, *European Union Terrorism Situation and Trend Report 2025* (European Union Agency for Law Enforcement Cooperation, 2025) 23.

[160] Institute for Economics & Peace (2024).

[161] United Nations General Assembly, 'Impact of Measures to Address Terrorism and Violent Extremism on Civic Space and the Rights of Civil Society Actors and Human Rights Defenders: Report of the Special Rapporteur on the Protection of Human Rights and Fundamental Freedoms while Countering Terrorism, A/HRC/40/52, pt. II.

[162] News, 'CBN Lifts Ban on Cryptocurrency Transactions' (*Vanguard,* 23 December 2023) https://www.vanguardngr.com/2023/12/cbn-lifts-ban-on-cryptocurrency-transactions/ accessed 11 January 2025.

[163] 'WATCH: Why We Redesigned Naira Notes - CBN Governor' (*TVC News Nigeria,* 29 January 2023), https://youtu.be/RVhulPw1XVE?si=T38A1g6EpzWqd6BK accessed 11 January 2025.

[164] Statista (2023).

[165] *HM Treasury v Ahmed* [2010] UKSC 2 para 4.

4.2.1.3 Proportionality

The final component of the suitability criterion emphasises the necessity of demonstrating, before implementation, that even when proposed AML/CTF measures are grounded in evidence and proven effective, any resultant limitations on FRF are both justifiable and proportionate to the security objectives sought. To avert defensive, rather than mitigative, AML/CTF strategies, it is essential to establish robust knowledge and a comprehensive understanding of the associated risks. This approach ensures the capacity to address such risks proportionately while safeguarding against excessive or unjustifiable infringements on FRF.

While AML/CTF measures yield significant benefits, they also carry unintended consequences that may conflict with international human rights objectives, undermining their broader effectiveness. When such measures are implemented without thorough consideration of their FRF implications through a rigorous risk-based approach, they risk becoming counterproductive. A notable example is, as earlier noted, the UK's sanctions on Roman Abramovich's interests in Chelsea FC. Although motivated by national security considerations, these sanctions failed to adequately account for the collateral impact on third-party stakeholders. These third parties, including employees, fans, and business partners, disproportionately bore the brunt of the sanctions, overshadowing their intended impact on the Kremlin, which the measures sought to target.

4.2.2 Operational Mechanism: Proposing Judicial Moderation Through Special AML/CTF Tribunals

Establishing a legislative framework for the protection of FRF is merely the foundational step in equipping states to pursue a security agenda that aligns with human rights norms. However, the critical determinant of success lies in the political will and practical commitment to uphold these frameworks, which often proves elusive. The pressing question, therefore, is: who should implement these standards, and what mechanisms should be recommended to ensure compliance?

Before adopting a national security measure to counter terrorism, the three strands of the suitability test—evidence-based (verifiable evidence), effectiveness, and proportionality—must be conjunctively satisfied. As previously analysed, many of the key AML/CTF measures currently employed by states would fail this test, as they inadequately balance the sanctity of FRF with national security objectives. In this context, it is imperative to recognise that a democracy committed to its principles may sometimes have to fight with 'one arm tied behind its back' to uphold its legitimacy and moral authority.[166]

To reconcile these competing imperatives, it is recommended that FATF include in its recommendations the need for governmental suspicions of terrorism to

[166] Limbach (2009), p. 27.

undergo judicial moderation using the three-pronged suitability test. Empirical evidence demonstrates that court-supervised CT efforts yield higher accuracy and greater success in preventing crimes.[167] Despite the commendable efforts of the UN in advancing human rights objectives and establishing the Mandate of the UNSR, this effort is not sufficient and clearly disjointed from the coordination of the global AML/CTF regime by the FATF. The FATF must clearly incorporate FRF recognition in its objectives and provide a recommendation for the creation of special tribunals to moderate intended AML/CTF measures before implementation. Judicial oversight not only enhances the legitimacy of AML/CTF measures but also ensures their alignment with international human rights obligations, thereby strengthening the overall efficacy of CT strategies.

States have established specialised organisations tasked with implementing their AML/CTF strategies. In the US, this responsibility lies with the Counterterrorism Finance Unit (CT Finance), while the UK entrusts it to the National Crime Agency (NCA). Similarly, Nigeria has vested this function in the National Counter-Terrorism Centre (NCTC). A critical limitation of these entities, however, is their reliance on reactive rather than proactive judicial oversight mechanisms, leaving significant actions to executive discretion without prior judicial moderation.

This chapter advocates for the establishment of judicial (or quasi-judicial) oversight mechanisms, either integrated within or operating independently, to review and moderate AML/CTF measures before their implementation. Such a framework would enhance the legitimacy, accountability, and alignment of AML/CTF measures with FRF. It is argued that embedding judicial oversight into AML/CTF strategies not only preserves the principle of separation of powers but also safeguards the right to the presumption of innocence, a cornerstone of democratic governance. This approach prevents a reversal of justice norms, ensuring individuals and entities are not presumed guilty until proven innocent, which would represent a fundamental departure from democratic ideals. According to Lord Hope of the UK Supreme Court, "the closer those measures come to affect what, in R v Secretary of State for the Home Department, Ex p Simms [2000] 2 AC 115, 131, Lord Hoffmann described as the basic rights of the individual, the more exacting this scrutiny must become" and "[i]f the rule of law is to mean anything, decisions as to what is necessary or expedient in this context cannot be left to the uncontrolled judgment of the executive".[168]

A logical follow-up action would be to incorporate an effective implementation mechanism within the FATF's standards to operationalise these safeguards.

[167] Home Office, 'Transparency Data: Counter-Terrorism Disruptive Powers Report 2023' (*GOV. UK*, 2024). See above discussions on 'evidentiality'.

[168] *HM Treasury v Ahmed* [2010] UKSC 2 para 45.

5 Conclusion

In response to global terrorism, states have intensified AML/CTF efforts as part of broader CT strategies, aiming to disrupt the financial lifelines of terrorist organisations. Particularly since the 9/11 attacks, numerous CT laws and policies have been enacted, targeting financial systems to prevent their exploitation for funding terrorism. However, these measures often infringe upon civil liberties and human rights, restricting freedoms such as privacy, association, and expression. Measures like asset freezes, surveillance programs, proscription orders, and emergency declarations frequently conflict with established international and municipal human rights standards.

While safeguarding national security and disrupting terrorist financing are essential, these objectives must not overshadow the protection of FRF. The rule of law and human rights protection are indispensable components of any security framework. Thus, the global AML/CTF regime must strive for a balance between addressing security needs and upholding the rights of citizens, as enshrined in international and domestic legal frameworks.

Scholars have contributed significantly to shaping what national security and AML/CTF decisions should entail, particularly regarding their formulation and implementation. Drawing from these contributions, this chapter develops a three-pronged suitability test—evidentiality, effectiveness, and proportionality—designed to assess the suitability of AML/CTF measures prior to implementation. This test ensures that security measures and the global AML/CTF regime do not render well-established human rights frameworks obsolete under the pretext of CT.

This chapter critically examines the global AML/CTF regime, exploring its alignment with national security and human rights ideals. It reviews overreaching AML/CTF measures and their impact on FRF, evaluates the proportionality of these measures, and proposes actionable recommendations to ensure a more balanced approach to combating terrorism financing while safeguarding human rights.

References

Address to a Joint Session of Congress and the American People (2001) United States Capitol, Washington D.C., 20 September 2001. https://georgewbush-whitehouse.archives.gov/news/releases/2001/09/20010920-8.html. Accessed 28 June 2025

Amnesty International (2019) "The Great Hack": Cambridge analytica is just the tip of the Iceberg. https://www.amnesty.org/en/latest/news/2019/07/the-great-hack-facebook-cambridge-analytica/. Accessed 29 June 2025

Ayoun D, Celle A, Lansari L (2018) Tense, aspect, modality, and evidentiality: crosslinguistic perspectives. John Benjamins Publishing Co., Amsterdam/Philadelphia

Bakare A (2021) Cryptocurrency Trading: CBN Orders Banks to Close Operating Accounts. (3)2 CBN Update 3(2):1–20, 2

Boyle MJ (2008) The war on terror in American grand strategy. Int Aff 84(2):191–209

Dawson J (2025) Proscribed terrorist organisations (Commons Library Research Briefing, 27 June 2025)
Donohue LK (2015) Section 702 and the collection of international telephone and internet content. Harv J Law Public Policy 38:117
FATF (2013) International best practices: targeted financial sanctions related to terrorism and terrorist financing (Recommendation 6)
Goldbarsht D (2020) Global counter-terrorist financing and soft law multi-layered approaches. Edward Elgar Publishing, Cheltenham
Hamilton C (2019) Contagion, counter-terrorism and criminology: justice in the shadow of terror. Springer Nature, Switzerland AG
Home Office (2016) Action Plan for Anti-Money Laundering and Counter-Terrorist Finance (HM Treasury, 2016)
Howard RD, Sawyer RL (2002) Terrorism and counterterrorism: understanding the new security environment. McGraw-Hill, Dubuque, United States
Institute for Economics & Peace (2024) Global terrorism index 2024: measuring the impact of terrorism. http://visionofhumanity.org/resources. Accessed 30 June 2025
Kraft M, Marks E (2011) US government counterterrorism: a guide to who does what. CRC Press, Taylor & Francis Group, Boca Raton
Limbach J (2009) Human rights in times of terror: is collective security the enemy of individual freedom? Goettingen J Int Law 1(1):17
Maogoto JN (2004–05) America's war on terror: rattling international law with raw power? Newcastle Law Rev 8(2):32
Mascaro L (2011) Patriot Act Provisions Extended Just in Time' (Los Angeles Times, 27 May 2011). https://www.latimes.com/archives/la-xpm-2011-may-27-la-na-patriot-act-20110527-story.html. Accessed 12 January 2025
Memmott M (2013) Report: NSA has broken into Google and Yahoo data centers. NPR, 30 October 2013. https://www.npr.org/sections/thetwo-way/2013/10/30/241855353/report-nsa-has-broken-into-google-and-yahoo-data-centers. Accessed 12 Jan 2025
Moore JN (1973) Law and National Security. Foreign Aff 51(2):408
National Crime Agency (n.d.) Money laundering and illicit finance. https://www.nationalcrimeagency.gov.uk/what-we-do/crime-threats/money-laundering-and-illicit-finance. Accessed 30 June 2025
Office of the United Nations High Commissioner for Human Rights (OHCHR) (n.d.) Human rights, terrorism and counter-terrorism Fact Sheet No 32. https://www.ohchr.org/sites/default/files/Documents/Publications/Factsheet32EN.pdf. Accessed 28 Mar 2017
Realuyo CB (2011) Following the terrorist money trail. Connections 10(2):105
Rébé N (2019) Counter-terrorism financing: international best practices and the law. Brill | Nijhoff, Netherlands
Roth J, Greenburg D, Wille S (2004) National commission on terrorist attacks upon the United States: monograph on terrorist financing. https://govinfo.library.unt.edu/911/staff_statements/911_TerrFin_Monograph.pdf. Accessed 28 June 2025
Ryder N (2025) Coordinated terrorist financing—an emerging threat or a glaring omission? Time to rethink the financial war on terrosism. In: Goldbarsht D, de Koker L, Ferrill J (eds) Combating financial crime: intended and unintended consequences. Springer Nature, Switzerland
Statista (2023) risk index score of money laundering and terrorist financing in Nigeria from 2018 to 2023. https://www.statista.com/statistics/1198369/risk-index-score-of-money-laundering-and-terrorist-financing-in-nigeria/. Accessed 11 Jan 2025
Stone R (2008) Textbook on civil liberties and human rights, 7th edn. Oxford University Press, Oxford, UK
U.S. Department of State (n.d.) Foreign terrorist organizations. https://www.state.gov/j/ct/rls/other/des/123085.htm. Accessed 3 Jan 2024

US Department of Treasury (2024) 2024 national terrorist financing risk assessment. https://home.treasury.gov/system/files/136/2024-National-Terrorist-Financing-Risk-Assessment.pdf. Accessed 30 June 2025

Woods MJ (2005) Counterintelligence and access to transactional records: a practical history of USA PATRIOT act section 215. J Natl Secur Law Policy 1:37

Yusuf Sulayman is a lawyer with years of experience teaching and practicing in Nigeria and the UK. He is a Sessional Teaching Fellow at the University of Portsmouth, UK, and an Executive Committee member of the Centre for Cybercrime and Economic Crime, University of Portsmouth. He was previously Programme Coordinator at the Centre for Security and Legal Studies, University of Abuja, Nigeria and consulted for the African Union towards validating key model legal frameworks. He has also worked for non-profits, especially in the education and policy spaces to provide sustainable and replicable solutions to challenging issues that affect mostly the underprivileged members of society. His major research areas are constitutionalism and human rights, with a focus on how normative social influence and judicial attitudes shape institutional performance and affect litigants' rights.

Charities, Non-profit Organisations and the FATF: Testing the Evidence Base and Proportionality of Risk-Based Counter-Terrorist-Financing Regulation

Jeanne Nel

Abstract In March 2024, the Australian Charities and Not-for-profits Commission (ACNC) reaffirmed the prevention of terrorist financing as a principal compliance priority for the 2024–25 fiscal year. This continued emphasis is notable given the absence of documented cases of deregistration for terrorism-related breaches since the ACNC's formation in 2012. This chapter critically interrogates the global regulatory emphasis on nonprofit organisations, arguing that the prioritisation of counter-terrorism financing (CTF) measures, driven largely by Financial Action Task Force (FATF) standards, may lack contextual proportionality and empirical justification. It examines how national regulatory frameworks have increasingly internalised FATF directives, often in the absence of sector-specific risk evidence. Using Australia as a case study, the analysis contends that such regulatory orientation may impose excessive oversight on charitable entities, posing significant barriers to charity and NPO operation and diverting attention from more salient governance concerns.

1 Introduction

In March 2024, the Australian Charities and Not-for-profits Commission (ACNC) released its compliance and enforcement priorities for the 2024–25 financial year. Consistent with previous years, "Preventing the misuse of charities for terrorism purposes" was again identified as an "overarching priority".[1] This ongoing focus is

[1] Australian Charities and Not-for-Profit Commission (ACNC) (2024). The web page has since been updated to reflect regulatory foci through 2026. Misuse of charities for finance terrorism remains an area of attention, but as a compliance review programme. "Overseas aid charities and

J. Nel (✉)
Department of Business Law and Taxation, Monash Business School, Monash University and Financial Integrity Hub (FIH), Melbourne, VIC, Australia
e-mail: Jeanne.Nel@monash.edu

D. Goldbarsht et al. (eds.), *Combating Financial Crime*, Ius Gentium: Comparative Perspectives on Law and Justice 131,
https://doi.org/10.1007/978-3-032-06858-3_6

notable given that minimal instances of Australian charities losing registration for terrorist financing have been reported since the ACNC's establishment in 2012.[2] Why, then, does terrorism remain a central compliance priority for Australia's charity regulator? The answer, it is submitted, lies in the influence of the Financial Action Task Force (FATF) and its global standard-setting on counter-terrorism financing.

This chapter critically examines the global prioritisation of charity and not-for-profit (NPO) regulation, particularly in response to the global combating of financing of terrorism standards of the intergovernmental FATF. It considers whether or not the current regulatory regime in relation to NPOs is appropriately evidence-based and proportionate in its focus on terrorist financing.

To answer this question, the chapter explores how governments have increasingly aligned their combating of financing of terrorism (CTF) regulatory frameworks and priorities with FATF standards and guidance, even in the absence of jurisdiction-specific evidence indicating significant risk. The chapter traces the evolution of Recommendation 8 from its inception in 2001 to the current version adopted in 2023, analysing regulatory developments through the Forty Recommendations, formal FATF guidance, and compliance at both regional and state levels through a risk-based lens. As a case study, the chapter focuses on Australia, where the ACNC has played a central role in implementing and enforcing regulatory measures. Despite limited evidence that the Australian charity sector presents a substantial terrorist financing risk, regulation of the sector to prevent terrorism and terrorist finance has been an enduring ACNC policy priority, displacing more pressing regulatory concerns and imposing disproportionate oversight on organisations that play an essential role in society.

The FATF was established by the G7 in 1989 to recommend steps that they can take to protect their financial systems against money laundering by drug syndicates. Their Recommendations (known as the Forty Recommendations) hardened into international financial standards. More than 200 jurisdictions globally are politically committed to meeting the FATF standards. The FATF implemented and oversees a peer review program evaluating the level of compliance of each jurisdiction. Jurisdictions that are assessed as insufficiently compliant are grey listed and,

terrorist financing" is highlighted under "Issues and alerts" on the regulator's "Areas of concern for charity regulation" page. The page contains information on broader areas of concern the regulator focuses on: ACNC (n.d. -a).

[2] Based on a review of information available in the public domain. Although the Australian Government in 2023 announced funding to enable increased disclosure of the ACNC's regulatory activities, current secrecy and privacy provisions contained in Part 7 of the *Australian Charities and Not-for-profits Act 2012* (Cth) ("ACNC Act") significantly limit the information that the ACNC may publish on compliance cases. The most recent Australian National Risk Assessment refers to "multiple charity registration revocations": AUSTRAC (2024), p. 43. However, the author's review of Australian Gazettes, ACNC and AUSTRAC reports and media reporting to collect aggregate data on ACNC compliance actions and charity revocations connected to terrorism since the ACNC's inception in 2012, could only speculatively identify one possible CTF-related revocation.

in severe cases, may be blacklisted. Such listing holds serious economic risks for the listed country and listing generally results in urgent remedial action to ensure appropriate compliance with the FATF standards.[3]

In 2001, in direct response to the 9/11 attacks on the USA, the FATF's mandate broadened to CTF.[4] In October 2001, weeks after the 9/11 attacks, it adopted a set of Special Recommendations on Terrorist Financing. One Special Recommendation (SR VIII) required countries to "review the adequacy of laws and regulations that relate to entities that can be abused for the financing of terrorism".[5] The Recommendation described non-profit organisations as "particularly vulnerable" and indicated that countries should ensure that they cannot be misused by terrorists.[6]

At the time, operational and fiscal regulation of NPOs varied globally, and few countries had bespoke frameworks in place to regulate their NPO sectors. Regulation tended to focus on tax aspects of charities qualifying for donations that are tax deductible. Casting NPOs and charities as particularly vulnerable to terrorist financing had a profound impact on a post-9/11 world. Countries took swift and broad action to counter this threat by creating new regulatory frameworks for NPOs. In February 2006, [7] the FATF adopted an interpretative note defining NPOs somewhat narrower for purposes of their standards: "The term non-profit organisation or NPO refers to a legal entity or organisation that primarily engages in raising or disbursing funds for purposes such as charitable, religious, cultural, educational, social or fraternal purposes, or for the carrying out of other types of 'good works".[8] By that stage, however, a broader approach has already settled as a compliance response to Special Recommendation VIII, also impacting on NPOs that fell outside FATF's 2006 definition.

In the years since 2001, countries, including Australia, have implemented increasingly extensive oversight of the charity and not-for-profit sector in response to FATF's risk labelling of NPOs and their NPO standards.[9]

A general and consistent criticism raised against the FATF's labelling in 2001 was that no compelling evidence was offered at the time to justify the vulnerability claim.[10] Critics argue that the regulation of NPOs has often been based on broad assumptions of vulnerability, without sufficient nuanced risk analysis or empirical evidence to support the extent of intervention imposed.[11]

[3] The legal nature of the FATF standards and the impact of listing is considered in paragraph 3.3 below.

[4] Mackintosh and Duplat (2013), p. 19.

[5] OECD and FATF (2001), p. 4.

[6] Hayes (2012), p. 30; Romaniuk and Keatinge (2018), p. 268; Barker (2022), p. 76.

[7] FATF (2006); Romaniuk and Keatinge (2018), p. 269.

[8] FATF (2001), p. 21.

[9] McGregor-Lowndes and Wyatt (2017), p. 266; Silver (2019), p. 755.

[10] Romaniuk and Keatinge (2018), p. 268; Barker (2022), p. 77.

[11] Hayes (2012), p. 45.

These concerns prompted the FATF to revise Recommendation 8 in 2016,[12] and again in 2023,[13] to clarify that not all NPOs are inherently at risk of terrorist financing abuse and to highlight its 2006 definition.[14] These revisions acknowledged that the original framing of SR VIII was overly generalised and had led to unintended negative consequences for the NPO sector, including overregulation.[15] Despite these reforms, correcting and winding back more than 20 years of institutionalised overregulation, primarily based on generalised perceptions of the sector's lack of integrity and vulnerability to abuse, has proven difficult.[16]

Further complicating the picture is the FATF's increasing emphasis on localised, context-specific risk-based regulation. Since 2012, countries and their regulated institutions are expected to identify, assess and respond to the actual risks relevant to their jurisdictions and institutions.[17] However, there remains a notable lack of independent, empirical research informing the assessment of the actual scale and nature of the risks FATF's standards seek to address, whether at the global level or within individual jurisdictions such as Australia. In practice, claims of risk continue to be recycled and reproduced without adequate scrutiny, allowing expansive, intrusive regulatory interventions to persist largely unchallenged. This critical gap in the evidence base is especially troubling given the indispensable role that NPOs play in delivering social, economic, and humanitarian outcomes.[18]

In this context, and in the face of ongoing regulatory priorities unsupported by robust risk analysis, this chapter examines the FATF's influence on the global regulation of NPOs through a risk-based regulatory lens, with particular attention to Australia's approach. It explores the history and unintended consequences of the FATF's regulatory approach for NPOs and charities,[19] focusing on the evidence base for the vulnerability claims that informed Special Recommendation VIII. The chapter argues that without a recalibration of the evidentiary foundations underpinning NPO regulation, the FATF's call for proportionate, risk-based oversight will remain largely rhetorical.

---

[12] FATF (2016).

[13] FATF (2023), p. 7.

[14] See notes 7 and 8 the associated main text.

[15] FATF (2023), p. 7. See also FATF (2021).

[16] See part 5.

[17] FATF (2013).

[18] FATF (2006), par 22; Harding (2022), p. 101; Berman (2002), p. 8; Romaniuk and Keatinge (2018), 265; Brass (2022), p. 148; Toepler et al. (2020), p. 649. See also Moldavanova et al. (2023), p. 5; Chitambara et al. (2022), p. 03.

[19] The FATF's 2016 definition of a non-profit organisation is "a legal person or arrangement or organisation that primarily engages in raising or disbursing funds for purposes such as charitable, religious, cultural, educational, social or fraternal purposes, or for the carrying out of other types of 'good works'. In Australia, the charity sector is a subsector of the bigger not-for-profit or for-purpose sector that falls under this definition: Nel de Koker J (2022), p. 770.

2 The Risk-Based Approach and Proportionality

One of the main criticisms of the regulation of NPOs, particularly their classification as a sector "particularly vulnerable[20]" to terrorist financing, is that it lacks proportionality. Comparatively speaking, banks and other financial services providers and for-profit companies, the bulk of which are small and subject to weak corporate governance, would appear as vulnerable to terrorist financing as NPOs.[21]

Critics argue that this approach imposes excessive regulatory burdens on NPOs without sufficient evidence to justify such measures, making it an inefficient and disproportionate response to the actual risk posed.[22] It is, therefore, appropriate to pause to explicate the FATF's risk-based approach to provide context to the argument in this chapter.

Recommendation 1 of the FATF Recommendations requires countries to

> ... identify, assess, and understand the money laundering and terrorist financing risks for the country, and [should] take action, including designating an authority or mechanism to coordinate actions to assess risks, and apply resources, aimed at ensuring the risks are mitigated effectively. Based on that assessment, countries should apply a risk-based approach (RBA) to ensure that measures to prevent or mitigate money laundering and terrorist financing are proportionate to the risks identified.[23]

The aim of the risk-based approach is to ensure the effective and efficient allocation of resources by directing regulatory efforts toward areas of genuine and demonstrable risk.[24] This approach requires governments and regulators to assess and mitigate risks proportionately, rather than applying blanket regulations across entire sectors.[25]

The FATF shifted from a prescriptive, rules-based anti-money laundering (AML) framework to a mandatory risk-based approach (RBA) in 2012. This shift was foreshadowed in 2003, when FATF permitted the optional application of risk-based measures in specific areas.[26] However, with the 2012 revision of the FATF Recommendations, the RBA was embedded as an overarching principle to become an essential foundation for implementing all anti-money laundering and counter-terrorism financing (AML/CTF) measures.[27] Since then, all countries and sectors

---

[20] OECD and FATF (2001), p. 4.

[21] Van Broekhoven et al. argue that the disproportionate approach is evident in the exceptional treatment of the NPO sector, which, since October 2001, has been subject to a dedicated Recommendation that applies exclusively to it (2023), p. 6.

[22] Hayes (2012), p. 45; Van Broekhoven et al. (2023), p. 12; Pavlidis (2023), p. 2; Alsancak and Reimer (2023).

[23] FATF (2012–2025), p. 10.

[24] FATF (2012–2025), p. 31. See also Ferwerda and Reuter (2024), p. 2002.

[25] De Koker and Goldbarsht (2024), p. 6.

[26] Committee of Experts on the Evaluation of Anti-Money Laundering Measures and the Financing of Terrorism (n.d.); Ferwerda and Reuter (2024), p. 2002.

[27] Committee of Experts on the Evaluation of Anti-Money Laundering Measures and the Financing of Terrorism (n.d.). Adopting a compulsory risk-based approach was to a great extent, the result of

are expected to identify, assess, and understand their money laundering and terrorist financing (ML/TF) risks and tailor their regulatory responses accordingly, rather than relying on a rigid, one-size-fits-all compliance model. The approach is reflected in the FATF guidance on assessments of technical compliance with the FATF Recommendations and review of the level of effectiveness of a country's AML/CTF/Counter Proliferation Financing (CPF) system,[28] in particular, in describing the characteristics of an effective system in the context of Immediate Outcome 10:[29]

> The country also has a good understanding of the terrorist financing risks and takes *appropriate and proportionate* actions to mitigate those risks. These include *focused, proportionate and risk-based* measures that prevent the raising and moving of funds through NPOs or methods which are at risk of being misused by terrorists, without unduly disrupting or discouraging legitimate NPO activities.

The context of a risk-based approach is particularly relevant to the regulation of NPOs as a CTF measure. Despite the expectation that regulatory frameworks should be tailored to actual risk levels, NPO advocates have consistently raised concerns that the regulation of the sector remains disproportionate, with risk assessments informing regulatory action lacking sufficient evidence.[30] This chapter shows that NPOs continue to be subject to broad, indiscriminate controls without sufficient risk assessments to justify such measures.[31] This ongoing tension highlights a key challenge in the implementation of the FATF's risk-based approach: while it formally calls for proportionate regulation, in practice, the overregulation of NPOs suggests a persistent failure to fully align policy with the principles of risk-based governance.

3 FATF Standard Setting: Regulating NPOs to Combat Terrorism and Financing of Terrorism: A Potted Version

This chapter focuses on overregulation of the NPO sector in the context of the FATF standards. Section 3, therefore, introduces with an explanation of the FATF standards and standard setting at an international level. Against this backdrop, section 4 discusses member states' responses to the standards and their implementation at a national level, and section 5 considers the impact and consequences of the member state responses to the FATF standards.

The focus of the NPO sector has mainly been on the FATF's action from 2001 onwards and it is sometimes held that there were no significant concerns about

---

global NPO advocacy for proportional, risk-based regulation of the sector: Romaniuk and Keatinge (2018), p. 272.

[28] FATF (2024), p. 161.

[29] "Terrorists, terrorist organisations and terrorist financiers are prevented from raising, moving and using funds". The outcome relates primarily to Recommendations 1, 4, 6 and 8.

[30] Van Broekhoven et al. (2023), p. 7.

[31] See paragraph 5 below.

NPOs and terrorist financing until the FATF adopted SR VIII in the aftermath of the 9/11 attacks.[32] Romaniuk and Keatinge, for example, observed that the 1999 International Convention for the Suppression of the Financing of Terrorism contains a passing reference to charities in its preambular paragraphs and that "The worlds of counterterrorism and civil society organizations were disconnected."[33]

However, rather than a passing reference, the preambular of the 1999 Convention quotes the entire paragraph 3(f) of the UN General Assembly Resolution 51/210 of 17 December 1996, in which the Assembly called upon all States to:

> take steps to prevent and counteract, through appropriate domestic measures, the financing of terrorists and terrorist organizations, whether such financing is direct or indirect, through *organizations which also have or claim to have charitable, social or cultural goals* ... and in particular to consider, where appropriate, adopting regulatory measures to prevent and counteract movements of funds suspected to be intended for terrorist purposes without impeding in any way the freedom of legitimate capital movements and to intensify the exchange of information concerning international movements of such funds.[34]

The paragraph confirms that, already in 1996, there were international concerns about terrorist financing links involving organisations "which also have or claim to have charitable, social or cultural goals".[35] It is accurate though that these concerns were not reflected until October 2001 in the FATF's standards.[36]

Although U.S. President Bill Clinton, then head of the G7, in June 1996 called for a stronger international campaign against crime and terrorism following the Dhahran bombing, referring to the Forty Recommendations as "40 very specific recommendations to combat crime and terror, to increase our efforts to prevent terrorists from committing their crimes",[37] the FATF's formal expansion to include terrorist financing did not occur until after the September 2001 attacks. In direct response to those attacks, the FATF's mandate was broadened to address both terrorist financing generally and, in that context, NPO regulation, reflecting a significant shift in global financial integrity policy.

---

[32] See e.g., Fries (2017), p. 29; De March (2017) p. 125.

[33] Romaniuk and Keatinge (2018), p. 267.

[34] UN General Assembly (1996), p. 5. The wording of paragraph 3(f) replicates the wording of the official document adopted by the group of seven major industrialized countries and the Russian Federation at the Ministerial Conference on Terrorism, held in Paris on 30 July 1996. The sentiments expressed and formulation contained in the FATF Recommendation and Guidance reminds of the expressions in par 3(f). (Emphasis added)

[35] In a self-regulatory context, Hayes (2012), p. 9 points to the World Bank's unpublished Draft Handbook on Good Practices for Laws Relating to NGOs.

[36] The FATF was founded in 1989 by the G7 to examine and develop measures to combat money laundering. Its mandate included analysing money laundering techniques and trends, reviewing national and international responses, and recommending measures to strengthen anti-money laundering efforts: Organisation for Security and Co-operation in Europe (OSCE) (2004), p. 1.

[37] See Apple (1996). It is worth mentioning that the 9/11 Commission Report notes that "Before 9/11, Treasury did not consider terrorist financing important enough to mention in its national strategy for money laundering": National Commission on Terrorist Attacks Upon the United States (2004), p. 186.

This section of the chapter examines the FATF's role in regulating NPOs to combat terrorism and terrorist financing. Therefore, the section commences in 2001, when the FATF's mandate was expanded to include terrorist financing.

The FATF Recommendations were reviewed in 1996, 2003 and 2012 and since 2012 they have been subject to continuous revision.[38] The text of the Recommendation on protecting NPOs from terrorist financing abuse (initially Special Recommendation VIII and since 2012, Recommendation 8) was revised in 2016 and 2022.[39] Before taking a closer look at the adoption and evolution of the NPO standard, it is however important to also position the role of the FATF's guidance notes.

3.1 The Role of Guidance Notes

FATF standards consists of the Recommendations, the Interpretative Notes that detail the Recommendations, and the Glossary that sets out key terms and their definitions. FATF standards are not legally binding, but countries are evaluated for their compliance with the standards, and as mentioned earlier, can be grey listed or blacklisted by the FATF depending on their level of non-compliance and political commitment to meet the standards.[40]

In addition to the standards, the FATF also issues non-binding guidance in the form of Guidance Notes and Best Practice Papers. Each of these components plays a distinct but interrelated role in guiding policymakers, regulators, and regulated entities.

In the context of this chapter, Recommendation 8 provides the overarching standard, the Interpretive Note to Recommendation 8 (INR 8) clarifies its application, and the Guidance Notes and Best Practice Papers offer guidance on effective and proportionate implementation.

INR 8, first adopted by the FATF in February 2006, defines NPOs for purposes of the standard, outlines risk-based approaches to oversight, and emphasises proportionality in regulatory measures. Over time, these notes have been revised to ensure compliance does not disproportionately burden civil society organisations.

The Best Practice Papers (BPPs) offer practical implementation guidance and real-world examples to help countries apply Recommendation 8 effectively. Unlike Interpretive Notes, which set binding interpretative frameworks, BPPs are advisory

[38] See also Nance (2018a), p. 138. A further comprehensive review is currently underway.

[39] Romaniuk and Keatinge (2018), p. 265, noting the 2016 revision as extraordinary: "something it [FATF] had never done before".

[40] The Special Rapporteur on the promotion and protection of human rights and fundamental freedoms while countering terrorism, in 2019, recognising the Forty Recommendations' power to "produce certain legal effects". made nine recommendations aimed at mitigating the reach and impact of "'soft law' counter-terrorism instruments". See Ní Aoláin (2019), pp. 20–22. The legal nature of the FATF standards and the impact of the enforcement mechanisms are considered below in par 3.3.

in nature and illustrate effective methods of compliance, self-regulation, and partnership between governments and NPOs. The BPPs have evolved in response to feedback from civil society, particularly emphasising risk-based approaches and mitigating unintended consequences. In addition, the FATF has also adopted non-binding Guidance Notes that provide guidance on relevant compliance aspects, for example its 2019 Terrorist Financing Risk Assessment Guidance.[41]

Against the backdrop of the FATF Regulatory Framework of standards and guidance the next section considers the evolution of Recommendation 8.

3.2 *The Evolution of Recommendation 8 from 2001 to 2023*

Four key events mark the evolution of Recommendation 8. An evolution that reflects a growing awareness of the importance to balance combating of abuse and protecting the vital role of legitimate NPOs. Its inception in 2001 introduced regulatory measures targeting NPOs as part of FATF's counter-terrorism financing framework. The consolidation of FATF standards in 2012 represented a formal transition, renumbering Special Recommendation VIII (SR VIII) as Recommendation 8. A major revision in 2016 acknowledged the need for a risk-based approach to prevent disproportionate restrictions on the sector. Further refinements in 2023 reinforced the principles of targeted and proportionate regulation, reflecting a growing recognition of the need to balance security objectives with the operational realities of NPOs. The following discussion examines these key developments in greater detail.

3.2.1 The Introduction of Special Recommendation VIII: 2001

Special Recommendation VIII (SR VIII) on NPOs was originally introduced in October 2001 as part of the FATF's Eight Special Recommendations on Terrorist Financing.[42] This set of Special Recommendations included a standard on terrorist financing through the non-profit sector:

> Countries should review the adequacy of laws *and* regulations that relate to entities that can be abused for the financing of terrorism. Non-profit organisations are particularly vulnerable, and countries should ensure that they cannot be misused:
>
> (i) by terrorist organisations posing as legitimate entities;
> (ii) to exploit legitimate entities as conduits for terrorist financing, including for the pur pose of escaping asset freezing measures; and

[41] FATF (2019).

[42] FATF (2002a, n.d.-b). See also Nance (2018b), p 121. In October 2004, Special Recommendation IX, focusing on border declaration or disclosure was added to increase the Special Recommendations (SR) on Terrorism Financing (TF) to nine. See Zolkaflila et al. (2015), p. 536.

(iii) to conceal or obscure the clandestine diversion of funds intended for legitimate purposes to terrorist organisations.[43]

Underscoring the broad support for the Special Recommendations, in February 2002, 65 jurisdictions from the FATF, FATF-style regional bodies, and the Offshore Group of Banking Supervisors, as well as nine international organisations, stressed the need for all countries in the world to adopt and implement the Special Recommendations. The Forum called on all non-FATF jurisdictions to participate in the self-assessment exercise on terrorist financing.[44]

The three outcomes of the FATF extraordinary session in October 2001 were: the decision to expand its mandate to include terrorist financing; the establishment of new international standards for combating terrorist financing (at the time, the Eight Special Recommendations on Terrorist Financing); and the development of a comprehensive Plan of Action to implement the Recommendations.[45] A key objective of the Plan of Action was the completion, in January 2002, by FATF member jurisdictions of the first phase of a self-assessment exercise against the Special Recommendations on combating terrorist financing.[46]

In February 2006 the FATF adopted an Interpretive Note (INR 8) to detail Recommendation 8. INR 8 defined NPOs for purposes of SR VIII:

> The term non-profit organisation or NPO refers to a legal entity or organisation that primarily engages in raising or disbursing funds for purposes such as charitable, religious, cultural, educational, social or fraternal purposes, or for the carrying out of other types of "good works". [47]

"Funds" was also defined:

> The term funds refers to assets of every kind, whether tangible or intangible, movable or immovable, however acquired, and legal documents or instruments in any form, including electronic or digital, evidencing title to, or interest in, such assets, including, but not limited to, bank credits, travellers cheques, bank cheques, money orders, shares, securities, bonds, drafts, letters of credit.[48]

In principle, the definition excluded some NPOs from the scope of its standard but the expansive range of its NPO and "funds" definition signalled to countries to be expansive in their approach.

The INR recognised the impact that this would have on the sector. It acknowledged that NPOs play a vital role in the world economy and in many national economies and social systems, often complementing the activity of the governmental and business sectors in providing essential services, comfort and hope to those in need around the world. However, it then recorded, without specific evidence or data, that the ongoing international campaign against terrorist financing has unfortunately

---

[43] FATF (2002a).

[44] Ibid.

[45] FATF (2002a), p. 2.

[46] FATF (2002a), p. 2.

[47] FATF (2001), p. 21.

[48] FATF (2001), p 4.

demonstrated that terrorists exploit the NPO sector to raise and move funds, provide logistical support, encourage terrorist recruitment or otherwise support terrorist organisations and operations. This misuse, it stated, not only facilitated terrorist activity but also undermined donor confidence and jeopardised the very integrity of NPOs. Therefore, protecting the NPO sector from terrorist abuse is both a critical component of the global fight against terrorism and a necessary step to preserve the integrity of NPOs.

The Interpretive Note recorded the following grounds for vulnerability of NPOs to terrorist financing abuse:

- NPOs enjoy the public trust, have access to considerable sources of funds, and are often cash-intensive.
- Some NPOs have a global presence that provides a framework for national and international operations and financial transactions, often within or near those areas that are most exposed to terrorist activity.
- Depending on the legal form of the NPO and the country, NPOs may often be subject to little or no governmental oversight (for example, registration, record keeping, reporting and monitoring), or few formalities may be required for their creation (for example, there may be no skills or starting capital required, no background checks necessary for employees).

Despite the conditionality and speculative nature of these identified vulnerability factors they are very general observations about a very large and diverse sector.[49] The vulnerability statements did not provide any evidence to support the assessment of the presence and the role of any of these factors in actual terrorist financing at that time. Undoubtedly, they would have played a role in a number of cases but no indication was given as to their actual impact, especially given the size and role of the sector as a whole.

3.2.2 The Consolidation of Recommendations and Mandating a Risk-Based Approach: 2012

Following a comprehensive revision of the FATF Recommendations, in February 2012, the FATF merged the original 40 Recommendations and the 9 Special Recommendations on Terrorist Financing, adopting a single, unified set of 40 Recommendations and new interpretive notes.[50] However, the review was a limited, focused exercise. It was aimed at clarifying the standard and ensuring its continued relevance. Most of the changes made were technical in nature; the high-level principles previously expressed in the Recommendations remained for the most part

[49] The size and diversity of the sector, globally and also in Australia, is widely acknowledged. See Salamon et al. (1999), p. 1; Nehme (2017), p. 159.

[50] International Monetary Fund (IMF) (2012), p. 3.

unchanged. Pertinent to this discussion, the FATF retained the wording when it re-issued SR VIII as Recommendation 8 in 2012.

From a risk-based regulation perspective, however, the revision constituted substantive changes. In particular, relevant to the regulation of NPOs, the 2012 revision introduced a Recommendation that requires countries to identify, assess, and understand the money laundering and terrorist financing risks they face and take appropriate measures to mitigate those risks.[51]

In 2014, the FATF published an analytical typologies paper on the risk of terrorist abuse in non-profit organisations (*Risk of Terrorist Abuse in Non-Profit Organizations*). Based on 102 case studies, along with limited survey and workshop findings, the paper identified four broad categories of NPO vulnerabilities: extended logistical networks; a large, transitory workforce, often reliant on volunteers and donors with minimal vetting and limited due diligence capabilities; high operational capacity, including access to substantial funding sources; and an organisational culture prone to poor decision-making and risk management due to a tendency to trust internal and external stakeholders.[52] Although the analysis helped deepen understanding of the FATF's concerns, it was limited in scope and data.[53] Despite these efforts, NPOs that demonstrated no vulnerabilities still faced the same regulatory requirements, with no reduction in compliance burden or exemptions from FATF-related regulations.

3.2.3 Major Revision of Recommendation 8: 2016 [Whole of Sector to a Subset]

The enduring blanket designation of NPOs as high-risk, despite lacking empirical support, drew persistent criticism from civil-society groups. They argued that it burdened the sector with unnecessary regulation and led to financial exclusion, as banks and other institutions deemed the perceived risk unmanageable.[54] Recognising these concerns, the FATF adopted a substantive revision of Recommendation 8 in 2016. The revised text formally acknowledged that not all NPOs are inherently at risk of terrorist financing abuse and underscored the need for a risk-based approach:[55]

> Countries should review the adequacy of laws and regulations that relate to non-profit organisations which the country has identified as being vulnerable to terrorist-financing abuse. Countries should apply focused and proportionate measures, in line with the risk-based approach, to such non-profit organisations to protect them from terrorist-financing abuse, including:
>
> (a) by terrorist organisations posing as legitimate entities;

[51] Ibid.

[52] FATF (2014).

[53] Center for Global Development (CGD) (2015), p. 37.

[54] Romaniuk and Keatinge (2018).

[55] Ibid.

> (b) by exploiting legitimate entities as conduits for terrorist financing, including for the purpose of escaping asset-freezing measures; and
> (c) by concealing or obscuring the clandestine diversion of funds intended for legitimate purposes to terrorist organisations.[56]

This revision sought to mitigate the unintended consequences of earlier regulatory frameworks by emphasising that restrictions should be proportionate and targeted, rather than applied indiscriminately across the entire sector. The INR, revised along with Recommendation 8, using language such as "focused measures", "identified threats" and "flexibility", clearly conveyed that measures "should not disrupt or discourage legitimate charitable activities".[57] However, this shift in the approach of the FATF and in the text of Recommendation 8 did not provide sufficient relief for the NPO sector. By 2016, regulators and financial institutions were accustomed to view NPOs as especially susceptible to terrorist financing. Many jurisdictions therefore continued to impose sweeping regulations that strayed from FATF's risk-based guidance.[58]

3.2.4 Further Update in the Unintended Consequences Review Program: 2023

In 2021 the FATF undertook a review of the unintended consequences of their standards,[59] including on NPOs.[60] It found that some countries intentionally and unintentionally, continued to incorrectly implement the Standards and justify restrictive legal measures to NPOs in the name of "FATF compliance", including through: intrusive supervision of NPOs; restrictions on NPOs' access to funding and bank accounts; and forced dissolution, de-registration or expulsion of NPOs.

Concerned about these findings, the FATF amended and clarified Recommendation 8 again in 2023 and issued clearer guidance on measures applying to NPOs.

The most recent update in 2023 further reinforced the principles of proportionality, risk sensitivity, and engagement with the NPO sector. This revision placed stronger emphasis on ensuring that counter-terrorism financing measures do not unduly restrict legitimate charitable activities and reaffirmed the need for evidence-based regulation:

> Countries should identify the organisations which fall within the FATF definition of NPOs and assess their terrorist financing risks. Countries should have in place focused, proportionate and risk-based measures, without unduly disrupting or discouraging legitimate NPO activities, in line with the risk-based approach. The purpose of these measures is to protect such NPOs from terrorist financing abuse, including:
>
> (a) by terrorist organisations posing as legitimate entities;

[56] Text of the revised Recommendation 8 adopted by the FATF Plenary (Busan, 22–24 June 2016).

[57] FATF (2012–2019), pp. 52–53.

[58] FATF (2021), Van Broekhoven et al. (2023), p. 14.

[59] CGD (2015), De Koker (2022), p. 266.

[60] FATF (2021).

(b) by exploiting legitimate entities as conduits for terrorist financing, including for the purpose of escaping asset-freezing measures; and
(c) by concealing or obscuring the clandestine diversion of funds intended for legitimate purposes to terrorist organisations.[61]

While these changes represent a growing recognition of the need for more balanced oversight, the challenge remains in translating the FATF's evolving guidance into practical, proportionate regulatory frameworks at the national level. The newer version is a step forward, but it's not a silver bullet for the consequences flowing from the initial versions of Recommendation 8.

Although the FATF's member countries were happy to accept changes in wording, the reality in member countries tells a different tale: that the FATF's initial labelling of NPOs as particularly vulnerable to terrorist financing provides a policy lens that endures. This is evident in the slow shift in messaging around Recommendation 8 in countries such as Australia, South Africa, and New Zealand. The response of an ACNC assistant commissioner in Australian Federal Senate hearings in November 2024 is telling:

> Terrorism and terrorism financing is an established priority area for the ACNC with regards to our compliance priorities.[62]

In South Africa,[63] the Financial Intelligence Centre, the country's financial intelligence unit, has not revised its stance following the FATF's amendment of Recommendation 8 in 2023. Public Compliance Communication (PCC) 41,[64] issued in December 2019, remains unchanged. Although softened with a subdued qualification later in the document, PCC 41 repeatedly states that:[65]

> Non-profit organisations (NPOs) have been identified by the Financial Action Task Force (FATF) as entities which are susceptible to abuse by criminals for terrorist financing and money laundering.

In New Zealand, the *Terrorism Financing Risk Summary*, published by the Department of Internal Affairs in July 2024,9 months after the 2023 FATF plenary changes, included an unqualified statement linking NPOs to terrorist financing and labelling that as "common":

> Abuse of not-for-profit organisations and shell companies are common methods of moving funds for terrorism financing. [66]

[61] FATF (2012–2025).

[62] Australian Federal Parliament, Economics Legislation Committee, 6 November 2024, p. 126 [Sekulic].

[63] For a comprehensive analysis of the South African NPO sector and CFT regulation, see Bissett et al. (2023).

[64] FIC (2019). PCCs are authoritative in nature and must be considered when interpreting the provisions of the FIC Act and assessing compliance with obligations imposed by the FIC Act. It is, therefore, an important regulatory statement.

[65] FIC (2019), p. 2.

[66] Department of Internal Affairs Te Tari Taiwhenua (2024), p. 4.

3.3 FATF Enforcement Mechanisms

To understand the far-reaching effect of the FATF Recommendations requires a brief explanation of the enforcement methods.

The FATF's Recommendations are technically non-binding under international law.[67] However, they are universally recognised as the international standard for the countering of terrorism financing and have been incorporated into UN Security Council resolutions[68] and the Global Counter-Terrorism Strategy.[69] Importantly, it is followed and implemented by all FATF member countries and, through the network of FATF-Style Regional Bodies (FSRBs), by some 200 countries around the world.

The FATF's primary method for enforcing compliance with its Recommendations is the mutual evaluation (MER) process,[70] which involves assessment by trained peer evaluators from member states, including those from the FATF, its FSRBs, the IMF, or the World Bank.[71] The evaluators undertake in-depth, structured assessments of member state compliance according to an established methodology.[72] These evaluation visits produce extensive reports, at the heart of which are the grading of compliance with each of FATF's Recommendations and the effectiveness of AML/CTF/CPF systems according to a linear ranked scale (compliant; largely compliant; partially compliant; non-compliant along with not applicable).[73]

Although the FATF standards constitute 'soft law',[74] the MER process employed by the FATF applies significant peer pressure on member countries that do not effectively implement these standards.[75] Since 2007, through a process of mutual evaluations, the FATF's International Co-operation Review Group (ICRG) has identified, examined, and worked with jurisdictions that were failing to adequately implement AML/CTF measures. A jurisdiction that enters this ICRG review process as a result of a disappointing mutual evaluation has 24 months to collaborate with the FATF or its FATF-style regional body (FSRB) to address the identified deficiencies and avoid possible public identification and formal review by the FATF. Countries that fail to

[67] SOS-Torture Network (2019), p. 2.

[68] E.g., "... and stressing the essential role of the Financial Action Task Force (FATF) in setting global standards for preventing and combatting money laundering, terrorist financing and proliferation financing and its Global Network of FATF-style regional bodies (FSRBs) and taking note with appreciation of the "FATF Consolidated Strategy on Combating Terrorist Financing" and its operational plan". UNSCR 2462. See also Goldbarsht (2017), pp 129-130, 134.

[69] SOS-Torture Network (2019), p. 2.

[70] De Koker (2024), p. 621.

[71] IMF (2011). See also Goldbarsht (2017), p. 133; Kyriakos-Saad (2005).

[72] FATF (n.d.-a). The methodology is reviewed and amended on an ongoing basis. See also Case-Ruchala D, Nance M (2024), p. 3.

[73] FATF (2024), p. 16.

[74] Non-binding, quasi-legal instruments, or mechanisms with formal enforcement mechanisms that is relatively weaker than conventional legal instruments: Jackson (2010), p. 41.

[75] Pavlidis (2023), p. 2.

make progress are included in the list of 'jurisdictions under increased monitoring', also known as the 'grey list'.

Commentaries point to the significant consequences of grey listing for countries,[76] notably isolation from financial markets.[77] A 2016 Center for Global Development Working Paper analysing SWIFT transfers found that grey listing, which occurs when a jurisdiction is placed under increased monitoring due to non-compliance with its standards, results in a 7–10 per cent drop in payment flows to an affected country from the rest of the world.[78] In practice, therefore, FATF and its regional bodies exert considerable influence, pressuring governments to adopt or amend national AML/CTF/CPF legislation.[79]

FATF-related pressure contributes to increasing state regulation of the charity and NPO sector: Given the extent to which countries are encouraged to take remedial action to achieve compliance, the evaluations lead to countries strengthening regulation in the pursuit of compliance rather than in responding to specific local circumstances and proven risk.[80] There appears to be a relationship between FATF's MER enforcement mechanisms and the regulatory measures that member countries adopt to avoid negative evaluations. Australia's regulatory history, particularly in charity regulation, serves as a compelling example of this dynamic. This case study will be further examined in section 4.1, within the context of Recommendation 8.

The next section considers national regulation and associated market responses.

4 State Member Regulatory Compliance and Market Responses

The FATF, through Special Recommendation VIII and Recommendation 8, played a major role driving increased NPO regulation globally.[81] The idea, advanced by a policy-shaping authority of considerable sway, that charities are intrinsically vulnerable has arguably prompted financial institutions to treat NPOS worldwide, irrespective of size, scope or mission as high-risk. This had profound, albeit unintended, consequences for international development and global governance agendas as it impacted on the regulation of NPOs, donations to NPOs, their relationships with stakeholders, and their cross-border activities.[82]

[76] De Koker et al. (2023), p. 81; Maslen (2023) pp. 8–11.

[77] De Koker and Turkington (2016), p. 248.

[78] Collin et al. (2016).

[79] SOS-Torture Network (2019), p. 2.

[80] Community World Service Asia (2020); Van Broekhoven et al. (2023), p. 12.

[81] Breen (2011), p. 949.

[82] Romaniuk and Keatinge (2018), p. 269; Hayes (2012); Sidel (2008), p. 9. In a summary of a cross section of responses to the regulation of NPO's post 9/11, Van der Does de Willebois points out that it caused many donors to be reluctant to donate to NPOs that operate in environments or countries associated with terrorist activity, some governments to impose unduly restrictive legislation, effec-

4.1 NPO and Charity Sector-Specific Regulatory Measures

A raft of countries established bespoke charity or NPO regulators post-9/11.[83] Several who had regulators in place introduced or strengthened charity oversight mechanisms in response to global CTF measures.[84]

Since 2014, the effectiveness of a country's actions to prevent terrorists from abusing the NPO sector was inter alia measured by '...the extent to which the country implemented a targeted approach, conducted outreach, and exercised oversight in dealing with NPOs that are at risk from the threat of terrorist abuse *without disrupting legitimate NPO activities*.'[85] However, a review of regulatory approaches of bespoke charity regulators provides insight into how the risk-based approach in place since 2012 in theory has had little effect on charity regulators' compliance foci and the narrative of charities and NPOs' vulnerability to terrorist financing abuse.

The compliance foci of such charity regulators evidence their disproportionate approach in this regard, showing a consistent prioritisation of terrorist finance in spite of an absence of evidence indicating it as a matter of concern. This is reinforced by continuing media and other public statements that, even after the 2023 changes to Recommendation 8, enforce the message that charities and NPOs lends themselves to being abused to support terrorist activity.

Hayes highlighted in 2012 that research revealed a direct link between FATF country evaluation reports and new national NPO regulations.[86] The Australian Charity and Not-for-profit Commission only came into being in December 2012, well after the completion of the research. However, when the pattern of regulatory attention afforded to CTF measures between 2012 and 2025 is reviewed, a clear correlation with mutual evaluations is discernible. It provides a strong case study.

---

tively seeking to control the activities and the funding of NPOs and alienated NPO's in the fight against terrorism and extremism and prevented humanitarian assistance: Van der Does de Willebois (2010), pp. 11–12.

[83] Examples include New Zealand (The Charities Commission (now the Charities Services under the Department of Internal Affairs) was established in 2005), Ireland (Charities Regulatory Authority (CRA) established by the *Charities Act 2009*), Singapore (Charity Act reforms and the establishment of a Charity Commissioner in the mid 2000s) and Malaysia (*Anti-Money Laundering and Anti-Terrorism Financing Act (AMLA) 2001*). See also Barker (2022), p. 76.

[84] E.g., the Charity Commission for England and Wales, existed before 9/11, but its powers were expanded significantly under the *Charities Act 2006* (UK) due to global counter-terrorism pressures. Similarly, the Canada Revenue Agency (CRA) bolstered scrutiny of charities' international activities. In the US, the IRS Exempt Organizations Division continued its oversight, but post-9/11 reforms included the *USA PATRIOT Act (2001)* and *Executive Order 13224*, which targeted charitable organizations suspected of links to terrorism.

[85] FATF (2013), p. 123.

[86] Hayes (2012).

4.1.1 Case Study: Australia

The ACNC, the national regulator for all charitable and not-for-profit entities (other than those that are government entities),[87] was established in December 2012 when the *Australian Charities and Not-for-profits Act 2012* (Cth) *('ACNC Act')* came into effect.[88] The objects of the *ACNC Act* are to maintain, protect, and enhance public trust and confidence in the Australian not-for-profit sector,[89] to support and sustain a robust, vibrant, independent and innovative Australian not-for-profit sector, [90] and to simplify and streamline regulation by reducing 'unnecessary regulatory obligations on the Australian not-for-profit sector'. [91]

In contrast to many other national regulators, the ACNC was not established in sole response to Special Recommendation VIII.[92] However, membership of the FATF and compliance with Recommendation VIII were certainly raised as a contributory argument for the regulator's establishment.[93] FATF compliance is also frequently mentioned in the ACNC's annual and compliance reports.[94]

Under the ACNC Act, the ACNC has various regulatory powers, including enforcement powers. The enforcement powers under Part 4–2 of the Act include the following:

- issuing a formal warning to a registered charity;[95]
- giving a direction to a registered charity;[96]
- accepting an enforceable undertaking from a registered charity, [97] and applying to a designated court for the enforcement of an undertaking;[98]
- applying for an injunction which relates to a registered charity;[99]

[87] Importantly, although the name of the *ACNC Act 2012* (Cth) indicates regulation of the broader not-for-profit sector, the reach of ACNC regulation is currently restricted to registered charities. The *Australian Charities and Not-for-profits Act 2012* (Cth) (*'ACNC Act')* charges the Commissioner with the responsibility to endorse and register not-for-profit entities and established a regulatory framework that can be extended to all not-for-profit entities in the future, initially, and that is still the case, the Commission only registers charities: Nel de Koker (2022), p. 768. See also Goldbarsht (2017), p. 147; ACNC (2023).

[88] Gilchrist (2014), p. 60; Aroney and Turnour (2017), p. 447.

[89] *ACNC Act 2012* (Cth) s 15-5(1)(a).

[90] Ibid s 15-5(1)(b).

[91] Ibid s 15-5(1)(c).

[92] Seibert (2016), p. 131.

[93] Hansard 2012; ACNC (2014), p 6. See also Pascoe (2017), p. 211; Barker (2022), p. 76; McGregor-Lowndes and Wyatt (2017), p. 266.

[94] ACNC (2014), pp. 6, 44.

[95] *ACNC Act 2012* (Cth) s 80-5.

[96] *ACNC Act 2012* (Cth) s 85-5.

[97] *ACNC Act 2012* (Cth) s 90-10.

[98] *ACNC Act 2012* (Cth) s 90-15.

[99] *ACNC Act 2012* (Cth) s 95-15.

- suspending or removing a responsible person;[100] and
- appointing one or more acting responsible people to replace a suspended or removed responsible person.[101]

Pertinent to the regulation of charities to combat terrorist financing, the Commissioner may revoke (cancel) a charity's registration if the Commissioner reasonably believes that a registered charity:[102]

- is not entitled to registration;[103]
- has provided information that was false or misleading in a material particular in its application for registration;[104]
- has contravened the ACNC Act or has not complied with a Governance Standard (or is more likely than not to contravene or not comply in the future);[105] or
- has a trustee in bankruptcy, a liquidator, or a person appointed, or authorised, under an Australian law to manage its affairs because it is unable to pay all its debts as and when they become due and payable.[106]

The impact of FATF membership and MERs and the weight of the FATF Recommendations are well illustrated by the Australia's national charity regulator's treatment of NPO regulation to combat CTF. The regulator's reports frequently highlight Australia's status as a founding member of the FATF which develops and promotes international AML/CTF/CPF standards. The reports also underscore that FATF members are required to ensure that non-profit organisations cannot be misused to generate, be conduits for, or conceal resources intended to finance terrorist activity.[107]

A review of the ACNC reports and compliance activities since 2012 shows compliance and enforcement priorities that are more a response to FATF risk guidance and the FATF MER than to actual findings of the domestic risk assessment.[108] This

[100] *ACNC Act 2012* (Cth) ss 100-10–100-15.

[101] *ACNC Act 2012* (Cth) ss 100-30.

[102] A charity may also request to have its registration revoked: *ACNC Act 2012* (Cth) s 35-10(1)(e).

[103] *ACNC Act 2012* (Cth) s 35-10(1)(a).

[104] *ACNC Act 2012* (Cth) s 35-10(1)(b).

[105] *ACNC Act 2012* (Cth) s 35-10(1)(c).

[106] *ACNC Act 2012* (Cth) s 35-10(1)(d).

[107] See e.g., ACNC (2014), pp. 6, 44, 94.

[108] Privacy regulations for ACNC-regulated entities hinder comprehensive reviews of compliance measures. While the ACNC does disclose certain findings, such as revoking a charity's registration, issuing warnings or directions, or accepting enforceable undertakings, statutory secrecy provisions prevent it from revealing details about individual complaints. This chapter is primarily based on information about the ACNC's compliance and enforcement statements and activities that had been published in the ACNC's annual reports, compliance reports, Charity Reports and on the ACNC website between 2013 and January 2025.

is evident in three ways: the stated compliance foci, the compliance activities, and the language and attention afforded in reporting to terrorist financing.[109]

4.1.1.1 Stated Compliance Priorities in Standalone Compliance Reports[110]

The stated compliance priorities in the Compliance reports since 2012 reflect an escalation of attention to terrorist financing that corresponds with the MER and FATF compliance feedback rather than evidence of abuse of NPOs for terrorist financing. The compliance foci stated in the inaugural ACNC compliance report correspond directly with the objects of the *ACNC Act*. It highlights its compliance priorities as:

> to raise awareness of governance standards and regulatory obligations, facilitate the lodgment of 2013 and 2014 Annual Information Statements, and address concerns involving serious non-compliance.[111]

The report analysed concerns raised from the commission's establishment in December 2012 through December 2014. It indicated that 1307 complaints (concerns) were lodged in that period, most commonly from members of the public, about misuse of charitable resources, fraud or financial mismanagement, lack of transparency, harm to beneficiaries, and sham charities and fundraising fraud.[112] Explicating the regulator's focus on charities operating overseas, the report echoes the sentiments raised in the 2014 AUSTRAC Report that charities constitute a "potential channel for terrorism financing".[113]

According to the 2012–14 Compliance Report, by early 2015, nine charities (0.014% of registered charities) had their registration revoked following a compliance investigation.[114] Notably, although the *ACNC Act* specifically cites "characterisation as engaging in, or supporting terrorist activities" as a basis for non-registration

[109] Developing a complete and accurate picture of compliance outcomes is further hindered by the fact that from 2018, the ACNC shifted away from detailed stand-alone compliance reports towards integrating compliance insights into other publications and sector updates, including annual reports, commissioner columns and sector insights reports.

[110] Until 2019, the ACNC released bespoke Compliance Reports that analysed its compliance and enforcement activities. Drawing on aggregated, de-identified data, these reports illuminated the ACNC's work and highlighted its compliance priorities. The last standalone report was the 2018 Charity Compliance Report, published in 2019. Since then, compliance reporting has been folded into other publications, the Australian Charities Report, the ACNC Annual Report, and periodic compliance reviews, rather than issued separately.

[111] ACNC (2015b), p. 4.

[112] ACNC (2015b), p. 8.

[113] ACNC (2015b), p. 18. The report cited: AUSTRAC (2014).

[114] ACNC (2015b), p. 7. This chapter focuses on revocations as a measure of terrorist financing-related compliance outcomes because the *ACNC Act 2012* s 35-1(a) determines that the Commissioner may revoke an entity's registration under the Act if the Commissioner inter alia reasonably believes that the entity is not being entitled to registration. The registration eligibility requirements, in turn, provide that organisations that are characterised by an Australian Government

or revocation,[115] and expected in view of the stated public interest, the report does not mention any instances of revocation following a finding of terrorist financing. Nevertheless, the report forecasts the 2015–16 additional compliance priorities to include "charities operating overseas".[116]

The 2015–16 report, published in 2017, does not reflect any significant change in concerns/complaints received or compliance outcomes with similar recurring concerns with nine compliance revocations across the reporting period (0.017%). Again, the report does not mention revocations owing to terrorist financing. However, notwithstanding the absence of terrorist financing-related revocations, in announcing the 2017–19 compliance foci, the 2015–16 report flags terrorism as a top compliance focus for the 2017–2019 period.[117]

In 2018, the *Charity Compliance Report 2017* recorded 7 charity registration revocations following a review of entitlement.[118] The report indicates that the focus on money laundering and terrorist finance abuse through participation in the 2017 National Risk Assessment of Australia's not-for-profit organisations enabled the regulator to "identify a number of registered charities *at risk of misuse* for terrorism financing or money laundering".[119] However, the report does not mention specific compliance outcomes following on actual misuse for terrorism financing or money laundering. Continuing the trend of previous compliance reports, the report announces that the 2018 compliance foci include misuse of a charity for terrorist purposes or to foster extremism as a top priority.[120]

The stated focus on prevention of terrorist financing abuse despite an absence of compliance outcomes that indicate terrorist financing as an issue was solidified in 2019. The 2018 Compliance Report, published in 2019, announced that "misuse of a charity for terrorist purposes or to foster extremism" is "so detrimental to trust and confidence in the charity sector that [they] are always considered a priority".[121] By 2018, the number of compliance revocations had increased. However, no reports were published, and compared against Australian Federal Police statistics, it appears no charities' status were revoked for engaging in terrorist financing by 2018.[122]

---

agency as engaging in or supporting terrorist or other criminal activities, are ineligible for registration under the *ACNC Act*: *ACNC Act 2012* s 25-5(3)(d).

[115] *ACNC Act* s 25-5(3)(d).

[116] ACNC (2015b), p. 17; Silver (2019), p. 759, contends that the focus is a response to the 2015 FATF MER criticising Australia for its inadequate monitoring of cross-border charity.

[117] ACNC (2017b), p. 21.

[118] ACNC (2018), p. 5.

[119] ACNC (2018), p. 15.

[120] ACNC (2018), p. 23.

[121] ACNC (2019b), p. 6.

[122] The ACNC collaborates with agencies like AUSTRAC and the Australian Federal Police to monitor and address risks related to terrorism financing within the charity sector. Given the privacy provisions in the *ACNC Act* that precludes the ACNC from publicly disclosing such information, the author searched AFP records for the period 2012 to 2024.

The 2018 Compliance Report was the last standalone publication by the ACNC. Since then, compliance actions and outcomes have been integrated into Annual Reports and other publications. However, as highlighted in the chapter introduction, and as the discussion in the next sections show, the emphasis on combating the misuse of charities for terrorist financing continues, even though the corresponding compliance outcomes have not yet been fully reflected.

4.1.1.2 Compliance Activities and Outcomes

The regulator highlights that its compliance and enforcement approach is risk-based and proportionate.[123] However, when reviewing the compliance and enforcement reports, a notable dissonance emerges between the evidence of charity misuse for terrorism, the actual enforcement outcomes, and the regulator's stated priorities. Despite the extremely low number of revocations, an unavoidable outcome of non-compliance with terrorism laws, the regulator continues to focus on charities operating overseas, terrorist financing, and collaboration with other agencies.

At the end of 2014, the ACNC participated in a CTF-related project with other government agencies and reviewed close to 7615 charities that "have international connections".[124] The review identified 130 (1.71%) charities that required closer consideration with 13 (0.17% of the 7.615 initially reviewed) resulting in an ongoing review. Notwithstanding this negligible outcome, "charities operating overseas" was included as a compliance focus area for 2015–2016.[125]

From July 2016, the ACNC collaborated with AUSTRAC and the ATO to complete a national risk assessment of Australia's not-for-profit sector.[126] The risk-assessment found that the key threats facing the NPO sector are largely fraud and theft of resources, with a low level of money laundering. The report statistics reflected that less than 0.4% of the funds sent overseas between 2012 and 2016 were flagged as suspicious and found that the extent of suspected terrorism financing involving NPOs in Australia is limited. Nevertheless, it doubled down on the assumption that charities are somehow innately at risk of terrorism financing misuse.[127] This approach is echoed in the regulator's stated compliance foci for 2017–19,

[123] ACNC (n.d.b).

[124] ACNC (2017b), p 15. It is worth mentioning that the Canadian National Security Intelligence Review Agency (NSIRA), reviewing the Canada Revenue Agency's (CRA) Review and Analysis Division (RAD), found that RAD, using a similar risk indicator, "conducting activities in or close to a foreign high-risk jurisdiction", does not have an evidence-based method for validating risk indicators: NSIRA(2025). Davis (2025) comments that such an approach could be described as "vibes-based".

[125] ACNC (2015b), p. 17.

[126] ACNC (2017b), p. 15.

[127] AUSTRAC (2017), p. 33.

which elevated "misuse of a charity for terrorist purposes or to foster extremism" to the second-listed priority.[128]

The 2018 Compliance Report, citing the significant risk misuse poses to public trust and confidence in the charitable sector, established charity misuse for terrorism or extremism as an ongoing compliance priority.[129] Confirming the influence of the 2014 MER and general FATF risk guidance,[130] misuse of charities for terrorism remains an "enduring" or "overarching" priority,[131] but it is less in the limelight than in 2015–2018, the years just following the MER.

4.1.1.3 The Narrative and Focus on Terrorism Financing in Reporting

When one considers the language used and attention afforded to terrorist finance in the specific Compliance Reports until 2018, the reports reflect a narrative of responding to FATF evaluation feedback from the fourth round of MERs in 2014 and 2015. Whereas the 2012–2014 ACNC Compliance Report contains nine references to terrorism and terrorist, the 2015–2016 Compliance Report, published in 2017, reflects a marked increase to 28 references. However, none of the references are in relation to actual findings of charity terrorist financing activity. The report explicates the ACNC's role in supporting FATF compliance in several bespoke sections of the report,[132] and highlights "proactively identifying risk".[133] The 2017 compliance report, published in 2018, peaks with 37 references to terrorist and terrorism. As with the 2015–16 report, the words appear in relation to the ACNC's role in supporting FATF compliance and proactive compliance activities. The last bespoke compliance report, the 2018 compliance report, published in 2019, contains fewer references, only 17. However, none of these mentions relate to a compliance outcome following funding for terrorist activity.

Looking at the annual Reports, the inaugural ACNC Annual Report,[134] a report where one would expect a clear mention of the establishment and the role of the regulator in relation to compliance with Recommendation 8, does not explicate the relationship nor mention the FATF. The report contains a single reference to combating terrorist financing—referencing an invitation to contribute on a related UN Forum.[135]

---

128 ACNC (2017b), p. 21; ACNC (2018), p. 17.

129 ACNC (2019b), p. 6.

130 FATF, APG (2015).

131 ACNC (2024).

132 ACNC (2017b), pp. 15, 22.

133 ACNC (2017b), pp. 15, 22. The case study focused on a charity that provides humanitarian aid into a country "considered to be high-risk for terrorism financing". However, the regulator's investigation and the report fall short of indicating a factual finding of terrorist financing: p. 27.

134 ACNC (2013).

135 ACNC (2013), p. 40.

However, from 2014, mentions of terrorism, terrorist financing, and the FATF in the Annual Reports increase. The *ACNC Annual Report 2013-14* introduces with a mention of the ACNC's role to, "like charity regulators in other countries", contribute to Australia's efforts to combat terrorist financing in compliance with international obligations under FATF.[136]

The lack of evidence and the dissonance between evidence and regulatory attention is underscored by two subsequent paragraphs in the report: under the section on top compliance issues in 2013–14, the report lists the top four compliance breaches as inappropriate use of charitable funds (funds used to purchase private assets for responsible person), lack of accountability to members (e.g., failing to convene as required in the constitution), responsible persons failing in their duties (e.g., failing to declare conflict of interest, or allowing the entity to operate while insolvent), and involvement with criminal activity (e.g., instances of employee theft due to governance failures).[137] No mention is made of terrorist financing. Despite the absence of instances of abuse of charities for terrorist financing, the following paragraph, headed "Safeguarding charities against terrorism financing", highlights Australia's status as a founding member of the FATF and states that the creation of the ACNC, and specifically the Register and compliance function, contributes to Australia's compliance with FATF Recommendation 8, which requires FATF members to ensure that non-profit organisations cannot be misused to generate, be conduits for, or conceal resources intended to finance terrorist activity.[138] This sentiment is repeated in the concluding paragraphs of the report.[139]

The *ACNC Annual Report 2014-15* dedicates a whole page to addressing the risk of terrorism financing.[140] Notably, the discussion introduces with an acknowledgement of a 2014 AUSTRAC report that flagged charities as a potential channel for terrorism financing. Although the AUSTRAC report qualified its finding, highlighting that terrorism financing affects only a "handful of charities and NPOs", not the entire sector, the ACNC report merely stated that while the incidence of terrorism financing through charities was low, the risk remains high.[141]

The placement of text in the *ACNC Annual Report 2015-16* again highlights the regulator's focus on terrorist-finance in relation to non-compliance without factual evidence: in the section on dealing with non-compliance, the statement reporting that the charity status of 10 organisations were revoked "following assessments of concerns", is directly followed by a paragraph highlighting Australia's membership of FATF, noting FATF reporting that there is a high risk of charitable funds being misused for terrorism financing, money laundering, or other non-charitable

136 ACNC (2014), p. 6.

137 ACNC (2014), p. 44.

138 ACNC (2014), p. 44.

139 ACNC (2014), p. 94.

140 Notably, a 2015 report by the Financial Action Task Force (FATF) noted that Australia had not prosecuted all types of terrorist financing offences, including the collection of funds for terrorist purposes: FATF, APG (2015).

141 ACNC (2015a), p. 52; AUSTRAC (2014), p 15.

purposes.[142] The report then highlights its collaboration with other government agencies to review close to 8000 charities that reported sending funds overseas, and that the regulator pro-actively reviewed 129 overseas operating charities. In addition, the report notes that following the proactive review, 10% of the 129 organisations were subject to ongoing review.[143] That would amount to 13 NPOs or 0.02%, of the approximately 55,000 charities then registered in Australia.

The *ACNC Annual Report 2016–17* continued the focus on terrorist financing. However, as with previous reports, the bulk of the use is in the context of FATF membership and compliance with the Recommendations.[144] Notably, the report contains a case study of a *mero motu* investigation of a large charity that provided humanitarian aid and relief in a country considered to be high-risk for extremism and terrorism financing. The charity's registration was revoked, but the report did not mention financing of terrorist activity as grounds for the revocation.[145]

Prioritising terrorism and affording attention to the enforcement of FATF standards between 2015 and 2017 paid off. The FATF re-rated Australia's compliance from non-compliant on Recommendation 8 to largely compliant in November 2018.[146]

After 2018, references to terrorism and terrorist declined from two in the 2018–19 Annual Report but none in the subsequent years, including in the most recent report of 2024. The 2018–19 Annual Report refers to FATF 3 times in one section that explains FATF and Australia's membership obligations.[147] Annual reporting after 2018 does not refer to the FATF at all.

5 The Impact and Consequences/Impact for NPOS and Charities

AML/CTF-related measures, on a daily basis, impede mission delivery of NPOs across the spectrum, be it peacebuilding, humanitarian, development, or organisations that support civil and human rights. The impact of the AML/CTF measures is mainly observed in two areas: human rights and financial exclusion. Sections 5.1 and 5.2 consider these areas in more detail.

[142] ACNC (2016), p. 11.

[143] Ibid.

[144] ACNC (2017a), pp. 60, 68.

[145] ACNC (2017a), p. 57.

[146] FATF (2018), p. 6.

[147] ACNC (2019a), p. 54.

5.1 *Disproportionate Regulation (Shrinking Civil Society Space, Denying Human Rights and Impeding Humanitarian Aid)*

In the aftermath of 9/11, countries implementing measures responding to Recommendation 8, often went beyond the FATF's scope and imposed more general NPO regulation to mitigate terrorist financing risks.[148] Sue Barker points out that countries' responses to 9/11 contribute to the backsliding of democracy. She explains that Recommendation VIII cast doubt over the entire nonprofit sector, prompting a contentious shift in governmental attitudes toward independent civil society organisations. Justifying a transition from passive registration systems to more active regulatory measures, the Recommendation resulted in broad, sweeping restrictions that significantly strained relations and eroded trust between governments and civil society.[149] This has had significant negative consequences for international development and global governance agendas as it impacted on donations to NPOs, their relationships with stakeholders and their cross-border activities.[150]

In many instances, countries overregulate in an attempt to avoid grey listing.[151] In some it appears that jurisdictions intentionally abuse the Recommendation to justify impeding civil rights.[152] In 2019, the Torture and Terrorism Working Group observed that

> In the name of counter-terrorism and security, they are arrested, arbitrary detained, prosecuted, sentenced to heavy prison terms, attacked, threatened and harassed, for documenting human rights violations and calling on their governments to fulfil their legal obligation to respect the fundamental rights of all citizens.[153]

The impact of the FATF Recommendations on Combatting Financing of Terrorism on human rights and civil society was evident within a decade of the 2001 Special Recommendations. Professor Martin Scheinin, the first Special Rapporteur on the

[148] Romaniuk and Keatinge (2018), p. 266.

[149] Barker (2023), p. 78.

[150] Romaniuk and Keatinge (2018), p. 269. Joel Charny (2019) highlights that the Recommendation's effect on the ability of humanitarian organisations to reach people in need, is and an unrecognized consequence of the "war on terror".

[151] Ní Aoláin (2019).

[152] Norwegian Refugee Council (NRC) (2018). The SOS-Torture Network (2019) cites the *Foreign Contribution (Regulation) Act 42 of 2010 (FCRA)* (India), as a law widely recognised as draconian, employed to stifle civil society and the NPO sector in India. The 2010 revisions of the Act were justified as required under FATF standards. The report also conveys how Bangladesh, a founding member of a FATF-style regional body, the Asia/Pacific Group (APG), responded to a critical 2009 MER to illustrate how Recommendation 8 is used to stifle free expression and severely restrict the work of civil society. See also Rutzen (2015), p. 31. Hayes (2012), p. 10, contends that the FATF Recommendations may have inadvertently assisted to provide repressive governments with broad powers to monitor and suppress charitable and non-governmental organisations. The article cites several specific examples of jurisdictions with exceptionally restrictive NPO regimes.

[153] SOS-Torture Network (2019), p. 1. See also Barker (2022), p. 78.

promotion and protection of human rights and fundamental freedoms while countering terrorism, a position established by the UN Commission on Human Rights in 2005,[154] raised concerns about the broad wording of anti-terrorism measures. He noted that these measures could be used to inhibit the rights to freedom of association and peaceful assembly.[155]

Since 2005, the Special Rapporteur on the promotion and protection of human rights and fundamental freedoms while countering terrorism have delivered multiple reports highlighting the negative impact of the unintended consequences of FATF Recommendations, in particular Recommendation 8 on human rights. In addition, humanitarian aid organisations' reports highlight how combatting terrorist financing through NPO regulation impedes humanitarian aid and risks lives.[156]

Reports of jurisdictions that employ regulatory measures justified as FATF Recommendation 8 compliance to clamp down civil society and associated breaches of human rights after 2012 when FATF adopted a compulsory risk-based approach and the 2016 revision of Recommendation 8, abound.[157] These reports underscore that the changes to Recommendation 8 had limited effect on the unintended consequences that flowed and continues to flow from the initial Recommendation in 2001. The question is whether the jurisdictions will continue to do so with FATF endorsement post the fourth round of evaluations.

5.2 Denial of Services, Financial Exclusion, Impacting Vulnerable Groups and Creating a Risk of Terrorist Abuse

Internationally, financial regulators and supervisors are stepping up regulation and supervision of financial institutions, leading to an increasing number of large fines.[158] To avoid such fines and the corresponding reputational damage, financial institutions carry out extensive due diligence on their customers to fulfil compliance requirements. These institutions, perceiving all NPOs as vulnerable to financial crime, tend to apply general commercial, if not more stringent, tests and risk assessment processes to the very different operating models of NPOs.[159] Consequently, NPOs face de risking (denials of services), limiting the role of NPOs in facilitating the attainment of the SDGs.[160] Van Broekhoven et al. observe that

---

[154] Romaniuk and Keatinge (2018), p. 274.

[155] Scheinin (2006).

[156] Mackintosh and Duplat (2013), NRC (2025). See also Rutzen (2015), Pavlidis (2023), p. 4.

[157] The Centre for Financial Crime and Security at the Royal United Services Institute (RUSI) examined 126 cases of "authoritarian abuses of the FATF standards" in 34 countries between 2013 and 2023: Reimer (2024).

[158] Duke Law International Human Rights Clinic and Women Peacemakers Program (2017), p. 27.

[159] Charity and Security Network (2017).

[160] Charity and Security Network (2019), Duke Law International Human Rights Clinic and Women Peacemakers Program (2017), p. 28; Human Security Collective, European Center for Not-for-Profit Law (2018); NRC (2025), p. 7.

> the focus on NPOs as being inherently more vulnerable to TF has trickled down into every facet of the financial-services industry.[161]

In the UK, the Charity Commission reported in March 2024 that 42% of trustees responding to the regulator's annual sector survey reported experiencing bad service.[162] In particular, 18% had found difficulty trying to open a new bank account, 15% found it challenging to comply with identity requirements set by their bank, and 6% experienced account freezes or blocking in the year between March 2023 and 2024.[163] Charities and NPOs in New Zealand frequently report being debanked, including owing to financial regulation standards, which led to a proposed legislation that require banks to provide financial services to consumers unless there is a "valid and verifiable commercial reason" for refusing or withdrawing services.[164]

Debanking adds another layer of complexity to the delivery of humanitarian aid. In Syria, the Norwegian Refugee Council reported in 2018 that banks refusing to provide services for organisations owing to their concerns about counter terrorist financing regulation represented another major hurdle to principled humanitarian action.[165] In January 2025, more than a year after the 2023 changes to Recommendation 8, the Muslim Charities Forum (MCF) reported that 68% of Muslim charities reported difficulties opening bank accounts, 42% experienced a complete withdrawal of banking services, and 42% also had significant challenges with transferring funds.[166] Responding to the UK Charity Commission's report on Banking Services to Charities and NPOs, Charity Finance Group explained that

> When banking services are inaccessible or fall short, people are forced to find alternative ways to manage money.[167]

The NRC's 2018 report made the link between debanking and growth in informal and unregulated payment methods clear. The report showed that organisations report that they are unable to transfer money to certain areas, including parts of Syria, causing them to use informal, unregulated methods, such as hawala or cash-carrying.[168]

---

[161] Van Broekhoven et al. (2023), p. 8. For a discussion of recent UK, Australian and New Zealand court decisions on de-banking, including the closure of charity accounts, see Styles (2025).

[162] Preston (2024).

[163] Charities Commission (2024).

[164] Financial Markets (Conduct of Institutions) Amendment (Duty to Provide Financial Services) Amendment Bill, New Zealand. See also Styles (2025).

[165] NRC (2018).

[166] Muslim Charities Forum (2025), Taaffe-Maguire (2025).

[167] Preston (2024).

[168] NRC (2018).

6 Where's the Evidence of the Risk?

As mentioned earlier, since the inception or the NPO-specific Recommendations, NPO advocates pointed to the poor, if not non-existent, empirical basis on which the Recommendations and subsequent post 9/11 CTF measures were grounded.[169] Commenting on the Special Recommendations adopted post 9/11, Sue Barker highlights that evidence that the NFP sector was in any way more likely to be exploited by terrorists than any other sector is lacking.[170]

Increasingly, the absence of evidence to justify these actions as proportionate to risk is striking. Already prior to 2012, international bodies and government agencies, including the US Treasury, acknowledged that NPOs may not pose a big a risk as initially portrayed.[171] In 2015, the US Treasury recognised self-radicalised, low-cost "lone-wolf" plots as a priority terrorist-financing concern, and warned that their small budgets blunt the effectiveness of classic counter-terrorist-finance tools.[172] The *2024 National Terrorist Financing Risk Assessment* identified "lone actors", self-radicalised individuals inspired by ISIS, al-Qaida or domestic violent-extremist ideologies, who plan and carry out attacks without organisational direction, as a primary domestic terrorism danger.[173] The report explicated that such individuals' operations are largely self-financed with small sums drawn from legal sources such as wages or personal savings.[174] The sums rarely trigger suspicious-activity alarms, rendering traditional asset-freezing and transaction-monitoring tools ineffective.[175]

Returning to Australia as a case study, the Australian Charity Regulator's compliance priorities provide an exemplar of a regulatory focus that is not based on evidence. The regulator frequently mentions the risk-based approach:

> The ACNC uses a risk-based approach to allocate its compliance resources in addressing complaints about charities.[176]

However, since its inception, charities operating overseas (with an "international connection") were a focus. A focus that remains in 2025, 13 years later. This in the clear absence of evidence that these charities are systemically misused for terrorist financing as illustrated by the responses during the 2024 Senate Hearings. The Deputy Commissioner reported at the hearings that 11 concerns were raised in the

---

[169] See paragraph 2.

[170] Barker (2023), p. 77.

[171] Hayes (2012), p. 29. In particular, in 2009, the United Nations Counter-Terrorism Implementation Task Force (CTITF) highlighted the lack of an evidentiary baseline to define the problem and the principle that oversight of NPOs should be proportional to the risk of abuse: CTITF Working Group (2009).

[172] US Department of the Treasury (2015), p. 45. A concern echoed by FATF (2015). See also Keatinge and Keen (2017).

[173] US Department of the Treasury (2024), p. 8.

[174] US Department of the Treasury (2024), p. 4.

[175] US Department of the Treasury (2024), p. 15.

[176] E.g., ACNC (2017), p. 16.

preceding year about 26 registered charities. Stated as a proportion, concerns were raised with the Regulator about 0.04% of charities registered with the ACNC. Of these, 11 concerns were related to links to terrorist organisations or activities associated with terrorist financing. No information was provided on how many organisations were connected to these 11 concerns. Only 8 of the concerns led to investigations. Even if each concern was linked to a different organisation, this represents only 8 out of 62,239 charities, or 0.01% of charities registered with the ACNC. Moreover, the Senate response indicated that no charities have had their registration revoked as a result of these investigations.[177]

The regulatory discourse on abuse of charities for terrorist finance has not shifted significantly in Australia since 2012. Regulatory prioritisation of this concern persists despite limited supporting evidence. The *ACNC Annual report 2014–15* echoed the finding of the 2014 AUSTRAC Report on terrorism financing in Australia that although the incidences of terrorism financing through charities were low, the risk remained high. Ten years on, despite the continued absence of evidence showing systemic or large-scale abuse of charities for terrorist financing, charities at risk of being misused to finance terrorism remain an ACNC compliance focus, highlighted as “a broader area of concern”.[178]

The FATF’s messaging about NPOs creates confusion about risk perceptions of the NPO sector, skewing the outcomes of the application of the risk-based approach to NPOs and charities. The 2002 FATF *Best Practices Paper on Combating the Abuse of Non-Profit Organisations* framed NPOs as a systemic vulnerability, opening with the statement that “The misuse of non-profit organisations for the financing of terrorism is coming to be recognised as a *crucial weak point* in the global struggle to stop such funding at its source.” [179] Subsequent revisions of FATF Best Practice Papers, responding to revisions of Recommendation 8, underscore risk-based differentiation, emphasising that not all NPOs are equally at risk. However, the 2025 FATF *Comprehensive update on terrorist financing risks* reverts to generalisation. The report acknowledges that the majority of NPOs represent a low TF risk and that misuse and exploitation is rare.[180] However, it repeatedly describes NPOs broadly as persistent vulnerabilities for terrorist abuse, without substantiated evidence of systemic risk.[181] This generalised framing may leave readers with an inflated risk perception of charities that is not supported by empirical data. The likelihood of incorrect implementation is increased by the document’s use of risk concepts defined in the 2019 FATF *Terrorist Financing Risk Assessment Guidance*. The 2019 Guidance suggests in relation to consequences of terrorist financing threats, that “Given the challenges in assessing consequences, countries

[177] Australian Federal Parliament, Economics Legislation Committee, 6 November 2024, p. 126 [Sekulic].

[178] ACNC (2015a), p. 52; ACNC (2024); ACNC (n.d.-a).

[179] FATF (2002b), par 1 (emphasis added).

[180] FATF (2025), p 101.

[181] FATF (2025), pp. 18, 64, 69, 102-4.

need not take a scientific approach when considering consequences, and instead may want to start with the presumption that the consequences of TF will be severe (whether domestic or elsewhere) and consider whether there are any factors that would alter that conclusion."[182] This suggestion is absent from the 2025 discussion of consequences but it is unclear whether it is an intentional omission. Together, these documents create a framework where systemic vulnerability and consequence severity compel heightened scrutiny of NPOs, even as other FATF guidance rejects blanket "high risk" labels in favour of targeted measures. When regulation is driven by perception rather than evidence, pouring money into FATF compliance elevates a possible risk of loss of life above certain, documented risks, diverting resources from known threats to a speculative one. In many countries this redirects funds that could address poverty, violent crime, and domestic violence toward burdening the very organisations capable of alleviating those problems.

7 Turning the Ship Around: Accurate Evidence-Based Risk Considerations

This chapter examined the global prioritisation of charity and NPO regulation, particularly in response to the global combating of financing of terrorism standards of the intergovernmental FATF. It considered whether or not the current regulatory regime in relation to NPOs is appropriately evidence-based and proportionate in its focus on terrorist financing.

The analysis shows that it is not. Although policy papers are steeped in the language of "proportionality" and "risk-based regulation", the measures applied to NPOs appear to be largely perception-driven. The FATF's peer-review machinery rewards formal, box-ticking compliance; it does little to test whether rules are calibrated to demonstrable risk or whether they are being deployed to curb civil and human rights.

To its credit, the FATF acknowledges the unintended consequences flowing from its Recommendations and dedicates significant resources to examining and mitigating de-risking, financial exclusion and over-regulation of NPOs. Yet two decades of ingrained perceptions cannot be erased with a few textual amendments, especially if institutional publications convey contradicting messages. Dismantling institutional bias and curbing the deliberate misuse of FATF standards will demand unequivocal guidance, rigorous country-level risk assessments, and clear thresholds for what constitutes an acceptable level of risk. Until those elements are in place, the promise of genuinely proportionate, evidence-based oversight of NPOs will remain rhetorical.

182 FATF(2019), pars. 15, 48.

References

Alsancak AF, Reimer S (2023) FATF's recommendation 8: a cure worse than the disease. https://www.rusi.org/explore-our-research/publications/commentary/fatfs-recommendation-8-cure-worse-disease

Apple RW (1996) Bombing in Saudi Arabia: the policy. https://www.nytimes.com/1996/06/28/world/bombing-saudi-arabia-policy-clinton-asks-summit-partners-join-battle-terrorism.html

Aroney N, Turnour M (2017) Charities are the new constitutional law frontier. Melbourne University Law Review 41(2):446–492

Australian Charities and Not-for-Profit Commission (ACNC) (2013) ACNC Annual report 2012-13. ACNC, Melbourne. https://www.acnc.gov.au/sites/default/files/documents/2021-07/ACNC%20Annual%20Report%202012-13%20-%20Complete%20%5BPDF%2C%202.5Mb%5D%20.pdf

Australian Charities and Not-for-Profit Commission (ACNC) (2014) ACNC Annual report 2013–14. ACNC, Melbourne. https://www.acnc.gov.au/sites/default/files/documents/2021-07/Download%20the%20ACNC%20Annual%20Report%202013%E2%80%9314%20%5BPDF%201.3MB%5D.pdf

Australian Charities and Not-for-Profit Commission (ACNC) (2015a) ACNC Annual report 2014-15. ACNC, Melbourne. https://www.acnc.gov.au/sites/default/files/documents/2021-07/Download%20full%202014-15%20ACNC%20Annual%20Report%20%5BPDF%203.3MB%5D.pdf

Australian Charities and Not-for-Profit Commission (ACNC) (2015b) Charity compliance report: December 2012–December 2014 and beyond. ACNC, Melbourne. https://www.acnc.gov.au/tools/reports/compliance-reports

Australian Charities and Not-for-Profit Commission (ACNC) (2016) ACNC Annual report 2015-16. ACNC, Melbourne. https://www.acnc.gov.au/sites/default/files/documents/2021-07/Download%20full%202015-16%20ACNC%20Annual%20Report%20%5BPDF%205.9MB%5D.pdf

Australian Charities and Not-for-Profit Commission (ACNC) (2017a) ACNC Annual report 2016-17. ACNC, Melbourne. https://www.acnc.gov.au/sites/default/files/documents/2021-07/Download%20full%202016-17%20%20ACNC%20Annual%20Report%20%5BPDF%208.45MB%5D.pdf

Australian Charities and Not-for-Profit Commission (ACNC) (2017b) Charity compliance report 2015 and 2016: protecting public trust and confidence in Australia's charity sector. ACNC, Melbourne. https://www.acnc.gov.au/tools/reports/compliance-reports

Australian Charities and Not-for-Profit Commission (ACNC) (2018) Charity compliance report 2017: protecting public trust and confidence in Australia's charity sector. ACNC, Melbourne. https://www.acnc.gov.au/tools/reports/compliance-reports

Australian Charities and Not-for-Profit Commission (ACNC) (2019a) ACNC Annual report 2016-17. ACNC, Melbourne https://www.acnc.gov.au/sites/default/files/documents/2021-07/2018-19_annualreport.pdf

Australian Charities and Not-for-Profit Commission (ACNC) (2019b) Charity compliance report 2018: maintaining, protecting and enhancing public trust and confidence in Australia's charity sector. ACNC, Melbourne. https://www.acnc.gov.au/tools/reports/compliance-reports

Australian Charities and Not-for-Profit Commission (ACNC) (2023) ACNC submission to the productivity commission's philanthropy inquiry submission #238. https://www.acnc.gov.au/sites/default/files/documents/2023-05/ACNC%20submission%20-%20Productivity%20Commission%27s%20Philanthropy%20Inquiry%20%282%29.pdf

Australian Charities and Not-for-Profit Commission (ACNC) (2024) ACNC compliance and enforcement focus for 2024–25. ACNC, Melbourne. https://www.acnc.gov.au/raise-concern/regulating-charities/acnc-compliance-and-enforcement-focus-for-2024-25#:~:text=In%202024%2D25%2C%20our%20compliance,and%20manage%20cyber%20security%20incidents

Australian Charities and Not-for-Profit Commission (ACNC) (n.d.-a) Areas of concern for charity regulation. ACNC, Melbourne. https://www.acnc.gov.au/raise-concern/regulating-charities/areas-concern
Australian Charities and Not-for-Profit Commission (ACNC) (n.d.b) Commissioner's policy statement: compliance and enforcement. ACNC, Melbourne. https://www.acnc.gov.au/about/corporate-information/corporate-policies/commissioners-policy-statement-compliance-and-enforcement
Australian Transaction Reports and Analysis Centre (AUSTRAC) (2014) Terrorism financing in Australia. AUSTRAC, Sydney. https://www.austrac.gov.au/sites/default/files/2019-07/terrorism-financing-in-australia-2014.pdf
Australian Transaction Reports and Analysis Centre (AUSTRAC) (2017) National risk assessment on money-laundering and terrorist financing 2017: Australia's non-profit organisation sector. AUSTRAC, Sydney. https://www.acnc.gov.au/sites/default/files/documents/2021-07/npo-risk-assessment_pdf_4.84mb.pdf
Australian Transaction Reports and Analysis Centre (AUSTRAC) (2024) Terrorism financing in Australia: Risk Assessment. AUSTRAC, Sydney. https://www.austrac.gov.au/sites/default/files/2024-07/2024%20AUSTRAC%20Terrorism%20Financing%20NRA.pdf
Barker S (2022) Focus on purpose – what does a world-leading framework of charities law look like? New Zealand law Foundation Research Reports 3. https://www.nzlii.org/nz/journals/NZLFRRp/2022/3.html
Barker S (2023) Designing an optimal charities framework. In: Langford R (ed) Governance and regulation of charities. Edward Elgar Publishing, Cheltenham, pp 84–108. https://doi.org/10.4337/9781035310746.00011
Berman HJ (2002) Doing "good" vs. doing "well": the role of nonprofits in society. Inquiry 39(1):5–11. http://www.jstor.org/stable/29772994
Bissett B, Steenkamp P, Aslett D (2023) An analysis of the 2021 south African FATF mutual evaluation report: terrorist financing and NPOs. J Financ Crime 30(6):1534–1548. https://doi.org/10.1108/JFC-11-2022-0265
Brass JN (2022) Do service provision NGOs perform civil society functions? Evidence of NGOs' relationship with democratic participation. Nonprofit Volunt Sect Q 51(1):148–169. https://doi.org/10.1177/0899764021991671
Breen OB (2011) Through the looking glass: European perspectives on non-profit vulnerability, legitimacy and regulation. *Brook J Int 36*(3): 947–991. https://brooklynworks.brooklaw.edu/bjil/vol36/iss3/6
Case-Ruchala D, Nance M (2024) The Limits of enforcement in global financial governance: Blacklisting in FATF as rational myth. *International Studies Quarterly 68*(3): 109–129. https://doi.org/10.1093/isq/sqae115
Center for Global Development (2015) Unintended consequences of anti–money laundering policies for poor countries. https://www.cgdev.org/sites/default/files/CGD-WG-Report-Unintended-Consequences-AML-Policies-2015.pdf
Charities Commission (2024) New data suggests nearly half of charities experience issues when banking. Press Release, 7 March. https://www.gov.uk/government/news/new-data-suggests-nearly-half-of-charities-experience-issues-when-banking
Charity and Security Network (2017) Financial access and de-risking: moving toward solutions for nonprofit organization. Issue Brief, 1 October. https://charityandsecurity.org/issue-briefs/financial-access-for-nonprofit-organizations/
Charity and Security Network (2019) Financial services deplatforming hurts aid, peacebuilding. Issue Brief, 19 August. https://charityandsecurity.org/issue-briefs/financial-services-deplatforming-hurts-aid-peacebuilding/
Charny J (2019) Counter-terrorism and humanitarian action: the perils of zero tolerance. Norwegian Refugee Council. https://www.nrc.no/opinions-all/counter-terrorism-and-humanitarian-action-the-perils-of-zero-tolerance

Chitambara P, Musonza C, Zamchiya P (2022) Punching holes to a fragile economy? Zimbabwe Human Rights NGO Forum. https://hrforumzim.org/wp-content/uploads/2022/12/Research-Report-Punching-Holes-into-a-Fragile-Economy.pdf

Collin M, Cook S, Soramaki K (2016) The impact of anti-money laundering regulation on payment flows: evidence from SWIFT data. Center for Global Development Working Paper No 445. https://doi.org/10.2139/ssrn.2893790

Committee of Experts on the Evaluation of Anti-Money Laundering Measures and the Financing of Terrorism (n.d.) Risk-based approach. https://www.coe.int/en/web/moneyval/implementation/risk-based-approach#:~:text=FATF%20was%20required%20to%20be,effective%20implementation%20of%20all%20recommendations

Community World Service Asia (2020) Impact of the FATF standards on the non-profit sector during COVID-19. Media release, 1 July. https://communityworldservice.asia/impact-of-the-fatf-standards-on-the-non-profit-sector-during-covid-19/

Counter-terrorism Implementation Task Force (CTITF) Working Group (2009) Tackling the financing of terrorism. Report, October https://unrcca.unmissions.org/sites/default/files/ctitf_financing_eng_final.pdf

Davis J (2025) Vibes-Based Audits: What NSIRA Found Inside the CRA's Charity Audits Division. Insight Monitor, 7 October. https://newsletter.insightthreatintel.com/p/vibes-based-audits-what-nsira-found?utm_source=post-email-title&publication_id=329102&post_id=175%E2%80%A6

De Koker L (2022) Editorial: regulatory impact assessment: towards a better approach for the FATF. J Money Laundering Control 25(2):265–267. https://doi.org/10.1108/JMLC-05-2022-149

De Koker L (2024) Editorial: FATF greylisting: time to revisit the approach. J Money Laundering Control 27(4):621–624. https://doi.org/10.1108/JMLC-07-2024-206

De Koker L, Goldbarsh D (2024) FATF'S risk-based approach: has the pendulum swung too far? In: Goldbarsht D, De Koker L (eds) Financial crime and the law: identifying and mitigating risks. Springer Nature, Cham, pp 247–262. https://doi.org/10.1007/978-3-031-59543-1_10

De Koker L, Turkington M (2016) Transnational organised crime and the anti-money laundering regime. In: Hauck P, Peterke S (eds) International law and transnational organised crime. Oxford University Press

De Koker L, Howell J, Morris N (2023) Economic consequences of greylisting by the financial action task force. Risks 11(5):Article 81. https://doi.org/10.3390/risks11050081

De March T (2017) The prevention of harm regulator. In: McGregor-Lowndes M, Wyatt B (eds) Regulating charities: the inside story. Routledge, New York, pp 119–137. https://doi.org/10.4324/9781315563923

Department of Internal Affairs | Te Tari Taiwhenua (2024) Terrorism financing risk summary. Report, 30 July https://www.dia.govt.nz/AML-CFT-Terrorism-Financing-Risk-Summary

Duke Law International Human Rights Clinic and Women Peacemakers Program (2017) Tightening the purse strings: what countering terrorism financing costs gender equality and security. https://law.duke.edu/sites/default/files/humanrights/tighteningpursestrings.pdf

Ferwerda J, Reuter P (2024) National assessments of money laundering risks: stumbling at the start. Risk Anal 44(9):2001–2007. https://doi.org/10.1111/risa.14302

Financial Action Task Force (FATF) (2001) FATF IX special recommendations. FATF, Paris. https://www.fatf-gafi.org/content/dam/fatf-gafi/recommendations/FATF%20Standards%20-%20IX%20Special%20Recommendations%20and%20IN%20rc.pdf.coredownload.pdf

Financial Action Task Force (FATF) (2002a) Annual report 2001–2002. FATF, Paris. https://www.fatf-gafi.org/content/fatf-gafi/en/publications/Fatfgeneral/Fatfannualreport2001-2002.html

Financial Action Task Force (FATF) (2002b) Best practices on combating the abuse of non-profit organisations. FATF, Paris. https://www.fatf-gafi.org/en/publications/Financialinclusionandnpoissues/Bpp-combating-abuse-npo.html

Financial Action Task Force (FATF) (2006) Annual Report 2005–2006. FATF, Paris. https://www.fatf-gafi.org/content/dam/fatf-gafi/annual-reports/2005%202006%20ENG.pdf

Financial Action Task Force (FATF) (2012–2025) The FATF recommendations: international standards on combating money laundering and the financing of terrorism & proliferation. FATF, Paris. www.fatf-gafi.org/en/publications/Fatfrecommendations/Fatf-recommendations.html

Financial Action Task Force (FATF) (2013) National money laundering and terrorist financing risk assessment. FATF, Paris. https://www.fatf-gafi.org/en/publications/Methodsandtrends/Nationalmoneylaunderingandterroristfinancingriskassessment.html

Financial Action Task Force (FATF) (2014) Risk of terrorist abuse in non-profit organisations. FATF, Paris. https://www.fatf-gafi.org/content/dam/fatf-gafi/reports/Risk-of-terrorist-abuse-in-non-profit-organisations.pdf.coredownload.pdf

Financial Action Task Force (FATF) (2015) Emerging terrorist finance risks. FATF, Paris

Financial Action Task Force (FATF) (2016) Outcomes of the plenary meeting of the FATF, Paris, 19–21 October 2016. FATF, Paris. https://www.fatf-gafi.org/en/publications/Fatfgeneral/Outcomes-plenary-october-2016.html#:~:text=Changes%20to%20the%20Methodology%20to,are%20not%20disrupted%20or%20discouraged

Financial Action Task Force (FATF) (2018) Anti-money laundering and counter-terrorist financing measures – Australia, 3rd enhanced follow-up report & technical compliance re-Rating. FATF, Paris. http://www.fatf-gafi.org/publications/mutualevaluations/documents/fur-australia-2018.html

Financial Action Task Force (FATF) (2019) Terrorist financing risk assessment guidance. FATF, Paris. www.fatf-gafi.org/publications//methodsandtrends/documents/Terrorist-Financing-Risk-Assessment-Guidance.html

Financial Action Task Force (FATF) (2021) High-level synopsis of the stocktake of the unintended consequences of the FATF standards. FATF, Paris. https://www.fatf-gafi.org/content/fatf-gafi/en/publications/Financialinclusionandnpoissues/Unintended-consequences-project.html

Financial Action Task Force (FATF) (2023) Combating the terrorist financing abuse of non-profit organisations. FATF, Paris. https://www.fatf-gafi.org/content/fatf-gafi/en/publications/Financialinclusionandnpoissues/Bpp-combating-abuse-npo.html

Financial Action Task Force (FATF) (2024) Methodology for assessing technical compliance with the FATF recommendations and the effectiveness of AML/CFT/CPF systems. FATF, Paris. www.fatf-gafi.org/en/publications/Mutualevaluations/Assessment-Methodology-2022.html

Financial Action Task Force (FATF) (2025) Comprehensive update on terrorist financing risks. FATF, Paris. https://www.fatf-gafi.org/content/fatf-gafi/en/publications/Methodsandtrends/comprehensive-update-terrorist-financing-risks-2025.html

Financial Action Task Force (FATF) (n.d.-a) Mutual evaluations. FATF, Paris. https://www.fatf--gafi.org/en/topics/mutual-evaluations.html

Financial Action Task Force (FATF) (n.d.-b) History of the FATF. FATF, Paris. https://www.fatf--gafi.org/en/the-fatf/history-of-the-fatf.html

Financial Action Task Force (FATF) and Asia Pacific Group (APG) (2015) Terrorist financing and financing of proliferation. In: Anti-money laundering and counter-terrorist financing measures – Australia, fourth round mutual evaluation report. FATF/APG, Paris/Sydney. www.fatf-gafi.org/topics/mutualevaluations/documents/mer-australia-2015.html

Financial Intelligence Centre (FIC) (2019) Guidance on combating the financing of terrorism and anti-money laundering measures relating to non-profit organisations. Public Compliance Communication No 41, 20 December. https://www.fic.gov.za/wp-content/uploads/2023/09/2019.12-PCC-PCC-41-NPOs-and-AML-CFT.pdf

Fries R (2017) Towards regulation. In: McGregor Lowndes M, Wyatt B (eds) Regulating charities: the inside story. Routledge, New York, pp 17–36. https://doi.org/10.4324/9781315563923

Gilchrist DJ (2014) Revolving door of change. Public Adm Today 40:60–61. https://doi.org/10.3316/ielapa.757253768073452

Goldbarsht D (2017) Who's the legislator anyway? How the FATF's global norms reshape Australian counter terrorist financing laws. Federal Law Rev 45(1):127–151. https://doi.org/10.1177/0067205X1704500106

Harding M (2022) Editorial: special issue on equity, charity and governance. J Equity 16(2):101–102

Hayes B (2012) Counter-terrorism, 'policy laundering' and the FATF: legalising surveillance, regulating civil society. Int J Not-for-Profit Law 14(1–2):5–48

Human Security Collective, European Centre for Not-for-Profit Law (2018) At the intersection of security and regulation: understanding the drivers of 'de-risking' and the impact on civil society organizations. Research report, 7 May. http://ecnl.org/publications/understanding-the-drivers-of-de-risking-and-the-impact-on-civil-society-organizations

International Monetary Fund (IMF) (2011) Anti-money laundering and combating the financing of terrorism (AML/CFT) – report on the review of the effectiveness of the program report, 11 May. https://www.imf.org/en/Publications/Policy-Papers/Issues/2016/12/31/Anti-Money-Laundering-and-Combating-the-Financing-of-Terrorism-AML-CFT-Review-of-the-PP4571

International Monetary Fund (IMF) (2012) Revisions to the financial action task force (FATF) standard – information note to the executive board. Policy paper, 17 July. https://www.imf.org/en/Publications/Policy-Papers/Issues/2016/12/31/Revisions-to-the-Financial-Action-Task-Force-FATF-Standard-Information-Note-to-the-PP4683

Jackson KT (2010) Global corporate governance: soft law and reputational accountability. Brooklyn J Int Law 35(1):41–106. https://brooklynworks.brooklaw.edu/cgi/viewcontent.cgi?referer=&httpsredir=1&article=1165&context=bjil

Keatinge T, Keen F (2017) Lone-actor and small cell terrorist attacks a new front in counter-terrorist finance? RUSI Occasional Paper, January. https://static.rusi.org/201701_op_lone-actor_and_small_cell_terrorist_attacks.1.pdf

Kyriakos-Saad N (2005) The methodology for assessing compliance with anti-money laundering and combating the financing of terrorism standards. In: Current developments in monetary and financial law. International Monetary Fund (IMF), New York, pp 265–277

Mackintosh K, Duplat P (2013) Study of the impact of donor counter-terrorism measures on principled humanitarian action. Norwegian Refugee Council Report, 15 July. https://www.nrc.no/resources/reports/study-of-the-impact-of-donor-counterterrorism-measures-on-principled-humanitarian-action

Maslen C (2023) The impact of grey listing by the Financial Action Task Force (FATF). U4 Helpdesk Answer 2023:21. https://knowledgehub.transparency.org/helpdesk/the-impact-of-grey-listing-by-the-financial-action-task-force-fatf

McGregor-Lowndes M, Wyatt B (2017) Conclusion. In: McGregor-Lowndes M, Wyatt B (eds) Regulating charities: the inside story. Routledge, New York, pp 261–291. https://doi.org/10.4324/9781315563923

Moldavanova A, Onishi T, Toepler S (2023) Civil society and democratization: the role of service-providing organizations amid closing civic spaces. Public Adm Dev 43(1):3–13. https://doi.org/10.1002/pad.2005

Muslim Charities Forum (MCF) (2025) Unfair banking practices are strangling charities—it's time for Droit Au Compte. MCF Blog, 10 February. https://www.muslimcharitiesforum.org.uk/2025/02/10/unfair-banking-practices-are-strangling-charities-its-time-for-droit-au-compte/

Nance MT (2018a) Re-thinking FATF: an experimentalist interpretation of the Financial Action Task Force. *Crime Law Soc Change 69*(2):131–152. https://doi.org/10.1007/s10611-017-9748-5

Nance MT (2018b) The regime that FATF built: an introduction to the financial action task force. *Crime Law Soc Change 69*(2):109–129. https://doi.org/10.1007/s10611-017-9747-6

National Commission on Terrorist Attacks Upon the United States (2004) The 9/11 Commission report. https://www.govinfo.gov/app/details/GPO-911REPORT/context

National Security and Intelligence Review Agency (NSIRA) (2025) Review of Canada Revenue Agency's Review and Analysis Division (RAD): Report - National Security and Intelligence Review Agency. NSIRA, Ottawa. https://nsira-ossnr.gc.ca/en/reviews/find-a-review/23-08/report/

Nehme M (2017) Australian charities and not-for-profits commission: enforcement tools and regulatory approach. Aust Bus Law Rev 45(2):159–187. https://www.proquest.com/scholarly-journals/australian-charities-not-profits-commission/docview/1903519706/se-2?accountid=12528

Nel de Koker J (2022) Regulating volunteer directors' duties in companies registered with the Australian charities and not-for-profits commission. Univ New South Wales Law J 45(2):764–797. https://doi.org/10.53637/YTHS8021

Ní Aoláin F (2019) Report of the Special Rapporteur on the promotion and protection of human rights and fundamental freedoms while countering terrorism. UN Report, 1 March. https://www.ohchr.org/en/documents/reports/ahrc4052-impact-measures-address-terrorism-and-violent-extremism-civic-space-and

Norwegian Refugee Council (NRC) (2018) Principles under pressure: the impact of counterterrorism measures and preventing/countering violent extremism on principles humanitarian action. NRC report, 12 June. https://www.nrc.no/resources/reports/principles-under-pressure

Norwegian Refugee Council (NRC) (2025) Humanitarian organisations' use of money service providers. NRC reference guide, 15 April. https://www.nrc.no/resources/reports/humanitarian-organisations-use-of-money-service-providers

OECD and FATF (2001) FATF Cracks down on Terrorist Financing (press statement, 31 October 2001) https://one.oecd.org/document/PAC/COM/NEWS(2001)91/en/pdf

Organisation for Security and Co-operation in Europe (OSCE) (2004) progress made by the fatf in developing and implementing international standards in the fight against terrorist financing. OSCE Brief, 12 March. https://www.osce.org/files/f/documents/8/7/25860.pdf

Pascoe S (2017) The digital regulator. In: McGregor-Lowndes M, Wyatt B (eds) Regulating charities: the inside story. Routledge, New York, pp 211–232. https://doi.org/10.4324/9781315563923

Pavlidis G (2023) The dark side of anti-money laundering: mitigating the unintended consequences of FATF standards. J Econ Criminol 2:100040. https://doi.org/10.1016/j.jeconc.2023.100040

Preston R (2024) Banks criticised by regulator as 42% of charities report experiencing poor service. Civil Socity UK, 7 March. https://www.civilsociety.co.uk/news/banks-criticised-by-regulator-as-42-of-charities-report-experiencing-poor-service.html

Reimer S (2024) Weaponisation of the FATF standards: a guide for global civil society. RUSI Report, 11 June. https://www.rusi.org/explore-our-research/publications/special-resources/weaponisation-fatf-standards-guide-global-civil-society

Romaniuk P, Keatinge T (2018) Protecting charities from terrorists … and counterterrorists: FATF and the global effort to prevent terrorist financing through the non-profit sector. Crime Law Soc Chang 69(2):265–282. https://doi.org/10.1007/s10611-017-9755-6

Rutzen D (2015) Aid barriers and the rise of philanthropic protectionism. Int J Not-for-Profit Law 17(1):5–44. https://www.icnl.org/wp-content/uploads/ijnl_Rutzen.pdf

Salamon L et al (1999) Global civil society: dimensions of the nonprofit sector. Centre for Civil Society Studies, Baltimore

Scheinin M (2006) Report of the Special Rapporteur on the promotion and protection of human rights and fundamental freedoms while countering terrorism. UN Report A/61/267, 16 August. https://documents-dds-ny.un.org/doc/UNDOC/GEN/N06/477/03/PDF/N0647703.pdf?OpenElement

Seibert K (2016) Navigating reform in contested spaces: reflections on not-for-profit sector regulatory reform in Australia, 2010–2013. In: Butcher JR, Gilchrist DJ (eds) The three sector solution. ANU Press, Canberra, pp 131–156

Sidel M (2008) Counter-terrorism and the enabling legal and political environment for civil society: comparative analysis of war on terror states. Int J Not-for-Profit Law 10(3):7–49. https://www.icnl.org/resources/research/ijnl/counter-terrorism-and-the-enabling-legal-and-political-environment-for-civil-society-a-comparative-analysis-of-war-on-terror-states

Silver N (2019) When charity no longer begins and ends at home: the Australian government's regulatory response to charities operating overseas. Adelaide Law Rev 40(3):755–782. https://law.adelaide.edu.au/ua/media/1398/ALR_40%283%29_07_Silver_Web.pdf

SOS-Torture Network (2019) FATF's recommendation 8 on non-profit organizations: A new tool to unfairly and dangerously shrink civil society space. Submission, 10 July. https://www.ohchr.org/sites/default/files/Documents/Issues/Terrorism/SR/Submissions/OMCT_GA74CT.pdf

Styles M (2025) De-banking 'risky' customers: contractual exclusion of customers by financial institutions and AML/CTF ramifications. In: Goldbarsht D, De Koker L, Ferrill J (eds) Combating financial crime: intended and unintended consequences. Springer, Cham

Taaffe-Maguire S (2025) Muslim charities still being debanked despite Farage furore. SkyNews, 29 January. https://news.sky.com/story/muslim-charities-still-being-debanked-despite-farage-furore-13293103

Toepler S et al (2020) The changing space for NGOs: civil society in authoritarian and hybrid regimes. Volunt Int J Volunt Nonprofit Org 31(4):649–662. https://doi.org/10.1007/s11266-020-00240-7

United Nation General Assembly (1996) 51st session measures to eliminate international terrorism. http://www.worldlii.org/int/other/UNGA/1996/282.pdf

United States Department of the Treasury (2015) National terrorist financing risk assessment. https://home.treasury.gov/system/files/246/National-Terrorist-Financing-Risk-Assessment-06-12-2015.pdf

United States Department of the Treasury (2024) National terrorist financing risk assessment. https://home.treasury.gov/system/files/136/2024-National-Terrorist-Financing-Risk-Assessment.pdf

Van Broekhoven L et al (2023) The future of FATF recommendation 8: a foresight piece. Human security collective report, November. https://www.hscollective.org/assets/Final_R8-Foresight_.pdf

Van der Does de Willebois E (2010) Nonprofit organizations and the combating of terrorism financing: a proportionate response. World Bank Working Paper No 208. https://openknowledge.worldbank.org/handle/10986/5926

Zolkaflila S et al (2015) A review on compliance rating: FATF special recommendation IX cross border declaration or disclosure. Procedia Econ Finance 31:535–550. https://doi.org/10.1016/S2212-5671(15)01199-5

Jeanne Nel is a senior lecturer in the Department of Business Law and Taxation at Monash University in Melbourne. She is a governance law scholar with an LLM in human rights law and a PhD in Law focused on the corporate regulation of volunteer charity directors' duty of care and diligence. Jeanne, an advocate of the High Court of South Africa, has lectured at several universities, including Monash and the University of Johannesburg in South Africa and Deakin University and La Trobe University in Australia.

Law Enforcement at the Forest-Finance Nexus in Papua New Guinea: Leveraging Tools Against Financial Crime in Defence of the Environment

Hannah Harris

Abstract This chapter explores the forest-finance nexus, using the case study of Papua New Guinea (PNG) to demonstrate how financial crimes—such as corruption, tax evasion, and money laundering—enable forest crime and secure the profitability of environmentally destructive practices such as illegal logging and the trade in illicit timber products. In response to the harmful impacts of forest crime in PNG and the continued inadequacy of PNG's forest law framework, authorities are experimenting with novel enforcement strategies. This chapter provides specific examples of how anti-money laundering, anti-corruption, and tax law frameworks, are being leveraged in PNG to undermine the profitability of forest crime and hold criminal enterprises accountable for their illicit and environmentally destructive acts. Building on examples from PNG, the chapter presents practical recommendations for leveraging the forest-finance nexus to better protect vital forest ecosystems and strengthen financial integrity on a global scale.

1 Introduction

The relationship between financial crime and environmental crime is becoming increasingly clear and well documented. The term forest crime usefully extends to both illegal logging and related criminal acts that enable or result from illegal activities that harm forest ecosystems. Related criminal acts at the intersection of environmental and financial crime include fraud, bribery and corruption, money laundering, and tax evasion. This chapter examines the forest-finance nexus in greater depth, using the case study of Papua New Guinea (PNG) to document and analyse the use of legal tools and enforcement strategies designed to combat financial crime, in

H. Harris (✉)
Macquarie Law School, Financial Integrity Hub (FIH), Asia Pacific Forest Crime Network (APFCN), Sydney, NSW, Australia
e-mail: hannah.harris@mq.edu.au

D. Goldbarsht et al. (eds.), *Combating Financial Crime*, Ius Gentium: Comparative Perspectives on Law and Justice 131,
https://doi.org/10.1007/978-3-032-06858-3_7

circumstances where those crimes are linked to illegal logging. Authorities in PNG have already begun using anti-financial crime tools to target forest crime, resulting in successful actions against perpetrators of these harmful acts. This creative approach is necessary, because PNG—like many other forest rich nations around the world—has consistently struggled to effectively enforce forestry sector regulation against the powerful actors and criminal enterprises that seek to exploit forest resources for profit, at the expense of forest ecosystems and the communities sustained by and reliant on these forests for survival and the maintenance of social and cultural expression and cohesion.

The chapter begins by introducing critical gaps in PNG's Forestry Law Framework to illustrate the need for a novel regulatory approach. Analysis highlights the three primary financial crimes—corruption, money laundering, and tax evasion—that facilitate illegal logging in PNG and enable the profitability of this criminal enterprise. The relationship between illegal logging and financial crime in PNG serves to highlight that, more often than not, financial crime *is* forest crime. This reality helps to explain the value of expanding research analysis and enforcement action beyond activities directly related to timber harvest, process, transfer, and sale.

Having outlined the nature of the problem represented by the forest-finance nexus, the chapter presents some avenues to solve this problem in PNG, directing enforcement of the legal tools designed to combat financial crime at the individuals and enterprises that facilitate or profit from illegal logging and related trade in illicit timber products. Analysis results in recommendations for leveraging the forest-finance nexus to enhance the effectiveness of law enforcement efforts against forest crimes—not only in PNG but on a global scale. In PNG, this approach requires the application of legal tools such as the *Anti-Money Laundering and Counter-Terrorist Financing Act* (AML/CTF Act) and the *Proceeds of Crime Act* to disrupt illicit financial flows generated by forest crime and build accountability in PNG's forestry sector. The chapter provides examples of actions already taken by PNG authorities, including the use of tax law to target forest crime and secure substantial penalties for perpetrators. By targeting the financial gains derived from the trade in illegally harvested timber, PNG authorities have demonstrated the deterrent and punitive potential of law enforcement at the forest-finance nexus.

The chapter is intended as an anchor point and a call to action, to encourage further scholarly research and strategic law enforcement at the forest-finance nexus. Opportunities exist far beyond PNG—extending not only to other forest-rich jurisdictions, but also to those jurisdictions whose economies and business enterprises profit from the facilitation of forest crime. Support is also needed from the international community and its laws and institutions, which have potential to coordinate transnational law enforcement cooperation and support national efforts to prevent and pursue criminal actors and enterprises engaged in or enabling forest crime. Efforts to combat both financial crime and forest crime must not proceed in a vacuum. Instead, the forest-finance nexus must be leveraged to hold criminal enterprises accountable for the social and environmental harms generated through their unscrupulous pursuit of profit, which comes at the cost of our planetary health, the livelihoods of forest reliant communities, the integrity of the global timber trade, and the stability of our international economic system.

2 Background to Forest Crime: It's Not Just About Logging

Illegal logging is a term that has been expanded in response to better understandings of the activities and harms that result when forest resources are exploited. Illegal logging goes beyond cutting down trees without proper permits or approvals. However, the scope of the term is not universally agreed and can range from restrictive to expansive. This chapter builds on definitions contained within destination country laws operating in the United States, European Union, United Kingdom, and Australia.[1] These laws represent a key element of the transnational regime to combat illegal logging. The chapter defines illegal logging to include all activities that relate to the harvest, transport, processing and sale of timber and timber derived products in contravention of laws in place in the jurisdiction in which the activity occurred. This definition is broad enough to capture most scenarios in which individuals or, more commonly, commercial enterprises, seek to exploit forest resources for profit.

Illegal logging has long been recognised as a significant challenge for PNG. In 1989, Justice Thomas Barnett published his interim report resulting from the Commission of Inquiry into aspects of the forestry industry. The report refers to logging companies in PNG as "robber barons; bribing politicians and leaders, creating social disharmony and ignoring laws and policy in order to gain access to, rip out, and export the last remnants of the province's valuable timber".[2] In the more than 35 years since the Barnett Commission of Inquiry, illegal logging has remained a substantial obstacle to the national cohesion and prosperity.

The harms of illegal logging, and the challenges faced by authorities seeking to combat illegal logging, are not unique to PNG. Enforcement challenges have been identified in jurisdictions spanning the Amazonian Region of South America (particularly Brazil and Argentina) through the Congo Basin in Africa, to Romania in Eastern Europe.[3] In each of the above examples, the impact of illegal logging, and the mechanisms by which illegal logging occurs, extend beyond those activities related to the harvest, processing, transfer, and sale of illicit timber products. As such, "forest crime" has become a popular term that encapsulates the full extent of the illegality that results from exploitation of forests. Forest crime can include all

[1] See United States Lacey Act 1900 (as amended 2008) ('Lacey Act'); European Union Timber Regulation 995/2010 ('UETR'); United Kingdom Timber and Timber Products (Placing on the Market) Regulations 2013 ('UK Timber Regulations'), United Kingdom environment Act 2021 and Forest Risk Commodity Regulation; Australian Illegal Logging Prohibition Act 2012 and Regulations.

[2] Barnett (1989), p. 466.

[3] Interpol (n.d.).

activities previously contained in the definition of illegal logging, but also extends to other crimes, including financial crimes, that facilitate acts of illegal logging and enable its continued profitability. By widening the lens of analysis from illegal logging to forest crime, new opportunities and enforcement strategies become visible, including the potential to leverage anti-money laundering law and other financial crime tools to deter and punish the activities that enable forest crime to flourish.

The international community is cognisant of the challenges posed by forest crime, which is now regarded as one of the most pressing issues facing our planet today. The United Nations Office on Drugs and Crime (UNODC) asserts that "wildlife and forest crime has become a low-risk, high profit transnational organized crime, which is overwhelming countries and communities, affecting biodiversity and development".[4] In 2023, at the meeting of the Asia-Pacific Economic Cooperation Expert Group on Illegal Logging and Associated Trade (APEC EGILAT), countries were urged to:

> [R]ecommit to ensuring the global forest products market does not become a financial playground to criminal elements who use illegally harvested forest products to drive other transnational crimes, perpetuate civil unrest, threaten global security, and fund terrorist organizations.[5]

Increased global attention on the risks and harms associated with forest crime can and does have local impacts. For example, the aforementioned destination country laws that prohibit the importation of illegally harvested timber are reshaping the global timber market and influencing trade in other agricultural goods. In the UK, destination country laws that were once restricted so specific types of wood and processed timber products have been expanded to include 'forest risk commodities' including palm oil and palm products.[6] This expansion of scope is warranted, given that palm plantations have been linked in many jurisdictions to destruction of substantial areas of natural forest.[7] Although implementation of this framework and the complimentary framework in the EU has been substantially delayed, such implementation remains on the agenda in both countries.[8] In PNG, palm plantations have been used as a tool to enable illegal logging, facilitating the abuse of certain licensing arrangements that allow for extraction and trade in valuable natural hardwood that would otherwise be deemed illegal.[9] Destination country laws are not the focus of this chapter, but their expanded scope illustrates the need for source countries like PNG to take action to combat forest crime, not only because of its environmental impact, but also because rampant forest crime may undermine valuable trade relationships, stifling the PNG economy.

---

[4] UNODC (2025).

[5] ITTO (2023).

[6] UK Environment Act (2021), Schedule 17.

[7] Vijay et al. (2016).

[8] European Commission (2025).

[9] Harris (2023).

The estimated value of wood exports from PNG in 2021 was USD560 million, plus an additional USD706 million from palm oil Harris (2024). More recent statistics suggest that the palm oil export market is growing in PNG, with a value of USD1.5 billion in 2022.[10] As such, palm oil represents the third largest export for PNG and the fastest growing export market in the country. Even with more than 80% of PNG's wood exports in 2021 (USD479 million) going to mainland China for further processing before export to the global market, more than USD35 million in value was exported directly to countries with prohibitions on importation of illegally harvested timber. Additionally, more than 64 percent of PNG's palm exports as of 2021 were to European Union countries and the United Kingdom, the very countries that prohibit the importation of forest risk commodities.[11]

The global trend towards prohibiting the import of illegally harvested timber is also likely to increase scrutiny of (and pressure on) Chinese timber products to ensure legality. In 2019, China made changes to its Forest Law for the first time in a decade, effectively banning the buying, transporting or processing illegal timber.[12] China has also taken diplomatic steps to signal its commitment to combating illegal logging and harmful deforestation at international for a including the EU–China High-Level Environment and Climate Dialogue and the 26th Conference of the Parties to the UN Framework Convention on Climate Change (COP26). At COP26, China (along with 141 other countries) signed the Glasgow Leaders' Declaration on Forests and Land Use, committing to "working collectively to halt and reverse forest loss and land degradation by 2030".[13]

The global context and economic ramifications provide strong incentives for action. The challenges of illegal logging and forest crime must be addressed, or PNG risks being locked out of key global markets, negatively impacting the economic viability of the forestry industry, and increasing the risk that deviant actors will infiltrate and capture the business operations in the PNG forestry sector. The changing regulatory environment and its trade implications have played a role in motivating novel law enforcement strategies and regulatory efforts in PNG. These efforts by authorities to leverage the forest-finance nexus are documented later in the chapter.

---

[10] National Statistics Office PNG (2023).

[11] National Statistics Office of PNG (2023), Workman (2023).

[12] Mukpo (2020).

[13] National Archives (2023) Glasgow Leaders' Declaration on Forests and Land Use. https://webarchive.nationalarchives.gov.uk/ukgwa/20230418175226/https://ukcop26.org/glasgow-leaders-declaration-on-forests-and-land-use/.

3 Forest Crime in PNG and the Limitations of the Forest Law Framework

Before introducing the innovations in enforcement by PNG authorities, which have resulted in effective enforcement actions against enterprises suspected of illegal logging, it is first helpful to describe the nature of forest crime in PNG and summarise the limitations of the Forest Law Framework which have necessitated law enforcement innovations.

In PNG, "illegal logging" is not expressly defined or criminalised in any legal code or regulation. The forestry sector—and the activities of harvesting, processing, and exporting timber in PNG—are governed by *The Forestry Act 1991*. Other relevant laws include *The Forestry (Amendment) Act 2000, The Forestry (Amendment) Act 2007, The Environment Act 2000* and the *Conservation and Environment Protection Act 2014*. A useful summary of the current legal framework governing forest legality in PNG is provided by the *Timber Legality Guidance Template for Papua New Guinea* published by APEC EGILAT.[14] However, for the purposes of this chapter, the important point is that PNG's ongoing challenges with illegal logging and forest crime are not due to a lack of legislation, but rather to limited in enforcement of this legislation.

3.1 Limitation 1: Lack of Enforcement

Implementation and enforcement of the Forest Law Framework falls primarily to the PNG Forest Authority (PNGFA) and the Provincial Forest Management Committees (PFMCs), with oversight from the National Forest Board (NFB). The laws noted above, and the guidelines and regulations that accompany them, govern the granting of licenses for the harvest, process, and export of timber products, as well as specifying the necessary approvals and payments to be made to secure these certifications of legality. While *The Forestry Act 1991* does not create a criminal offence of 'illegal logging' it does establish offences for non-compliance under Sections 114, 122, and 125 that may result in a fine or imprisonment. Non-compliance with the Act can also enable revocation of the relevant license.

Unfortunately, there has been little to no enforcement of the *Forestry Act* in PNG. In a 2022 report, the UNODC concluded that:

> The penalties available under the Forestry Act are not commensurate with the high value of timber resources, the vast profits generated from illegal logging activities, the very large scale of many foreign- owned logging operations in PNG, and the environmental damage caused when offences are committed. Furthermore, it was reported that there have been no

[14] APEC Expert Group on Illegal Logging (2021) Timber legality guidance template. https://www.apec.org/docs/default-source/groups/egilat/2021/0308apec-experts-group-on-illegal-logging-and-associated-trade-egilattimber-legality-guidance-templa.pdf. Accessed 29 July 2025.

> successful prosecutions of illegal logging or other forestry crimes in the PNG court system.[15]

There is, in fact, one documented case of a National Court order against the company Concord Pacific for illegally logging 500 times the legally allotted forest area as part of a 'road line clearance' issued in 1994.[16] However, the local company found to have breached the *Forestry Act* was quickly wound up and the fine was never actually paid.[17] This example illustrates how corporate structures can, and often are, manipulated to limit the effectiveness of environmental law frameworks ill-equipped to navigate the complexities transnational business enterprises and foreign investment. This foreshadows one of the advantages of deploying laws against financial crime in defence of the environment, as such laws are often more attuned to the subtleties of commercial operations and can rely on the added support of inter-government cooperation and collaboration with multi-lateral organisations empowered to assist in efforts to combat financial crime.

As documented above, limited enforcement of the Forest Law Framework is the first of three key limitations that undermine the effectiveness of the framework in PNG. For the purposes of this chapter, there are two additional limitations that warrant analysis: the failure of the framework to acknowledge the connection between illegal logging and other forms of criminal activity; and the lack of transparency, accountability, and oversight of the authority responsible for the framework's implementation and enforcement. These additional limitations are detailed further below, with reference to their wider significance to other forest rich jurisdictions that also struggle to combat forest crime and its harms.

3.2 Limitation 2: Failure to Acknowledge the Connection Between Illegal Logging and Other Crimes

One of the most substantial limitations of the Forestry Law Framework in PNG is its inadequacy in addressing the role played by criminal activities in facilitating illegal logging. The relationship between illegal logging and other forms of criminal activity is well documented in many countries that rely heavily on the economic contributions of forestry sector. Studies have linked illegal logging to the crimes of bribery and corruption, fraud, money laundering, trafficking, theft, and violence:[18]

> Forest crime has all the hallmarks of organized and sophisticated crime, sharing many characteristics with other transnational criminal activities, frequently involving fraud, money-

[15] UNODC (2022a).

[16] Hance (2011).

[17] Lawson (2014) Illegal logging in Papua New Guinea. Energy, Environment and Resources EER PP 2014/04. https://www.chathamhouse.org/sites/default/files/home/chatham/public_html/sites/default/files/20140400LoggingPapuaNewGuineaLawson.pdf.

[18] Kailemia (2019).

> laundering, corruption, and counterfeiting. Large economic incentives, remoteness, lack of traceability, demographic pressure, and the lack of available tools, methods, or even standardized definitions to assess forest loss, among others, make forests fertile ground for corruption.[19]

The nexus between criminal activity and illegal logging has also been associated with participation by organised criminal enterprises operating transnationally:

> Illegal activities…range in complexity from local illegal harvesting through to international and highly organized criminal syndicates with established commercial supply chains.[20]

The transnational nature of interactions between criminal enterprise, corporations, and individual actors, complicates enforcement efforts targeting illegal logging and forest crime. These actors engage directly and indirectly across the entire timber supply chain from initial harvest through transport, processing, and point of sale. Often, interactions traverse multiple jurisdictions and involve a convoluted web of licit and illicit activities and transactions.

In PNG, the crime most frequently associated with illegal logging is corruption.[21] Acts of bribery and corruption are criminalised in PNG under the *Criminal Code Act 1974*, providing one potential avenue for collaborative law enforcement. A range of other criminal activities have also been associated with illegal logging in PNG, including: tax evasion (*Income Tax Act 1959*); money laundering (*Proceeds of Crime Act 2005, Criminal Code Act 1974* and *Anti-Money Laundering and Counter Terrorist Financing Act 2015*); and fraud, theft, violence, and intimidation (*Criminal Code Act 1974*). Many of these crimes have also been identified as contributing to or resulting from illegal logging in other forest rich nations.

The *Forestry Act* and supporting regulations focus on process and procedures administered by the PNG Forest Authority (PNGFA) to assure legality. However, the processes and procedures that are established by the law are complex, involving many different steps and verification points, without acknowledging or accounting for the myriad ways that criminal conduct can circumvent legal compliance at any stage—particularly through corrupt or fraudulent means. Currently, the Forestry Law Framework provides for a 34-step process for ensuring timber legality in the case of Forest Management Agreements (FMA). However, several independent reports provide illustrative examples of how this process is susceptible to circumvention and manipulation through criminal acts including bribery and corruption, fraud, violence, coercion, and intimidation.[22] Most timber exports from PNG are not coming from FMA areas. In 2022, only around 22% of log exports were from FMA areas, while 40% were from areas governed by licenses that pre-date the *Forestry Act* altogether and 35% were from Forest Clearance Authority (FCA) areas. This illustrates the limited value of the 34-step process, and the fact that the process is being largely circumvented. A common mechanism for circumvention of the FMA

[19] United Nations Office on Drugs and Crime (2022a).

[20] Ibid.

[21] Harris (2019).

[22] Lawson (2014), Forest Legality (2013).

process is to fraudulently claim that the forest areas to be logged will be converted to agricultural or other land-use, thus allowing the issuance of an FCA. There are numerous reported examples where this conversion never occurs.[23]

The Oakland Institute has exposed how foreign companies often engage in bribery and corruption to obtain timber licenses in PNG.[24] Global Witness has demonstrated how companies manipulated landowner consent through corrupt practices, including deception or bribery, to secure the appearance of legality for their operations where legitimate consent through negotiation would not have been possible.[25] Interpol also highlights that corruption, facilitated by organised criminal networks, can occur at any stage in the timber supply chain, presenting a substantial challenge to effective law enforcement efforts.[26] While Interpol is concerned with global trends in the illegal timber trade, the link between illegal logging and organised crime has been identified within PNG, with reports noting the connection between illicit timber harvesting activities in PNG and the trafficking of drugs, arms, and people. Smuggling is a key component of this organised criminal activity, with one report stating: "It has been observed that fuel, food, machinery and other material are not purchased domestically but are smuggled into PNG on the logging ships".[27] As such, illegal logging in PNG contributes to a wider illicit network of organised criminal activity with serious implications for the safety and security of the Asia Pacific region.

Tax evasion is another form of criminal activity that occurs in the context of illegal logging and forestry crime. Investigations by the PNG government and international NGOs have repeatedly revealed how companies involved in the timber industry in PNG engage in tax evasion to increase profitability. Recently, the Internal Revenue Commission of PNG imposed a large financial penalty on a logging company found to be engaged in illicit tax evasion through transfer pricing, providing conclusive evidence that tax evasion is a significant concern in the PNG forestry sector.[28]

Fraud and forgery in export and import documentation is also a significant concern, as is the fraudulent acquisition of logging licences under the pretence of, for example, agricultural development, when in fact there is no honest intent to develop the area for agriculture. The misuse of Special Agricultural Business Leases (SABLs) is a particularly impactful example of this form of criminality, although no prosecutions were ever secured for the offence of Fraud related to SABLs (or any other criminal offence) despite all SABLs being deemed illegal. More recently, evidence has emerged of fraudulent use of Forest Clearing Authorities (FCAs) under the pretence of agricultural development, despite a lack of informed consent by

[23] Global Witness (2012), Jubilee Australia (2023)

[24] Oakland Institute (2017).

[25] Global Witness (2019).

[26] Interpol (n.d.) Forestry crime.

[27] Financial Analysis and Supervision Unit (2021) Annual report 2021.

[28] IRC (2023).

landowners or any meaningful demonstration of intention to develop the land for agricultural use.[29]

This challenge extends beyond the PNG Forestry Law Framework. Interview research has demonstrated the impact of corruption and fraud on effective enforcement of laws designed to prohibit the import of illegally harvested timber:

> …participants mentioned the limitations of both destination country laws and certification schemes due to corruption and fraud. One interviewee went as far as to say: "if you solve corruption, you solve everything". Others recounted stories of forged certification stamps and noted the additional challenge of language barriers when attempting to validate documents from foreign jurisdictions.[30]

Money laundering also has strong links to forestry crime in PNG and globally. Money laundering is generally defined as "the act by which the proceeds of crime are made to appear legitimate".[31] Due to the substantial profits generated from illegal logging and forest crime, money laundering is necessary to enable criminal enterprises to deploy the profits generated, contributing to the continued financial incentive to engage in forest crime. The Bank of Papua New Guinea's National Money Laundering and Terrorist Financing Risk Assessment of 2017 established that the logging industry was a sector at high risk for money laundering activities in PNG, reflecting similar risks associated with logging and forestry crime on a global scale.[32]

The use of violence and intimidation by logging companies to secure landowner consent is also serious issue. Reports have brought to light instances where violence and threats have been used to suppress community dissent against logging activities. A Forest Trends report from 2004 notes, "allegations of police squads being used to beat and intimidate landowners and employees who complained about the activities of the logging company".[33] More recently, a 2017 report highlights that violence and intimidation remain a concern for rural forest reliant communities in PNG:

> People's resistance has been met with violence and intimidation. In a number of cases, local villagers resisting these land deals through peaceful protests have been arrested, beaten, or relocated.[34]

Human rights abuses are also a concern in the forestry sector in PNG.[35] The impact of forest crime on human rights has been identified as an issue of global concern, with scholars and advocacy groups highlighting the ways in which forest crime and corruption generate human rights risks and abuses that require a coordinated

[29] Jubilee Australia (2023).

[30] Harris (2024), p. 13.

[31] Asia Pacific Group on Money Laundering (APG): https://apgml.org/about-us/page.aspx?p=acbf69ba-a694-4db0b1be-f27172dde9fc.

[32] Harris (2022).

[33] Forest Trends: https://www.forest-trends.org/wp-content/uploads/imported/png-volume-1-pdf.pdf, p. 55.

[34] Oakland Institute (2017).

[35] Jubilee Australia (2023), Global Witness (2020).

response, addressing the harmful human impacts that result from exploitation of forests, in addition to the well understood environmental impacts.[36]

Despite the strong evidence of the link between illegal logging and various other criminal activities, both in PNG and globally, the forest law framework does not adequately acknowledge or engage with the connection between the forestry sector and facilitative and derivative criminal activities in PNG. In fact, the PNGFA recently defended against accusations of illegality and criminality in the forestry sector, stating that the critical views presented in certain reports "are not fair and there is no justification…merely perceptions with no concrete evidence".[37] This denial conflicts with the extensive and unsuccessful efforts of government to enhance the legal framework governing the forestry industry in PNG in response to extensive evidence of illegality and public outcry over criminality and harm in forest reliant communities. A headline search of *The National* news site—the primary news platform for PNG—turns up 43 headlines containing "illegal logging" between 2012 and 2024. The same search for the other major newspaper *The Post-Courier* turns up 27 headlines.[38] A wider search of global news sites that reference "illegal logging" and "Papua New Guinea" together returns 331 results. As such, the connection between crime and forestry in PNG is well established in the realms of public perception, even if it is invisible to the operation of the Forest Law framework.

3.3 *Limitation 3: Limited Transparency, Accountability, and Oversight of the Responsible Authority*

The third noteworthy limitation of the forest law framework in PNG is the lack of transparency, accountability, and oversight of the regulatory authority responsible for enforcement of the framework, the PNGFA.

The Forestry Law Framework was designed to regulate an industry that generates substantial revenue for the government through license fees and tax revenue, although there is evidence that much of this tax revenue is being lost to criminal evasion, transfer pricing, and other corporate misconduct by logging companies operating in PNG.[39] The reality is that the restrictive elements of the framework designed to protect the environment and forest-reliant communities from unsustainable logging practices are largely incompatible with the facilitative elements of the framework designed to enable a productive and profitable forestry industry.

[36] UNODC (2022b), UNODC (2022a).

[37] PNG Forest Authority, Media Statement: Major reforms at PNGFA already addressing Act Now Concerns (November, 2023): https://actnowpng.org/sites/default/files/PNGFA%20Media%20Response%20to%20AN%20Timber%20Legality%2 0Risk%20Assessment.pdf

[38] Search conducted on 21 February 2024 via the website search functions at the following addresses: https://www.postcourier.com.pg/; https://www.thenational.com.pg/

[39] World Bank (2018) p48.

This conflict is apparent within the wording of the long title of the *Forestry Act 1991* itself, which is said to be an Act to both "manage, develop and protect the Nation's forest resources and environment" and to "utilize the Nation's forest resources to achieve economic growth, employment creation and industrial and increased 'down stream' processing of the forest resources". Even in reference to protecting the Nation's forests, the focus is on forests as an "asset" and the commercial value of forest resources is a central concern of the Act. An economic growth focus can undermine objectivity in administration of legal frameworks, particularly in sectors that are substantial contributors to the economy.

Furthermore, sections 6 and 7 of the *Forestry Act 1991*, which establish the PNGFA and its functions, create a conflict between the objectives of administering the Act and enforcing it. It is arguable that the responsibilities of the PNGFA under Section 7(1) subsections (d), (e), and (i)—broadly, the authority to grant licenses and control market participation, should be carried out separately to those under Section 7(1) subsections (g) and (h)—broadly, the oversight and enforcement of the Act and related customs and export. The overlapping responsibilities may contribute to increased risk of corruption between the PNGFA and industry participants.

Considering the risks of conflict inherent to the *Forestry Act 1991* and allegations of corruption that have plagued the forestry sector and the PNGFA for decades, independent oversight and scrutiny are essential. Oversight should be focused on ensuring that the inherent conflict of interest between revenue generation and environmental protection established by the Forestry Law Framework is not compromising the quality of law enforcement in the forestry sector. Unfortunately, there are limited mechanisms for ensuring such oversight, and the mechanisms that do exist are not being utilised effectively. For example, a Risk Assessment published in 2023 notes that efforts by the Judiciary to enhance transparency around the granting of logging licenses have not had any impact on the conduct of the PNGFA and other government agencies:

> In July 2021, the Deputy Chief Justice sitting as a judge in the National Court issued an order calling for 'an immediate ban' on any logging in Timber Rights Purchase areas until the Forest Authority and a number of other government agencies provided the court with a series of detailed reports on the environmental impacts of all logging operations in the country. It was reported in February 2023, that while the Forestry Authority had not complied with the terms of the court order and logging in TRP areas was continuing, no enforcement action had been taken by the court.[40]

There are also several examples of PNGFA payments to logging companies that have been deemed to be unlawful by the National Court but have not resulted in an action against the Authority to address this apparent maladministration.[41] Given the above documented limits of the Forestry Law Framework in PNG, efforts to combat illegal logging and forestry crime must be expanded to include the use of criminal law mechanisms and related transnational legal tools, enabling enforcement efforts

[40] Act Now! PNG (2021).

[41] PNGi (2020).

to target the criminal activities that facilitate illegal logging and undermine effectiveness of and compliance with the Forestry Law Framework.

In summary, the PNG context presents some substantial barriers to effectively combatting illegal logging, particularly when the focus is limited to compliance with the *Forestry Act*, administered by the PNGFA whose interests are self-proclaimed to be focused on the economic value and development potential of the forestry sector. However, the above analysis demonstrates opportunities to leverage existing criminal law mechanisms to combat illegal logging in PNG, supplementing the forestry law framework while responding to the known relationship between illegal logging and other forms of criminal activity—in particular the crimes of corruption, tax evasion, and money laundering. Expanding the application of the criminal law to activities that contribute to illegal logging in PNG is likely to overcome some of the documented limitations of the Forest Law Framework, it may also lead to increased awareness (and responsiveness) of key stakeholders, regarding the risks of engaging in illegal logging and criminal acts that facilitate forest crime. Stakeholders including government, industry, civil society, global financial institutions, international donors and other multilateral organisations, all have an important role to play in overcoming illegal logging and forest crime in PNG and the wider Asia Pacific region.

Given the positive potential of widening the focus of law and enforcement strategies to include other forms of criminality related to illegal logging, the next section details the specific laws and strategies that PNG could deploy to achieve this objective, noting steps already taken by PNG authorities to apply certain laws targeting financial crime against entities suspected of profiting from forest crime with impunity. It is hoped that the examples and recommendations set out below will provide inspiration for the ongoing development of a more expansive and collaborative enforcement approach, both in PNG and further afield.

4 The Forest-Finance Nexus: Deploying Financial Crime Enforcement Strategies

Early in the chapter it was noted that certain regulators and enforcement actors in PNG have begun utilising creative enforcement strategies that appear promising for targeting illegal logging at the forest-finance nexus. The most notable example of this promising approach in PNG comes from enforcement of tax law violations against a major logging company suspected of engaging in forest crime.

In mid-2023, the Inland Revenue Commission (IRC) imposed a K140 million (USD 40 million) tax assessment against an undisclosed logging company "for engaging in illicit tax evasion, specifically through transfer pricing".[42] More recently, in February 2024, the IRC—in cooperation with the Immigration and Citizenship

[42] IRC (2023).

Authority (ICA)—issued a K11.79 million tax assessment against a mining company found to have engaged in tax avoidance and visa violations.[43] The successful enforcement action is the first for *Project Masta*, which focuses on investigating foreign worker and employer compliance with tax law, demonstrating both a collaborative approach between enforcement authorities and a focus on transfer pricing: a specific form of tax crime strongly associated with illegal logging, not only in PNG but in may forest rich jurisdictions globally.

The IRC explains transfer pricing tax evasions as "the act of manipulating the prices at which goods or services are transferred between related parties or companies within a multinational group. The purpose of this manipulation is to reduce the taxable income of one party, typically in a high-tax jurisdiction, by artificially inflating expenses or lowering revenues. By doing so, the company aims to shift profits to lower tax jurisdictions, thereby evading or minimizing its tax liabilities".[44] A World Bank report referenced by the Financial Action Task Force (FATF) estimates that "governments lose between USD 6 and 9 billion annually in tax revenue from illegal logging alone". (FATF 2021) The report highlights the typologies of financial crime most commonly associated with illegal logging:

> The use of tax havens or transfer pricing by companies in the fishing and forest sectors are common practices to reduce tax bills, increasing the potential financial losses…In some cases, payments for illegal activities are made directly to overseas accounts by a foreign entity, and never enter the formal national financial systems. In addition, the laundering of illegal revenues can undermine the integrity and stability of financial systems in local countries.[45]

Collaboration between the IRC and the ICA in enforcement of tax law against transfer pricing also demonstrates the value of inter-agency cooperation—particularly given that the connection between illegal logging and abusive labour practices. For example, the US Department of State has reported practices in the logging sector in PNG that suggest illegality linked to human trafficking and corruption. The US Department of State report alleges:

> law enforcement accepted bribes from incoming vessels in Papua New Guinea waters and logging companies, which greatly hindered anti-trafficking efforts in those industries. Logging companies bribed officials to bypass inspections and not take law enforcement action against employees accused of crimes, such as sexual abuse and exploitation, including potential trafficking crimes.[46]

Given this reality, a tax law approach is valuable—targeting the corporate actors and criminal enterprises profiting from immigration violations and other criminal activity, and further research into the role of immigration law and law enforcement to target illegal logging and forest crime is also warranted.

---

[43] NBC (2024).

[44] IRCPNG:https://irc.gov.pg/news/media-releases/major-logging-operator-chargedk140m-for-tax-evasion

[45] World Bank (2019).

[46] US State Department (2024).

4.1 Tax Evasion and Tax Law Violations: Law Enforcement Opportunities

From a tax law perspective, the various mechanisms for establishing an offence and penalty for breach of the *Income Tax Act 1959* ('*Tax Act*') are complex and extensive. In fact, there would be some value in reviewing and streamlining taxation law in PNG to reduce complexity and make reporting and enforcement more efficient and effective. However, it is worth noting some of the most impactful provisions for use in the context of illegal logging and forest crime in PNG, which may also be mirrored in other jurisdictions with similar crime typologies and tax law frameworks, suggest the possibility of establishing more direct connections between tax law and specific high-risk sectors for forest crime in other jurisdictions.

Division 14 of the *Tax Act* gives powers to the customs authority to restrict the movement of overseas ships when there are suspicions of tax law violations or unpaid tax assessments. Under Section 196, a customs officer "shall not grant a clearance to the ship until he is satisfied that any tax that has been or may be assessed under this Division has been paid, or that arrangements for its payment have been made to the satisfaction of the Commissioner General".[47] Such provisions may be used to restrict departure of illegally harvested timber from the jurisdiction of PNG and demonstrate the value of cooperation between the IRC and Customs and border authorities.

Other notable provisions are those contained in Part VI and VII of the Tax Act, addressing penalties and enforcement powers. Section 262 establishes an additional 20% tax for unpaid assessments and Section 264 establishes that unpaid tax "may be sued for and recovered in any court of competent jurisdiction by the Commissioner General suing in his official name". Section 264A allows for inclusion of additional costs in these proceedings. This prohibitive penalty tax is a valuable disincentive for failure to pay an established tax assessment. Part VII establishes clear offences and penalties for tax crime, enabling the IRC to take legal action against entities that misreport or attempt to avoid legitimate taxation. Some of these offence provisions include procedural offences that promote enhanced disclosures by business entities and are likely to assist authorities with detection and enforcement activities. For example, section 313 establishes an offence of failure to provide information or comply with requirements within the Act. Perhaps the most relevant and direct offence for pursuing tax crime committed in relation to forest crime is Section 317, establishing the offence of lodging a false tax return, a necessary component of transfer pricing as a criminal strategy to profit from illicit timber harvest and trade. Other relevant offences include False Declarations under Section 319, which can result in imprisonment for up to 4 years and understating income under Section 320.

While the Tax Act has potential to enhance efforts to combat illegal logging and related activities at the forest finance nexus, the limitations of this approach should also be noted, especially if other jurisdictions intend to leverage similar laws.

---

[47] Papua New Guinea Income Tax Act 1959 Part III Division 14 Section 196.

Reflecting on the transfer pricing enforcement action introduced above, the IRC noted that investigation was challenging and costly:

> During the audit, the taxpayer was not cooperative and provided limited information…The taxpayer even denied the existence of any association with the overseas parties and disclosed their residence to be in certain jurisdictions. However, thanks to the IRC's progress in international tax cooperation in recent years, powerful tools like the exchange of information standard (which allows for the IRC to obtain information on foreign taxpayers from tax administrations in other jurisdictions) allowed the IRC to confirm the existence of the association.[48]

This case illustrates the importance of international cooperation in tax investigations and highlight the value of simplifying the taxation framework to remove loopholes, streamline reporting, and increase the efficiency of oversight processes. As such, PNG's ratification of two major international treaties addressing tax issues is commendable and provides an avenue for access to continued support and capacity building.[49] To increase efficiency and effectiveness of tax law enforcement in PNG, it may be helpful to draw further on international expertise and support, including through expanded cooperation with the OCED and Tax Inspectors without Borders Program and by utilising membership of the Global Tax Forum other cooperative organisations to seek guidance and share best practices on legal structure and enforcement.[50]

Finally, linking of the taxation frameworks with other regulatory frameworks should be promoted in PNG. Joint investigations (as in the case of the cooperation between the IRC and ICA) are powerful and should be continued. Efforts to combat forest crime are likely to benefit from a global shift towards a more collaborative and dynamic law and enforcement strategy; one that views forest crime and financial crime not as distinct areas of risk and harm, but as connected elements of a strategy deployed by criminal enterprises in the pursuit of illicit profits.

Given PNG's history of ineffective forest law and unsuccessful enforcement of the Forestry Law Framework, it is reasonable to assume that without this innovative approach, the misconduct of the entities subject to enforcement action would have remained unpunished. The strategy of the IRC provides a tangible and hopeful example of a path forward for deterring forest crime, one that targets the ill-gotten gains that are the primary motivator of this form of organised criminality. How then, could this novel enforcement strategy be leveraged by other authorities in PNG and expanded to jurisdictions throughout the timber supply chain?

---

[48] IRC (2023).

[49] OECD (2023).

[50] IRC (2025).

4.2 Corruption and the Role of Anti-corruption Agencies

Given the successful collaboration between the IRC and ICA, and the potential for further collaboration with the Customs Authority, it is recommended that anti-corruption agencies such as PNG's recently established Independent Commission Against Corruption (ICAC) also be actively included in enforcement efforts at the forest-finance nexus. As noted earlier in this chapter, corruption represents a substantial barrier to the effectiveness of the Forest Law Framework and has also been highlighted as a key inhibitor of efforts to combat forest crime in other jurisdictions.

Engagement between other enforcement authorities and the ICAC may enable more effective action against forest crime, particularly if the legal framework governing the ICAC is adapted to provide it with greater disclosure and enforcement powers. However, the likelihood that engagement with the ICAC will have a meaningful impact remains uncertain. PNG has a complex history with anti-corruption agencies and effective action by relevant authorities. As such, a more immediately actionable approach would be to focus on Anti-Money Laundering (AML) laws, which also have generalisable application to other jurisdictions due to the relatively consistent legal frameworks that exist to combat money laundering on a global scale, recognising the transnational nature of the financial transactions that enable illicit transfer of ill-gotten profits from criminal activity.

4.3 Money Laundering Law and Enforcement Strategies

There are three laws in PNG that comprise the AML Framework which may be deployed to combat illegal logging and associated criminal conduct: the *Anti-Money Laundering and Counter Terrorist Financing Act 2015 ('AML/CTF Act');* the *Criminal Code 1974* as amended by the *Criminal Code (Money Laundering and Terrorist Financing) (Amendment) Act 2015*; and the *Proceeds of Crime Act 2005* as amended by the *Proceeds of Crime (Amendment) Act 2015*. Deploying these laws to combat illegal logging is likely to have a significant impact, with PNG's Money Laundering and Financing of Terrorism National Risk Assessment identifying illegal logging as "one of the country's most significant proceeds-generating crime threats for money laundering".[67]

The AML regime established by the above-mentioned laws was intended to bring PNG in line with international AML standards, to enhance capacity to detect and deter money laundering and terrorist financing, and to expand the obligations of financial institutions to support these efforts.[68] In fact, the National Risk Assessment referenced above was the result of new reporting requirements established by Section 6 of the *AML/CTF Act*. Another valuable dimension of the AML regime is the AML/CTF Act's establishment of the Financial Intelligence and Supervision Unit (FASU) within the PNG Central Bank. The FASU has been active in investigating and enforcing the regime, including against BSP Financial Group (Bank of the South Pacific).

Reporting on the sanctions against BSP, the Australian Financial Review reports:

> FASU said the sanctions were in response to 'significant levels of financially- motivated crime suffered by PNG'. It singled out 'money laundering, corruption, tax evasion/avoidance, organised crime, illegal logging and wildlife trafficking'.[51]

It is not only valuable, but in fact essential, for PNG to utilise its AML regime to target illegal logging and forest crime. Criminal Enterprises are deriving substantial financial value from forest crime, the profits of which can be linked to other illicit and harmful activities that undermine the safety and security of PNG and the wider region.

Another benefit of utilising the AML regime is that it directly targets corporate entities (commercial banks and other financial institutions) who are enabling illegal logging through their business activities. These financial institutions can be incentivised by the AML regime—through risk of sanctions combined with loss of correspondent banking relationships that enable their operations and profit generation—to become allies in the fight against illegal logging and forest crime. When banks become gatekeepers against illegal activity, the profitability of this activity is undermined, and the incentive to engage in illegal logging and forest crime can be largely eliminated.

The forest-finance nexus is well understood by the FASU, with the Acting Director of the agency making the following statement in a 2022 speech:

> Papua New Guinea is a country blessed with richness in natural resources and is home to one of the largest rainforests in the world. But unfortunately, our forests are being exploited by unscrupulous individuals and foreign logging companies facilitated by a network of tax-havens, local and foreign banks, lawyers, accountants, corrupt officials and politically exposed persons.[52]

Unfortunately, that same speech articulates some of the limitations of the AML/CTF regime in the context of illegal logging and forest crime:

> The bulk of the proceeds of illegal logging never return to PNG … the private sector do not want to forgo, or even risk, the profits to be made from the facilitation of illegal logging in PNG … Tax-haven jurisdictions do not want to cease providing anonymous companies and anonymous banking services to logging companies involved in illegal logging in PNG … Foreign jurisdictions do not typically want to expend valuable law enforcement resources to address a crime that has been committed in some tiny, far-off nation … The evidence required to prove beyond reasonable doubt that logs have been taken illegally is difficult to obtain and even more difficult to use…[53]

[51] AFR (2021). NAB and CBA exposed over PNG money laundering. Retrieved from https://www.afr.com/companies/financial-services/nab-and-cba-exposed-over-png-money-laundering-20210712-p588x2.

[52] Wilson (2022).

[53] Ibid.

Despite these limitations, the AML/CTF regime has already had a documented impact on business practices in PNG. A 2021 investigation demonstrates bank awareness of the legal and financial risk exposure presented by the forestry sector in PNG:

> Westpac PNG indicated that it had ceased, or started closure activity, for any banking relationship (including transaction services) with entities involved in the logging/timber industry who do not meet Forest Stewardship Council (FSC) or Programme for the Endorsement of Forest Certification (PEFC) standards. ANZ PNG also indicated it had reviewed its exposure to the sector and now only has a banking relationship with one customer involved in logging, which holds FSC certification.[54]

In Australia, enforcement of the *AML/CTF Act* by the FASU against BSP Financial Group has garnered press attention, highlighting the flow-on implications for Australian banks:

> The largest lender in the Pacific, BSP Financial Group, has been ordered to remove senior managers following breaches of anti-money laundering laws in Papua New Guinea, putting further pressure on Commonwealth Bank of Australia and National Australia Bank to cut ties with the troubled institution.[55]

Whilst repatriating assets stolen through illegal logging and corruption in PNG remains a substantial challenge, the *AML/CTF Act* creates a powerful incentive for enhanced compliance with reporting standards that reduce the risk that locally domicile banks and other corporate entities will inadvertently or intentionally participate in the provision or laundering of funds derived from or intended to enable illegal logging activities.

Additional dimensions of the Act that could benefit efforts to combat illegal logging include utilisation of provisions for enhanced due-diligence (Sections 26–29); prohibiting engagement with shell banks (Section 38) and disclosure of beneficial ownership (Section 59). Based on its powers under Section 59, the FASU should also be encouraged to develop a beneficial ownership database of companies operating in the forestry sector in PNG. Beyond this, the FASU could use its powers under Section 73 to develop compliance rules specific to financing of forestry activities or provision of financial services to entities associated with the forestry sector, with a view to establish enhanced due-diligence with respect to such entities and activities.

While there are many fruitful avenues to pursue within the AML/CTF Act alone, both the *Criminal Code (Money Laundering and Terrorist Financing) (Amendment) Act 2015* and the *Proceeds of Crime Act* provide additional opportunities to leverage the forest-finance nexus. For example, section 508B of the Criminal Code establishes the offence of money laundering, in a manner that is sufficiently broad to cover all offences under the *Forestry Act*. As such, a person or corporation found to be engaged in (or consenting to or enabling) the concealment, disguise, conversion, transfer, removal from PNG, bringing to PNG, receiving, acquiring, using or

[54] ACT NOW! PNG (2021).

[55] AFR (2021).

possessing of illegally harvested timber or funds derived from illegally harvested timber, could prosecuted for money laundering under the *Criminal Code*.

All other criminal activities documented as occurring to facilitate illegal logging in PNG are also subject to at least 6 months imprisonment and thus would also meet the requirement for a predicate offence under the AML provisions. Relevant crimes include failure to comply with reporting and due diligence obligations under the *AML/CTF Act,* bribery and corruption, fraud, tax evasion, violence and intimidation, trafficking, and theft. The benefit of this overlap is that it may enable PNG authorities to successfully prosecute illegal logging and forest crime through the AML provisions of the *Criminal Code*, in cases where enforcement of the *Forestry Act* is unlikely due to the limitations discussed early in this chapter. Additionally, investigations under the *Criminal Code* for money laundering could extend not only to actors suspected of direct involvement in illegal logging, but also to actors facilitating illegal logging through related criminal activities, the companies that transport and otherwise 'deal with' illegally harvested timber, and the banks and financial institutions that service these actors.

Finally, the amended *Proceeds of Crime Act* provides for the forfeiture of property used in connection with criminal activity, as well as depriving persons of the proceeds and benefits derived from such activities. The most relevant provisions of the amended Act in the context of illegal logging and forest crime are contained in Part III which sets out the confiscation scheme under Division 1, allowing for the Court to control property related to a criminal prosecution and ultimately enables the forfeiture of the proceeds of crime to the state. It is appealing to potentially be able to repatriate the proceeds of illegal logging and forest crime to PNG, considering the scale of the financial losses calculated as a result of such crime. One report asserts that in PNG "recent studies and analysis conducted with UNODC estimate that illicit proceeds generated from forestry crimes exceed the funds earned in the legal timber market".[56] A World Bank study expands:

> By concentrating on the financial aspects of criminal enterprises, law enforcement officials are not only better able to investigate and discover the full scope of the criminal activity—how much timber is being harvested and how much money is being generated—but also where the proceeds are hidden, and who has been involved in recycling those proceeds into the legitimate economy. This knowledge enables prosecutors to proceed with confiscating and actually recovering the ill-gotten gains. Stripping criminals of the proceeds of their crime raises the cost of conducting this illegal business and consequently helps to deter further criminal activity.[57]

Targeting the proceeds of crime is also a valuable tool in addressing corruption linked to illegal logging. If bribe payments can be effectively detected, seized, and forfeited, the incentive to participate in corrupt schemes is reduced. However, there are substantial challenges with practical implementation of the *Proceeds of Crime Act* in PNG, particularly when funds have already left the country and enforcement requires cooperation with enforcement authorities in other jurisdictions. Detection

[56] Financial Action Task Force (n.d.) Money laundering from environmental crime.

[57] World Bank (2012).

can also be a significant challenge. The FASU has highlighted restraint of the proceeds of crime as a key objective in its Strategic Report 2023–2027 and has further suggested legislative amendment may be necessary to ensure the FASU is sufficiently empowered to enforce the Act.[58] Additionally, it may be valuable to increase transnational cooperation around the Act with enforcement agencies in other jurisdictions. "Return of assets is possible only when there is close and effective cooperation between States involved".[59] This is a particularly important point considering the nature of the forestry sector in PNG, which is largely extractive with limited productive engagement with the domestic economy. Indications are that entities engaged in illegal logging use the PNG financial system to move only small amounts of money—often routed through tax havens to be used to pay only for those goods and services that cannot be easily smuggled into PNG on logging ships. Expenditure on costs, such as the salary and wages for workers are paid into accounts in the foreign employee's home country from accounts held by the logging companies offshore. It has been observed that fuel, food, machinery, and other material are not purchased domestically but are smuggled into PNG on the logging ships.[60]

The above insights from the FASU's investigation and analysis reflect broader trends regarding the operating practices of criminal enterprises engaged in illegal logging and forest crime. The FATF report: "Money Laundering from Environmental Crime" provides insights that mirror the findings of the FASU:

> In addition to the challenges in separating legitimate and illicit financial flows due to comingling, the placement of funds in a different jurisdiction from where then underlying crime was committed creates an additional barrier to identification and prosecution while also facilitating a secondary crime of tax evasion.[61]

The PNG Forest Authority itself notes that "logging operations in PNG are foreign-dominated"[62] citing Rimbunan Hijau (RH) Cakara Alam and Vanimo Forest Productions as the dominant operators. Each of these operators have been subject to various investigations and court actions for misconduct in their logging operations and all are ultimately owned by Malaysian companies. As such, cooperation between authorities in Malaysia and PNG should be encouraged, as it would benefit efforts to combat money laundering and the financing of illegal logging operations by these questionable foreign entities in PNG.

To motivate such cooperation, it may be valuable to emphasise the connection between illegal logging and organised criminal enterprise. Research in other jurisdictions has shown that "the growing involvement of organized crime in illegal logging and related activities…greatly increased levels of violence, displacement,

[58] Papua New Guinea Forest Authority (2020) National forest plan 2021–2030.

[59] UNODC (2010).

[60] FASU (2021).

[61] Financial Action Task Force (2021).

[62] PNG Forest Authority, Media Statement: Major reforms at PNGFA already addressing Act Now Concerns (November, 2023): https://actnowpng.org/sites/default/files/PNGFA%20Media%20Response%20to%20AN%20Timber%20Legality%2 0Risk%20Assessment.pdf

vulnerability to being trafficked and deforestation".[63] A US State Department report links the PNG forestry sector to similar forms of criminal activity:

> Malaysian and Chinese logging companies arrange for some foreign women to enter the country…After their arrival, many of these women—from countries including Indonesia, Malaysia, Thailand, China, and the Philippines—are turned over to traffickers who transport them to logging and mining camps, fisheries, and entertainment sites and exploit them in sex trafficking and domestic servitude. Sex traffickers also reportedly exploit foreign children in Papua New Guinea. Chinese, Malaysian, and local men are subjected to forced labor at commercial mines and logging camps.[64]

The link between organised crime and illegal logging was highlighted by the 2023 Pacific Transnational Crime Network event which reported discussion of "child exploitation, illicit drugs and illegal logging".[65] By focusing on the link between illegal logging and criminal enterprise may enhance effective cooperation with jurisdictions where the proceeds of illegal logging activities are being laundered and used to fund other criminal activities. Other opportunities for cooperation include working through international treaties such as the United Nations Convention against Corruption (UNCAC) to which both PNG and Malaysia are party.

Finally, linking illegal logging in PNG to bank lending practices in Malaysia may encourage the Malaysian financial sector to enhance compliance practices on both AML and environmental risk assessments. Such efforts could also be expanded beyond Malaysia to other financial centres at risk of funding the enterprises that contribute to illegal logging and forest crime, not only from the perspective of sustainable business, but also from the perspective of reducing risk exposure to criminal activity. A recent report by Forest & Finance highlights the importance of targeting the role of banks and finance companies in combating forest crime and related environmental harm on a global scale:

> Given the prolific harms documented in their clients' forestry and agribusiness operations – often spanning several decades – banks and investors appear to be systematically ignoring egregious harms in order to maintain highly profitable business relationships. Meanwhile, a litany of corporate-devised initiatives offers financial institutions platforms to make lofty pledges on sustainability without any real transparency or accountability, enabling business-as-usual greenwashing.[66]

This report reflects much of the insight and recommendations provided by an earlier 2021 report into the financing of illegal logging in PNG, which highlighted the role of corresponding banks (particularly in Australia) that may facilitate illegal logging in PNG and, by doing so, breached Australian anti-money laundering law:

> Providing credit or other banking services to logging companies is a major liability for commercial banks operating in PNG…The commercial banks' exposure to the logging sector also creates risks for the banking system as a whole…Until illegal logging is stamped out, bank involvement in the logging sector is a liability…some banks have already taken

[63] Global Initiative (2020).

[64] US State Department (2020).

[65] Australian Federal Police (2023)

[66] Forests and Finance (2023).

> positive steps...For these banks, continued due diligence is vital, including scrutinising the actual impact of the logging operations they continue to finance. It is also important they identify and end banking relationships with companies in the same corporate family as the logging companies, to avoid supporting the industry through the back door.[67]

There is a clear argument in favour of a coordinated transnational approach to combat money laundering associated with illegal logging and forest crime in PNG and the wider Asia Pacific. This coordinated approach requires participation of law enforcement and financial sector stakeholders in foreign jurisdictions, including Malaysia and Australia. Such collaboration may be extended beyond the Asia Pacific region too—to integrate comparative insights from other affected jurisdictions and development of generalisable legislative and law enforcement strategies to combat crime at the forest-finance nexus.

5 Leveraging the Forest-Finance Nexus: A Call to Action

This chapter has sought to illuminate opportunities for strategic action and policy development at the forest-finance nexus—using the example case of PNG. However, this chapter also seeks to re-orient and re-focus scholarly research in the fields of financial *and* environmental crime. The chapter is intended as both a call to action and an anchor point for further investigation of the forest-finance nexus. As such, the following section identifies some areas for further scholarly analysis and recommendations for action—that build on the PNG experience. The author herself is actively engaged in ongoing projects that intersect several of these areas. Collaboration must be encouraged, between scholars, practitioners, and stakeholders from government and industry (especially the financial services sector) to advance knowledge and understanding of the powerful interactions between illicit finance and environmental harm. Only through continued research, policy action, and reflective analysis, can we hope to secure a future where forests and financial integrity are both safeguarded from criminal actors and enterprise.

5.1 Transnational Enforcement Mechanisms

First, research should be advanced to address the question of how best to leverage transnational enforcement mechanisms to advance cooperation between States and overcome the challenges that currently undermine cooperative efforts at the forest-finance nexus. One question is how might PNG leverage UNCAC to better combat forest crime and intercept the illicit proceeds generated from such criminal activity? Articles 43 through 55 of UNCAC enable State Parties (of which PNG is one) to

[67] Act Now! PNG (2021).

request cooperation in the investigation and prosecution of corruption-related offences, including for the purposes of asset recovery and information sharing. Given that corruption is one of the primary facilitators of forest crime, leveraging UNCAC to assist with the cross-border dimensions of such criminal activities seems both promising and prudent. Regional initiatives like the Pacific Transnational Crime Network, led by the Australian Federal Police, present further avenues to embed environmental crime within broader regional security frameworks.[68] The FATF's peer-review and technical assistance programs should also be analysed for their potential to strengthen law enforcement collaboration at the forest-finance nexus—including through asset tracing and joint prosecutions.

5.2 *Corporate Liability Models*

The growing global movement toward corporate accountability offers another important area for legal research at the forest-finance nexus. The role of corruption in facilitating forest crime could be a particularly fruitful relationship to leverage in this regard. Australia's *Crimes Legislation Amendment (Combatting Foreign Bribery) Act 2024* introduces a "failure to prevent" foreign bribery offence (s 70.5A, *Criminal Code 1995* (Cth)) that could be used to prosecute companies engaged in bribery of government officials in PNG—including bribes paid to facilitate illegal logging and other forest crimes (Attorney-General's Department 2024). Similarly, the EU Corporate Sustainability Due Diligence Directive (CSDDD) requires companies to identify and mitigate environmental and human rights risks in global supply chains.[69] In Australia, the new mandatory climate reporting framework contained within the *Corporations Act 2001 (Cth)*, includes a requirement for regulated entities to lodge an annual sustainability report including a statement of material financial risks or opportunities relating to climate, accompanied by a Directors' declaration. While forest crime and illegal logging is not expressly in scope, the relationship between deforestation and climate change is well established, and the framework is illustrative of the trend towards mandating entities to consider environmental risks arising from business operations—with legal consequences for non-compliance. Given the rapid expansion of import regulations targeting illegally harvested timber and forest risk commodities suggests that the strength and number of mandatory due diligence obligations will also increase, once again following in the footsteps of the EU, UK, and Australia.

Under international law, current efforts to establish an International Anti-Corruption Court (IACC) include a draft Statute that would extend liability to corporations and other legal entities as well as individuals. The current draft also includes a "failure to prevent" offence, which would greatly expand the

[68] Australian Federal Police (2023).

[69] European Commission (2023).

responsibility of corporations to engage in robust risk assessment, compliance, and due diligence practices on a global scale. The draft Statute also includes money laundering as an offence within the court's jurisdiction—if the IACC is established and these provisions are successfully incorporated they will represent a powerful mechanism for pursuit of those commercial actors who engage in or enable forest crime. These developments raise pressing questions about risk and compliance strategies for entities such as banks and other businesses with potential exposure to individuals and entities engaged in forest crime. The increased legal risk for indirect enablers and facilitators of forest crime provides an opportunity to engage industry participants as allies in detection and prevention efforts at the forest-finance nexus.

5.3 *Comparative Analysis for Global Application*

While PNG's enforcement innovations at the intersection of forest crime and financial crime are context-specific, the use of financial crime frameworks to combat forest crime is broadly replicable across other affected jurisdictions. Indonesia, Malaysia, countries in the Congo Basin in Africa, and those in the Amazon region of Latin America all face similar enforcement challenges when attempting to combat forest crimes—as in PNG, many of these challenges stem from the financial motivation behind forest crime and the financial crime strategies used to facilitate forest crime and secure the proceeds of such environmentally destructive acts. The FATF has documented the link between environmental crime and financial crime in multiple regions including Southeast Asia, Central Africa, South America, and Eastern Europe. Typologies identified by the FATF include transfer pricing, use of offshore accounts, and trade-based money laundering—all requiring the participation of entities in secondary jurisdictions where shell companies are established and illicit funds are transferred, hidden or re-routed.[70]

In Latin America, Brazil has begun working with INTERPOL and UNODC to target environmental crime networks using financial investigation techniques.[71] There is an opportunity here for comparative legal research to address questions such as how legislative frameworks and institutional structures that have enabled PNG's approach might be adapted and applied in other jurisdictions. And, further, how regional cooperation might be leveraged to build shared enforcement capacity—for example through groups such as APEC EGILAT. This expert group provides a valuable platform for policy dialogue and enforcement cooperation. Its work includes promoting timber legality frameworks, strengthening supply chain transparency, and facilitating cross-border collaboration among forestry and customs agencies across the Asia-Pacific region. While the group's agenda has not yet expanded to engage with the intersection of forest crime and financial crime, such

[70] Financial Action Task Force (2021).

[71] United Nations Office on Drugs and Crime (2023).

engagement should be encouraged and joined up with efforts to ensure the resilience of APEC nations to both financial and environmental crime threats.

5.4 Strengthening AML and Tax Frameworks: Reform Options

Although financial enforcement tools are powerful, their impact in PNG and similar jurisdictions depends on robust legal and institutional infrastructure. The FASU has acknowledged the need for stronger legislative powers to restrain proceeds of crime, while tax authorities have called for simplification of overly complex reporting rules.[72] AML enforcement can be further strengthened through improved transparency measures, such as beneficial ownership registers—a reform backed by the FATF as a priority recommendation.[73] The UK has recently introduced environmental risk factors into its Suspicious Activity Reporting (SAR) regime[74] and PNG could explore similar mechanisms, perhaps using the FASU's powers under s 73 of the *AML/CTF Act* to impose sector-specific compliance rules on logging-related financial flows. Future research could also assess the feasibility of joining initiatives like the Tax Inspectors Without Borders program or the OECD Global Forum on Transparency.[75]

5.5 Community-Centred Enforcement and Restitution

A more inclusive enforcement strategy must centre forest-reliant communities, many of whom suffer direct harm from illegal logging, land grabs, and associated violence. Yet current financial enforcement strategies rarely involve these communities or allocate recovered proceeds for reparative purposes. The UNODC and Transparency International have emphasised the need to link anti-corruption work with access to justice and victim participation.[76] Models from other jurisdictions—such as the Philippines' Community-Based Forest Management Agreements or Colombia's restitution mechanisms in post-conflict zones—could inform approaches for community restitution or reinvestment of recovered assets. Additionally, there is a need to explore legal tools that could empower landowners and customary groups to bring claims or participate in monitoring and enforcement, potentially through constitutional, tort, or environmental rights frameworks. Aligning financial

[72] Bank of PNG (2023).

[73] Financial Action Task Force (2022) Recommendation 24—Transparency and Beneficial Ownership of Legal Persons.

[74] National Crime Agency (2022).

[75] OECD (2023).

[76] United Nations Office on Drugs and Crime (2023), Transparency International PNG (2022).

enforcement with environmental justice objectives would help ensure that the forest-finance nexus is not only a legal tool, but a pathway toward equity and repair.

6 Conclusion

PNG's forests sit at the heart of global environmental, economic, and social systems. As this chapter has shown, illegal logging and forest crime are not only ecological disasters — they are also directly linked to the commission of financial crimes including fraud, corruption, money laundering, and tax evasion.

This chapter has documented the extent and complexity of the forest crime challenge in PNG and the limitations of the existing Forest Law Framework in this country. PNG is not alone in the challenges it faces. The relationship between forest crime and financial crime presents challenges for the protection vital forest ecosystems, but also allows for promising opportunities to coordinate enforcement approaches and leverage the legal tools designed to combat financial crime, deploying them against the commercial entities and criminal enterprises that profit from exploitation of vital forest ecosystems.

From the analysis of PNG, several avenues for transnational action emerge. First, it is recommended that a more collaborative approach be taken to combat forest crime, not only within States, but between enforcement agencies operating in multiple jurisdictions, supported by regional bodies, international organisations, and transnational legal mechanisms that facilitate cooperation to combat financial crime. Integration of forest crime enforcement with transnational AML and anti-corruption regimes alike will incentivise increased compliance by business enterprises seeking to avoid legal exposure deriving from facilitation of forest crime or inadvertent laundering of the proceeds of such crimes. The strengthening and expansion of mandatory social and environmental due diligence obligations have similar potential, as do novel models of corporate liability such as the "failure to prevent" model enacted in Australia and the UK and contemplated for inclusion under the jurisdiction of the IACC. Such legal innovations should be encouraged. By targeting the funds generated from forest crime, the profitability of illegal logging and related activities may be reduced, shifting the cost benefit calculations away from forest crime as a profitable criminal enterprise. Targeting enforcement efforts at the forest-finance nexus is also likely to motivate the financial services sector to cooperate as co-regulators and quasi-enforcement agencies in the effort to combat both financial and forest crime.

As banks and other financial service providers become increasingly aware of the extent of criminality in the forestry and agriculture sectors, they will be incentivised to engage with forest crime risk factors in their AML risk assessments and enhance their compliance policies and practices to avoid the significant costs associated with breaches of AML obligations. Collaboration with this sector provides national enforcement agencies with increased transnational reach and is likely to have flow on effects for the forestry sector and other industries at risk of facilitating forest crime. When business enterprises rely on access to financial services to conduct their operations, they will be necessarily responsive to increasingly stringent standards of transparency and integrity in their business practices.

Other actions points include the strengthening of domestic enforcement bodies—like the FASU and IRC in PNG—with the goal of enhancing collaborative investigative capacity and information sharing. Transnational enforcement partnerships should also be strengthened. For PNG and the wider Asia Pacific region, Australia and Malaysia are obvious partner jurisdictions—being the locations where financial flows that derive from forest crime are often channelled; exposing legitimate businesses in the financial services sector to increased risk of complicity. Finally, community and wider stakeholder participation should be prioritised to ensure that enforcement efforts translate into restorative justice for the environment and impacted communities. In PNG, this could include involving customary landowners in investigations, redirecting recovered assets to community development, and safeguarding land rights to strengthen protections against illegal timber harvesting and forest exploitation.

Taken in concert with ongoing scholarly research, these actions can strengthen and re-invigorate efforts to combat forest crime—while providing a new focal point for financial crime enforcement efforts—targeting criminal enterprises that exploit our legitimate economy and financial institutions to profit from the destruction of forest ecosystems at the cost of local communities and the integrity of the global economy.

References

ACT NOW! PNG (2021) The money behind the chainsaws. https://actnowpng.org/sites/default/files/publications/The%20Money%20Behind%20the%20Chainsaws.pdf. Accessed 29 July 2025

AFR (2021) NAB and CBA exposed over PNG money laundering. Retrieved from https://www.afr.com/companies/financial-services/nab-and-cba-exposed-over-png-money-laundering-20210712-p588x2. Accessed 29 July 2025.

APEC Expert Group on Illegal Logging (2021) Timber legality guidance template. https://www.apec.org/docs/default-source/groups/egilat/2021/0308apec-experts-group-on-illegal-logging-and-associated-trade-egilattimber-legality-guidance-templa.pdf. Accessed 29 July 2025

Australian Federal Police (2023) Enhancing partnerships with Pacific law enforcement agencies to combat transnational crime. https://www.afp.gov.au/news-centre/media-release/enhancing-partnerships-pacific-law-enforcement-agencies-combat. Accessed 29 July 2025

Australian Government Attorney-General's Department (2024) Crimes Legislation Amendment (Combatting Foreign Bribery) Act 2024 – fact sheet. https://www.ag.gov.au/crime/publications/failure-prevent-foreign-bribery-fact-sheet. Accessed 29 July 2025

Bank of Papua New Guinea (2023) FASU strategic plan 2023–2027. https://www.bankpng.gov.pg/wp-content/uploads/2023/03/FASU-Strategic-Plan-2023-2027.pdf. Accessed 29 July 2025

Barnett TE (1989) Commission of inquiry into aspects of the forestry industry, interim report no. 4: timber exploitation in New Ireland Province, vol. I

European Commission (2023) Corporate sustainability due diligence. https://commission.europa.eu/business-economy-euro/doing-business-eu/corporate-sustainability-due-diligence_en. Accessed 29 July 2025

European Commission (2025) Proposal for a Regulation of the European Parliament and of the Council amending Regulation (EU) 2023/1115 as regards certain obligations of operators and traders. Retrieved from https://environment.ec.europa.eu/document/download/15e6d00c-28bc-48db-9b32-b485742d372b_en?filename=Proposal%20for%20a%20Regulation%20-%20EUDR.pdf. Accessed 15 December 2025

Financial Action Task Force (2022) Recommendation 24 – transparency and beneficial ownership of legal persons. https://www.fatf-gafi.org/en/publications/Fatfrecommendations/FATF-Recommendation-24-Beneficial-ownership-legal-persons.html. Accessed 29 July 2025

Financial Action Task Force (n.d.) Money laundering from environmental crime. https://www.fatf-gafi.org/content/dam/fatf-gafi/reports/Money-Laundering-from-Environmental-Crime.pdf.coredownload.pdf. Accessed 29 July 2025

Financial Action Task Force (FATF) (2021) Money laundering from environmental crime. FATF https://www.fatf-gafi.org/en/publications/Environmentalcrime/Money-laundering-from-environmental-crime.html. Accessed 1 Aug 2025

Financial Analysis and Supervision Unit (2021) Annual report 2021. https://www.bankpng.gov.pg/wp-content/uploads/2023/03/Financial-Analysis-and-Supervision-Unit-Annual-Report-2021.pdf. Accessed 29 July 2025

Forest Legality (2013) Papua New Guinea timber legality risk assessment. https://forestlegality.org/sites/default/files/pdf/papua-new-guinea.pdf. Accessed 29 July 2025

Forests and Finance (2023) Banking on biodiversity collapse 2023. https://forestsandfinance.org/wp-content/uploads/2023/12/BOBC_2023_vF.pdf. Accessed 29 July 2025

Global Initiative (2020) Organized crime, trafficking, and deforestation in Mexico. https://globalinitiative.net/analysis/oc-trafficking-deforestation-mexico/. Accessed 29 July 2025

Global Witness (2012) Bending the truth: forest governance in Papua New Guinea. https://www.globalwitness.org/en/campaigns/forests/bending-the-truth/. Accessed 1 Aug 2025

Global Witness (2019) A major liability: illegal logging in papua new guinea threatens China's timber sector and global reputation. https://www.globalwitness.org/en/campaigns/forests/major-liability-illegal-logging-papua-new-guinea-threatens-chinas-timber-sector-and-global-reputation/. Accessed 1 Aug 2025

Global Witness (2020) Papua New Guinea hosts APEC meeting on illicit timber trade while allowing illegal loggers to destroy its forests. https://www.globalwitness.org/en/press-releases/papua-new-guinea-hosts-apec-meeting-illicit-timber-trade-while-allowing-illegal-loggers-destroy-its-forests/. Accessed 29 July 2025

Hance J (2011) Logging company fined $100 million for illegal logging in Papua New Guinea. Mongabay. https://news.mongabay.com/2011/06/logging-company-fined-100-million-for-illegal-logging-in-papua-new-guinea/. Accessed 1 Aug 2025

Harris A (2019) Corruption and the forestry industry in Papua New Guinea: transnational actors, local dynamics and environmental impact. Asia Pac J Environ Law 22(1):48–65

Harris H (2022) Illegal logging, corruption and the limitations of destination country laws in the Pacific context. New Zealand Yearbook Int Law 4:64–96

Harris H (2023) Corporate liability within the ICAC framework. Transnat Cri Law Rev 2(1):74–89. https://ojs.uwindsor.ca/index.php/nlj/article/view/7906/5606. Accessed 29 July 2025

Harris H (2024) Illegal logging and the criminal law context in PNG, report commissioned for ActNOW! PNG. https://actnowpng.org/publications/publication-illegal-logging-and-criminal-law-context-papua-new-guinea. Accessed 1 Aug 2025

Internal Revenue Commission of Papua New Guinea (IRC) (2023) Major logging operator charged K140 million for tax evasion. https://irc.gov.pg/news/media-releases/major-logging-operator-charged-k140m-for-tax-evasion. Accessed 1 Aug 2025

Internal Revenue Commission of Papua New Guinea (IRC) (2025) Continued cooperation with Tax Inspectors Without Borders programme to support forest and mining sector audits. https://www.pwc.com/pg/en/publications/png-pulse-keeping-you-informed/png-pulse-april-2025.html. Accessed 1 Aug 2025

International Tropical Timber Organization (2023) ITTO encourages sustainable wood use at meeting of APEC Expert Group. https://www.itto.int/news/2023/08/21/itto_encourages_sustainable_wood_use_at_meeting_of_apec_expert_group/. Accessed 29 July 2025

Interpol (n.d.) Forestry crime. https://www.interpol.int/en/Crimes/Environmental-crime/Forestry-crime. Accessed 29 July 2025

Jubilee Australia (2023) Forestry sector corruption in Papua New Guinea. https://www.jubileeaustralia.org/storage/app/uploads/public/64f/66f/96a/64f66f96ad950779028158.pdf. Accessed 29 July 2025

Kailemia M (2019) Problem-oriented policing of transnational environmental crimes: a social harms approach. Int J Comp Appl Crim Just 43(2):145–158. https://doi.org/10.1080/01924036.2018.1515093

Lawson S (2014) Illegal logging in Papua New Guinea. Energy, environment and resources EER PP 2014/04. https://www.chathamhouse.org/sites/default/files/home/chatham/public_html/sites/default/files/20140400LoggingPapuaNewGuineaLawson.pdf. Accessed 29 July 2025

Mukpo A (2020) China's revised forest law could boost efforts to fight illegal logging. Mongabay. https://news.mongabay.com/2020/03/chinas-revised-forest-law-could-boost-efforts-to-fight-illegal-logging/. Accessed 1 Aug 2025

National Archives (2023) Glasgow leaders' declaration on forests and land use. https://webarchive.nationalarchives.gov.uk/ukgwa/20230418175226/https://ukcop26.org/glasgow-leaders-declaration-on-forests-and-land-use/. Accessed 29 July 2025

National Crime Agency (2022) Guidance on suspicious activity reports (SARs) and environmental crime. https://www.nationalcrimeagency.gov.uk/who-we-are/our-expectations/suspicious-activity-reports. Accessed 29 July 2025

National Statistical Office of Papua New Guinea (2023) International merchandise trade highlights: palm oil and timber exports, 2021–2022. National Statistical Office of Papua New Guinea. https://www.nso.gov.pg/statistics/economy/international-merchandise-and-trade/2023-release/. Accessed 1 Aug 2025

NBC News PNG (2024) Mining company charged for income tax evasion. https://www.nbc.com.pg/post/11353/mining-company-charged-for-income-tax-evasion. Accessed 1 Aug 2025

OECD (2023) Global forum on transparency and exchange of information for tax purposes: Papua New Guinea 2023. https://www.oecd.org/tax/transparency/documents/exchange-of-information-on-request/papua-new-guinea-peer-review.pdf. Accessed 29 July 2025

Okland Institute (2017) Taking On the Logging Pirates: Land defenders in Papua New Guinea Speak Out

Papua New Guinea Forest Authority (2020) National forest plan 2021–2030. https://www.pngfa.gov.pg/images/documents/National_Forest_Plan_2021_2030.pdf. Accessed 29 July 2025

PNGi Central (2020) Illicit K10.6m payment: further evidence the Forest Authority is a rogue body. https://pngicentral.org/reports/illicit-k10-6-payment-further-evidence-forest-authority-is-a-rogue-body/. Accessed 1 Aug 2025

Radio New Zealand (2023) Papua New Guinea's forest crime crisis worsens amid weak governance. https://www.rnz.co.nz/international/pacific-news/489178/png-forest-crime-crisis-worsens-amid-weak-governance. Accessed 29 July 2025

Transparency International PNG (2022) Corruption perceptions index 2022. https://www.transparencypng.org.pg/wp-content/uploads/2023/02/CPI-2022.pdf. Accessed 29 July 2025

United Nations Office on Drugs and Crime (2023) Global study on crimes that affect the environment 2023. https://www.unodc.org/documents/Environmental_Crime/Global_Study_2023.pdf. Accessed 29 July 2025

United Nations Office on Drugs and Crime (UNODC) (2022a) Rapid assessment: criminal justice response to wildlife and forestry crime in Papua New Guinea. UNODC Regional Office for

Southeast Asia and the Pacific. https://www.unodc.org/res/environment-climate/asia-pacific_html/PNG_Assessment.pdf. Accessed 1 Aug 2025

United Nations Office on Drugs and Crime (UNODC) (2022b) Wildlife and Forest crime toolkit: impacts on human rights. UNODC https://www.unodc.org/documents/Wildlife/Toolkit_e.pdf. Accessed 1 Aug 2025

US State Department (2020) Trafficking in Persons Report: Papua New Guinea, available at: https://www.state.gov/reports/2020-trafficking-in-persons-report/papua-new-guinea/

US State Department (2024) Trafficking in Persons Report: Papua New Guinea, available at: https://www.state.gov/reports/2024-trafficking-in-persons-report/papua-new-guinea/

UNODC (2010) Follow the Money Trail: the challenges in illegal logging investigations, available at: https://www.unodc.org/roseap/uploads/archive/documents/indonesia/forestcrime/Following_the_money_in_illegal_logging.pdf

UNODC (2025) Sustainable Development Goals, SDG 14 and 15, available at: https://www.unodc.org/unodc/en/about-unodc/sustainable-development-goals/sdg14-and-15.html#:~:text=Wildlife%20and%20forest%20crime%20has,trade%20in%20animals%20and%20plants

Vijay V, Pimm SL, Jenkins CN, Smith SJ (2016) The impacts of oil palm on recent deforestation and biodiversity loss. Public Library of Science ONE 11(7):e0159668. https://doi.org/10.1371/journal.pone.0159668. Accessed 1 Aug 2025

Wilson A (2022) *Illicit financial flows and environmental crime*. Statement presented at the 31st Session of the Commission on Crime Prevention and Criminal Justice, UNODC. https://www.unodc.org/documents/commissions/CCPCJ/CCPCJ_Sessions/CCPCJ_31/expert_discussions/statements/day2/Wilson_ONEA.pdf. Accessed 1 Aug 2025

Workman D (2023) Papua New Guinea's top 10 exports. World's Top Exports (WTEx) https://www.worldstopexports.com/papua-new-guineas-top-10-exports/. Accessed 1 Aug 2025

World Bank (2012) Justice for Forests, available at: https://openknowledge.worldbank.org/server/api/core/bitstreams/848d6ecd-c541-54e5-aa63-7bb249393882/content

World Bank Group (2018) Papua New Guinea Economic Update: Reinforcing Resilience. World Bank Group. https://pubdocs.worldbank.org/en/482771571323560234/WBGReport1017Digital.pdf. Accessed 1 Aug 2025

World Bank Group (2019) Illegal logging, fishing, and wildlife trade: the costs and how to combat it. World Bank Group. https://pubdocs.worldbank.org/en/482771571323560234/WBGReport1017Digital.pdf. Accessed 1 Aug 2025

Dr Hannah Harris is a Senior Lecturer at Macquarie Law School and a research fellow with the Financial Integrity Hub (FIH). Her research area is transnational law and corporate regulation. Her current work includes analysis of legislative responses to transnational challenges, including illegal logging and modern slavery, and the impact of foreign bribery enforcement action on corporate compliance policies and practices.

Surveilling the Citizen: Constitutional Tensions Within the Canadian AML Regime

Sanaa Ahmed

Abstract Anti-money laundering regulation allows global and local regulators as well as states to amass volumes of data on the private, financial affairs of individuals. Using Canada as a case study, this chapter argues that financial-sector surveillance undermines the state's commitment to the constitutionally guaranteed right to privacy.

1 Introduction

The global anti-money laundering and counter terrorism financing (AML/CTF) regime allows global and local regulators to amass volumes of data on the private, financial affairs of individuals. Within jurisdictions, domestic AML/CTF laws and regulation strip away or erode many constitutional and procedural safeguards but also amplify the potential for enhanced policing and/or abuse. This is particularly so because the surveillance obligations prescribed under global and domestic regulation—especially recordkeeping and reporting requirements—are broadly conceived, amorphously worded, and do not carry attendant commitments as to the use of this data by either global or local regulators.[1] Using Canada as a case study, this

[1] The sociologist David Lyon defines surveillance as "the operations and experiences of gathering and analysing personal data for influence, entitlement and management" and control. David Lyon (2018) *The Culture of Surveillance*. Polity Press, Cambridge. P. 6. Surveillance is also described as an organisational practice that often results in people being categorised or "sorted" in ways that facilitate different forms of treatment for different individuals. Significantly, other authors underscore the point that surveillance is a form of power and is never "neutral". Bennett et al. (2014). P. 6–7. Moored to this history, financial-sector surveillance—or the surveillance of capital flows—

S. Ahmed (✉)
University of Calgary, Calgary, AB, Canada
e-mail: sanaa.ahmed@ucalgary.ca

D. Goldbarsht et al. (eds.), *Combating Financial Crime*, Ius Gentium: Comparative Perspectives on Law and Justice 131,
https://doi.org/10.1007/978-3-032-06858-3_8

chapter argues that financial sector surveillance undermines the Canadian state's commitment to the constitutionally guaranteed right to privacy.

The issue acquires particular complexity in light of public-private partnerships, whereby private sector actors (both institutions such as banks as well as individual 'enablers' such as lawyers, accountants etc) are tasked with the enforcement of AML regulation and/or with the policing of laundering on behalf of the state. Such public-private partnerships remain of continued and growing significance to the global AML/CTF regulator, the Financial Action Task Force (FATF). In her opening address at the 2025 FATF Private Sector Collaborative Forum, FATF president Elisa de Anda Madrazo emphasised the importance of collaboration between the public and private sectors and was quoted as saying: "Without the private sector, the FATF mandate to tackle money laundering and the financing of terrorism and proliferation could not be achieved. The private sector is at the forefront of the fight against financial crimes. In this fight, public authorities and private sector play on the same team".[2]

However, this emphasis elides two crucial issues. First, in many liberal democracies such as Canada, the privatisation of enforcement/policing functions is constitutionally infirm.[3] Second, the extent of surveillance mandated by global and domestic

is based on the identification of at-risk categories, the preemptive exclusion of illegitimate players and what has been referred to as the development of 'exceptionalism within the governmentality of everydayness' so as to protect the international financial architecture from blacklisted players and entities. As such, financial surveillance practices—including targeted economic sanctions and private-sector policing—are deemed a key intelligence-gathering tool that is investigative, analytical and proactive. Amicelle and Favarel-Garrigues (2012), pp. 105–106.

[2] Financial Action Task Force (2025) https://www.fatf-gafi.org/en/publications/Fatfgeneral/pscf-march-2025.html; see also Chadderton (2025), chapter 3, and Goldbarsht and Goodrick (2025), chapter 4.

[3] As documented in the mainstream media and academic literature, public policy and law in many areas of governance has been privatised and/or found porous to influences external to the state. Examples include tax policy, anti-union legislation as well as the rollback of climate change mitigation efforts. While neoliberalism helped birth the idea of private jails, private policing and private prosecution, private sector involvement in the criminal law realm has generally proven problematic. AML laws and regulation exemplify this. First, the laws and regulation deviate obviously from basic principles of criminal law—for example, the vaguely couched objectives of the law, the shifting of the burden of proof from the state on to an accused etc—and end up encroaching on constitutionally guaranteed rights such as due process, equal treatment under the law and the right to a fair trial. Second, the criminal law portfolio is the exclusive remit of the federal government in Canada (as opposed to provincial or territorial governments) and money laundering is a predicate offence. The outsourcing of law-making (see footnote 62 in chapter "Charities, Nonprofit Organisations and the FATF: Testing the Evidence Base and Proportionality of Risk-Based Counter-Terrorist-Financing Regulation") and law-enforcement is constitutionally infirm since criminal law was traditionally conceived as a salient feature of the sovereign state, simultaneously constituted by and constitutive of the state. In the Hobbesian and Lockean construction, the primary purpose of the modern state is to provide peace, security and public order. The outsourcing of criminal law-making and law enforcement functions may thus be seen as dereliction of state responsibility, particularly since criminal law and law enforcement derive their value *from their provision by public officials*. Similarly, as theorists such as Rousseau, Locke and Rawls contend, the social contract is a relationship whereby the people sacrifice or forego the enforcement of some rights in exchange for longer-term security and the guarantee of protection *by the state*. The terms of this contract cannot, as such, be unilaterally varied to substitute the state with *private-sector*

AML/CTF regimes poses serious threats to civil liberties. Not only does surveillance infringe on the privacy rights of individuals, by *enlisting* the private sector to function as the eyes and ears of the state, the Canadian state sidesteps its own constitutional and legal duties regarding the collection, use, and disclosure of information that could jeopardise the privacy of individuals. This enlisting thus affects significant rights, for example, the right to due process, equal treatment under the law and the right to a fair trial. As discussed below, while Canadian law provides safeguards regarding the collection, use, and disclosure of personal information by private sector organisations about individuals, these laws apply to the collecting organisations alone and in respect of their commercial activities only. That is, the protections afforded by the law do not extend to the collection, use, and disclosure of data collected in compliance with AML/CTF regulation. Nor do these protections apply to disclosure of data to governmental agencies. Significantly, the AML/CTF legal framework not only features carve-outs for the sharing of this data with governmental agencies, it also authorises some sharing between private sector actors. Critically, *there is no law governing the collection and use of this data by governmental agencies other than the constitutional right to privacy*.

This chapter discusses financial sector surveillance in light of the Supreme Court of Canada's (SCC) jurisprudence on the constitutionally guaranteed right to privacy. The first, largely descriptive part, showcases the legal architecture that underpins the AML/CTF regime in Canada and the privacy protections available under the law. The second part tracks the global evolution of surveillance practices and financial sector surveillance, while the third shows how the law enables financial sector surveillance through the collection, use, and disclosure of data by private organisations on behalf of the state. The fourth part examines how the Canadian AML/CTF regime runs afoul of privacy protections contained in the law, and the fifth offers a possible way towards constitutional sufficiency. The concluding part argues that the Canadian state's constitutional obligation to safeguard privacy necessarily extends to the collection, use and disclosure of this data by private organisations.

2 The Law of the Land

A founding member of the FATF in 1989, Canada has a seemingly strong AML/CTF regime that is simultaneously plugged into global networks. Besides the FATF, Ottawa is also a member of the Asia Pacific Group on Money Laundering,[4] as well

delegates, particularly when it comes to the performance of a core responsibility of the state. I discuss these issues in a forthcoming article.

[4] Financial Action Task Force (n.d.). The stated function of the APG is to "ensure the adoption, implementation and enforcement of internationally accepted anti-money laundering and counter-terrorist financing standards.... The effort includes assisting countries and territories of the region in enacting laws to deal with the proceeds of crime, mutual legal assistance, confiscation, forfeiture and extradition; providing guidance in setting up systems for reporting and investigating suspicious transactions and helping in the establishment of financial intelligence units." While the list of

as many of the global organisations that devise AML/CTF regulations. Additionally, Canada hosts the Egmont Group,[5] and its own financial intelligence unit (FIU)—the Financial Transactions and Reports Analysis Centre of Canada (Fintrac)—sees part of its work as contributing to other multilateral fora such as the FATF, the APG and the Caribbean FATF, besides participating in international policy making and the provision of technical assistance to other FIUs.[6]

Bolstering this regime further is a gamut of domestic laws and regulations. The federal AML/CTF regime in Canada allows domestic regulators (and their global partners) to amass volumes of information about citizens. At present, 13 federal departments and agencies in addition to provincial, regional, and municipal regulatory agencies and law enforcement bodies are involved with the AML effort in Canada.[7] The AML/CTF regime rests on three interdependent pillars: policy and coordination (entailing the assessment of money laundering and terrorist financing risks, domestic and international policy development, as well as coordination); prevention and detection (entailing the promotion, supervision, and enforcement of AML/CTF compliance and the collection, analysis, and dissemination of financial and other intelligence); and investigation and disruption (entailing the identification, investigation, prosecution, and sanctioning of money laundering and terrorist financing offences).[8] Given the nature and breadth of activities covered under the

members includes several states seen as recalcitrant, and thus in need of such assistance, presumably the same does not apply to states such as Canada, the US, Australia, and New Zealand, which are also FATF members, and can be reliably presumed to be the ones *providing* assistance.

[5] Egmont Group (n.d). The group is meant to facilitate international cooperation and the secure exchange of expertise and financial intelligence to combat money laundering and terrorist financing.

[6] Financial Transactions and Reports Analysis Centre of Canada (n.d.-a).

[7] Cullen Commission (2022), specifically Exhibit 1019, Affidavit #1 of Lesley Soper, affirmed May 11, 2021, Exhibit B, pp. 8–15. The federal agencies and departments include the Canada Border Services Agency, Canada Revenue Agency, Canadian Security Intelligence Service, Department of Finance Canada, Department of Justice Canada, Financial Transactions and Reports Analysis Centre of Canada, Global Affairs Canada, Innovation, Science and Economic Development Canada, Office of the Superintendent of Financial Institutions, Public Prosecution Service of Canada, Public Safety Canada, Public Services and Procurement Canada and Royal Canadian Mounted Police. Additionally, Statistics Canada, Canada Mortgage and Housing Corporation and the Bank of Canada are also known to have some AML/CTF responsibilities. See, for example, Bank of Canada, “Anti-money laundering and anti-terrorist financing controls framework”, online https://www.bankofcanada.ca/about/governance-documents/anti-money-laundering-and-anti-terrorist-financing-controls-framework/. Meanwhile, provincial and municipal law enforcement bodies, provincial Crown Attorney’s offices or prosecution services as well as provincial regulators (especially those with a role in the oversight of the financial sector such as provincial securities regulators) also have key AML/CTF responsibilities. Department of Finance Canada (2023). *Consultation on Strengthening Canada’s Anti-Money Laundering and Anti-Terrorist Financing Regime*, p. 9. Online at https://www.canada.ca/en/department-finance/programs/consultations/2023/strengthening-canada-anti-money-laundering-and-anti-terrorist-financing-regime/consultation-on-strengthening-canadas-anti-money-laundering-anti-terrorist-financing-regime.html.

[8] Department of Finance Canada (2023). *Consultation on Strengthening Canada’s Anti-Money Laundering and Anti-Terrorist Financing Regime*, p. 9. Online at https://www.canada.ca/en/department-finance/programs/consultations/2023/strengthening-canada-anti-money-laundering--and-anti-terrorist-financing-regime/consultation-on-strengthening-canadas-anti-money-laundering-anti-terrorist-financing-regime.html.

three pillars, financial sector surveillance is essential to the effective operation of each.

While the seamless operation of the AML/CTF regime is undergirded by a complex matrix of federal statutes and associated regulation,[9] the *Proceeds of Crime Money Laundering and Terrorism Financing Act*[10] (PCMLTFA) and eight associated regulations[11] are the primary law governing this area. Enacted in June 2000 and last amended in February 2025, the PCMLTFA comprises mostly procedural law and is divided into six parts. The first part describes the requirements regarding recordkeeping, identity verification, registration, and the reporting of financial transactions (including suspicious transactions), and the second part sets out detailed obligations regarding the reporting of currency and monetary instruments. The third part establishes the Canadian FIU– Fintrac—and includes detailed prescriptions regarding the use and disclosure of information. The fourth part deals with violations under the statute, compliance, and penalties while the fifth part describes offences and punishment. The concluding part features details regarding the transitional provisions, consequential and conditional amendments, and the coming-into-force provision.

Privacy, meanwhile, is constitutionally guaranteed as a foundational value under the *Canadian Charter of Rights and Freedoms* (Charter) and receives additional statutory protection through the *Privacy Act* as well as the *Personal Information Protection and Electronic Documents Act* (PIPEDA), both being federal laws. Additionally, each province and territory has enacted privacy legislation, which is overseen by a commissioner or ombudsperson;[12] some have statutory privacy torts,[13] while others rely on the common law for the enforcement of privacy torts.[14] Since 1984,[15] Canadian jurists have also developed a deep vein of jurisprudence around

---

[9] Other legislation that affects the overall operational efficacy of the AML/CTF regime include the Access to Information Act, Canada Business Corporations Act, Canadian Security Intelligence Act, Charities Registration (Security Information) Act, Customs Act, Extradition Act, Freezing Assets of Corrupt Foreign Officials Act, Immigration and Refugee Protection Act, Income Tax Act, Justice for Victims of Corrupt Foreign Officials Act, Library and Archives of Canada Act, Mutual Legal Assistance in Criminal Matters Act, National Defence Act, National Security and Intelligence Committee of Parliamentarians Act, Security of Canada Information Disclosure Act, Seized Property Management Act, Special Economic Measures Act, State Immunity Act and United Nations Act. Also of significance are the Criminal Code, the Canadian Charter of Rights and Freedoms, the Privacy Act and the Personal Information Protection and Electronic Documents Act. Cullen Commission (2022), specifically Exhibit 1019, Affidavit #1 of Lesley Soper, affirmed May 11, 2021, Exhibit B, pp. 8–15.

[10] S.C. 2000, c 17.

[11] The *Proceeds of Crime (Money Laundering) and Terrorist Financing Regulations* SOR/ 2002-184 are the most relevant for the purposes of this article. As such, any reference to Canadian AML regulations should be read as a reference to these, unless the context otherwise suggests.

[12] Privacy Commissioner of Canada (2024).

[13] These include British Columbia, Manitoba, Saskatchewan and Newfoundland and Labrador. In Quebec, privacy rights are enshrined in the Charter of Human Rights and Freedoms and Civil Code. Laidlaw (2021), "The future of the tort of privacy".

[14] These include Ontario and Alberta. SVR Lawyers (2024).

[15] *Hunter v Southam Inc* [1984] 2 SCR 145 is among the earliest cases that address the issue of privacy.

privacy issues. Even so, as will be demonstrated below, the nature and structure of financial sector surveillance frustrates or limits many of the protections applicable under the law.

Given the very nature of privacy, a sharp definition of the term is hard to come by in even the broader academic literature on privacy. In Solove's canvassing of the philosophical underpinnings of the concept, he skirts the Scylla of "intimacy[16]" as well as the Charybdis of "right to be left alone" and argues for privacy to be viewed as "a set of family resemblances" categorised in terms of the harms caused by privacy violations.[17] As discussed below, financial sector surveillance is problematic on all four counts. As such—and particularly in view of the privacy protections ostensibly available under the law—the extent of financial surveillance prevalent in Canada *should* have been a non-starter. But the structural peculiarities of the financial sector surveillance regime enable the untrammelled growth of the same.

The constitutional right to privacy is generally understood to stem from the provision dealing with unreasonable search and seizure[18] and is meant to protect people against unjustified intrusions on their privacy interests,[19] which includes informational privacy.[20] Canadian jurisprudence on informational privacy describes three interrelated but conceptually distinct understandings of privacy: privacy as secrecy; privacy as control; and privacy as anonymity. Privacy as secrecy is the idea that information disclosed in confidence will be held in trust and confidence by those to whom it is disclosed while privacy as control is the idea of control over, access to, and use of information.[21] This aspect of privacy "derives from the assumption that all information about a person is in a fundamental way his own, for him to communicate or retain for himself as he sees fit".[22] Comparatively, privacy as anonymity allows individuals to act in public spaces without being identified and surveilled. While all information is not protected under the Charter, "personal and confidential

[16] Solove (2007), p. 755. This is the idea that the content of privacy cannot be captured by exclusive focus on either information, access or intimate decisions because privacy entails all three; hence privacy should be understood as content that covers "*intimate* information, access and decisions".

[17] Solove (2007), pp. 757–760. The detailed taxonomy Solove develops features four general categories of privacy problems with 16 subcategories. The four general categories are Information Collection (with the two subcategories Surveillance and Interrogation); Information Processing (with the five categories Aggregation, Identification, Insecurity, Secondary Use, Exclusion); Information Dissemination (with the seven subcategories Breach of Confidentiality, Disclosure, Exposure, Increased Accessibility, Blackmail, Appropriation and Distortion); and Invasion (with the two subcategories Intrusion and Decisional Interference).

[18] Section 8 of the *Charter* reads: "Everyone has the right to be secure against unreasonable search or seizure." https://www.justice.gc.ca/eng/csj-sjc/rfc-dlc/ccrf-ccdl/check/art8.html.

[19] Hunter v Southam Inc [1984], p. 159.

[20] *R. v. Tessling* [2004] 3 SCR 432, paras 20–24. The two other categories are personal privacy and territorial privacy.

[21] See Section 8, Charterpedia, available at https://www.justice.gc.ca/eng/csj-sjc/rfc-dlc/ccrf-ccdl/check/art8.html.

[22] *R v Spencer* [2014] 2 SCR 212, para 40.

information" and information regarding the "biographical core" of an individual has been determined as protected.[23]

Significantly, in *Spencer*, the SCC held that the nature of the privacy interest engaged by state conduct "turns on the privacy of the area or the thing being searched and the impact of the search on its target, not the legal or illegal nature of the items sought".[24] As the court reasoned, merely entering a public space did not mean the individual expected to be personally identified and subjected to extensive surveillance. As such, the court held that a "reasonable expectation of privacy"[25] attaches to even subscriber information — name, address, and contact information — associated with an individual Internet Protocol (IP) address. Their logic was that given the vast amounts of *other* information online, state actors in possession of this subscriber information could triangulate information to get "personal and confidential information" about an individual. Accordingly, they held that a request for this information from an Internet Service Provider would constitute a "search under section 8".[26] In *Bykovets*, the court found that even an IP address carries a reasonable expectation of privacy.[27]

3 What Privacy?

For a fuller appreciation of the significance of the current financial sector surveillance architecture, one needs to situate it within the broader field of surveillance studies. An expansive and far-reaching surveillant empire constructed under the aegis of the law in a liberal democracy such as Canada would have once beggared belief. But since 9/11, the field itself has undergone several waves of profound transformation, both in response to the contemporaneous evolution of surveillance practices by both state and non-state actors as well as advances in technological capacity. With each discovery of practices ranging from the warrantless wiretaps

[23] *R. v. Plant* [1993] 3 SCR 281, pp. 292–4. "In fostering the underlying values of dignity, integrity and autonomy, it is fitting that s. 8 of the *Charter* should seek to protect a biographical core of personal information which individuals in a free and democratic society would wish to maintain and control from dissemination to the state. This would include information which tends to reveal intimate details of the lifestyle and personal choices of the individual."

[24] *R v Spencer* [2014] 2 SCR 212, para 36.

[25] *R. v. Tessling* [2004] 3 SCR 432, paras 18 and 19. Citing the "the totality of the circumstances" approach taken in *R v Edwards*, the SCC in *Tessling* foregrounded the need to assess reasonableness in view of (1) the existence of a subjective expectation of privacy; and (2) the objective reasonableness of the expectation.

[26] *R v Spencer* [2014] 2 SCR 212, para 42–46.

[27] R v Bykovets [2024] SCC 6.

authorised by the Bush Administration[28] to the Snowden disclosures regarding global surveillance by the US National Security Agency,[29] from Covid-related surveillance[30] to surveillance capitalism,[31] from Cambridge Analytica[32] to border patrol drones and outdoor security cameras, public understandings regarding the nexus between surveillance, privacy, and consent have been fundamentally altered.

For the most part, the issue of surveillance was once neatly ordered by ownership: state versus non-state surveillance.[33] Snowden made real the kind of state surveillance that had until then only found representation in dystopian fiction or popular culture.[34] While surveillance was originally understood as applicable to foreign states and agents, the discovery of surveillance programs after 9/11 showed that ordinary citizens were also objects of surveillance for their own states.[35] Much of the 'logic' grounding such surveillance was located in national security discourses—for example, the 'need' for enhanced law enforcement powers or executive discretion,[36] given the "perceived exceptional nature of national emergencies"—but soon came to be extended to criminal offences.[37] Comparatively, non-state surveillance drew on the 'logic' of profit to justify tracking individual data for marketing purposes by using smart devices, store loyalty cards, and facial recognition software.[38] The differing 'logics', in turn, were used by state and non-state actors to justify their entryway to surveillance: states surveilled to keep citizens safe and corporations surveilled to bolster their bottom line. Financial sector surveillance is an exception because it muddies the state/non-state segregation.

---

[28] Daniel J. Solove (2007), p. 745.

[29] Austin (2015), p. 103

[30] Arjun Kharpal (2020).

[31] Zuboff (2019) defines surveillance capitalism as "[a] new economic order that claims human experience as free raw material for hidden commercial practices of extraction, prediction, and sales".

[32] Johnson and Duncan (2025).

[33] I use ownership as an umbrella term that covers the authorship of the surveillance as well as its enforcement. For example, the decision to surveill cities such as London or the decision to track Covid patients is a state-*authored* decision. Installing security cameras on the streets or using drones, CCTV footage, location data and credit card information, on the other hand, are enforcement decisions also taken by the state. Similarly, tracking customer behaviour in stores or monitoring employee productivity are authorship decisions by non-state actors. Using facial recognition software on customers or installing monitoring software on company-issued devices that use screen capture and keystroke logging to track employee behaviour are enforcement decisions by non-state actors.

[34] For example, George Orwell's description of the surveillance state in *1984* and the Tom Cruise starrer *Minority Report* showcasing a fictionalised model of predictive policing.

[35] Austin (2015), p. 104.

[36] See, for example, the Human Rights Watch (2015) report documenting US excesses after 9/11.

[37] Austin (2015), pp. 104–105 calls this the blurring of the line between national security and criminal offences, both domestically and internationally.

[38] Zuboff (2019), p. 19.

The use of the word 'muddies' is deliberate here. As seen above, the ownership of financial sector surveillance is ostensibly split into authorship and enforcement functions, with states assuming the former while the latter is assigned to non-state actors. Functionally, however, the bifurcation is not so clean. First, while the logic for surveillance is said to be national security, authorship of the decision to conduct surveillance stems from FATF pressure, not Parliament of its own volition.[39] Since the FATF is an actor external to the state, authorship is thus rendered a state/non-state hybrid product. Second, while enforcement for financial sector surveillance is mostly outsourced to non-state reporting entities, the provision of a controlling role for the state in enforcement through Fintrac makes for another hybrid product. Third, unlike other sorts of national security surveillance, financial sector surveillance grants considerable latitude for the exercise of discretion *by non-state actors* in their enforcement of the same. This muddying of imperatives, authors and enforcers makes financial surveillance an exception to the general rules regarding surveillance.

To be clear, however, this muddying only throws an *additional* layer of complexity over *an already intractable problem*. Austin contends that state surveillance is a form of "lawful illegality" since it is seriously problematic from a rule of law perspective. This is because the systemic features of surveillance programmes—secrecy,[40] legal complexity,[41] and jurisdiction-specific control[42]—militate against the rule of law tenet that states are also subject to the law. Simply put: by interpreting broadly-worded legislation to their advantage, states conduct secret surveillance using multiple institutions, often, across national boundaries while only remaining (notionally) accountable to domestic constituencies. Being 'subject to the law' thus remains a normative ideal—there is neither contestation of the state's interpretation

[39] This was admitted on the floor of Parliament by Roy Cullen, who was the Parliamentary Secretary to the Minister of Finance, while narrating the background to the promulgation to the PCMLTFA in 2001. He said: "In 1997 the 26 member financial action task force on money laundering, the FATF of which Canada is a founding member, found Canada to be lacking in certain key areas and strongly encouraged us to bring our anti money laundering regime in line with international standards. As a result of pressure here and internationally, the government brought in Bill C-22 [the bill that was the basis for the PCMLTFA] in the last parliament." Hansard no 59, transcript for May 10, 2001, 37th Parliament, 1st Session; available at https://www.ourcommons.ca/documentviewer/en/37-1/house/sitting-59/hansard#T1510.

[40] The shroud of secrecy cast over surveillance programmes, argues Austin, is essential to preserving and facilitating state claims regarding their 'lawfulness'. This claim of lawfulness rests on either a unilateral interpretation of the law or claims of deference to that one-sided interpretation within a structurally biased accountability framework. Austin (2015), p. 106.

[41] Legal complexity, as Austin uses it, refers to (a) the multiplicity of state institutions responsible for aspects of a surveillance programme, and (b) legislation that is susceptible to being abused by the state "behind its wall of secrecy and protective official statements". The combined operation of the two undermine state accountability. Austin (2015), pp. 110–111.

[42] Issues regarding jurisdiction are particularly problematic from an accountability perspective since surveillance programmes are often global in orientation (party due to the global communications networks and partly due to cooperation agreements between states) while oversight and accountability mechanisms remain firmly rooted within jurisdictions. Austin (2015), pp. 117–8.

nor adjudication of the same by an objective body such as a court of law—with severe implications for accountability for incursions into privacy.[43]

Financial sector surveillance disperses and attenuates even this filamentous accountability by, first, adding non-state actors into the fray, and second, by introducing new modes of consent-based engagement with the surveilled. The interposing of non-state actors between the state and the citizen fundamentally alters the nature of the surveillance relationship. Even the moth-eaten legal framework Austin speaks of governs *state* surveillance; *it does not extend to surveillance at the behest of the state by non-state actors*. More simply, a state needs to justify invasive surveillance against the touchstone of national security—even if disingenuously—and satisfy claims regarding constitutionality; a non-state actor is not subject to such requirements. Further, the legal framework governing consent to surveillance is materially different as it applies to non-state actors. Given the fundamental imbalance of power between states and citizens, the differing 'logics' of surveillance and the *supposedly* 'vanilla' nature of information collected by non-state commercial actors, the rules regarding consent are far more stringent for states than they are for non-state actors.

4 Codifying Financial-Sector Surveillance

The fourfold, stated object of the PCMLTFA is "to implement specific measures to detect and deter money laundering and the financing of terrorist activities and to facilitate the investigation and prosecution of money laundering offences", to help rout organised crime by providing law enforcement agencies (LEAs) with information about the proceeds of crime, to help fight transnational crime—particularly money laundering and terrorism financing—and to protect the Canadian financial system from current and future abuse by launderers and "terrorists".[44] While the need for surveillance is in embedded in all four objectives, the first objective explicitly includes measures such as: the establishment of record keeping and client identification requirements for financial services providers as well as businesses, professions, and activities "susceptible to being used for money laundering or the financing of terrorism"; the reporting of suspicious financial transactions as well as cross-border movements of currency and monetary instruments; as well as the establishment of an overseer agency—Fintrac—to ensure compliance and dealing with reported information.

However, the substantive heft that would ground primary legislation of this sort is missing. For example, what is "money laundering"? The PCMLTFA refers to the

[43] While the potential accountability-related challenges are many, this chapter only relates to the privacy-related dimensions of accountability.

[44] Section 3, *PCMLTFA*. While the characterisation of politically motivated militant actors as "terrorists" is a political act in itself, this discussion is beyond the pale of this paper.

Criminal Code (Code) but the latter does not expressly define the phrase either.[45] The absence of substantive provisions coupled with the ambiguously worded, expansive objectives render the statute particularly susceptible to subjective interpretation by regulators[46] and LEAs but also by those tasked with conducting surveillance.

For example, when the broad objective is to "detect and deter" laundering by the specific implementation of reporting, record keeping, and client identification measures, the question of which financial services providers/businesses/professions/activities qualify as "*susceptible to being used* for money laundering or the financing of terrorist activities [emphasis added]"—and thus merit this scrutiny—is left open under existing law.[47] In the absence of formal legal criteria or parameters demarcating *susceptibility* and a formal assignment of roles and responsibilities for this particular issue, it is unclear who is to *determine* susceptibility, under what statutory authority, using what criteria and, critically, how this assessment can be contested, reviewed, or challenged.[48] Without these legal

[45] The Interpretation section of the *PCMLTFA* defines a "money laundering offence" as "an offence under subsection 462.31(1) of the *Criminal Code*". While the specified provision of the *Code* is helpfully titled "Laundering proceeds of crime", the description of the offence lacks any reference to "money laundering", "money" or even "laundering". It simply states: "Every one commits an offence who uses, transfers the possession of, sends or delivers to any person or place, transports, transmits, alters, disposes of or otherwise deals with, in any manner and by any means, any property or any proceeds of any property with intent to conceal or convert that property or those proceeds, knowing or believing that, or being reckless as to whether, all or a part of that property or of those proceeds was obtained or derived directly or indirectly as a result of (a) the commission in Canada of a designated offence; or (b) an act or omission anywhere that, if it had occurred in Canada, would have constituted a designated offence".

[46] Fintrac, for example, sees providing "comprehensive guidance" to businesses subject to the PCMLTFA among its core responsibilities and claims to have fielded over 10,000 enquiries from businesses regarding reporting obligations, reporting systems, registration requirements and other regulatory requirements. Financial Transactions and Reports Analysis Centre of Canada (2024) Annual Report 2023-24.

[47] Section 3(a)(i), *PCMLTFA*.

[48] An example of how this has played out is that of lawyers: while the original *PCMLTFA* tasked lawyers with reporting laundering by their clients, a 2015 Supreme Court ruling held that doing so would constitute breach of client-attorney privilege. (See *Canada (Attorney General) v. Federation of Law Societies of Canada* 2015 SCC 7.) Provincial law societies and the Federation of Law Societies of Canada stepped into this breach and became responsible for reviewing, commenting on and testifying to the adequacy of the measures in place. As professional bodies with mandatory membership, the societies and Federation do espouse commitments to the "public interest". However, the question that remains unaddressed is why an unelected, non-representative body of any stripe *should* be allowed to determine what is in the larger interests of "the public", especially when some of these interests may run counter to the pecuniary and professional interests and obligations of said members.

safeguards, these functions are performed by regulators and LEAs, often with little oversight or recourse.[49]

Comparatively, the issues of subjectivity inherent to the question of what gets flagged as a "suspicious" financial transaction[50] have received serious scholarly attention, particularly in the contexts of debanking and derisking. Across jurisdictions, researchers point to inadequate training, defensive reporting, compliance overload, as well as regulatory overload as some of the factors that contribute to problematic subjective determinations, both at an individual level as well as a jurisdictional level. These scholars also point to the attendant implications for accountability and lack of meaningful recourse.[51]

However, these issues merit further scrutiny due to the increasing involvement of the private sector. In Canada, between 24,000 and 30,000 private sector entities[52] across 30 economic sectors and financial products have surveillance obligations under the law, which include customer identification and verification, record-keeping and reporting of financial transactions including suspicious transactions.[53] These private sector reporting entities include financial institutions but also Designated Non-Financial Businesses and Professions (DNFBPs).[54] For the year

[49] This subjectivity on part of the regulators and LEAs manifests in ever-widening circles of susceptibility across jurisdictions. While the finance and real estate industries have been in the regulatory crosshairs since the inception of the suspicious transaction reporting regime, the last 10 years have seen the emergence of a motley of other 'industries' such as art dealerships, football clubs and film production now understood as significant money laundering threats. However, these shifts appear unsupported by evidence or data beyond anecdotal nuggets about one-off instances from LEAs themselves. In the UK, for example, the Serious Fraud Office's determination that private school tuitions are a possible conduit for laundering (personal communication with author) does not seem to factor in *just how many* school-going children a potential launderer would need to have in order to run a successful laundering operation!

[50] Section 3(a)(ii), *PCMLTFA*.

[51] See, for example, Amicelle and Favarel-Garrigues (2012), pp. 105–124; de Koker and Casanovas (2024); Whyte (2024); Anthony (2025).

[52] Department of Finance Canada (2023).

[53] Financial Transactions and Reports Analysis Centre of Canada (2024) Annual Report 2023–24, p. 4.

[54] Section 5, *PCMLTFA*. These surveillance obligations extend to authorised foreign and local banks; cooperative credit societies; savings and credit unions and caisses populaires; life companies, foreign life companies, life insurance companies; companies to which the *Trust and Loan Companies Act* applies; trust companies; loan companies; persons and entities dealing in securities or any other financial instruments or those that provide portfolio management or investment advising services; persons and entities (whether they have a place of business in Canada or not) that provide foreign exchange dealing, remit or transmit funds, transport currency, money orders, travelers checks or other similar negotiable instruments, issue or redeem money orders, travelers checks or other similar negotiable instruments, deal in virtual currencies, or any prescribed services. The requirement to surveil also applies to persons and entities engaged in a prescribed business, profession or activity and such persons/ entities while they're engaged in a "prescribed activity". See Section 5 (i) and (j), *PCMLTFA*. While the *PCMLTFA* does not describe what the prescribed businesses, professions or activities are, the associated regulations include accountants and accountancy firms; real estate brokers or sales representatives; real estate developers; mort-

2023–2024, a total of 48,839,373 financial reports were submitted to Fintrac by the reporting entities.[55]

The reporting structure outlined in the PCMLTFA envisages these private sector institutions collecting information for reporting to Fintrac. Besides mandatory reporting of all financial transactions over $10,000,[56] the PCMLTFA also makes reportable all financial transactions where the reporting entities have "reasonable grounds to suspect" the commission or attempted commission of money laundering, terrorism financing, or sanctions evasion.[57]

The obligations regarding reporting, recordkeeping, and client verification are equally exacting. The regulations (including six schedules) require reporting entities to collect several kinds of information about their clients, depending on the purpose of the said collection (for example, whether the information is intended to ground the reporting of a suspicious transaction or is part of general recordkeeping by the reporting entity). Regarding cash transactions over $10,000, the first set of required information comprises basic identification details about the person or entity conducting the transaction (including their name, type of person/ entity, government-issued identification documents, contact details, details regarding their business, etc.[58]) as well as not-so-basic details (for example, whether they qualify as a Politically Exposed Person or the Head of an International Organisation[59]). If the person or entity is conducting the transaction on behalf of another, further details about the that person/entity are also required as well as details regarding the relationship between the two.[60] Similar information is also sought regarding the beneficiary of the transaction.[61] If the transaction is conducted via an Electronic Funds

gage administrators, mortgage brokers and mortgage lenders and dealers in precious metals and precious stones. Sections 47, 53, 59, 64.1, 65 and 70, *Proceeds of Crime (Money Laundering) and Terrorist Financing Regulations* SOR/ 2002-184. Further, the requirements also apply to casinos as well as establishments that run lottery schemes (including those conducted over the internet or using other digital networks) or run more than 50 electronic gaming devices such as slot machines as well as to Crown departments, agents and mandatories that accept deposit liabilities, issue or sell money orders or redeem them from the public or that sell prescribed precious metals while carrying out a prescribed activity. Employees of a person or entity described above are similarly expected to fulfil surveillance obligations. Section 5, *PCMLTFA*.

[55] The largest by volume were large cash transactions reports (6.2 million), Electronic Funds Transfer reports (41.5 million) and Suspicious Transaction reports (631,137). Other reports included cross-border currency reports, casino disbursements reports and large virtual currency transactions reports. Annex B, *Financial Transactions and Reports Analysis Centre of Canada Annual Report 2023-24*, p. 42.

[56] These includes cash as well as virtual currency transactions.

[57] Section 7, *PCMLTFA*.

[58] Sections 1–8, Part A, Schedule 1, Proceeds of Crime (Money Laundering) and Terrorist Financing Regulations SOR/ 2002-184.

[59] Section 9.3, *PCMLTFA*.

[60] Sections 1–11, Part F, Schedule 1, Proceeds of Crime (Money Laundering) and Terrorist Financing Regulations SOR/ 2002-184.

[61] Sections 1–11, Part G, Schedule 1, Proceeds of Crime (Money Laundering) and Terrorist Financing Regulations SOR/ 2002-184.

Transfer, additional information is required. This includes details regarding the type of device used to request the transaction online, the identification number of the device, and the IP address used by the device.[62]

The second set mandates the collection of information about the transaction (including the time the transaction was attempted or conducted, type and amount of fiat currency, the purpose of the transaction, the named source of funds, as well as their account numbers) as well as the details of accounts associated with that transaction (including account numbers, their owners, the contact details of owners, their business or occupation, the name of their employer, their government-issued identity documents, the type of account, etc.).[63]

The qualification criteria for exemption from such exhaustive reporting is equally stringent. For example, should a bank want to sidestep filing such a report every time a client conducts a business transaction over the $10,000 limit, the bank will have to satisfy a series of progressive conditions. These include providing information to Fintrac showing that the client is a business entity, the account is a business account, that the client has held that account for at least 2 years or that the client banked with another financial entity for a continuous period of 2 years, that the bank has records showing that the client has consistently deposited $10,000 or more "on an average of at least twice a week during the preceding 12 months", that such deposits are consistent with the client's established business practices, and that the bank has taken "reasonable measures" to determine the source of funds. The bank will also need to provide the total value and total number of the client's cash deposits over the preceding 12 months.[64]

The informational requirements for general recordkeeping are similarly rigorous. Financial entities are to keep records including signature cards of clients, official corporate records for corporations, a record of the intended use of the account, every deposit slip, cheque, debit and credit memo, a record of the client's financial capacity, trails of international electronic funds transfers for amounts great than $1000,[65] every transaction associated with a credit card,[66] and even assessments regarding the clientele and markets served by foreign financial institutions that the reporting entity has a correspondent banking relationship with.[67] A money service business that provides crowdfunding platform services, meanwhile, is additionally

---

[62] Schedules 2 and 3, Proceeds of Crime (Money Laundering) and Terrorist Financing Regulations SOR/ 2002–184.

[63] Sections 1–10, Part B, Schedule 1, Proceeds of Crime (Money Laundering) and Terrorist Financing Regulations SOR/ 2002-184.

[64] Section 8 read with Schedule 5, Proceeds of Crime (Money Laundering) and Terrorist Financing Regulations SOR/ 2002-184.

[65] Section 12, Proceeds of Crime (Money Laundering) and Terrorist Financing Regulations SOR/ 2002-184.

[66] Section 13, Proceeds of Crime (Money Laundering) and Terrorist Financing Regulations SOR/ 2002-184.

[67] Section 16, Proceeds of Crime (Money Laundering) and Terrorist Financing Regulations SOR/ 2002-184.

tasked with keeping records of the purposes for which funds are being raised.[68] Real estate developers are to keep records regarding every person they sell as property to,[69] while mortgage brokers are to keep records of every mortgage on real property or a hypothec on immoveable property.[70] The recordkeeping requirement for casinos include records of every deposit slip for every account opened by the casino, including an international electronic funds transfer of more than $1000.

According to the PCMLTFA, the primary function of Fintrac is to collect, analyse, assess, and—if need be—disclose the information collected to LEAs and other government institutions or agencies for further investigation or for law enforcement purposes.[71] To this end, Fintrac is entitled to ask the reporting entities for information missing from the filed reports. Fintrac may also incorporate information provided by FIUs of other jurisdictions as well as information provided by LEAs, government institutions, or agencies. There is also a catchall for "other information voluntarily provided" to Fintrac.[72] Additionally, Fintrac may collect "publicly available" information, including from commercially available databases, as well information from databases maintained for law enforcement or national security purposes by federal or provincial governments, foreign governments, and international organisations.[73] Significantly, Fintrac is meant to retain the reports filed by the reporting entities as well as the information it collects for a period of 10 years.[74]

The PCMLTFA thus positions Fintrac at the heart of a vast informational or surveillant empire and much of the information collected poses a clear threat to privacy, which is both a constitutionally and statutorily protected right. But the primary problem with the PCMLTFA's Fintrac model is the reliance on private sector actors for much of the information collected. While Fintrac can add information received from LEAs and other governmental institutions and agencies, both domestic and foreign, the centrepiece of this surveillance project are private businesses. Accordingly, the PCMLTFA, the regulations, and even Fintrac's annual reports devote the most space to the public-private partnership that forms the backbone of the AML/CTF regime. However, as discussed below, by *enlisting* the private sector

[68] Section 36.1, Proceeds of Crime (Money Laundering) and Terrorist Financing Regulations SOR/2002-184.

[69] Section 64, Proceeds of Crime (Money Laundering) and Terrorist Financing Regulations SOR/2002-184.

[70] Section 64.6, Proceeds of Crime (Money Laundering) and Terrorist Financing Regulations SOR/2002-184.

[71] Section 40, *PCMLTFA*.

[72] This is a reference to information provided to Fintrac by LEAs, national security agencies as well as members of the public about alleged criminals and terrorists and this information is said to often form the starting point for Fintrac's own analysis. In its annual report for 2023–2024, Fintrac said it received 2485 voluntary information records, which were used to establish connections between individuals and entities and to develop "actionable financial intelligence" for disclosure recipients. The RCMP is consistently the recipient of the largest volume of disclosures. Financial Transactions and Reports Analysis Centre of Canada (2024) Annual Report 2023-24, p. 8.

[73] Section 54, *PCMLTFA*.

[74] Section 54(1)(d), *PCMLTFA*.

to function as the eyes and ears of the state, the Canadian state sidesteps its own constitutional and legal duties regarding the collection, use, and disclosure of information that could jeopardise the privacy of individuals.

5 Dismantling Privacy

Functionally, Fintrac is meant to be independent from LEAs and operate at an arm's length from them, while protecting personal information under its control from unauthorised disclosure.[75] As such, the PCMLTFA features a detailed section regarding the disclosure and use of information by Fintrac. For example, the Attorney General,[76] the Canadian Security Intelligence Service (CSIS),[77] and the Canada Revenue Agency (CRA)[78] may only seek additional information from Fintrac by making an application to a judge. That said, the carve-outs and exceptions in the law significantly undermine Fintrac's seeming commitment to privacy.

First, where Fintrac determines that there are reasonable grounds to suspect that designated information under its control would be relevant to the investigation or prosecution of a money laundering, terrorist financing, or sanctions evasion offence, it can pass along the information to the police, the CRA, Agence du revenue du Quebec, Canada Border Services Agency (CBSA), the Communications Security Establishment, the Competition Bureau, provincial securities regulators, ministers responsible for the Special Economic Measures Act or the Justice for Victims of Corrupt Foreign Officials Act (Sergei Magnitsky Law), Department of Environment, as well as the Department of Fisheries and Oceans.[79]

Second, where Fintrac has reasonable grounds to suspect the information is "relevant to threats to the security of Canada", Fintrac is authorised to share information with CSIS, the police, CBSA, the Department of Citizenship and Immigration, the Department of National Defence and the Canadian Forces, and the Office of the Superintendent of Financial Institutions.[80]

Third, Fintrac may also share information with institutions and agencies of foreign states and international organisations,[81] with authorities specified by the

[75] Section 40(a) & (d), *PCMLTFA*.

[76] Section 60(2), *PCMLTFA*. The investigation must be regarding money laundering, terrorism financing or sanctions evasion.

[77] Section 60.1, *PCMLTFA*. The investigation must be regarding a threat to the security of Canada and requires the prior approval of the Minister of Public Safety and Emergency Preparedness.

[78] Section 60.3, *PCMLTFA*. The investigation must be regarding tax evasion and requires the prior approval of the Minister of National Revenue.

[79] Section 55(3), *PCMLTFA*.

[80] Section 55.1, *PCMLTFA*.

[81] Section 56.1, *PCMLTFA*.

Minister of Finance,[82] with supervisory bodies,[83] with the CRA, the Bank of Canada,[84] as well as courts.[85] Fourth, any vestigial privacy protections are eroded further by the use of vague but expansive catchalls: matters related to "national security" are exempt from disclosure bans,[86] as are those that could "materially affect public policy or the strategic direction" of Fintrac,[87] and those that pose potential "risks to the integrity of the Canadian financial system".[88] Finally, Fintrac is also allowed to share any information that the Minister or a finance department officer "consider[] relevant for the purpose of carrying out the Minister's powers and duties".[89]

The point that merits underscoring is that *the information Fintrac collects, analyses, and disseminates is not of state provenance*. As such, this information foundationally lacks the legitimacy or authority that is accorded to, for example, information acquired through police investigations. Four issues deserve particular consideration here. First, the very condition of being external to the state renders questionable the synchronicity of objectives essential to quality reporting and information collection. When crime control is a state priority, for example, state institutions such as the police or border security agencies are understood to mirror the objectives of the state in their investigations. While the possibility of *individual* bias tainting investigations and the information collected cannot be completely extinguished, the alignment of *institutional* priorities with those of the state is generally a given. The same assumption cannot be made regarding private sector commercial enterprises which have profitability as their abiding priority.[90] While a state may want to completely weed out laundering, banks and casinos also stand to lose profitable business by outing launderers and so, arguably, would have an interest in underreporting laundering. This is because banks and casinos (as well as other commercial entities) make money off even illicit funds. The financial intermediation function of a bank (that is, lending money held in deposits by the bank)

82 Section 58.1, *PCMLTFA*.

83 Section 65, *PCMLTFA*.

84 Sections 65–65.1, *PCMLTFA*.

85 Section 68.1, *PCMLTFA*.

86 Section 53.32, *PCMLTFA*.

87 Section 52(2) and (3), *PCMLTFA*.

88 Section 53.31, *PCMLTFA*.

89 Section 53.1, *PCMLTFA*. Unlike most Canadian statutes that describe the extent of powers available to the minister, neither the *PCMLTFA* nor its eight associated regulations define these powers and duties. However, the part of the *PCMLTFA* telling titled "Protection of Canada's Financial System" contains the minister's broad power to issue written directives "in order to safeguard the integrity of Canada's financial system" and allows them to take notice of "any circumstance that the Minister considers relevant" and to impose "any terms and conditions … that the Minister considers appropriate." Furthermore, the directive is to prevail over the regulations where the two are in conflict. Sections 11.42–11.48, *PCMLTFA*.

90 This point is corroborated by the testimony of Nicholas Maxwell to the Cullen Commission: "Reporting entities are adrift [sic] to report on everything under the sun and to not be aware of the priorities that really make a difference to Canada." Cullen Commission (2022), Evidence of Nicholas Maxwell, Transcript, January 14, 2021, p. 67.

does not discriminate between monies from illicit sources and those from licit sources; both generate as much revenue for the bank. Similarly, casinos net the same amount of fees from those using illicit monies for play as they do from 'regular' clients. This claim is borne out by investigations into the 'Vancouver model' of money laundering in Canada, the 'Toronto Method' of laundering through mortgage fraud at HSBC Canada, as well as the 2024 discovery of laundering at TD Bank. In each instance, it was discovered that the laundering had been taking place undisturbed for periods extending from 7 to 9 years. While the foregoing would suggest a clear conflict of interest between reporting entities and the state when it comes to the reporting of laundering, even the most charitable interpretation cannot extend much beyond a 'misalignment of objectives'.[91]

Second, there is necessarily a material difference between information collected during a purpose-specific investigation and compliance-triggered reportage. The capabilities of a professional financial crimes investigator are obviously different from those of a jeweller with basic AML compliance training and this difference would reflect in the quality of information both would cull. But the more significant differences would be those of *objective* and *motive*. Policing and surveillance are not the primary function of any reporting entity; as such, the generation of information is only incidental to the conduct of their core business, not an essential objective. Ensuring *quality* is thus unlikely to be a key concern.

Meanwhile, the issue of motive is inextricably entangled with the underlying profit imperative. The incentive structure at most commercial establishments pegs financial rewards and professional success for employees to revenue generation for the institution.[92] A suspicious transaction report thus represents a potential loss of revenue (and, as a corollary, professional and/or financial rewards) as well as a loss of productive workdays in the preparation of the report. The impetus towards gathering quality information and filing accurate reports is thus far less clear-cut than it is made out to be by proponents of public-private partnerships.

Third, there is a fundamental difference in state and private sector approaches to surveillance. Ensuring the privacy of individuals is a key consideration for a state. For example, although the Code allows LEAs to undertake electronic surveillance in criminal investigations, the exercise of this power is subject to stringent controls.[93] Only designated police officers and agents may conduct electronic surveillance, that too, only for certain serious offences. Further, judicial authorisation is a *sine qua non* for electronic surveillance and its granting depends on the judge being satisfied that the surveillance is in the best interests of the administration of justice, that other investigative procedures have failed or are unlikely to succeed, or that urgency renders other investigative measures

---

[91] I've discussed this idea in more detail elsewhere. See Ahmed (2023a, b).

[92] For example, the bonus for a banker or their professional advancement within the organisation depends on the volume of deposits they mobilise and/or the financial products they sell. Flagging suspicious transactions or saving the bank from potential fines for non-compliance are not part of this calculus.

[93] Part VI, Criminal Code. See also Public Safety Canada (2022), Annual Report on the Use of Electronic Surveillance—2022.

impractical. Even so, the authorisation is time-limited and may carry additional terms and conditions. A final safeguard is the requirement for the Minister of Public Safety and Emergency Preparedness to present an annual report on the use of electronic surveillance to Parliament.

Financial sector surveillance by private sector entities, on the other hand, is not subject to similar safeguards.[94] The implication appears that money laundering offences are 'serious' enough to warrant what Lyon calls "a culture of surveillance",[95] where the collection of information is an unmitigated good that requires no qualification. There are neither stipulations about who may collect this information (say, a bank manager, as opposed to a bank teller) nor requirements for judicial authorisation, let alone parliamentary oversight. Allowing Fintrac to collect sensitive information through third parties thus enables Fintrac to sidestep the safeguards and procedures applicable to other information-collecting state institutions and agencies. There is considerable room for a fruit of the poisonous tree analysis[96] here and the impacts on privacy and state accountability are apparent (discussed below). But the deepest cut is perhaps the *layering of subjectivities to create an objective fault standard*.

Canadian jurisprudence has consistently held that "reasonable suspicion" must be grounded in "objective, ascertainable facts".[97] That is, to ensure the integrity of the finger-pointing process, even a subjective assessment regarding suspicion must be based on "facts" that should be obvious to an objective observer. But for the reasons discussed above, subjectivity invariably affects even 'facts' regarding financial transactions:[98] the 'objective fact' of a hockey bag full of cash being presented at a casino till, for example, does not qualify as suspicious unless the casino chooses to flag it as such. Accordingly, Fintrac's determination of what constitutes "reasonable suspicion" is founded on its subjective reading of *subjective assessments by private sector actors presented as 'evidence'*. More simply: the quality of

[94] For more on privacy preservation in the private sector, see Brand, de Koker, and Herse (2025) in this book.

[95] Lyon's focus is on surveillance in everyday, mundane activities such as walking down a street, listening to music or buying in stores. (Or, indeed, the conduct of routine financial transactions.) He holds this form of surveillance as distinct from the surveillance conducted via "the octopus tentacles of global intelligence and policing networks" or corporate marketing. The culture of surveillance, as Lyon describes it, studies how everyday surveillance is imagined and experienced but, simultaneously, how these mundane activities affect and are affected by surveillance. Lyon (2018), p. 2.

[96] This is the legal principle that prevents evidence acquired through illegal or unconstitutional means—such as illegal wiretaps—being used by the state in a criminal prosecution.

[97] *R v Chehil*, 2013 SCC 49. See also *R. v. Simpson*, 1993 CanLII 3379 (ON CA), *R. v. Ahmad*, 2020 SCC 11 and *R. v. Kang-Brown*, 2008 SCC 18.

[98] In their 2018 empirical study of financial policing practices, Amicelle and Iofolla (2018), p. 852 claim that all bank staff they interviewed admitted that the degree of subjectivity embedded with the suspicion-base model of intervention—that is, the lack of certainty and consensus as to how much data and, by extension, 'how much suspicion' was required to act—was the most difficult aspect of their job.

information collected by third parties is problematic even without the two, consecutive layers of subjective interpretation by the reporting entity and Fintrac.

Fourth, this tainted, subjective assessment is subsequently circulated far and wide. As discussed above, Fintrac is entitled to share this 'information' with governmental agencies, both local and foreign.[99] However, even more controversially, since the February 2025 amendments to the PCMLTFA, this information can also be shared among private sector entities, that too without the consent of the individual whom it is about.[100] This effectively means a person's banker, accountant, real estate broker and jeweller are now authorised by law to discuss details about their clients—*without their knowledge or consent*—as long as four basic conditions are met. One, the information should have been collected in the course of the reporting entity's "activities"; whether this refers to an entity's commercial activities—for example, selling a mortgage—or for Fintrac reporting activities is unclear. Two, the disclosure to other entities needs to be "reasonable for the purpose of detecting or deterring money laundering, terrorist financing or sanctions evasion",[101] with each entity presumably making calls about 'reasonableness', detection, and deterrence themselves. Three, informing the client about the disclosure would "risk compromising the ability to detect or deter money laundering, terrorist financing, or sanctions evasion", where, again, the reporting entity itself is entitled to determine risk as well as self-assess its ability to detect and deter. The final condition is that the disclosure is to be made in accordance with "the regulations", which have yet to materialise.[102]

The reporting entity that is the recipient of such information is further allowed to collect or use this information—again, without the knowledge or consent of the concerned individual—as long as the collection or use are in conformity with the as-yet unspecified regulations. And just as long as these disclosures, collection, and use are conducted in "good faith", no entity or person can be held criminally or civilly liable for their conduct.[103]

To be fair, this information sharing sounds useful on paper. Were a person suspected of money laundering to be debanked by the Royal Bank of Canada, for example, they would be unable to move their account to Bank of Montreal, if the two banks were in conversation. That said, the potential encroachment on privacy as well as other civil rights are enormous. Effectively, the said individual would be denied banking services *across Canada*, based on a singular assessment by the Royal Bank.

[99] See footnote 76 in chapter "Law Enforcement at the Forest-Finance Nexus in Papua New Guinea: Leveraging Tools Against Financial Crime in Defence of the Environment".

[100] Section 11.01 of the PCMLTFA came into force on April 1, 2025. These private sector entities are listed in footnote 53 in chapter "The Illusory Truth Effect and Financial Integrity Objectives and Consequences".

[101] Section 11.01(b), PCMLTFA.

[102] The latest set of regulations issued under this act are the *Proceeds of Crime (Money Laundering) and Terrorist Financing Reporting of Goods Regulations, SOR/2025-67*, which deal with trade-based money laundering.

[103] Section 11.01(2), *PCMLTFA*.

The real-time impact of debanking in contemporary cashless societies is often underestimated, particularly as it applies to false positives. A person wrongly or mistakenly suspected of money laundering, for example, could find themselves unable to access their money, use credit cards to pay bills, or need to secure high-interest loans while attempting to transfer mortgages or lines of credit. Businesses could find themselves unable to make payroll or service debt. According to the *Globe & Mail*, the Financial Consumer Agency of Canada, the federal financial services watchdog, received more than 800 grievances about debanking between 2018 and 2023.[104] While academic scholarship in the last 10 years has focused on the many pitfalls associated with debanking[105], far less is known about the practice in the public sphere. For example, defensive reporting practices at banks[106] remain a serious concern as does the fact that financial regulators and banking ombuds offices have limited oversight over debanking decisions and even more limited powers to reverse them.[107] It is far easier to get on the banking no fly list than it is to get off the list. Some academics have accordingly deployed the phrase "civil death" to describe those who have had their assets frozen, reputations damaged, and have been deprived of passports, work and income.[108] Given that the 2025 amendments to the PCMLTFA further provide reporting entities immunity from civil and criminal liability for such "good faith" subjective assessments, the scope for accountability for 'bad' or flawed decision-making is severely compromised.

6 Towards *Charter* Compliance

Ensuring that all laws are *Charter* compliant ought to be a priority for the state. However, the existing structure of financial sector surveillance makes things complicated. As set out in the foregoing sections, most—if not all—of the information provided by private sector actors to Fintrac as part of their reporting role and/or

[104] Alini, Posadzki and Marotta (2025).

[105] See, for example, de Koker, Howell, and Morris (2023), p. 81.

[106] The practice refers to the overreporting of 'suspicious' transactions by reporting entities with a view to reducing their exposure to risk. In an ideal world, a banker suspicious of their client or a particular transaction would conduct their own enquiries and investigations *before* generating a Suspicious Transaction Report for the regulator. In practice, however, many such *potentially suspicious* clients and transactions get flagged prior to meaningful enquiries or investigations. This helps the banker reduce the time spent on an individual case and avoid the risk (and associated liability) of not reporting a transaction that is *actually* suspicious. Enabling such behaviour are the official Fintrac guidelines for reporting: among the markers of "suspicious behaviour" for financial entities are "Client exhibits nervous behaviour", "Client has a defensive stance to questioning" and "client exhibits a lack of concern about higher than normal transaction costs or fees." https://fintrac-canafe.canada.ca/guidance-directives/transaction-operation/indicators-indicateurs/fin_mltf-eng#s2

[107] Alini et al. (2025).

[108] Amicelle and Favarel-Garrigues. (2012) p. 110 and accompanying footnotes.

retained by the entity as part of their PCMLTFA-mandated record keeping role would either qualify as "personal and confidential" or subject to the "reasonable expectation of privacy".[109] Indeed, the Office of the Privacy Commissioner of Canada has found "certain aspects" of the PCMLTFA "inherently privacy-invasive".[110] But to merit constitutional protection, a 'search' for evidence of criminal activity (or 'seizure' of said evidence)[111] needs to be conducted by an "agent of the state".[112] While Fintrac staff *would* count as agents of the state for the purposes of this analysis, they do not *directly* examine an individual's "person or property" for evidence or seize this evidence; their role begins only *after* that initial search and seizure has *been* conducted by the private entities.[113] While the inspection of docu-

---

[109] An example I give to students in my seminar course on money laundering is that of credit card statements that banks are meant to keep records of under the *PCMLTFA*. My credit card bill, for example, would reveal my penchant for fine dining but also my political views in terms of my media subscriptions. By triangulation with other publicly available information, it would be easy to figure out the geographical areas I live, work and play in (for example, frequent $12–13 payments to Uber on weekday mornings suggest a workplace that is within a 10-min car ride radius), the kinds of healthcare issues I have (for example, is a weekly $150 payment to a chiropodist, a physiotherapist or a mental health professional?), where I shop but also, sometimes, what I'm buying (for example, monthly payments would suggest a subscription; a quick Google search would show whether it is to a food delivery service or to a porn website; multiple subscriptions could be suggestive of either a food or porn addiction). In each example, the "intimate details of the lifestyle and personal choices of the individual" described in *R v Plant* would be up for state scrutiny.

[110] Office of the Privacy Commissioner of Canada (2023).

[111] 'Search' refers to the examination conducted by "agents of the state" of an individual's person or property to look for evidence [Peter W. Hogg and Wade Wright (2019). S 48:4] and includes the right to inspect documents as part of an administrative scheme set up by statute to regulate commercial and industrial activity [*Comité paritaire de l'industrie de la chemise v Potash*, [1994] 2 SCR 406, pp. 440–441]. Meanwhile, a 'seizure' is the taking away of things, without consent [*R v Dyment*, [1988] 2 SCR 417, p. 431] that could be used as evidence by the said agents [Hogg & Wright, s 48:4] and includes documents [Thomson *Newspapers Ltd. v Canada (Director of Investigation and Research, Restrictive Trade Practices Commission)*, (1990) 1 SCR 425].

[112] An agent of the state is a person authorised to act for or in place of the state. Crown attorneys and police officers exercising statutory powers as agents of the government qualify as agents of the state. Canadian courts have been strict in defining and affirming the circumstances under which a person may be considered an agent of the state, requiring "an identifiable, direct relationship between the agent and the state that can be found in a statute or clearly shown by convention". Gilbert and Kerr (2009), available at https://www.iankerr.ca/book-chapters. "In determining whether or not the informer is a state agent, it is appropriate to focus on the effect of the relationship between the informer and the authorities on the particular exchange or contact with the accused. … I would accordingly adopt the following simple test: would the exchange between the accused and the informer have taken place, in the form and manner in which it did take place, but for the intervention of the state or its agents?" *R v Broyles*, [1991] 3 SCR 595.

[113] To appreciate the significance of this process, analogise Fintrac's investigation of money laundering using information from a bank to that of a police officer investigating cocaine trafficking in a city such as New York. With a single gram 'baggie' costing between USD 100 and 120 (inclusive of delivery charges), users are likely to be resident in reasonably affluent neighbourhoods and choosing home delivery. Under the existing process, the police officer's investigation would then be *led by* the suspicions of the concierges of upmarket condominiums. Not only would the concierge be legally obligated to surveill the residents of the building, they would also be required to

ments could qualify as a 'search', the PCMLTFA is not an "administrative scheme" set up to "regulate commercial and industrial activity". Money laundering is a criminal offence under the Code; a statute designed to help detect a criminal offence is thus necessarily penal—and not administrative—in nature (were the exercise truly administrative in nature, for example, Fintrac would be obligated to verify all transactions itself, not just the ones flagged by the reporting entities for a high-level review).

To be clear: the nature of the information being collected is such that would merit *constitutional protection* were it being collected by the state. That is, the state would need to necessarily meet the high bar required to justify such an encroachment on the privacy rights of an individual and it would also need to adhere to exacting rules regarding the collection of the information.[114] For example, the courts have frequently torpedoed attempts by law enforcement to deploy or coopt other agents of the state to do their 'dirty work'. Where the prerequisites for conducting searches are subject to strict rules to ensure the constitutionality of the process, a law enforcement agency cannot sidestep these constitutional requirements by enlisting another state agent, who is not subject to such strict rules, to conduct the search on their behalf.[115]

The courts have been equally careful in dealing with 'hybrid' government bodies—such as Fintrac—that have regulatory or administrative functions in addition to criminal investigative functions under regulatory or administrative statutes.[116] Where the nature of the state action changes from regulatory or administrative inspection to criminal investigation, officials are expected to abandon their authority to use administrative or regulatory inspection powers and seek—for the most part—the prior judicial authorisation appropriate to criminal investigations.[117] Or

---

keep records of all activities outside of a mandated threshold (for example, a list of visitors who don't 'belong' or a list of all residents who receive visitors after midnight) and share their suspicions and records with the police as the starting point of *the police's* review and analysis process.

[114] For further debate on privacy rights, see Gallant (2025) in this book.

[115] In *R v Colarusso*, for example, the court found that while a coroner as an agent of the state was statutorily empowered to seize blood and urine samples of the accused as part of their investigation into the death of a victim in an impaired driving incident, the police's taking of the samples for the purposes of their own investigation, without independent authorisation, violated the constitutional guarantee against unreasonable search and seizure. https://decisions.scc-csc.ca/scc-csc/scc-csc/en/item/1097/index.do. Similarly, in *R v Ling*, the court held that evidence collected by auditors with the Canada Revenue Agency could not used for a criminal investigation by the Special Investigations Section of Revenue Canada. https://decisions.scc-csc.ca/scc-csc/scc-csc/en/item/2016/index.do.

[116] Section 8, Charterpedia. https://www.justice.gc.ca/eng/csj-sjc/rfc-dlc/ccrf-ccdl/check/art8.html

[117] In *R v Jarvis*, the court shot down the state's argument that there was "no rigid audit/investigation distinction" under the *Income Tax Act* and held that "officials 'cross the Rubicon' when the inquiry in question engages the adversarial relationship between the taxpayer and the state" in that the enquiry is a determination of criminal liability. At such time, the SCC said, tax officials would be expected to relinquish their inspection and requirement powers under the Act. Paras 88–89. https://decisions.scc-csc.ca/scc-csc/scc-csc/en/item/2015/index.do

the state body could—as Fintrac is authorised to under the *PCMLTFA*—pass along the evidence they have to the appropriate authorities for investigating offences.[118]

Significantly, the jurisprudence is consistently clear that a seizure does not have to be directly from the person whose rights are implicated,[119] and that such a 'taking' would count as a seizure whether the thing/information is provided pursuant to a police demand, request, or voluntarily.[120] In *Cole*, the SCC was even more explicit regarding the role of third parties. It held that voluntary disclosure of information to the state by a person who has acquired lawful possession of information *for their own purposes* does not vest in the state a "delegated or derivative power" to appropriate that information for the purposes of a criminal investigation.[121] "Where a lower constitutional standard is applicable in an administrative context, … the police cannot invoke that standard to evade the prior judicial authorization that is normally required for searches or seizures in the context of criminal investigations".[122] So, conceivably, a police officer asking a third party (such as a bank) for information regarding an individual or the bank voluntarily providing the information to an officer would count as 'seizure'.

Since the *Charter* does not have a requirement for prior judicial authorisation baked into its text, the evidence discovered by unreasonable search or seizure is not necessarily inadmissible.[123] Simultaneously, however, the courts have also held that prior judicial authorisation is required to make a search "reasonable" and that "state intervention" in the form of a search cannot be used to justify fishing expeditions and must be based on "credible probability" that evidence will be found.[124] The 'reasonableness' of the search and seizure is thus conditioned by a balancing of the importance of the state's objective against the impact on an individual's privacy interest[125] and turns on whether the action is, first, authorised by law; second, the law itself is reasonable; and third, the manner in which the search is carried out is reasonable.[126]

---

[118] See footnote 49 in chapter "Law Enforcement at the Forest-Finance Nexus in Papua New Guinea: Leveraging Tools Against Financial Crime in Defence of the Environment".

[119] In *Dyment* [1988], the court held that a police officer taking a patient's blood sample from a medical practitioner, who drew it without the patient's knowledge or consent, amounted to unreasonable 'seizure' and was inadmissible as evidence for an impaired driving charge.

[120] Charterpedia. https://www.justice.gc.ca/eng/csj-sjc/rfc-dlc/ccrf-ccdl/check/art8.html

[121] *R v Cole* [2012] 3 SCR 34, para 67. The case was about a school board turning over to the police a laptop issued by the school to an instructor thought to contain compromising photos of a student. The court found that the school board and principal had an "administrative" interest in ensuring safety within the school and could search and seize the laptop *themselves*.

[122] *R v Cole*, para 69.

[123] Section 24(2) of the Charter states that evidence obtained via a Charter violation will only be excluded if it brings the administration of justice into disrepute. Thus, if the agent of state can demonstrate that they acted in good faith or were unaware they were in breach of the Charter, courts will sometimes admit the evidence. Hogg and Wright (2019), s 48:1.

[124] Hunter v Southam Inc.

[125] *R. v. Rodgers*, [2006] 1 SCR 554; *Hunter v. Southam*, pp. 159–60.

[126] *R. v. Collins*, [1987] 1 SCR 265, para 23.

While the law does provide for consensual searches, this consent must be both voluntary and informed, which requires—among other things—that the rights-holder be aware of *their right to not consent*.[127] The SCC has unequivocally held that a third party can neither consent to a search on behalf of another nor waive a constitutional protection on behalf of another:

> The adoption of a doctrine of third party consent in this country would imply that the police could interfere with an individual's privacy interests on the basis of a consent that is *not* voluntarily given by the rights holder, and *not* necessarily based on sufficient information in his or her hands to make a meaningful choice. … I would therefore reject the Crown's contention that a third party could validly consent to a search or otherwise waive a constitutional protection on behalf of another.[128]

Finally, the state is also prohibited from widespread dissemination and disclosure of information: in *Mills*, for example, the SCC held that disclosure of seized records to "individuals outside of those to whom, or for purposes other than for which, they were originally divulged may interfere with a reasonable expectation of privacy".[129] The fact that information may already be available to some segment of the public "does not preclude further harm to the privacy interest by additional dissemination that would increase access to the information".[130]

The implications of this jurisprudence regarding the financial sector surveillance regime appear significant initially. First, the nature of the information collected, used and disclosed qualifies it for categorisation as personal and confidential information regarding the biographical core of an individual that carries a reasonable expectation of privacy, particularly since much of this information is being capable of being triangulated using other sources. Second, relying on third parties to provide information about an individual does not absolve the state of its responsibilities; the conduct would still qualify as search or seizure regardless of whether the information was provided pursuant to a demand or request by an LEA or voluntarily to Fintrac. Third, where a third party such as a financial institution has acquired the information for their own administrative purposes, the state may not appropriate that information for a criminal investigation; it would still need to apply for a judicial warrant for the same. The institution can neither waive constitutional protections available to its client nor can it consent to a search on their behalf. Fourth, the state is also barred from dissemination and disclosure to others and from sharing the information for purposes other than what it was originally shared for. For example, Fintrac should be unable to share the information with its counterparts in other jurisdictions and the administrative/regulatory bodies such as provincial beneficial ownership registries should be unable to share ownership details with the police and revenue authorities investigating money laundering.

[127] Hogg and Wright (2019), s 48:35.

[128] *R v Cole*, paras 78–79.

[129] *R v Mills*, [1999] 3 SCR 668, para 108.

[130] *R v JJ*, 2022 SCC 28, para 60.

The above would suggest that financial surveillance would be subject to similar controls and would thus be *Charter* compliant in its effects. However, this assessment is undermined by the structure of the AML/CTF regime, specifically, the inclusion of private actors and the reliance on consent-based surveillance. First, the *Charter* does not apply to private entities.[131] Private actors such as accountants or banks, for example, have no legal obligation to comply with *Charter* niceties when it comes to the collection, use, and dissemination of information.[132] Theoretically, PIPEDA is meant to ensure that private sector organisations[133] do not encroach on privacy rights while collecting, using, or disclosing "personal information"[134] about an individual "in the course of [their] commercial activities".[135] But for PIPEDA, securing the consent of the surveilled is an adequate guarantee of privacy in and of itself. As such, the statute predicates the collection, use, or disclosure of personal information on the "knowledge and consent of the individual".[136] Not only must the information be collected, used, and disclosed for "explicitly specified, and legitimate purposes"[137] that "a reasonable person would consider appropriate in the circumstances",[138] the validity of consent depends on, first, whether the individual has been informed of the purposes for which their information will be used or disclosed[139] and, second, the said individual understanding the "nature, purpose and consequences" of their consent.[140] However, PIPEDA simultaneously carves out a

---

[131] *R.W.D.S.U. v. Dolphin Delivery Ltd.*, [1986] 2 S.C.R. 573, paras 26–29.

[132] Gilbert and Kerr, (2009) p. 8.

[133] Scassa (2013). An organisation is defined as including "an association, a partnership, a person and a trade union" and specifically excludes government institutions subject to the *Privacy Act*. Section 2(1) and section 4(2)(a), *Pipeda*. *Pipeda* applies to federal works, undertakings and businesses across Canada and to organisations that carry out commercial activities interprovincially or internationally. It also applies to intra-provincial commercial activities in any province that has not enacted substantially similar legislation.

[134] "Personal information" is defined as "information about an identifiable individual, but does not include the name, title or business address or telephone number of an employee of an organization." *Pipeda*, Section 2(1).

[135] "Commercial activity" is defined as "any particular transaction, act or conduct or any regular course of conduct that is of a commercial character, including the selling, bartering or leasing of donor, membership or other fundraising lists." *Pipeda*, Section 2(1). Whether collecting *additional* information about individuals that is specific to AML/CTF qualifies as "in the course of commercial activities" is questionable but has not been litigated as of yet.

[136] Clause 4.3, Schedule 1, *Pipeda*.

[137] Clause 4.3.3, Schedule 1, *Pipeda*.

[138] Section 3, *Pipeda*.

[139] Clauses 4.4, 4.5 and 4.3.2, Schedule 1, *Pipeda*.

[140] Section 6.1, *Pipeda*. Prominent critics of Canada's "outdated" privacy laws have argued that the details regarding consent are buried deep within an organisation's privacy policy, couched in legal jargon, often describe ways of sharing data or purposes of sharing that are impenetrable to lay readers and pose significant challenges to 'opting out' of the surveillance project. See, for example, Scassa (2024b).

series of detailed exceptions to this rule: instances when information can be collected[141], used,[142] and disclosed[143] without either the knowledge or the consent of the

---

[141] Section 7(1)(a), (b), (b.2), (d) and (e) of *Pipeda* set out the most relevant exceptions as applicable to financial sector surveillance under the *PCMLTFA*. The full text of section 7(1) reads as follows: "For the purpose of clause 4.3 of Schedule 1, and despite the note that accompanies that clause, an organisation may collect personal information without the knowledge or consent of the individual only if (a) the collection is clearly in the interests of the individual and consent cannot be obtained in a timely way; (b) it is reasonable to expect that the collection with the knowledge or consent of the individual would compromise the availability or the accuracy of the information and the collection is reasonable for purposes related to investigating a breach of an agreement or a contravention of the laws of Canada or a province; (b.01) it was disclosed under paragraph (3)(d.21); (b.1) it is contained in a witness statement and the collection is necessary to assess, process or settle an insurance claim; (b.2) it was produced by the individual in the course of their employment, business or profession and the collection is consistent with the purposes for which the information was produced; (c) the collection is solely for journalistic, artistic or literary purposes; (d) the information is publicly available and is specified by the regulations; or (e) the collection is made for the purpose of making a disclosure (i) under subparagraph (3)(c.1)(i) or (d)(ii), or (ii) that is required by law".

[142] Section 7(2)(a), (b), (b.2), (c.1) and (d) of *Pipeda* set out the most relevant exceptions as applicable to financial sector surveillance under the *PCMLTFA*. The full text of section 7(2) reads as follows: "For the purpose of clause 4.3 of Schedule 1, and despite the note that accompanies that clause, an organisation may, without the knowledge or consent of the individual, use personal information only if (a) in the course of its activities, the organisation becomes aware of information that it has reasonable grounds to believe could be useful in the investigation of a contravention of the laws of Canada, a province or a foreign jurisdiction that has been, is being or is about to be committed, and the information is used for the purpose of investigating that contravention; (b) it is used for the purpose of acting in respect of an emergency that threatens the life, health or security of an individual; (b.1) the information is contained in a witness statement and the use is necessary to assess, process or settle an insurance claim; (b.2) the information was produced by the individual in the course of their employment, business or profession and the use is consistent with the purposes for which the information was produced; (c) it is used for statistical, or scholarly study or research, purposes that cannot be achieved without using the information, the information is used in a manner that will ensure its confidentiality, it is impracticable to obtain consent and the organisation informs the Commissioner of the use before the information is used; (c.1) it is publicly available and is specified by the regulations; or (d) it was collected under paragraph (1)(a), (b), (b.01) or (e)".

[143] Section 7(3)(a), (b), (c.1), (c.2), (d), (d.1), (e.2), (h.1) and (h.2) of *Pipeda* set out the most relevant exceptions as applicable to financial sector surveillance under the *PCMLTFA*. The full text of section 7(3) reads as follows: "For the purpose of clause 4.3 of Schedule 1, and despite the note that accompanies that clause, an organisation may disclose personal information without the knowledge or consent of the individual only if the disclosure is (a) made to, in the Province of Quebec, an advocate or notary or, in any other province, a barrister or solicitor who is representing the organisation; (b) for the purpose of collecting a debt owed by the individual to the organisation; (c) required to comply with a subpoena or warrant issued or an order made by a court, person or body with jurisdiction to compel the production of information, or to comply with rules of court relating to the production of records; (c.1) made to a government institution or part of a government institution that has made a request for the information, identified its lawful authority to obtain the information and indicated that (i) it suspects that the information relates to national security, the defence of Canada or the conduct of international affairs, (ii) the disclosure is requested for the purpose of enforcing any law of Canada, a province or a foreign jurisdiction, carrying out an investigation relating to the enforcement of any such law or gathering intelligence for the purpose of enforcing any such law, (iii) the disclosure is requested for the purpose of administering any law of Canada or a province, or (iv) the disclosure is requested for the purpose of communicating with the next of kin or authorised representative of an injured, ill or deceased individual; (c.2) made to

individual. As Scassa (2024a) cautions, PIPEDA is primarily permissive in its orientation; the only real or meaningful check on surveillance by private actors is the constitutional guarantee of privacy.[144]

Second, and as a corollary to the foregoing, is the issue of *how* the *Charter* is to be extended to apply to private sector actors in the conduct of surveillance. Gilbert and Kerr's agent of the state idea[145] initially sounds persuasive: since banks, accoun-

---

the government institution mentioned in section 7 of the *Proceeds of Crime (Money Laundering) and Terrorist Financing Act* as required by that section; (d) made on the initiative of the organisation to a government institution or a part of a government institution and the organisation (i) has reasonable grounds to believe that the information relates to a contravention of the laws of Canada, a province or a foreign jurisdiction that has been, is being or is about to be committed, or (ii) suspects that the information relates to national security, the defence of Canada or the conduct of international affairs; (d.1) made to another organisation and is reasonable for the purposes of investigating a breach of an agreement or a contravention of the laws of Canada or a province that has been, is being or is about to be committed and it is reasonable to expect that disclosure with the knowledge or consent of the individual would compromise the investigation; (d.2) made to another organisation and is reasonable for the purposes of detecting or suppressing fraud or of preventing fraud that is likely to be committed and it is reasonable to expect that the disclosure with the knowledge or consent of the individual would compromise the ability to prevent, detect or suppress the fraud; (d.21) made to another organisation under subsection 11.01(1) of the *Proceeds of Crime (Money Laundering) and Terrorist Financing Act*; (d.3) made on the initiative of the organisation to a government institution, a part of a government institution or the individual's next of kin or authorised representative and (i) the organisation has reasonable grounds to believe that the individual has been, is or may be the victim of financial abuse, (ii) the disclosure is made solely for purposes related to preventing or investigating the abuse, and (iii) it is reasonable to expect that disclosure with the knowledge or consent of the individual would compromise the ability to prevent or investigate the abuse; (d.4) necessary to identify the individual who is injured, ill or deceased, made to a government institution, a part of a government institution or the individual's next of kin or authorised representative and, if the individual is alive, the organisation informs that individual in writing without delay of the disclosure; (e) made to a person who needs the information because of an emergency that threatens the life, health or security of an individual and, if the individual whom the information is about is alive, the organisation informs that individual in writing without delay of the disclosure; (e.1) of information that is contained in a witness statement and the disclosure is necessary to assess, process or settle an insurance claim; (e.2) of information that was produced by the individual in the course of their employment, business or profession and the disclosure is consistent with the purposes for which the information was produced; (f) for statistical, or scholarly study or research, purposes that cannot be achieved without disclosing the information, it is impracticable to obtain consent and the organisation informs the Commissioner of the disclosure before the information is disclosed; (g) made to an institution whose functions include the conservation of records of historic or archival importance, and the disclosure is made for the purpose of such conservation; (h) made after the earlier of (i) 100 years after the record containing the information was created, and (ii) 20 years after the death of the individual whom the information is about; (h.1) of information that is publicly available and is specified by the regulations; or (h.2) [Repealed, 2015, c. 32, s. 6] (i) required by law."

[144] Scassa (2024a). While privacy protections contained in provincial laws would theoretically apply to provincially regulated entities such as accountants or lawyers, even these protections would prove inadequate in face of the fact that the *PCMLTFA* is federal law and would thus supersede provincial laws.

[145] The authors discuss the role of Internet Services Providers as agents of the state in the context of R v Weir, 2001 ABCA 181. The court of appeal found that since the ISP forwarded the evidence of child pornography to the police at their request, it was functioning as an agent of the state and had conducted a warrantless search (para 11). Gilbert and Kerr (2009) p. 1, 8.

tants, jewellers, etc., are collecting, using, and disclosing personal information at the behest of the state, they should qualify as 'agents of the state' and should, as such, be subject to constitutional requirements.[146] That said, the key difference between the ISP in Gilbert and Kerr's reading and that of the entities governed by the *PCMLTFA* is that the latter are not collecting the information at the "request" of the state through its agents. Under the *PCMLTFA*, they are *legally obligated* to provide this information to the state. The question posed under the 'Broyles test'[147] asks: would the exchange between the accused and the informer have taken place, in the form and manner in which it did take place, *but for the intervention of the state or its agents*? The reporting structure described by the *PCMLTFA* does not contemplate the state 'intervening' in the relationship between the accused and the 'informer' entity; the state is *already present* in the nexus between the individual, the entity and Fintrac. To rephrase: the entity is not just collecting the information in the course of a *normal* commercial relationship with the individual; the entity is also collecting (and storing) *additional* information as part of its legal requirement to report (and keep records of) certain sorts of transactions to the state. Even more simply: this information is collected *at the behest of the state*, not *on its behalf.*

This crucial distinction is why an agent of the state characterisation is inadequate to pursuing state accountability when it comes to invasive financial sector surveillance. Fortuitously, however, the *Charter* itself as well as the jurisprudence of the SCC identify certain other entities that are bound by the *Charter*.[148] This is because section 32(1) of the *Charter* explicitly claims to apply to "matters within the authority" of "the particular legislative body that created them", including "entities that are controlled by government or that perform truly governmental functions".[149] As such, not only does the *Charter* apply to legislation enacted by governments, it also applies to the action taken under statutory authority, that is, "regulations, by-laws, orders, decisions and all other action (whether legislative, administrative or judicial)".[150] The broad wording of section 32(1), reasoned the SCC, was to prevent Parliament, the legislatures and all governments (federal, provincial, and territorial) from shirking their *Charter* obligations by delegating some of their legislative responsibilities or powers to entities not ordinarily subject to the *Charter*.[151] And so,

[146] The Federation of Law Societies in the 2015 case before the Supreme Court said the *PCMLTFA* turned lawyers into "unwilling agents of the state". Significantly, the SCC did not address the issue in its judgement. See footnote 47 in chapter "The Illusory Truth Effect and Financial Integrity Objectives and Consequences".

[147] See footnote 66 in chapter "Law Enforcement at the Forest-Finance Nexus in Papua New Guinea: Leveraging Tools Against Financial Crime in Defence of the Environment".

[148] Section 32(1) of the *Charter* states: "This *Charter* applies: (a) to the Parliament and government of Canada in respect of all matters within the authority of Parliament including all matters relating to the Yukon Territory and Northwest Territories; and (b) to the legislature and government of each province in respect of all matters within the authority of the legislature of each province."

[149] Dickson v Vuntut Gritchin First Nation [2024] SCC 10, para 42.

[150] Eldridge v British Columbia (Attorney General) [1997] 3 SCR 624, para 21.

[151] *Dickson* [2024], para 44–5. Citing *McKinney v University of Guelph* [[1990] 3 SCR 229], the court held that the Charter is meant to provide a check over state power over the individual and so, the "entry point" for the application of the Charter must be "flexible, purposive, and generous, rather than technical, narrow, or legalistic".

while the court has consistently found "private activity" excluded from the *Charter* and held that the application of the *Charter* is limited to "government action",[152] it has also—equally consistently—identified ostensibly 'private' entities that are bound by the *Charter*.[153]

As articulated by the court, a private sector entity will be governed by the *Charter* if it is either 'government'[154] or if its activities can be ascribed to the government because they are "*governmental in nature* [emphasis added]".[155] In the latter case, it is the "nature of the activity" that must be scrutinised to determine whether it involves the implementation of a "specific statutory scheme or a government program".[156] While private organisations are ordinarily exempt from the application of the *Charter*, in the context of AML/CTF surveillance functions, these actors perform 'governmental functions'. That is, *the invasive surveillance regime administered by these actors are an expression of the government policy articulated in the objectives of the PCMLTFA*.

The three-factor test for "governmental in nature" established in *Eldridge* and confirmed in *Dickson* is also met here. As discussed above, these private sector entities have considerable discretion under the PCMLTFA about how to conduct surveillance. While some of the reporting entities (such as financial corporations) are created by statute and all of their actions at issue are taken pursuant to statutory authority under the PCMLTFA, others (such as accountants) are implementing the government's specific AML/CTF program and exercise "powers of statutory compulsion".[157] As such, the application of *Charter* standards is entirely appropriate to the conduct of financial sector surveillance.

[152] McKinney v University of Guelph, [1990] 3 SCR 229.

[153] These have variously included public hospitals [*Eldridge*], municipalities [*Godbout v. Longueuil (City)*, [1997] 3 SCR 844], labour unions [*Lavigne v. Ontario Public Service Employees Union*, [1991] 2 SCR 211] and Indigenous governments [*Dickson*] but not public universities [*McKinney*].

[154] To qualify as 'government', an entity must either be characterised as government by its very nature (that is, they are democratically elected by members of the public and are accountable to their constituents; have general taxing powers; they are empowered to make, administer and enforce laws within a jurisdiction; and they derive their existence and lawmaking powers from Parliament or the provinces and exercise delegated powers) or because of the degree of government control over the entity. *Dickson* [2024], paras 63–64.

[155] The two-pronged test was first articulated in *Eldridge* [1997] but subsequently finessed in *Dickson* [2024].

[156] *Eldridge* [1997], para 44. The expansion of the Eldridge factors in *Dickson* are worth reproducing in full: "[T]he Court has previously recognised an entity's activities as being subject to the *Charter* where the entity: exercised discretion under government legislation about how to provide services; was created by statute and all of its actions at issue were taken pursuant to statutory authority; or implemented a specific government program and exercised powers of statutory compulsion. In such circumstances, an entity cannot escape *Charter* scrutiny merely because it is not part of government or controlled by government. Even if an entity is otherwise independent from government, the presence of a delegated statutory power of compulsion means that the entity has a coercive power of governance that is not possessed by private individuals, corporations, or organisations. It is this power that makes the *Charter* applicable to bodies exercising statutory authority." *Dickson* [2024], paras 65–68.

[157] This means that the entity has a coercive power of governance that is not possessed by private individuals, corporations, or organisations. *Dickson* [2024], para 67.

7 Conclusion

As per its 2021 follow-up report to the FATF, Canada's compliance with FATF Recommendations remains patchy: it has been deemed compliant with 11 Recommendations, largely compliant with 23, partially compliant on five Recommendations and non-compliant on one.[158] As such, there is considerable anxiety in policy circles about the possible outcome of the fifth round of mutual evaluation scheduled for November 2025.[159]

Meanwhile, with a slew of significant amendments to existing laws and frameworks, Canada appears to be hurtling towards a minimal privacy destination that is in direct contravention of its *Charter* commitments. In the bid to maximise information sharing—between private sector entities, between private sector entities and LEAs, and with other jurisdictions—Ottawa runs the serious risk of trampling over the constitutionally guaranteed privacy rights of Canadians. While there is lip service to the protection of privacy, the structure of the AML/CTF regime allows for deeply problematic, invasive surveillance despite the existence of the *Charter*, the *Privacy Act*, and *PIPEDA*. Even more worrying is the fact that these legislative developments have been accompanied by largely performative, tokenistic attempts at public consultation: none of the real concerns and criticisms have been addressed nor does there appear to be significant public engagement over such issues.[160]

As this chapter indicates, financial sector surveillance poses significant and real risks to people and their lives. At a bare minimum, the Canadian state needs to step up to its constitutional commitments.

[158] Financial Action Task Force (2016).

[159] See, for example, Trichur (2025) in the *Globe and Mail.*

[160] The last public consultation regarding Canada's AML/CTF regime was conducted under the aegis on the Department of Finance Canada in June 2023. See https://www.canada.ca/en/department-finance/programs/consultations/recent.html. While an Advisory Committee on Money Laundering and Terrorist Financing (ACMLTF) has been set up as a "high-level discussion forum to address emerging issues and provide general advice" regarding Canada's AML/CTF regime, there is no public record of its deliberations or proceedings. The committee features a mix of public and private-sector representatives and, according to its terms of reference, is supposed to meet twice a year at least. See https://www.canada.ca/en/department-finance/programs/committees/advisory-committee-money-laundering-terrorist-financing.html. Meanwhile, it is significant that the latest round of privacy-encroaching amendments to the PCMLTFA under the omnibus Bill C-2 introduced on June 3, 2025, which is currently at the second reading stage in Parliament, have only managed to catch the attention of 11 members of Parliament. See Hansard no 009, transcript for June 5, 2025, 45th Parliament, 1st Session, online https://www.ourcommons.ca/documentviewer/en/45-1/house/sitting-9/hansard, Hansard no 013, transcript for June 11, 2025, 45th Parliament, 1st Session, https://www.ourcommons.ca/documentviewer/en/45-1/house/sitting-13/hansard and Hansard no 018, transcript for June 18, 2025, 45th Parliament, 1st Session, online https://www.ourcommons.ca/documentviewer/en/45-1/house/sitting-18/hansard.

References

Ahmed S (2023a) Running with the hare, hunting with the hounds: the Canadian state and money laundering. In: Leuprecht C, Ferrill J (eds) Dirty money: financial crime in Canada. McGill-Queen's University Press, Montreal, pp 91–120

Ahmed S (2023b) Harmonious coexistence: law and laundering in Canada. In: Robert C (ed) Transnational and cross-border crime: Canadian perspectives, pp 277–302

Alini E, Posadzki A, Marotta S (2025) Debanked. The Globe and Mail https://wwwtheglobeandmailcom/investing/personal-finance/article-debanked-why-some-canadians-are-losing-their-bank-accounts-without/. Accessed 29 July 2025

Amicelle A, Favarel-Garrigues G (2012) Financial surveillance: who cares? J Cult Econ 5(1):105–124

Amicelle A, Iafolla V (2018) Suspicion-in-the-making: surveillance and denunciation in financial policing. Br J Criminol 58:845–863

Anthony N (2025) Fair access to banking. Cato Institute. http://www.jstor.org/stable/resrep65727

Austin LM (2015) Lawful illegality: what Snowden has taught us about the legal infrastructure of the surveillance state. In: Geist M (ed) Law, privacy and surveillance in Canada in the post-Snowden era. University of Ottawa Press, Ottawa

Bennett CJ, Haggerty KD, Lyon D, Steeves V (eds) (2014) Transparent lives: surveillance in Canada. Athabasca University Press

Brand M, de Koker L, Herse C (2025) Privacy-preserving data analytics: a case study in anti-money laundering and counter terrorist and proliferation financing innovation in Australia. In: Goldbarsht D, de Koker L, Ferrill J (eds) Combating financial crime: intended and unintended consequences. Springer, Cham

Canada (Attorney General) v. Federation of Law Societies of Canada [2015] SCC 7

Comité paritaire de l'industrie de la chemise v Potash [1994] 2 SCR 406

Cullen Commission (2022) Commission of inquiry into money laundering in British Columbia. https://cullencommission.ca/. Accessed 29 July 2025

de Koker L, Casanovas P (2024) De-risking, de-banking and denials of bank services: an over-compliance dilemma? In: Goldbarsht D, de Koker L (eds) Financial crime, law and governance. Ius Gentium: comparative perspectives on law and justice, vol 116. Springer, Cham. https://doi.org/10.1007/978-3-031-59547-9_3

de Koker L, Howell J, Morris N (2023) Economic consequences of greylisting by the financial action task force. Risks 11(5):81. https://www.mdpi.com/2227-9091/11/5/81

Department of Finance Canada (2023) Consultation on strengthening Canada's anti-money laundering and anti-terrorist financing regime, p 9. https://www.canada.ca/en/department-finance/programs/consultations/2023/strengthening-canada-anti-money-laundering-and-anti-terrorist-financing-regime/consultation-on-strengthening-canadas-anti-money-laundering-anti-terrorist-financing-regime.html. Accessed 29 July 2025

Dickson v Vuntut Gritchin First Nation [2024] SCC 10

Egmont Group (n.d.) About the Egmont Group. https://egmontgroup.org/about. Accessed 29 July 2025

Eldridge v British Columbia (Attorney General) [1997] 3 SCR 624

Financial Action Task Force (2016) Canada's measures to combat money laundering and terrorist financing. https://www.fatf-gafi.org/en/countries/detail/Canada.html. Accessed 29 July 2025

Financial Action Task Force (2025) Private Sector Collaborative Forum reinforces importance of public-private collaboration in the fight against financial crime. https://www.fatf-gafi.org/en/publications/Fatfgeneral/pscf-march-2025.html. Accessed 29 July 2025

Financial Action Task Force (n.d.) Asia/Pacific Group on money laundering. https://www.fatf-gafi.org/en/countries/global-network/asia-pacific-group-on-money-laundering%2D%2Dapg-.html. Accessed 29 July 2025

Financial Transactions and Reports Analysis Centre of Canada (2024) Annual report 2023–24

Financial Transactions and Reports Analysis Centre of Canada (n.d.-a) Mandate. https://www.fintrac-canafe.gc.ca/fintrac-canafe/1-eng. Accessed 29 July 2025

Financial Transactions and Reports Analysis Centre of Canada (n.d.-b) Money laundering and terrorist financing indicators—Financial entities. https://fintrac-canafe.canada.ca/guidance-directives/transaction-operation/indicators-indicateurs/fin_mltf-eng#s2. Accessed 29 July 2025
Gallant M (2025) New Zealand and Manitoba unexplained wealth law: surveying the rights landscape. In: Goldbarsht D, de Koker L, Ferrill J (eds) Combating financial crime: intended and unintended consequences. Springer, Cham
Gilbert D, Kerr IR (2009) Deputising the private sector? ISPs as agents of the state. In: Desafíos del derecho a la intimidad y a la protección de datos personales en los albores del siglo XXI. Perspectivas del derecho latinoamericano, europeo y norteamericano
Hogg PW, Wright W (2019) Constitutional law of Canada, 5th edn
Human Rights Watch (2015) No more excuses: a roadmap to justice for CIA torture. https://www.hrw.org/report/2015/12/01/no-more-excuses/roadmap-justice-cia-torture. Accessed 29 July 2025
Hunter v Southam Inc [1984] 2 SCR 145
Johnson C, Duncan B (2025) Gun lobbyists and Cambridge Analytica weaponized gun owners' private details for political gain. ProPublica. https://www.propublica.org/article/guns-lobbying-cambridge-analytica-nssf-privacy-elections. Accessed 29 July 2025
Kharpal A (2020) Use of surveillance to fight coronavirus raises concerns about government power after pandemic ends. CNBC. https://www.cnbc.com/2020/03/27/coronavirus-surveillance-used-by-governments-to-fight-pandemic-privacy-concerns.html. Accessed 29 July 2025
Laidlaw E (2021) The future of the tort of privacy. National Magazine. https://nationalmagazine.ca/en-ca/articles/law/opinion/2021/the-future-of-the-tort-of-privacy#:~:text=Alberta%20is%20also%20out%20of,and%20Freedoms%20and%20Civil%20Code. Accessed 29 July 2025
Lyon D (2018) The culture of surveillance. Polity Press, Cambridge
McKinney v University of Guelph [1990] 3 SCR 229
Office of the Privacy Commissioner of Canada (2023) Public consultation on Strengthening Canada's Anti-Money Laundering and Anti-Terrorist Financing Regime: Submission of the Office of the Privacy Commissioner of Canada (OPC) to Finance Canada. https://www.priv.gc.ca/en/opc-actions-and-decisions/submissions-to-consultations/sub_fc_230810/. Accessed 29 July 2025
Privacy Commissioner of Canada (2024) Provincial and territorial privacy laws and oversight. https://www.priv.gc.ca/en/about-the-opc/what-we-do/provincial-and-territorial-collaboration/provincial-and-territorial-privacy-laws-and-oversight/. Accessed 29 July 2025
Public Safety Canada (2022) Annual report on the use of electronic surveillance – 2022
R v Ahmad [2020] SCC 11
R v Broyles [1991] 3 SCR 595
R v Bykovets [2024] SCC 6
R v Chehil [2013] SCC 49
R v Cole [2012] 3 SCR 34
R v Collins [1987] 1 SCR 265
R v Dyment [1988] 2 SCR 417
R v JJ [2022] SCC 28
R v Kang-Brown [2008] SCC 18
R v Mills [1999] 3 SCR 668
R v Plant [1993] 3 SCR 281
R v Rodgers [2006] 1 SCR 554
R v Simpson [1993] CanLII 3379 (ON CA)
R v Spencer [2014] 2 SCR 212
R v Tessling [2004] 3 SCR 432
RWDSU v Dolphin Delivery Ltd [1986] 2 SCR 573
Scassa T (2013) Privacy and publicly available personal information. Can J Law Technol 11(1):1–23
Scassa T (2024a) Privacy for the digital age: the supreme court of Canada's decision in R. v. Bykovets. https://www.example.com. Accessed 29 July 2025

Scassa T (2024b) Public sector use of private sector personal data: towards best practices. Dalhousie Law J 47(2):652

Solove DJ (2007) I've got nothing to hide' and other misunderstandings of privacy. San Diego Law Rev 44:745–772

SVR Lawyers (2024) Civil privacy law in Alberta: where do we go from here? https://www.svr-lawyers.com/news-highlights-posts/2024/11/27/civil-privacy-law-in-alberta-where-do-we-go-from-here#:~:text=Jones%20also%20acknowledged%20other%20civil,legitimate%20concern%20to%20the%20public. Accessed 29 July 2025

Thomson Newspapers Ltd v Canada (Director of Investigation and Research, Restrictive Trade Practices Commission) [1990] 1 SCR 425

Trichur R (2025) International review of Canada's anti-money laundering system will put regulators in the hot seat. Globe and Mail. https://www.theglobeandmail.com/business/commentary/article-will-task-force-review-reduce-money-laundering-canada/. Accessed 29 July 2025

Whyte J (2024) Debanked: the economic and social consequences of anti-money laundering regulation. IEA Discussion Paper, No. 125. Institute of Economic Affairs, London

Zuboff S (2019) The age of surveillance capitalism: the fight for a human future at the new frontier of power. Public Affairs, New York

Sanaa Ahmed is an Associate Professor of law at the University of Calgary, where she teaches courses on money laundering and criminal law. She takes an interdisciplinary approach to money laundering and terrorism financing regulation and focuses on the intersection of law, public policy and economics in her study of the regulatory, constitutional and governance issues at the heart of global regulation. A former journalist, TedX speaker and Killam Laureate, Ahmed is the author of peer-reviewed articles published in the *Dalhousie Law Journal*, *Journal of Economic Criminology*, *Journal of Modern African Studies*, *Oxford Bibliographies in Criminology*, *Socio-Legal Review* and the *Vienna Journal of International Constitutional Law* as well as book chapters published in edited volumes published by the University of Toronto Press, McGill-Queen's University Press and Irwin Law. She holds a PhD from Osgoode Hall Law School York University, an LLM from University of Warwick and a BA LLB from University of Karachi.

New Zealand and Manitoba Unexplained Wealth Law: Surveying the Rights Landscape

Michelle Gallant

Abstract Amidst the panoply of tools deployed in the contemporary financial war on crime, unexplained wealth mechanisms have begun to feature prominently. Such mechanisms are thought central to the strengthening of strategic assaults on assets and property linked to criminal activity. That strengthening typically results from the altering of the traditional rules of engagement in the context of property entitlements tainted by allegations of crime. Unexplained wealth devices generally provide that liability to forfeiture attaches to property upon satisfaction of a low standard of proof and that, to retain ownership, property owners must meet a different, higher, standard.

As with all tools devised to confront crime, unexplained wealth regimes ought to comply with the rule of law. Since the fight against finance has been ongoing for several decades, many other modern instruments have been vetted through court challenges for their congruence with rights-based norms and the rule of law. Fresh and new to the discourse, the rights-based story of unexplained wealth law is merely beginning to unfold.

This chapter explores this emerging story. Consistent with the theme of this volume, it locates unexplained wealth mechanisms within the wider context of the financial war on crime. Organised around two representative models—New Zealand and the Canadian province of Manitoba—it charts the central features of unexplained wealth devices and the alteration of the conventional rules of engagement. Against that backdrop, the essay identifies potential themes of collusions with the rule of law. It begins with an introduction to the new devices.

M. Gallant (✉)
Faculty of Law, University of Manitoba, Winnipeg, MB, Canada
e-mail: Michelle.Gallant@umanitoba.ca

D. Goldbarsht et al. (eds.), *Combating Financial Crime*, Ius Gentium: Comparative Perspectives on Law and Justice 131,
https://doi.org/10.1007/978-3-032-06858-3_9

1 Unexplained Wealth Mechanisms: Definitions, Context and Imperatives

As the phrase implies, unexplained wealth mechanisms typically target wealth whose specious origins demand an explanation. Framing that speciousness is the basic idea an accumulation of wealth not readily connectable to some lawful source of income must derive from crime.[1] Whereas the vast amounts of assets held by the successful technology tycoon call for no accounting, the fortune amassed by the individual in receipt of social assistance or otherwise having no obvious sufficient source of wealth calls for justification. If not adequately explained, that wealth must be presumed to originate in some nefarious deeds.

There is no consensus, no universal definition, of unexplained wealth mechanisms.[2] Many devices catalogued within this domain explicitly incorporate the phrase ‘unexplained wealth’. Others do not yet are understood to constitute such devices. A search of the internet for ‘unexplained wealth law’, for instance, draws attention to New Zealand but the legal instrument identified contains no mention of ‘unexplained wealth’.[3] Ireland is regularly described as an early adopter, but the phrase unexplained wealth is not part of Irish law.[4]

Commonly, if not universally, unexplained wealth regimes tend to be characterised by certain shared elements. First, many function on the basis of an order to disclose information about the source of wealth used in connection with some acquisition of property.[5] In species, such an order compels an individual to explain—through the provision of documentation or other evidence—the sources of resources used to purchase property. These can be called disclosure orders, or sometimes more directly, unexplained wealth orders.[6] A second common feature is the attaching of legal presumptions, or some shifting of the burden of proof, onto property owners. This might be framed as imposing an onus—shifting the onus of proof—onto a claimant to prove that the property does not derive from illicit sources. The failure to discharge that onus results in the cancellation of existing entitlements to property. Classic language to establish this is forfeiture: the failure to discharge the onus entails the immediate termination—forfeiture—of interests in property. A third common, although again not always present, ingredient is some reliance on an observed disparity between an individual’s known legitimate sources of income and the possession of property that exceeds what those legitimate sources would allow. It is that difference, so to speak, that begs an explanation.[7] Again, in the absence of

---

[1] Dornbierer (2021) pp. 25026.

[2] See generally, Brun (2023) pp. 16–17.

[3] Proceeds of Crime (Recovery) Act 2009, No 8.

[4] Hamilton (2011) pp. 122–141; see also Dornbierer [2021] p. 82.

[5] For instance, the New Zealand and Manitoba models considered herein.

[6] Ibid.

[7] For example, the Manitoba model.

a universal classification system, or perhaps an international model, these elements are common rather than constant.

Notably, some states recognise a criminal offence of 'illicit enrichment', a phrase often used interchangeably to refer to the crime of 'unexplained wealth'.[8] This descends principally from international law in the context of corruption. International law acknowledges of the crime of 'illicit enrichment,' a crime defined as an acquisition of wealth by a public official that cannot reasonably be explained.[9] That crime, 'illicit enrichment,' is sometimes called an unexplained wealth law.

Notably, too, a tight connection exists between corruption and unexplained wealth mechanisms. Unexplained wealth devices can apply to any crime. They are often reserved for corruption and the misdeeds of public officials. Vast estates can be accumulated through the exploitation of public office and pillaging of public coffers. To avoid any potential accountability, and to hide their wealth, officials send the riches to foreign shores. The location of the specific crime of 'illicit enrichment' within the international convention on corruption speaks tellingly of attempts to hold such perpetrators to account. On foreign shores, sometimes the tangible evidence of any pillaging is that a foreign public official appears to have assets beyond what their legitimate public salary might allow—*qua* 'unexplained wealth'.

The United Kingdom unexplained wealth mechanism originates principally from concerns about corrupt political actors.[10] The Canadian province of British Columbia has an unexplained wealth mechanism that applies to any alleged criminal wealth yet contains features directly referrable to the acquisition of unexplained wealth by public officials.[11] The crime of illicit enrichment is an important tool in efforts to deal with financial crime. The focus herein is on unexplained wealth mechanisms that do not formally constitute criminal offences. They respond the underlying idea of unexplained wealth—to the possession of resources that demand an explanation—but do not criminalise that possession.

[8] A comprehensive list of jurisdictions with criminal illicit enrichment laws can be found at: Basel Institute on Governance, Annex 1, A complication of Illicit Enrichment Legislation and Other Relevant Legislation, pp. 6–94: https://learn.baselgovernance.org/pluginfile.php/59301/mod_resource/content/1/Illicit_Enrichment_Annex-1-PAGES.pdf

[9] Corruption Against Convention (2004) Art 20. The crime associated with unexplained wealth 'illicit enrichment' elicits rights based considerations; see Boles (2014). This feature is not a mandatory element of the Convention.

[10] Proceeds of Crime Act 2002, s 362 B.

[11] *Civil Forfeiture Act,* SBC 2024 c 1 s 24. The province of British Columbia introduced civil forfeiture in 2005 and consolidated various amendments into the new 2024 law.

1.1 The Global Finance-Centric Strategy

The development of regimes centred in some manner on wealth of spurious origins sits within wider strategic anti-financial crime efforts that stretch back over several decades. Marshalled chiefly under the auspices of international law, unexplained wealth mechanisms complement that strategy and mimic its ambitions.

The beginning of the struggle with finance is rooted in 1980s preoccupations with the global trade in illegal drugs.[12] While the idea that finance, financing, or money plays a role in crime is hardly new, an explicit and organised modern assault on this aspect of crime began with awareness of the financial dimensions of the drugs trade. That the global trade produced enormous profits beget the mobilisation of a finance-centric control strategy initiated by an instrument attentive to drugs-related money laundering—the crime of concealing, or 'cleansing' money derived from drug crimes—and the enabling of the forfeiture, or confiscation, of drug proceeds.[13]

From that launching point, the modelling of strategic devices aimed at the financial element of crime swiftly gained momentum. A subsequent series of international instruments broadened the centring on the drugs trade, corruption, organised crime, terrorism, proliferation, and virtually any serious criminal enterprise.[14] Sophisticated finance-centric machinery developed. With the accretion of knowledge about the financial element of crime, shortfalls and weakness were identified, and the machinery honed. The initial focus on drug moneys and drugs money laundering morphed into the laundering of resources linked to serious offences. An initial template that enabled the post-conviction forfeiture, or post-conviction confiscation, of the proceeds of crime softened into the enabling of non-conviction-based takings of assets linked to crime. Enhanced financial transparency rules, rules designed to enhance the visibility of criminal money as it travelled through the financial system, evolved. Global machinery sharpened to attend to modern financial innovations—the likes of virtual currency and crowdfunding platforms.

An important organisational by-product of this progressive development is standardisation of the strategy into global norms known as the Financial Action Task Force (FATF) Recommendations.[15] The norms represent the distillation and consolidation of the global initiative. Built over decades, the recommendations constitute the bedrock minimum standard set of finance-centric tools that states must enact.

[12] See generally Gilmore 2011, pp. 53–67.

[13] Convention Against Illicit Traffic in Narcotic Drugs and Psychotropic Substances, 1988.

[14] International Convention for the Suppression of the Financing of Terrorism, 1999; Convention Against Transnational Organized Crime, 2000; Convention Against Corruption, 2004. A sequence of United Nations Security Council Resolutions, amongst other instruments, shaped this development: for instance, SC Res 1373 (terrorist financing); SC Res 1696 and 1737 (state-based proliferation financing) and SC Res 1540 (non-state-based proliferation financing).

[15] International Standards on Combatting Money Laundering and the Financing of Terror and Proliferation, 2012 (updated to November 2023): https://www.fatf-gafi.org/en/publications/Fatfrecommendations/Fatf-recommendations.html.

Unexplained wealth mechanisms are thematically co-terminus with this global machinery. They readily fit within the trend of devising specific legal strategies attentive to property—to assets and money—linked to crime. The global standards, however, do not speak directly of unexplained wealth devices. The closest they come to endorsing such mechanisms is the request that states, in designing domestic asset confiscation regimes, consider requiring that offenders demonstrate the lawful origins of property liable to confiscation.[16]

1.2 The Imperatives Underlying Growth

Individual states are free to exceed global standards. Any state can choose to craft their own unique instruments as a complement to the global architecture. A growing number of states appear to be embarking on this path.[17] Amongst others, Western Australia started down this path in 2000 with other Australian jurisdictions later following suit;[18] in Africa, Kenya embraced unexplained wealth law in 2007;[19] the United Kingdom journey began in 2017.[20]

Undergirding this swelling popularity are common motifs, all loosely clustered around the idea of the need for new, perhaps more practical and effective tools. A constant, as mentioned previously, is corruption. A profound North-South, or developed-developing, country lens tends to be influential.[21] No country is immune to the wiles of political corruption. The theft of public resources tends to be more chronic in developing nations, a phenomenon in part attributable to colonialism.[22] The proceeds of corruption habitually settle in jurisdictions of the global north. That settling parallels the investment trajectories of lawfully sourced riches. Prime destinations for significant wealth tend to be the expensive real estate, and other markets, of rich developed nations.[23] Developing nations decry these trajectories and seek the

---

[16] Ibid. Recommendation 4, Interpretative Guidance. Serious controversy surrounding crime of illicit enrichment precluded agreement that it be considered a global standard: see Dornbierer (2021) p. 12.

[17] Brun (2023) pp. 17–18.

[18] Criminal Property Confiscation Act 2000 no 068.

[19] Anti-Corruption and Economic Crimes Act, No 3 of 2003, Cap 65.

[20] Criminal Finances Act 2017, c 22.

[21] This lens permeates global institutional initiatives. The Stolen Asset Recovery Initiative, established in 2007, perhaps the most active global agent in curbing corruption through a focus on assets recovery acknowledges this reality, prefacing much of its work with a reference to this fact: see, for example, Tracking Anti-Corruption and Asset Recovery Commitments (2011) pp. 11 ('Much of the proceeds of corruption are laundered through the world's financial centers. It is estimated that USD 20 billion to USD 5 billion are stolen annually from developing nations and hidden in financial centres').

[22] See, for example, Kamga (2019). Some argue that a North/South, developed/developing country pervades the entire global finance-centric project; see Ahmed (2025).

[23] For example, London, United Kingdom: Unexplained Wealth Orders (2022) pp. 8–9.

repatriation of stolen public goods. Sometimes the only evidential hint of the spoils in richer markets is the disconnect between a political actor's apparent wealth and their legitimately sourced earnings. Responding to the global dynamics of corruption, questioning that wealth where it amasses, through unexplained wealth mechanisms, makes sense and helps redress global inequities.

Attending to the sophistication of the modern financial world and the targeting the chief pins of organised crime plays a role. It is firmly established that the modern criminal entrepreneur relies on corporate entities and trusts, on professional financial facilitators, and on convoluted global pathways to protect their earnings.[24] This makes the tracing of allegedly tainted assets challenging, time-consuming, sometimes verging on futile. Any relaxation of the rules applicable to the capture and forfeiture of tainted property allows a modern governance regime keep pace with the realities of the global financial system. Relatedly is the bedrock notion that the chief pins of organised crime, those who benefit most, who orchestrate the underlying crime, and who deploy the legions of financial intermediaries are too far removed from the actual crimes to be amenable to criminal prosecution or to conventional non-conviction based forfeiture.[25] At the same time, they have direct of knowledge of the source of income used to acquire valuable property. Compelling disclosure about the provenance of funds puts the burden squarely on their shoulders of justify their wealth. It is a practical response.

Restoring international reputation can be a factor.[26] The failure to effectively thwart financial crime can result in demonisation, international shaming, and being listed as a jurisdiction prone to money laundering.[27] Countries anointed as perennial repositories of criminal assets risk sanction and exclusion from global financial machinery. A mechanism that eases an assault on tainted property can signal an end to tolerance of criminal finance and can deflect distain.[28]

Variations on these imperatives shape the New Zealand and Manitoban embrace of unexplained wealth devices. New Zealand is an attractive global destination for investment. Despite reasonably robust anti-criminal finance tools, improvement was deemed necessary to deal with gangs and the transnational character of their crimes. Excavating information from foreign jurisdictions about the source of earnings was

---

[24] Transparency International UK (2019); OECD (2021).

[25] Cullen Commission (2022) p. 1616; Brun (2023) p. 26.

[26] Unexplained Wealth Orders (2023) p. 25.

[27] The Financial Action Task Force assesses states for money laundering risks and publicly lists risky jurisdictions: https://www.fatf-gafi.org/en/topics/high-risk-and-other-monitored-jurisdictions.html

[28] Arguably reputational concerns heavily underpinned British Columbia's embrace of unexplained wealth law. A 2019 report associated a novel kind of money laundering—the laundering of money from China through underground banking and drugs cartels—with the British Columbia city of Vancouver. This became known as the 'Vancouver model'. That report bred heightened interest in provincially-based laundering ultimately triggering a comprehensive inquiry into money laundering in the province. The idea that British Columbia was a haven for tainted financial activity cast distain and influenced the immediate adoption of a provincial unexplained wealth regime: German (2019) p. 46; see also, generally, Cullen Commission (2022).

difficult.[29] Debates surrounding unexplained wealth provisions refer to the challenge of international pathways and of obviating the need to deploy legions of forensic accountants by placing the task squarely on criminals to prove their resources are lawfully obtained.[30] Debates in Manitoba reflect similar motifs. While not a prime destination for international investment nor a jurisdiction particularly disposed to the foreign dimensions of finance-centric criminality, new tools were thought essential to confront organised crime and its central beneficiaries and to sever relationships between wealth and crime.[31] A Manitoba premier specifically acknowledged the value of asking 'gangsters' to explain their wealth and hold them accountable.[32]

In neither jurisdiction did corruption play any obvious influential role.

2 Two Models: New Zealand and the Canadian Province of Manitoba

In 2023, New Zealand stepped onto the terrain of unexplained wealth mechanisms. Through comprehensive amendments, New Zealand modified its existing civil forfeiture mechanism by introducing key features of an unexplained wealth regime: disclosure of source orders and related legal presumptions. The third ingredient, the incorporation of language referencing disparities between lawful sources of income and wealth owned, does not feature therein. Nor is the phrase 'unexplained wealth' used.

In 2021 the Canadian province of Manitoba introduced the initial vestiges of an unexplained wealth regime.[33] In 2024, the province enacted changes that specifically speak of unexplained wealth orders, of legal presumptions and of disparities between lawful sources of income and property acquisitions.[34]

As with many such regimes, the new provisions reside within existing non-conviction-based forfeiture law. They form part of lengthy elaborate legislative

---

[29] Departmental Disclosure Statement September 2022, Criminal Proceeds (Recovery) Amendment Bill, p. 4 https://disclosure.legislation.govt.nz/assets/disclosures/bill-government-2022-163.pdf.

[30] See generally, Hansard Debates, Criminal Proceeds (Recovery) Amendment Bill—Third Reading, 28 March 2023: https://www.parliament.nz/en/pb/hansard-debates/rhr/combined/HansDeb_20230328_20230328_24.

[31] See generally, Legislative Assembly of Manitoba Debates and Proceedings, Hansard, Vol LXXVIII, April 5, 2024; New Release—Manitoba 'Province Distributes New Legislation That Would Ensure Proceeds of Crime Benefit Manitobans, Not Criminals, March 9, 2021: https://news.gov.mb.ca/news/index.html?item=50938.

[32] 'Fact-Checking Wab Kinew's Promises on Crime During Manitoba Leaders' Debate', September 22, 2023: https://perma.cc/9V5W-KT5M.

[33] Criminal Property Forfeiture Amendment Act, SM 2021 c 50.

[34] *Unexplained Wealth Act (Criminal Property Forfeiture Act and Corporations Act Amended)* SM 2024 c 19. The *Act* also introduced changes designed to enhance corporate transparency.

schemes aimed at assets tainted by crime. Amidst the intricate structure are central components of an unexplained wealth mechanism. Although the details of the overarching law necessarily inform any potential collisions with the rule of law, only the foundational pieces of the new devices are canvassed.

2.1 *The New Zealand Model*

In 2009, New Zealand, through the enactment of the *Criminal Proceeds (Recovery) Act* enabled the civil forfeiture of tainted property.[35] The *Act* defines 'tainted property' as property that is acquired from significant criminal activity, or directly or indirectly derived from significant criminal activity and is liable to forfeiture (s 5). The *Act* defines the nature of forfeiture as a civil proceeding (s 10) and provides that the proceeding is in no way dependent upon any related criminal proceedings. The *Act* enables the prior restraint of property, with or without notice to any interested owners (s 18–42) Prior to the recent amendments, the civil, non-conviction-based approach, provided for the perfection of the forfeiture if, in a trial of the action, a court was satisfied, on a balance of probabilities, that the property constituted 'tainted property'.

In 2023, the *Criminal Proceeds (Recovery) Amendment Act* introduced a slate of changes.[36] Significantly, it bifurcated forfeitures into type 1 and type 2, with type 1 introducing an unexplained wealth mechanism. The configuration is reasonably straight-forward. First, and similar to a previous iteration, a restraining order against specific property must be applied for. A restraining order obtains if a court is satisfied that there is reason to believe that property qualifies as 'tainted property' (s24). Second, an order, called a disclosure of source order, can be applied for (s 109A). A disclosure of source order is an order to provide source information. Source information includes the circumstances surrounding the acquisition of property, the source of any funds or other property used in that acquisition and documentation relating to the acquisition (s 109 A(4)).

For a disclosure of source order to be made, a court must be satisfied that there are reasonable grounds to believe that a respondent—a property owner or someone within an interest in the property—resides outside of New Zealand, whether temporarily or permanently, or is otherwise absent from the jurisdiction (s 109 A (3)). The other element, a central feature of unexplained wealth law, consists of the presumption that the property is tainted property and therefore liable to forfeiture, if the court concludes that, on a balance of probabilities, the respondent was served with the disclosure of source order and failed to comply with its terms (s 50D). While the attaching of the presumptions is otherwise automatic, the regime does allow for

[35] Public Act 2009 No 8.

[36] Public Act 2023 No 6.

some discretion. The presumptions do not apply if the court is satisfied that it is not 'in the interest of justice' to do so (s 50 (2 D)).

The disclosure of source order fastens onto foreign residents, or persons otherwise outside of New Zealand. Rather than contemplate unexplained wealth generally, the orders uniquely apply in that context. The narrow focus accommodates the realities alluded to previously—the difficulties of collecting information about possible criminal wealth from foreign places.

The 2023 regime sits squarely within the ambit of unexplained wealth law. Respondents, or property owners, are compelled to share information about the source of moneys used to acquire property. Legal presumptions attach to the failure to adequately respond to a disclosure order.

2.2 The Manitoba Model

Similar to New Zealand, Manitoba's unexplained wealth device was born of changes to existent civil forfeiture law. Initial amendments were introduced in 2021 and revised in 2024.[37] Manitoba civil forfeiture law, introduced in 2004, enables the forfeiture of the proceeds of unlawful activity.[38] Unlawful activity connotes offences acknowledged under federal criminal law and quasi-criminal offences acknowledged by provincial law (s 1).[39] The proceeds of unlawful activity are defined as property, acquired in whole or in part, as a result of unlawful activity (s 1). The apparatus operates as a civil mechanism, enabling the temporary seizure of property and the perfection of the forfeiture through a civil trial governed by the civil standard of proof (s 17.12). To succeed, it must be proven, to the civil standard of a balance of probabilities, that the proceeds were acquired through unlawful activity. Akin to New Zealand, civil forfeiture is non-conviction based, in no way dependent any prior, or related, criminal conviction for any offence that underlies the forfeiture.

The amendments fuse an unexplained wealth mechanism onto the Manitoba civil forfeiture regime. Prior to the commencement of civil forfeiture proceedings, or during their currency, an application can be made for an order specifically defined as an unexplained wealth order (s 2.3(1)). An explained wealth order compels a respondent—a property owner or a responsible officer (the latter a reference to property held by a corporate entity)—to provide a written statement explaining, in part, how they acquired a certain property, the nature of their interest in that

[37] Criminal Property Forfeiture Amendment Act, SM 2021 c 50; Unexplained Wealth Act (Criminal Property Forfeiture Act and Corporations Act Amended) SM 2024 c 19.

[38] Criminal Property Forfeiture Act, CCSM c C306.

[39] Canadian constitutional law confers the power to create criminal offences onto the federal Parliament. The provinces have the constitutional authority to create quasi-criminal offences, or to enact prohibitions within their legislative competence: *R v S (S)* [1990] 2 SCR 254. This distinction has its roots in s 91 (Powers of Parliament) and s 92 (Exclusive Powers of the Provincial Legislatures) of the Canadian constitution: *Constitution Act* 1867 30 & 31 Victoria c. 3 (UK).

property and the sources, and amounts, of the respondent, or a responsible party's, lawfully obtained income and assets.

Once an application is made, the court, unless it is not in the interests of justice, must make an unlawful wealth order if it is satisfied that there are reasonable grounds to suspect that a series of conditions exist (s 2.5 (1)). Those conditions are: that respondent is the owner of the property; that the fair market value of the property exceeds $125,000; that the known sources of lawfully obtained income and assets would be insufficient to enable the acquisition of the interest in property and that the respondent, or a person who does not deal with the respondent at arm's length, is, or has been involved in, unlawful activity. Differing from the New Zealand structure, Manitoba's regime explicitly incorporates the idea of a disparity between lawful sources of income and wealth held, the element common to many unexplained wealth regimes. However, distinct from its counterpart, unexplained wealth orders are not confined to situation involving a foreign owner or someone not physically present in the jurisdiction. Orders can apply to anyone.

The making of an unexplained wealth order triggers a second component, a rebuttable presumption. The issuance of an order contemplates a subsequent forfeiture trial to which the rebuttable presumption attaches. A failure to comply with an unexplained wealth order sparks the presumption that the property constitutes the proceeds of crime and is, therefore, forfeit (s 17.18). Structurally similar to New Zealand, failure to discharge the order triggers the presumption that the property qualifies as unlawfully obtained property and is forfeit.

3 The Important Mechanics of Proof

In contending with the financial dimensions of crime, unexplained wealth mechanisms are potent devices. Part of that potency lies in the displacement of the criminal law and the criminal legal norms that ordinarily govern criminal prosecutions. Although they occur as responses to crime the mechanisms are not tethered to a criminal conviction. Consequences that attach to 'crime' typically attach upon a successful criminal prosecution, a proceeding governed by stringent rules such as the gathering of sufficient evidence to prove beyond doubt that some crime has occurred. Unexplained wealth law, in Manitoba, New Zealand, and generally, preclude the operation of criminal mechanics. Divesture of assets happens in a civil context within a civil proceeding. In this, potency is enhanced through the displacement the criminal rules of engagement and the incorporation of the dictates of a civil process. More fundamental, however, is a potency that results from the alteration of the conventional *civil* rules of engagement and matters intimately linked to proof.

Conventional civil rules of engagement maintain that to alter the *status quo*, to deprive someone of some interest in property, to hold someone to account in a civil action, the initial burden of proof, sometimes called the onus of proof, lies with the complainant. The entity seeking to disrupt the existing state of affairs, the entity alleging that some wrongful act has occurred, and that property ought to be removed, or property interests terminated, bears the initial burden of proof. That burden is discharged, or the claim proven, when that entity satisfies the civil standard of proof, a threshold generally known in law as the balance of probabilities. If that burden is not discharged, if that standard of proof is not crossed, then the action fails. In the context of property alleged tainted by crime, conventional civil rules dictate that the province or the state bears the initial burden of proof and must meet the civil standard of a balance of probabilities. A delineation of the specific mechanics of the New Zealand and Manitoba models reveals a potency achieved by changing the familiar civil rules of engagement.

Under the Manitoba model, an explained wealth order obtains upon reasonable grounds to suspect that a series of conditions exist in relation to property. The initial burden of proof lies with the province. Reasonable grounds to suspect is the lowest legal standard in Canadian law. It has been described as something being merely 'possible', or a possibility.[40] Reasonable grounds to *believe* is a slightly higher standard, connoting something more in line 'probable' or a probability.[41] Under the mechanics of the Manitoba regime, once this minimal standard is met, the burden of proof shifts onto the property owner. At this stage, the respondent must satisfy the terms of the unexplained wealth order. To discharge the order, it is not sufficient for a property owner to establish that there are *reasonable grounds to suspect* the inverse, that lawful earnings underpin the acquisition. Rather, the compliance burden is discharged by applying the civil standard of proof of a balance of probabilities. Any failure to satisfy the conditions of the order attracts a presumption that the property constitutes the proceeds of unlawful activity.

Simply put, at no point is the province necessarily compelled to demonstrate, by a balance of probabilities, that property derives from crime. Once reasonable grounds to suspect are established, it is property owners who must justify their entitlement. The *status quo*, the existing state of the distribution of property entitlements, is not altered by conventional civil legal rules. Rather, the province establishes reasonable grounds to suspect, establishes the *possibility* that some acquisition of property has been secured by unlawful source of income. The burden then lies with the property owner. To maintain pre-existing entitlements, the owner must prove—in accordance with the civil threshold of proof—the legitimacy of that entitlement.

The central mechanics of New Zealand's model differ slightly but occasion a similar change to the normal civil rules. Property is seized (s24) and a disclosure of source order issues if the court is satisfied that there are reasonable grounds to *believe* that it constitutes tainted property (s 109A). The initial onus of proof lies with the state and the threshold precipitating an order is higher—reasonable grounds to believe as opposed to reasonable grounds to suspect—than the Manitoban device. Still, it is a low threshold. If the court is satisfied on the balance of probabilities that a property owner has failed to comply with the order, the property is presumed to be

[40] Boisvert (2022) pp. 2–3; *R v Chehil* [2013] 3 SCR 220 para 27–28.

[41] Boisvert (2022) pp. 3–4; *R v MacDonald* [2014] 1 RCS 37, para 85.

tainted property (s 50). The state has the burden of demonstrating non-compliance with the order. If non-compliance is proven, the presumptions attach. The presumption can be rebutted if the respondent shows, in accordance with the civil standard of proof, that the property is not tainted property.

The New Zealand model is slightly more complex than its Manitoban equivalent. Significantly, a disclosure of source order issues upon proof, to the slightly higher standard of reasonable grounds to believe, that property qualifies as tainted property.[42] Once issued, the civil standard of proof governs compliance with the disclosure of source order, not the more fundamental question of whether the property is tainted by an association with crime. In the event of non-compliance, a property owner clearly bears the onus of proving, on a balance of probabilities, that property is not tainted by that association. Again, at no point in the procedure contemplated by the unexplained wealth mechanism is the state required to prove, applying the civil standard of proof, the tainted origins of property. The procedural rules do not correlate with the usual mechanics of a civil legal process. The *status quo* can be permanently disturbed although the alleger of misdeeds, the state, has never justified that disturbance by reference to the civil standard.

This delineation reveals the starkly revolutionary character of unexplained wealth models. They deviate from the conventional rule of law of ordinary civil legal governance. The reasonable grounds to suspect standard and the reasonable grounds to believe standard typically govern interim legal processes—the standard that governs, for instance, the securing of a warrant and other police powers.[43] Here, a *permanent* divestiture of property can occur in the presence of an extremely low legal standard. Obviously, these rules of engagement are structurally efficacious in assuring the forfeiture of unexplained wealth.

4 Rights-Based Tensions and the Rule of Law

In a modern age shaped by rights, it is usually not sufficient to merely fashion more efficacious legal devices. Although new approaches may have their origins in the perceived failings of existing tool and may advance ambitions as a matter of practice, new instruments ought to be consonance with rights. The golden threads of societies organised around rule of law ideals demand that state action abide by the rule of law. It might be productive to simply seize and forfeit houses, gold stores, and expensive yachts so to thwart criminal prosperity. It might not be tolerable for productivity to trump rights.

[42] *R v Williams* [2007] NZCA 52 para 213.

[43] Lower standards can sometimes be engaged when security concerns are at stake: *A (SC 70/2022) v Minister of Internal Affairs* [2024] 1 NWLR 372 (Supreme Court of New Zealand).

Challenges in other jurisdictions have begun to materialise.[44] The Manitoba and New Zealand models remain untested.[45] Discernment of potential collisions is a precarious endeavour. The nuances of distinct mechanisms and overarching social realities shape challenges and influence outcomes. Arguably several rights-based themes might be ascendent and apt to inform challenges to unexplained wealth mechanisms.

4.1 Criminal Tools and Compliance with Criminal Standards and Rights

Conspicuous in challenges to civil forfeiture law, or non-conviction-based takings of property linked to crime, the percussor to unexplained wealth law, are inquiries related to whether non-conviction-based takings ought to comply with criminal legal rights.[46] As alluded in the context of the mechanics of proof, law classically loosely divides into two camps—criminal and civil, or criminal and civil and administrative—and applies different substantive and procedural protections onto each. Higher and more demanding legal protections ordinarily govern criminal matters than civil, administrative, or regulatory matters. This is a well-known derivative of the severity that can attach to a criminal conviction—including a deprivation of liberty. Civil matters, by contrast, are typically governed by less exacting standards and attract less stringent protections because less is presumed to be at stake. To be accused of negligence or breach of contract—civil matters—carries little social stigma and the consequence of civil liability is usually a fine or some financial payment rather than time in prison.

On their face, unexplained wealth mechanisms clearly contemplate operating within the lower realm of rights-based protections. A habitual piece of any criminal device is the standard of proof of beyond doubt, or the highest, most exacting standard of proof. Defendants typically have the legal right to be presumed innocent until this threshold is crossed. The New Zealand and the Manitoba models both depend upon standards that are remarkably lower than this. Through the intersecting mechanics, proprietary interests are permanently cancelled on proof rules even lower than the common civil standard of a balance of probabilities. The mechanisms specifically incorporate legal standards of civil proceedings, as opposed to the criminal standard of beyond a reasonable doubt. Both operate within the confines of

[44] *Hajiyeva v National Crime Agency* [2020] EWCA 108. Campbell and Clancy identify a series of concerns provoked by the United Kingdom model: see Campbell and Clancy [2024] pp. 41–48.

[45] Campbell (2010) explored problematic aspects of New Zealand civil forfeiture (non-disclosure order-assisted) regime.

[46] United States v Ursery [1996] 518 US 267; Gale v The United Kingdom [2012] Application no. 25092/12; Chatterjee v Ontario (Attorney General) [2009] 1 SCR 624; Gogitidze and Others v Georgia [2015] Application no 36862/05.

legal systems that acknowledge a higher order of protections govern criminal matters.[47]

In neither jurisdiction, however, does the formal structure of a law determine its substantive character for the purposes of criminal legal rights. It is the task of the courts to discern any underlying criminal character. Framing an unexplained wealth mechanism as a non-criminal device is not necessarily dispositive of its non-criminal nature for the purpose of a rights-based analysis including the triggering of the criminal legal standard of proof.[48]

Despite cogent and compelling arguments, courts tend to resist characterising civil forfeiture as a criminal proceeding.[49] Shaping this characterisation is the idea that the target is property, not people, and that no one risks exposure to a criminal conviction nor any criminal consequence descending. In Canada, the courts have gone so far to conclude that even the forfeiture of property on the basis that it might be used in some *future* crime comes within the realm of civil jurisdiction.[50]

It is true that the New Zealand and Manitoba devices differ from civil forfeiture. In furthering the financial war on crime, they ease the route to any takings of tainted property. Arguably, there would need to something therein, in the reliance on less stringent standards, on disclosure orders, and on legal presumptions, that would accentuate a criminal character. It is not obvious what might suffice to occasion such a characterisation. No one risks exposure to a criminal conviction. No one risks exposure to a deprivation of liberty. Certainly allegations of criminal, as opposed to civil, wrongdoing underpin unexplained wealth mechanisms. The consequences, a deprivation of valuable property, are severe. But those allegations underpin civil forfeiture. Deprivations of significant property occur through civil forfeiture. Civil forfeiture has not generally been determined to embody an orientation sufficient to cast it into the criminal camp. Since unexplained wealth law fuses onto civil forfeiture, it is difficult to fathom how they somehow accentuate some underlying criminal character sufficient to attract criminal legal protections.

4.2 The Right Against Self-Incrimination

Disclosure of source orders and unexplained wealth orders compel the sharing of information. Respondents, to comply with the terms of any order, must ferret out and disclose materials relating to the origins of funds used in some acquisition of property. That compulsion invites consideration of the right against

[47] *New Zealand Bill of Rights Act 1990* no 109, s 21–27; *Canadian Charter of Rights and Freedoms,* being Schedule B to the *Canada Act 1982*, 1982, c. 11 (U.K.) s 11.

[48] See R v Wigglesworth [1987] 2 SCR 541; Z v Dental Complaints Assessment Committee [2008] NZSC 55; Ko, (2015).

[49] King (2012, 2014); *Chatterjee v Ontario (Attorney General)* [2009] 1 SCR 624.

[50] British Columbia (Director of Civil Forfeiture) v Angel Acres Recreation and Festival Property Ltd [2023] BCCA 70 (CanLII).

self-incrimination, the legal protection against the extraction of evidence used to incriminate the individual from whom it is extracted.[51] New Zealand and Canada, along with the other nations, recognise the protection against self-incrimination.

While disclosure orders clearly prompt self-incrimination concerns, the protection tends to reside firmly within the context of criminal, as opposed to civil, proceedings.[52] The protection contemplates enticing the emergence of truth and anticipates, in the pursuit of truth, granting a form of immunity unto truth-sayers against the imposition of *criminal* accountability. It does not usually extend onto civil accountability. In the context of unexplained wealth orders, the compulsion connects to matters of a civil order. Business records, for instance, relevant to the discernment of civil liability to taxation, do not attract this protection.[53]

There is a context within which this right could attain some traction. Materials, information, obtained pursuant to a disclosure of source, or an unexplained wealth, order, could potentially inform a subsequent, or related, criminal prosecution.[54] Afterall, the information, shared under compulsion, constitutes evidence. Once obtained, it might reveal new dimension or otherwise trigger interest in prosecuting a respondent for underlying criminal misdeeds. New Zealand and Manitoba's devices specifically prohibit the use of any compelled information in actions related to the imposition of criminal accountability.[55] Any actual use of information obtained under compulsion to inform a subsequent, or related, criminal prosecution could violate of the protection against self-incrimination.

4.3 *Privacy Rights*

The compelling sharing of otherwise private information, information about the business affairs, the financial affairs, of property owners irritates privacy. Differing from self-incrimination, the criminal versus civil dichotomy is irrelevant to any protection of privacy rights since privacy applies to civil matters. The functional value of unexplained wealth devices lies in the fracturing of the layers of secrecy and anonymity that shelter financial matters and property acquisitions from scrutiny.

[51] See, for example, Hajiyeva v National Crime Agency [2020] EWCA 108; National Crime Agency v A [2018] All ER (D) 21; National Crime Agency v Baker & Ors [2020] EWHC 822.

[52] For example, *Martineau v MNR* [2004] SCC 81; *Cropp v Judicial Committee* [2008] 3 NZLR 774 (noting that the right applies to communications and not to the compelled production of 'bodily' evidence as part of safety regulations).

[53] Ibid; Thompson Newspapers Ltd v Canada (Director of Investigation and Research, Restrictive Trade Practices Commission) [1990] 1 SCR 425.

[54] In the context of the 2022 BC provincial inquiry into money laundering, the Commission solicited an opinion of the constitutionality of unexplained wealth law which identified conflicts principally arising from evidence derived from a civil action informing a subsequent, or related, criminal matter: Cromwell [2021] pp. 1790–1801.

[55] Proceeds of Crime (Recovery) Act, s 165A; Criminal Property Forfeiture Act, s 2.8.

Their intent is to extract financial information that is otherwise extremely difficult to obtain.

Canada and New Zealand accommodate privacy rights, in part through discrete privacy laws, in part within the remit of the governance of search and seizure powers, and in part through common law doctrines.[56] In no instance are financial privacy rights absolute.[57] Effective state regulatory, administrative and civil governance requires some access to fulsome information. Compliance with regulatory mechanisms attentive to matters such as taxation and business affairs requires some state intrusion onto privacy interests.[58] Moreover, tighter protections generally govern more personal information as opposed to financial and business information although there are invariably links between finance and personal affairs.

While disclosure orders, and unexplained wealth orders, intrude upon privacy, they form part of a state-based regime aimed 'governing' the relationship between property and crime. A key consideration is likely the compliance dimension—whether the compelled disclosure of information constitutes a reasonable restraint on privacy.

4.4 *Property Rights*

Unexplained wealth regimes affect property rights. Successful negotiation of their mechanics leads to the termination of property entitlements. The intermingling of disclosure orders and presumptions results in the permanent deprivation of interests—ownership—in property. Interference with property rights is their very objective.

Canadian constitutional law does not enshrine property rights protections. The Canadian *Bill of Rights,* while not a constitutional instrument, provides for the peaceful enjoyment of property and the right not to be deprived thereof except by due process of law.[59] A hint of New Zealand's l disposition towards the relevance of property rights to unexplained wealth law might lie in a recent proposal to amend the New Zealand *Bill of Rights*. In proposing to add property rights, the text defines the amendment as *Right to Lawfully Acquired Property*.[60]

The tension between property rights and unexplained wealth law is ineluctable. Arguably, the only imaginable challenge might lie in the relationship between the mechanics and the termination of property entitlements. Is it tenable, consistent

[56] For New Zealand, see Law Commission [2008] pp. 10–16. For Canada, see Normey (2012) and *Jones v Tsighe* [2012] ONCA 32.

[57] For further debate on this, see Brand, de Koker, and Herse (2025), Sulayman (2025), and Ahmed (2025).

[58] See discussion in *R v McKinlay Transport Ltd* [1990] 1 SCR 627.

[59] SC 1960 c 44 s 1.

[60] New Zealand Bill of Rights (Right to Lawfully Property Acquired Property) Amendment Bill, 2023, 271-1.

with any bedrock conceptions of property rights, that entitlements terminate when the state's claim rests on 'reason to suspect' or 'reason to believe' that some unlawful source of income informs an acquisition of property? Due process of law ordinarily anticipates the right to be heard, to contest a taking of property, and the corresponding right to have disputes mediated by an independent third party—a court. The New Zealand and Manitoban models accommodate such due process concerns. Penultimately, however, they displace conventional standards and burdens of proof—the rules of engagement—and permit takings regulated by slight evidential underpinnings. This makes property rights subservient to 'reason to suspect' or 'reason to believe'. It is possible that such subservience might be unacceptable.

4.5 Rights and Reasonable Limits

Rights exist in a pluralistic environment of competing rights and interests, a context within which individual rights co-exist with broad societal interests. In free and democratic societies, rights are traditionally subject to reasonable limits. While conventional criminal legal rights, privacy rights, rights related to self-incrimination and to property can be infringed by a state exercise of power, that infringement can, at times, be justified and, thereby, congruent with a healthy legal order.

Both New Zealand and Manitoba operate within such a context.[61] The recognition that an aspect of unexplained wealth regimes infringes upon rights, or otherwise violates the rule of law, is not, on its own, sufficient. Reasonable limits on rights are ordained by law and any attenuation or inference with rights can, despite that inference, be justifiable in a free and democratic society.

Reasonable limits narratives typically implicate a balancing act between rights and the underlying objective of a law. Relevant to that analysis could be certain features of the Manitoba and New Zealand models. In the context of Manitoba, the tethering of unexplained wealth orders to property in excess of $125,000 ties the objective—foreclosing on serious financial crime—to the structure of the law. To a degree, the threshold tailors the law to the precise ambitions. With New Zealand, the law is tied to 'foreign' defendants, or property owners temporarily or permanently, not within the jurisdiction of New Zealand. In a modern global environment, the difficulties of pursuing offenders, including their possible proceeds of crime, is well-known. Given that context, rights concerns, and the tailoring of the regime to foreign exigencies, might demonstrate that it constitutes a reasonable and justifiable limit.

[61] In Canada, constitutional Charter rights are subject to 'reasonable limits prescribed by law as can be demonstrably justified in a free and democratic society: *Charter*, s 1. In New Zealand, the rights conferred by the Bill of Rights are similarly 'subject only to such reasonable limits prescribed by law as can be justified in a free and democratic society:' s 5.

The rule of law story may rest on assessments related to such balancing acts, the weighing of possible rights infringements, the specific ingredients of the regimes and the public interest in securing enhanced control over criminal phenomenon. In discerning congruence with rights, are the urgencies of the financial war on crime, the underlying phenomenon of the drugs trade, of corruption, of the trade in illegal weapons, sufficiently dire to justify a limit on the rights of property owners? Given the generative impacts of finance on crime, does the public interest in curbing crime justify a restraint on rights that would not otherwise obtain? Are the perils of prosperous crime are sufficiently deleterious to the public good to justify limits on rights?

4.6 Interests of Justice and Undue Hardship

Finally, although not a rights-based consideration, arguably a salvific feature of unexplained wealth mechanisms lies in discretionary 'interests of justice' or 'undue hardship' provisions. Given the relation between disclosure, or unexplained wealth, orders, and the reality of the mechanics of proof, clearly a harsh and disturbing character enlivens such regimes. Built into the New Zealand and the Manitoba mechanisms is some relief against that harshness through judicial discretion. While the confluence of the legal mechanics can result in the permanent divestiture of assets occurring outside of the normal conditions of a conventional civil action, build-in discretionary powers might alleviate the concerns that this unusual structure attracts.

New Zealand law contemplates the exclusion of certain property from type 1 forfeiture due to undue hardship (s 51). Having considered the entirely of the circumstances related, a court can exclude discrete property interests from forfeiture if the inclusion is likely to cause undue hardship. Similarly, Manitoban law grants the court the discretion to refuse forfeiture if it would not be in the interests of justice (s 14(1)).

Precisely what circumstances might trigger 'undue hardship' or the 'interests of justice' exception remains to be seen. Arguably, for instance, while self-incrimination might not be directly triggered, the exercise of discretion might be influenced by related concerns.[62] Any putative harsh impacts could shape an exercise discretion in favour of a property claimant. An example of circumstances could be intervening circumstances in which criminal financing informed a divorce settlement or some other similar settlement of property-based entitlements. Judicial discretion in the context of unexplained wealth law arguably mediates against unjust outcomes.

[62] *Hajiyeva v National Crime Agency* [2020] EWCA Civ 108.

5 Conclusion

In honing the global finance-centric strategy, domestically fashioned unexplained wealth mechanisms constitute powerful complementary weaponry. They service the ambitions of the financial war on crime by facilitating the removal of property linked to criminal activity. At the same time, there are profound and disturbing elements to the mechanisms. That existing property entitlements can be displaced through a process wherein the initiating actor, New Zealand or the province of Manitoba, has only marshalled sufficient evidence to justify a suspicion, or a reasonable belief, that property derives from crime evokes troubling matters with respect to the rule of law. Any popular appeal of such devices need be credibly confirmed to accord with the bedrock principles of the rule of law. The evolving story of unexplained wealth mechanisms ought to be rigorously scrutinized for its consonance with rights.

References

Ahmed S (2025) The fatal flaw of 'glocal solutions' to illicit financial flows. J Econ Criminol 7:100116. https://www.sciencedirect.com/science/article/pii/S294979142400068X

Ahmed S (2025) Surveilling the citizen: constitutional tensions within the Canadian AML regime. In: Goldbarsht D, de Koker L, Ferrill J (eds) Combating financial crime: intended and unintended consequences. Springer, Cham

Boisvert A (2022) The reasonable grounds to believe standard in Canadian criminal law, Commissioned Paper, Public Order Emergency Commission. https://publicorderemergencycommission.ca/files/documents/Policy-Papers/The-Reasonable-Grounds-to-Believe-Standard-in-Canadian-Criminal-Law-Boisvert.pdf. Accessed 30 July 2025

Boles J (2014) Criminalizing the problem of unexplained wealth: illicit enrichment offences and human rights violations. New York Univ J Legis Public Policy 17(4):835–880

Brand M, de Koker L, Herse C (2025) Privacy-preserving data analytics: a case study in anti-money laundering and counter terrorist and proliferation financing innovation in Australia. In: Goldbarsht D, de Koker L, Ferrill J (eds) Combating financial crime: intended and unintended consequences. Springer, Cham

Brun J et al (2023) Unexplained wealth orders: toward a new frontier in asset recovery. https://star.worldbank.org/publications/unexplained-wealth-orders-toward-new-frontier-asset-recovery. Accessed 30 July 2025

Campbell L (2010) The recovery of "criminal" assets in New Zealand, Ireland and England: fighting organized and serious crime in the civil realm. Vic Univ Wellington Law Rev 41:15–36

Campbell L, Clancy A (2024) The principled and practical limits to explained wealth orders. Univ Western Aust Law Rev 52(1):29–52

Cromwell T (2021) Constitutionality of possible changes to the British Columbia civil forfeiture act: unexplained wealth orders, information sharing and combining law enforcement and civil forfeiture personnel. Commission of Inquiry, pp 1745–1804

Cullen A (2022) Commission of inquiry into money laundering in British Columbia, final report. https://cullencommission.ca/files/reports/CullenCommission-FinalReport-Full.pdf. Accessed 29 July 2025

Dornbierer A (2021) Illicit enrichment: a guide to laws targeting unexplained wealth. Basel institute on Governance. https://baselgovernance.org/publications/illicit-enrichment-guide-laws-targeting-unexplained-wealth. Accessed 29 July 2025.
German P (2019) Dirty money—part 2: turning the tides: an independent review of money laundering in B.C. Real Estate, Luxury Vehicle Sales and Horse Racing https://news.gov.bc.ca/files/Dirty_Money_Report_Part_2.pdf. Accessed 29 July 2025
Gilmore W (2011) Dirty money: the evolution of international measures to counter money laundering and the financing of terrorism. Council of Europe
Hamilton B (2011) Comparative evaluation of unexplained wealth orders. https://www.ojp.gov/pdffiles1/nij/grants/237163.pdf. Accessed 29 July 2025
Kamga S (2019) Illicit financial flows, asset recovery, the power game and the right to development in Africa. Comp Int Law J 52:193–124
King C (2012) Using civil processes in pursuit of criminal law objectives: a case study of non-conviction based asset forfeiture. Int J Evid Proof 16:337–363
King C (2014) Civil forfeiture and article 6 of the ECHR: due process implications for England and Wales and Ireland. Leg Stud 34(3):371–394
Ko I (2015) "Tainted" assets, "dirty" money and the civil-criminal dichotomy: a novel approach to the classification of civil forfeiture proceedings under the criminal proceeds (recovery) act 2009. Aukland Univ Law Rev 21:193–224
Law Commission Te-aka-matua-o-te-ture (2008) Privacy concepts and issues: review of the law of privacy, stage 1. https://www.lawcom.govt.nz/assets/Publications/StudyPapers/NZLC-SP19.pdf. Accessed 29 July 2025
Normey R (2012) Privacy law in Canada. LawNow 37(2):33–40. The Angolan Data Protection Act: first impressions
OECD (2021) Ending the shell game: cracking down on the professionals who enable tax and white collar crime. OECD, Paris. https://www.oecd.org/content/dam/oecd/en/publications/reports/2021/02/ending-the-shell-game_79ff90e4/79e22c41-en.pdf. Accessed 29 July 2025
Sulayman Y (2025) Re-evaluating human rights in global counter-terrorism financing: a case for preliminary judicial moderation. In: Goldbarsht D, de Koker L, Ferrill J (eds) Combating financial crime: intended and unintended consequences. Springer, Cham
Tracking Anti-Corruption and Asset Recovery Commitments: A Progress Report and Recommendations for Action (2011) https://star.worldbank.org/sites/default/files/2020-12/OECD-StAR%202009%20Report%20Tracking%20Accra%20Commitments.pdf. Accessed 29 July 2025
Transparency International UK (2019) At Your Service: Investigating How UK Businesses and Institutions Help Corrupt Individuals and Regimes Launder Their Money and Reputations. https://www.transparencyinternational.org.uk/sites/default/files/pdf/publications/At-Your-Service-TI-UK.pdf. Accessed 29 July 2025

Michelle Gallant is a professor in the Faculty of Law, University of Manitoba, in Winnipeg, Canada. She teaches, researches and publishes in the areas of money laundering law, tax law, and philanthropy. Among other work, Michelle was a member of the Research Cluster of 2022 Public Order Emergency Commission and contributed to the 2023/2024 Public Inquiry into Foreign Inference.

De-banking 'Risky' Customers: Contractual Exclusion of Customers by Financial Institutions and AML/CTF Ramifications

Megan Styles

Abstract De-banking is undertaken by financial institutions pursuant to contractual terms and conditions, often in response to money laundering or terrorism financing concerns, and in furtherance of AML/CTF obligations imposed on such institutions. This chapter provides an overview of recent judicial consideration of de-banking in the United Kingdom (UK), New Zealand (NZ) and Australia. Whilst the case law is in its infancy (and limited), in some cases banks have been successful in defeating legal challenges to de-banking. In others it can be considered whether there is a willingness from courts to tacitly import a duty of good faith or a 'reasonableness' requirement for banks in their contractual arrangements with customers holding banks to a higher standard in their contractual arrangements with customers than ordinary commercial parties. Consideration is given to whether there may be an emerging perception and expectation that financial institutions have a societal/corporate responsibility over and above other contracting parties. This chapter examines the interaction between contractual relationship of bank and customer and the not inconsiderable requirements imposed on financial institutions under the Anti-Money Laundering and Counter-Terrorism Financing Act 2006 (Cth) (AML/CTF Act). Ultimately, the balancing of contractual arrangements between parties, AML/CTF obligations, and considerations of fairness together present complexities over and beyond those in an ordinary contractual relationship. Consideration is given to whether there may be a need for legislative intervention around de-banking in Australia both to protect banking customers and to provide clarity and guidance for financial institutions. The chapter will primarily examine the Australian context but with reference to international case law developments in the United Kingdom (UK) and New Zealand (NZ).

M. Styles (✉)
Monash University, Melbourne, VIC, Australia
e-mail: megan.styles@monash.edu

D. Goldbarsht et al. (eds.), *Combating Financial Crime*, Ius Gentium: Comparative Perspectives on Law and Justice 131,
https://doi.org/10.1007/978-3-032-06858-3_10

1 Introduction

'De-banking' is a term that has been defined as "a bank's decision to decline to offer, or continue to provide, a banking service".[1] De-banking can occur for a variety of reasons[2] but often arises in instances where there is a risk, or perceived risk, of money laundering or terrorism financing.[3] Financial institutions reported to an enquiry into potential policy responses to de-banking in Australia reasons including anti-money laundering and counter-terrorism financing (AML/CTF) risks, sanctions compliance, corruption, modern slavery, reputation, fraud and scams, and other regulatory obligations and expectations.[4] The power of banks over their customers is significant, and banks are potentially able to shut down accounts with little notice, with no reasons given and ban customers indefinitely.[5] The extent of de-banking in Australia is unclear, with the Australian Government agreeing in 2023 with a recommendation to work towards data collection on de-banking.[6] Whilst the data may be unknown, it has been understood that there is likely an overcompliance by banks with AML/CTF requirements, or a risk-averse approach leading to high levels of de-banking.[7] As Dahdal notes "de-banking is the surest form of de-risking…[b]anks can reduce the risk of client malfeasance to zero by restricting all banking services from clients deemed 'high risk'".[8] This is an issue that has been specifically identified with respect to particular sectors, such as the FinTech sector and new technologies.[9] Digital currency exchanges, for example, have reported significant difficulties in their banking relationships with one exchange alleging that over 65 banks denied services, without regard to KYC practices, DCE registration or AML/CTF policies.[10] Migrant communities in Australia may have been disproportionally impacted by de-banking.[11] The money remittance industry has also experienced high levels of de-banking.[12] De-banking has also been described as a particular concern in the Asia-Pacific, with financial exclusion a considerable issue

[1] Shaw (2024). For background see in general De Koker and Goldbarsht (2024). Excessive de-banking has been identified as a risk by FATF, with 2025 amendments introduced to address de-risking and promote financial inclusion: FATF (2025).

[2] Scott (2025).

[3] Parasol (2022).

[4] Council of Financial Regulators (2022).

[5] Senate Select Committee on Australia as a Technology and Financial Centre (2021), para 4.3.

[6] Australian Government (2023).

[7] De Koker and Casanovas (2024), p. 45.

[8] Dahdal (2024), p. 599.

[9] Senate Select Committee on Australia as a Technology and Financial Centre (2021), para 4.16; Parasol (2022), p. 1325.

[10] Senate Select Committee on Australia as a Technology and Financial Centre (2021), para 4.8.

[11] Dahdal (2024), p. 599.

[12] Fujii-Rajani (2017), p. 204.

in some island nations posing significant socioeconomic risks.[13] Ultimately, excessive de-banking can lead to the channelling of excluded customers into the cash economy and less regulated services, having unintended AML/CTF consequences.[14] FATF, in its 2025 guidance, identifies de-risking as contrary to a risk-based approach and calls for financial institutions to avoid the wholesale exclusion of particular sectors and assess customers on individual and actual risk.[15]

There are many issues at play when a bank decides to de-bank a customer. There are commercial interests of the bank and customer, social responsibilities of banks to offer products, ethical considerations in relation to banks supporting criminal activity, cultural norms relating to transactions that may be deemed suspicious, and obligations on financial institutions to information share and cooperate with law enforcement investigations and enquiries.

Notwithstanding these issues, ultimately, customers and financial institutions are in a contractual and commercial relationship[16] and financial institutions do have legitimate legal rights in relation to the exiting of customers depending on the terms of the contract, usually set out in the terms and conditions of the banking service provided when the customer has signed up to the provision of banking services. Generally speaking, the common law position is that "a contract by a bank to provide banking services to a customer is terminable by the bank upon reasonable notice", unless there is some contractual or statutory restriction.[17] However, this contractual relationship is set within a broader context of AML/CTF regulations, ethical considerations, and compliance and reporting obligations.

The chapter provides an overview of recent judicial consideration of de-banking in the United Kingdom (UK), New Zealand (NZ), and Australia. Given that the case law across the jurisdictions is in its infancy, the judicial commentary emerging from other common law countries is of particular interest. De-banking cases have been considered in the context of general contract law principles but in particular, the case law may suggest an eagerness for such cases to be argued on the basis of an implied duty of good faith,[18] or a Braganza 'reasonableness'[19] requirement on banks in their contractual arrangements with customers, in an attempt to hold banks to a higher standard in their contractual arrangements with customers than other contracting parties. Certainly, in Australia, the case law as a whole has not finally determined the applicability of such legal principles in contract law,[20] let alone in cases of de-banking, and generally, the observation in each case has been that it has not

[13] Johnson (2024); Pacific Islands Forum Secretariat (2023).

[14] De Koker and Casanovas (2024), p. 116; De Koker et al. (2017).

[15] FATF (2025).

[16] Dahdal (2024).

[17] Peart (2023).

[18] Renard Constructions (ME) Pty Ltd v Minister for Public Works (1992) 26 NSWLR 234; Esso Australia Resources Pty Ltd v Southern Pacific Petroleum NL [2005] VSCA 228.

[19] Braganza v BP Shipping Ltd [2015] 1 WLR 1661.

[20] Renard Constructions (ME) Pty Ltd v Minister for Public Works (1992) 26 NSWLR 234; Esso Australia Resources Pty Ltd v Southern Pacific Petroleum NL [2005] VSCA 228.

been necessary to finally determine the issue. For this reason, given the likelihood of further de-banking cases, such legal principles may receive continued judicial attention in this area, particularly in light of societal expectations on financial institutions that may lead to a greater inclination to import public law understandings of 'reasonableness' into contractual dealings. Consideration will be given in this chapter to whether, given the complexities in this area, there may be a need for legislative intervention in de-banking. Tensions between the AML-CTF framework, challenges for reporting entities and adverse legal outcomes for legitimate bank users adversely impacted by de-banking measures will be considered in the context of recent case law developments. Such issues will be examined primarily in the context of AML/CTF regulations and financial institutions operating in Australia but with reference to developments in the international context relating to these topical and emerging issues.

2 The Australian Legislative Context

Australia's AML/CTF legislation does not mandate de-banking.[21] The Department of Home Affairs has stated:

> The blanket de-banking of whole industry sectors and classes of customers goes beyond the risk-based approach to AML/CTF regulation, which is premised on a customer-by-customer assessment of risk and appropriate mitigation measures, rather than the complete disengagement from risk. At the same time, the AML/CTF Act does not require any financial institution to provide services to particular customers—this would go well beyond the scope of AML/CTF regulation.[22]

Whilst the AML/CTF Act does not explicitly legislate de-banking, financial institutions have a variety of AML/CTF obligations that impact on their decision on whether or not to exit a customer such as having an AML/CTF compliance program,[23] customer due diligence and monitoring requirements, responding to information requests from law enforcement, transaction monitoring, and carrying out ongoing money laundering risk assessments, for example.[24] Many of the breaches of the AML/CTF Act listed under current and concluded enforcement proceedings on the AUSTRAC website refer to "serious and systemic non-compliance with Australia's AML/CTF laws".[25] If a bank fails to de-bank high-risk customers, this can be a breach of legislative customer due diligence requirements and there are

---

[21] Senate Select Committee on Australia as a Technology and Financial Centre (2021) para 4.75.

[22] Senate Select Committee on Australia as a Technology and Financial Centre (2021) para 4.75.

[23] S 81(1) provides that a reporting entity must not commence providing a service unless it has an AML/CTF program.

[24] See the AML/CTF Act, Div 6 (Ongoing Customer Due Diligence), Part 3 (Reporting Obligations), Div 2 (Suspicious Matter Reports), Div 3 (Threshold Transactions), Div 8 (Risk Assessments), for example.

[25] AUSTRAC (2025a).

a range of potential consequences, including fines for non-compliance.[26] Section 36(1) of the AML/CTF Act provides that a reporting entity must monitor customers with a view to identifying, mitigating, and managing risks in relation to money laundering or financing of terrorism and do so in accordance with the AML/CTF Rules. This effectively means that ongoing customer due diligence must be conducted in light of the AML/CTF Rules, which can lead to de-banking. Pursuant to r 15.10, a reporting entity is obliged to consider whether a relationship with a customer will be continued rather than allowing the transactions to continue. In addition to their general AML/CTF obligations, financial institutions have an obligation not to aid and abet criminal activity, and banks and their agents are not absolved from being held criminally responsible for participation in money laundering activities.[27] So while de-banking is not specifically mandated in legislation, it can be necessary to ensure that a bank is complying with its ongoing due diligence obligations and indirectly a requirement of banks in complying with the statutory rules. What is not legislated is the risk threshold or degree of suspicion or concern necessary to be held by a bank before they exit a customer and this is where criticism is levelled in terms of potential overcompliance by banks.

The AML/CTF Act provides protections for reporting entities that comply with reporting obligations. For example, where information has been reported to AUSTRAC in a suspicious matter report (SMR) (and other types of transaction report), the person, office, employee, or agent is taken not to be in possession of that information at any time for the purposes of money laundering, terrorism financing and certain other offences against the Criminal Code.[28] Section 236 provides for a defence in proceedings if proven that reasonable precautions were taken and due diligence exercised to avoid a contravention. Section 235 provides for protection from liability in proceedings where duties are exercised in good faith to comply with the Act and provides that no action can lie against a person, or officer, employee, or agent in a criminal or civil suit in relation to anything done, or omitted to be done, in good faith…in compliance with a requirement under the AML/CTF Act, Regulations, or Rules. Pursuant to s 248, the AUSTRAC CEO may provide exemptions, in writing, to a specified person as to one or more provisions. It is in this context, that financial institutions (perhaps unsurprisingly) appear to have taken risk-averse approaches and have been criticised as engaging in excessive de-banking or de-risking.[29] Major Australian banks have faced significant fines for breaches of AML/CTF obligations[30] and this has been a factor identified as leading to risk averse approaches by banks.[31]

[26] Dahdal (2024).

[27] For an overview of corporate criminal liability in Australia, for example, see Nicholson and Wilcock (2022).

[28] S 51.

[29] See De Koker and Casanovas (2024).

[30] See Parasol (2022).

[31] De Koker and Casanovas (2024).

A scenario that arises with some frequency, is when a financial institution receives information from law enforcement or investigative agencies that gives rise to a financial institution making the decision to de-bank a customer. Technically, in such circumstances a 'Chapter 75 Notice' can be issued enabling a bank an exemption from their obligations in such circumstances (including enabling the bank to continue the banking relationship if they so choose). However, the number of such notices issued appears to be low and this does not always occur.[32] A Chapter 75 Notice is an exemption granted to a reporting entity following a request from a law enforcement agency and allows the bank to avoid forcibly exiting a customer who as a result of the request may be suspected of involvement in criminal activity.[33] This is because de-banking in such circumstances may have the potential to alert the account holder to law enforcement interest and have the potential to compromise an investigation.[34] Chapter 75 notices will soon be replaced by a 'keep open notice' where it is reasonably suspected that the provision of the designed service by the reporting entity would assist in the investigation of a serious offence.[35] Like a Chapter 75 Notice, the keep open notice will not compel a reporting entity to provide a designated service.[36]

In an instance where the decision to de-bank has been prompted by law enforcement involvement, s 123 'the tipping off provision' may have previously statutorily prohibited the giving of any reasons (or detailed reasons) to an exited customer (even if there are legitimate reasons) or prevent the financial institution from putting those reasons before a court interpreting whether a customer has been exited in accordance with contractual terms (and thus place the bank at a significant disadvantage in litigation where it is unable to place relevant material before a bank). Whether or not a financial institution is required to give reasons for de-banking can be understood by reference to the contractual terms and conditions which may include an explicit requirement to give reasons, or a requirement to give reasons may be found by a court through the implication of a term, such as a term of good

[32] In 2020–21, AUSTRAC received 74 requests and issued 126 notices under Chapter 75: see AUSTRAC (2021a). Chapter 75 notices are soon to be replaced with 'Keep open' notices, effective from 31 March 2026, with notices being able to be directly issued by law enforcement: Australian Government (2024). The Anti-Money Laundering and Counter-Terrorism Financing Rules 2024 recently provided for the form of 'keep open' notices and are subject to finalisation at the time of writing.

[33] Chapter 75 specifies that the AUSTRAC CEO may exempt reporting entities from particular sections of the AML/CTF Act where a requesting officer of an eligible agency reasonably believes that providing a designated service to a customer would assist the investigation of a serious offence. It does not mandate that a bank continue to provide a designated service—neither will a 'keep open notice': Explanatory Memorandum, *Anti-Money Laundering and Counter-Terrorism Financing Act 2006* and Explanatory Memorandum, Anti-Money Laundering and Counter-Terrorism Financing Amendment Act 2024.

[34] AUSTRAC (2021a).

[35] AML/CTF Amendment Act, s 39B.

[36] AUSTRAC, *Anti-Money Laundering and Counter-Terrorism Financing Rules 2024*, Exposure Draft, Schedule 1—Forms, Form 1—Keep open notice.

faith or a reasonableness requirement. Often, the reason for de-banking is unclear and there can be a grey area as to whether it has occurred for a legitimate reason (say, AML/CTF reasons), or for example an illegitimate reason such as a 'protected characteristic' subject to anti-discrimination laws such as sex, race, religion.[37] Ultimately, financial institutions may be faced with statutory limitations on the information they can provide an exited customer and are obliged to comply with AML/CTF regulations and to assist in ensuring that the financial system is not used for illicit purposes, and on the other, a customer may be found to have an entitlement to reasons and/or may have engaged in criminal activity that has given rise to the decision to de-bank.

Very recent amendments have been made to the AML/CTF Act, including the replacement of section 123. Under the new provision, disclosure of information is an offence where the disclosure "would or could reasonably be expected to prejudice an investigation".[38] New subsection 6 provides that "except where it is necessary to do so for the purposes of giving effect to this Act, a person is not to be required to disclose to a court or tribunal information mentioned in subsection (2)". This amendment has been described as "intended to provide greater flexibility for reporting entities seeking to disclose information for legitimate purposes, including sharing information within reporting groups to effectively identify, mitigate and manage their collective risks".[39] The new provision also provides for broad exceptions for disclosures between reporting entities and disclosure of certain information by specified persons (including legal practitioners and accountants) to dissuade a customer from engaging in unlawful conduct.[40] These changes enabling the broad disclosure of information between reporting entities may have significant ramifications in that where information is shared in such a way, there may be a risk of complete financial exclusion for some even in the absence of a criminal conviction or in circumstances where a reporting entity may have reached an incorrect conclusion.[41] Given the operation of subsection (6), there are no clear changes to allow disclosure of relevant information to a court. For this reason, the amendments appear unlikely to have any significant impact on the judicial treatment of de-banking cases, in that there may still be instances where a bank is unable to disclose the reason for exiting a customer to a court, even where it is a legitimate one.

[37] Dahdal (2024).

[38] S 123(1)(6).

[39] Australian Government (2024).

[40] S 123(5).

[41] Asher discusses the wide-reaching impact of a CIFAS marker in the UK to 'hamstring' an offender with all their bank accounts potentially closing or being suspended within minutes, where a record of an individual's name and other personal details may be uploaded to the National Fraud Database. There is no right to a fair trial or equality of arms in such circumstances: Asher (2025), p. 3.

3 Judicial Consideration in Australia: The De-Banking Case Law

There has been limited judicial consideration of de-banking in Australia, and no High Court consideration. In the existing case law, the interaction between contract law principles and the AML/CTF regime has provided some complexity to cases of de-banking.

In 2022, the ACT Civil and Administrative Tribunal considered the case of Flynn.[42] Mr Flynn had made a complaint to the Human Rights Commission alleging that Westpac had unlawfully discriminated against him by refusing to provide him with banking services because of his occupation as a digital currency exchange provider. Westpac relied on protection under s 235(1)(e) of the AML/CTF Act which provides protection from liability where an action has been taken 'in good faith' in carrying out the obligations under the AML/CTF Act. Westpac considered that the Tribunal should have regard to the AML/CTF Act framework in which Westpac operated, Westpac's policies and procedures responding to its legal and regulatory obligations, the terms and conditions of its commercial relationship with Mr Flynn, and the services Westpac had decided to provide to consumers and the circumstances in which it has decided to do so.[43] Westpac argued that its actions were in compliance with s 82 of the AML/CTF Act because Westpac identified Mr Flynn as high risk during the course of enhanced due diligence. Ultimately, the Tribunal was found not to have jurisdiction to determine the issue, being a matter under s 235(1)(e) of the AML/CTF Act, because the matter arose under a law of the Commonwealth and so would involve the Tribunal exercising federal jurisdiction.[44] It is of note that in this case, although it was ultimately not decided, s 235 was considered to have some potential operation to protect Westpac from liability. The matter does not appear to have proceeded in the Supreme Court, where the court would have had jurisdiction to hear the matter.

In 2023, the New South Wales Supreme Court considered the case of Human Appeal International Australia v Beyond Bank Australia (Human Appeal).[45] The case highlights some of the difficulties for financial institutions in balancing their responsibilities to customers and compliance with AML/CTF obligations.[46] Human Appeal International Australia was a customer of Beyond Bank Australia Ltd ('Bank'). The customer alleged that the Bank wrongfully 'de-banked' them, exercising a contractual discretionary power to close their accounts, even though the

[42] Flynn v Westpac Banking Group [2022] ACAT 21.

[43] Flynn v Westpac Banking Group [2022] ACAT 21 [31].

[44] Flynn v Westpac Banking Group [2022] ACAT 21 [64].

[45] Human Appeal International Australia v Beyond Bank Australia Ltd (No 2) 415 ALR 134; [2023] NSWSC 1161; Human Appeal International Australia v Beyond Bank Australia Ltd (No 3) [2023] NSWSC 1622.

[46] Scott refers to the possible regulatory conflicts faced by banks: Andrew, Scott, 'De-Banking/De-Risking: Issues for the 119th Congress' (2025).

accounts were said to be in credit and being operated in accordance with the trading terms. Reasons were not provided for the closing of the accounts.

The customer argued that the Bank was only entitled to terminate Human Appeal's banking facilities if it was acting in good faith and reasonably with a focus on the Bank's contractual obligations to the customer. Reliance was placed on the duty of cooperation and good faith generally implied in commercial contracts. Secondly, it was argued that the trading terms of the Bank (including its Code of Practice) were breached by the Bank's termination of the facilities without justification or reasons. In this regard, the court was asked to compel the Bank to vary its terms and conditions so as to require reasonable grounds for, and proper notice of, termination.

The Bank contended that its decision had to be understood in the context of its obligations under the AML/CTF Act. The Bank was issued with a Notice to Produce during the proceeding relating to its decision to terminate the facilities. The Bank contended it had complied with the notice in accordance with its statutory obligations and that the AML/CTF Act prevented it from even stating whether or not there were additional documents caught by the notice which had not been produced. It maintained that there were no documents to produce which had not already been produced.

The Court ultimately found that the purported termination of the banking facilities was invalid and that the provisions in clause 25 of the terms and conditions, concerning the termination of customer bank accounts, contravened the bank's obligations under the Code of Practice.[47] The court made orders that the purported termination of the plaintiff's banking facilities was invalid and that a clause of the Bank's terms contravened their obligations pursuant to the Customer Owned Banking Code of Practice to the extent that it did not, in the circumstances of the case, require the defendant to specify the reasons for the closure of the plaintiff's bank accounts.[48] Human Appeal succeeded with respect to both claims. Of significance was a concession by Counsel for the Bank that the Bank could only terminate the facilities if it had a 'valid commercial reason'. This, Parker J commented made "it unnecessary to decide whether such a requirement attached to all banker-customer relationships".[49] His Honour Parker J did however note that a customer of the particular bank might have been in a stronger position than the customer of a commercial bank based on the contractual context and the provisions of the Bank's constitution. In relation to the first ground (that there were contractual duties that prevented the Bank from terminating the customer's facilities without reasonable grounds) it was said to be 'common ground' that the evidentiary burden was on the customer to prove the absence of a valid commercial reason but the bank bore an evidentiary onus and had advanced no admissible evidence. It was concluded that

[47] Human Appeal International Australia v Beyond Bank Australia Ltd (No 2) 415 ALR 134; [2023] NSWSC 1161.

[48] Human Appeal International Australia v Beyond Bank Australia. Ltd (No 3) [2023] NSWSC 1622.

[49] Human Appeal International Australia v Beyond Bank Australia. Ltd (No 3) [2023] NSWSC 1622 [12].

the bank lacked reasons. In relation to the second ground, it was found that the termination provisions in the bank's terms did not strike a 'fair balance' between the parties' interests as required by a clause in the Code of Practice.

His Honour Parker J made some observations about the failure to disclosure particular documents by the bank in response to the Notice to Produce. The bank noted its obligations under the AML/CTF Act with respect to disclosure. Parker J referred to s 123 in particular, noting that this provision did not appear to prevent disclosure to a court and commented that it was "well established that, absent contrary intention, a reference to a "person" will not include a court".[50] Further, s 123(1) expressly concerned disclosure to a court. His Honour commented that he did not read the provision as preventing disclosure, in general terms, of the administrative burden of the Commonwealth Act, together with other reporting obligations, on a reporting entity. His Honour commented that he found "it difficult to accept that, if in fact the Bank decided to terminate Human Appeal's banking facilities because of that administrative burden, none of the documents produced in the review, and none of the records recording the decision, could be disclosed at all, even in partially redacted form".[51] Further, it was noted that there was also no evidence "that, if the terms of the Act did prevent disclosure, partial or total, the CEO of AUSTRAC had been asked (under s 248) to modify its application, so as to permit such disclosure".[52]

The significance of the Human Appeal case remains to be seen. The case did not decide whether such requirements applied to all banker-customer relationships and this was specifically noted in the judgment. In future cases, the wording of the particular contractual context is likely relevant and the enquiry will be influenced by the specific factual circumstances of a case. Further, the nature of the particular bank and relevant code of practice was considered relevant and a potential distinction was drawn between a commercial bank and a customer owned bank.

The case and the observations made raise some interesting questions around the operation of the AML/CTF Act. It is clear from the case that there was significant concern from the Bank in relation to the Bank's statutory obligations (and the corresponding offence provisions) that led to the potential withholding of information from the court. Although there is some commentary by Parker J with respect to the tipping off provisions, it seems apparent that the bank considered its obligations to be such that it could not make certain disclosures to the court (and presumably had received legal advice to that effect). A conservative approach (perhaps fairly) appears to have been taken by the bank to the offence provisions. Of note is the fact that s 235 was not discussed in Human Appeal, despite the significant discussion of good faith and the fact that the bank raised the AML/CTF context as significant. It is unclear if this provision may have worked to absolve the bank from any liability

---

[50] Human Appeal International Australia v Beyond Bank Australia Ltd (No 2) [2023] NSWSC 1161 [72].

[51] Human Appeal International Australia v Beyond Bank Australia Ltd (No 2) [2023] NSWSC 1161 [76].

[52] Human Appeal International Australia v Beyond Bank Australia Ltd (No 2) [2023] NSWSC 1161 [76].

or whether there was again insufficient evidence advanced by the bank for this provision to assume any relevance. While the future judicial consideration of Human Appeal remains to be seen, it is of note that the argument concerning an "implied duty of cooperation and good faith generally implied in commercial contracts"[53] seems to have been afforded some weight in the case. Human Appeal raises issues concerning the tipping off provisions, their interpretation and questions around whether a bank can rely on information obtained under the Act in a proceeding brought by a customer, or whether there is a risk of contravening s 123.

In Marundrury,[54] in the Federal Court of Australia, the applicants had commenced proceedings against the Commonwealth Bank of Australia alleging to be victims of 'cuckoo-smurfing'. It was claimed that the respondent had breached duties under the AML/CTF Act in failing to report suspicious activity on the applicant's bank accounts. Marundrury concerned an application for leave by the applicant to file a proposed second amended statement of claim, and the respondent sought summary dismissal of the proceeding. The bank argued that it may wish to rely on the immunity in s 235 of the AML/CTF Act but that to make out that defence it would need to disclose information falling within s 123(1)(b). His Honour Mochinsky J found that there was a reasonable prospect of an exemption or modification under s 248 of the AML/CTF Act being granted by the AUSTRAC CEO permitting the Bank to disclose to the Court and the applicant's legal representatives on a confidential basis information relevant to the allegation in revised paragraph 47 of the Proposed Pleading and any defence raised by the Bank in reliance on s 235. Leave was therefore granted to give leave to the applicants to file the Proposed Pleading, while relieving the Bank of the obligation to plead revised paragraph 47 and preserving the right of the Bank to apply for a stay of the proceeding in the event that it was unable to obtain an exemption or modification from the CEO of AUSTRAC. An application by the bank for the summary dismissal of the proceeding was dismissed. It appears in such cases, reliance on s 248 may therefore be made to seek an AUSTRAC CEO exemption to use relevant material in court proceedings.

Most recently in *Merciful Group Incorporated v Norfina Limited t/as Suncorp Bank*, the New South Wales Supreme Court considered that Suncorp had established that it had 'acted rationally, honestly and in good faith' and 'for a proper purpose' in de-banking Merciful (a registered charity) in circumstances where Merciful was sending large amounts of money to a third-party money remitter consistent with the well-known money laundering technique of layering and for onward transmission to high risk countries to which the bank itself would not send money. Further, the source of Merciful's wealth was unable to be established through open source searches and among other factors, large sums of money were being spent on high-value luxury goods. Merciful was unable to establish any breach of contract by

[53] Human Appeal International Australia v Beyond Bank Australia Ltd (No 2) [2023] NSWSC 1161 [14], [113].

[54] Marundrury v Commonwealth Bank of Australia (No 3) [2023] FCA 807 (13 July 2023).

the bank, who was seen to be acting in the context of its AML/CTF obligations. His Honour Hammerschlag CJ discussed the requirements for the implications of terms in a contract and was nevertheless satisfied that the bank had acted in accordance with its obligations.[55]

The few Australian cases that have emerged (and those from the international context discussed below), while fact specific, are indicative of the complex context in which such cases arise, balancing the rights of the customer, contractual terms and conditions, overlapping legislative regimes and banking policies and procedures. Ultimately, the success of any one party to such a proceeding may depend largely on what information is able to be properly put before the court as admissible evidence, the terms of the contractual relationship, and the reasonableness of a bank's decision as compared with the impropriety on the part of the customer. In circumstances where financial institutions have simply taken a risk averse approach to closing an account, there may be insufficient evidence to demonstrate reasonableness of any account closures. Having noted the above however, it is difficult to make significant observation of the Australian case law, given the limited judicial consideration to date.

4 International Context and Developments

De-banking is an international issue.[56] The Financial Action Task Force (FATF) standards require countries to adopt relatively uniform AML/CTF/CPF laws.[57] The FATF has cautioned against the "wholesale cutting loose of entire countries and classes of customer, without taking into account, seriously and comprehensively, their level of money laundering and terrorist financing risk".[58] De-banking has received judicial attention overseas. In the UK and NZ, it is of note that an implied term of good faith/reasonableness has been applied to commercial contracts generally and discussed in the de-banking cases.

The case law in the UK has generally ruled in favour of banks and described as showing a "trend that the court will uphold a bank's decision to exercise its contractual rights".[59] However, what is again clear from a review of the UK cases (and in other jurisdictions) is that each case turns on the specific contractual terms to be interpreted and the specific facts of the case. The position in NZ and Australia, remains less clear and in each of these jurisdictions (including the UK) it is a topical issue that is likely to see further judicial commentary.

---

[55] Merciful Group Incorporated v Norfina Limited t/as Suncorp Bank [2025] NSWSC 841.

[56] Council of Financial Regulators (2022).

[57] De Koker and Casanovas (2024).

[58] Financial Action Task Force (2015).

[59] Herbert Smith Freehills (2023).

4.1 The UK

New regulations were introduced in the UK in 2024 requiring improved transparency around account closures.[60] This followed the controversial de-banking of Nigel Farage, former Brexit Party leader, on political grounds.[61] Certainly, there has been a concern that some cases of de-banking may arise due to opposing ideological views held by a bank as opposed to other arguably more legitimate reasons for de-banking[62]. Whether or not this is an issue remains ripe for further research, with the UK Financial Conduct Authority recently observing that initial findings were that ideological differences were not a primary reason for de-banking with financial crime being the key reason for de-banking.[63] In 2021/22, banks in the UK closed 343,000 accounts with the reason in about half being that the bank was unable to satisfy itself that the customer was not involved in money laundering or other financial crimes.[64] This can be contrasted with the fact that only 1083 people in the UK were convicted of money laundering in the 2021/22 period.[65] It remains to be seen what the issue was in the remaining half of those cases.

Legislative changes in the UK included requiring detailed reasons for terminations and restrictions on contracting out of the new requirements, and additional notice requirements.[66] Exceptions to the requirements include in circumstances where it is suspected that the customer has committed an offence, or the service is being used in connection with a serious crime.[67]

Shah & Anor v HSBC Private Bank (UK) Ltd,[68] an English High Court case, concerned a long running dispute between HSBC Private Bank and Mr Shah. Mr Shah had claimed that money laundering reports filed by the bank had led to damage causing him financial loss in excess of US$300 m, and he sought to recover these monies from the bank. This claim was dismissed. The High Court considered that the bank could be put to proof that it held the relevant suspicion of money laundering and that it was arguable that the bank had a duty to provide information to Mr Shah once tipping off was no longer in issue. The Court agreed with the bank that an implied term suggested by Mr Shah (that the bank had an implied duty to provide him with information with respect to its dealings with the Serious Organised Crime Agency) would cut across the statutory regime, operate as a disincentive to report

[60] Payment Services (Amendment) Regulations 2024 amending the Payment Services Regulations 2017.

[61] Payment Services (Amendment) Regulations 2024 amending the Payment Services Regulations 2017.

[62] See discussion of de-banking on moral or political grounds in Dahdal (2024).

[63] Whyte (2024), p. 6.

[64] Whyte, (2024), p. 6.

[65] Whyte (2024) p. 27.

[66] Eversheds Sutherland (2024).

[67] Eversheds Sutherland (2024).

[68] Shah & Anor v HSBC Private Bank (UK) Ltd [2012] EWHC 1283 (QB).

suspicious activity, and undermine the integrity of the reporting regime. It was held that there was an implied term that permitted the bank to refuse to provide information where it might contravene the tipping-off provisions of the *Proceeds of Crime Act 2002* ('POCA'). The implied term was found in the bank-customer contract permitting it to refuse to execute a payment instruction pending permission from the Serious Organised Crime Agency under s 335 and further, the bank was not obliged to provide the customer with details of its disclosure to the agency. Where information provided under s 333 might amount to a 'tipping off' offence, the bank was obliged to refuse to provide it. This case is particularly interesting because the implied term was implied to give effect to the broader legislative regime in which the bank operated, as compared with those cases in which an implied term of good faith has been implied in favour of a customer. This case, whilst not strictly considering the issue of de-banking, is of note given that it again highlights the distinction between contractual terms and conditions and anti-money laundering obligations/ tipping off provisions.

In N v The Royal Bank of Scotland plc,[69] the bank had frozen accounts held with it by N and terminated the banking relationship. N commenced proceedings challenging the actions of the Bank. The National Crime Agency had participated in some aspects of the proceedings because the alleged context was money laundering and the proceedings had implications for the working of the POCA and the criminal law more generally.[70] The Court observed that "the authorities continue to examine the important question of whether rationality or objective reasonableness or neither is required when a contract gives the right to a contracting party (rather than a third party) to reach a decision" but that the facts were such that it was not necessary to enter further into these questions.[71] Ultimately, it was found that the bank had considered there were "exceptional circumstances for closing the accounts" as required by the terms and the view was "held in good faith, and was a rational view".[72] Further, if a standard of objective reasonableness was required, the Bank's view did meet that standard and it had acted in a "reasonable manner".[73] Ultimately, the "bank's decision was itself a proper response to circumstances for which N, not the Bank, must take responsibility". It was further noted that "the wider, public, interests of the prevention of crime and the protection of the victims of crime are a further crucial part of the picture".[74] It is of note that the Court considered the uncertain case law with respect to good faith and reasonableness requirements but nevertheless found that the bank had acted in accordance with the terms even if such terms were applied (to whatever legal standard).

[69] N v The Royal Bank of Scotland Plc [2019] EWHC 1770.

[70] N v The Royal Bank of Scotland Plc [2019] EWHC 1770 [3].

[71] N v The Royal Bank of Scotland Plc [2019] EWHC 1770 [15].

[72] N v The Royal Bank of Scotland Plc [2019] EWHC 1770 [95].

[73] N v The Royal Bank of Scotland Plc [2019] EWHC 1770 [80].

[74] N v The Royal Bank of Scotland Plc [2019] EWHC 1770 [105].

Harvey v Santander UK plc[75] concerned a breach of contract claim brought by a customer against a bank who had frozen their account due to a suspicion of suspected fraud or criminal activity. The High Court dismissed an application by the claimant for an interim mandatory injunction to force the bank to unfreeze the account. The claimant, Harvey, had opened the account not long after being struck-off from the Solicitor's Roll as a result of involvement in promoting investment schemes dishonestly. The account was ultimately used in such a way that the bank had made Suspicious Activity Reports to the National Crime Agency. The bank was unable to disclose this fact to Harvey because it would have been at risk of penalties under the domestic proceeds of crime and AML legislation if it tipped Harvey off to the action it was taking. As a result, the bank advised Harvey that it was unable to provide reasons for the freezing of the account. In a relatively brief decision, the interim mandatory injunction was refused on the basis that the court did consider there to be a high likelihood that the claimant would "succeed in satisfying a court at trial that the Defendant ha[d] not been exercising its contractual rights under its 2022 General Terms and Conditions to freeze the account, to close it and to decline to execute the Claimant's instructions".[76] None of the explanations provided by the Claimant provided any assurance that the funds were not proceeds of crime and that the proposed property transactions were not an attempt at laundering the funds. Of note in this case is the clear evidence that was before the court of Mr Harvey's alleged wrongdoing and suspected criminal activity.

In Uzbekov v Revolut Limited,[77] the High Court considered the closure of Mr Uzbekov's account by Revolut. The material before the court was that Revolut had blocked and closed the account because "after considering media reports, it formed the view that Mr Uzbekov might be involved in money laundering, that the funds in his account might constitute criminal property and that his continued use of the account might damage its reputation and goodwill".[78] The claim was issued 3 years after the closure of the account and Mr Uzbekov accepted that Revolut's conduct had caused him no compensable loss. Ultimately, the court found that there was no real prospect of declaratory relief and the claim was struck out as an abuse of process. The court made observations that a judgment against Revolut would not bind any third party and even "insofar as it had precedential value, it would be unlikely to determine whether another UK bank, applying its own terms and conditions.... had acted wrongfully in terminating his account with that bank on the basis of whatever information was available to it at the relevant time...".[79]

Again, the situation in the UK continues to develop and there is no clear judicial precedent in cases of de-banking.

[75] Harvey v Santander UK Plc [2023] EWHC 2947 (KB).

[76] Harvey v Santander UK Plc [2023] EWHC 2947 (KB) [35].

[77] Uzbekov v Revolut Ltd [2024] EWHC 98 (KB).

[78] Uzbekov v Revolut Ltd [2024] EWHC 98 (KB) [2].

[79] Uzbekov v Revolut Ltd [2024] EWHC 98 (KB) [48].

4.2 New Zealand

Recent decisions in New Zealand have considered whether a bank should be prevented from terminating its banking arrangements with a customer.[80] In a 2016 case, E-Trans International Finance Ltd v Kiwibank Ltd [2016] 3 NZLR 241, the New Zealand High Court held that the bank was entitled to terminate its contract with a money remitter, on notice, without reasons. Kiwibank had changed its policy in relation to money remitters due to risks they posed under the Anti-Money Laundering and Countering Financing of Terrorism Act 2009 (NZ AML/CFT Act). The bank was conducting a staged review and de-banking money remitter clients inconsistent with its risk appetite. The High Court dismissed a breach of contract claim and found that the bank had an absolute right to terminate, subject to giving notice. Observations were made that the bank had acted legally, but highlighted legislative action and policy choices were required and non-justiciable.[81] The policy response was to discourage blanket de-banking policies against money remitters, but changes were not made to the legislation in response.[82] The High Court considered the public policy considerations relating to integrity in financial markets, the importance economic role of remittances for communities relying on them and the promotion of competition in the market. Such cases highlight the key dilemmas and tensions that arise with respect to de-banking.[83]

In the 2023 case of Targa Capital Limited,[84] Westpac had identified a link between its customer and an individual sanctioned in Australia. After seeking further information, Westpac informed Targa that it would cease its relationship with them. Targa sought an interim injunction preventing Westpac from de-banking them, claiming it was a breach of contract. The High Court rejected the interim injunction and found that Targa's breach of contract claim was not seriously arguable. Under the contract, Westpac had a discretion to terminate if it believed there were 'reasonable grounds' to do so and was obliged to exercise its discretion in a reasonable and consistent way. It was argued that the Discretion Clause required 'reasonableness simpliciter' and Westpac argued that the Discretion Clause only imported the standard required by the default rule for contractual discretions. Ultimately, the Court did not need to decide this point, because even if the Discretion Clause required reasonableness simpliciter and required an assessment of both the procedure and substance of Westpac's decision, reasonableness had been made out.

A few months later, in The Christian Church Community Trust v Bank of New Zealand,[85] the NZ High Court upheld an application for an interim injunction by the Gloriavale Christian community preventing BNZ from de-banking it. Some

[80] See Peart (2023).

[81] See Fujii-Rajani (2017).

[82] See Fujii-Rajani (2017).

[83] De Koker et al. (2017).

[84] Targa Capital Limited v Westpac New Zealand Limited [2023] NZHC 230.

[85] Christian Church Community Trust v Bank of New Zealand [2023] NZHC 2523.

commentary has noted that this was "despite BNZ having ostensibly stronger contractual powers than Westpac" in Targa.[86] BNZ's standard terms and conditions provided that BNZ could close a customer's account or immediately suspend or restrict the account or any other product or service 'for any reason' and provided a non-exhaustive list of examples. There was no clause requiring the bank to exercise its powers reasonably, as there was in Targa. The Court acknowledged the earlier cases providing that banks have a right to terminate on reasonable notice, unless modified by the contract. However, the court held that, as the termination clause provided examples, this implied that either there needed to be a valid reason for termination, or that BNZ would need to act reasonably when making a decision to terminate. Further, the court was unable to accept the argument that there was an absolute termination right, rather than a contractual discretion and finally, it was seriously arguable that the default rule, or the expanded default rule, applied to any decision by BNZ to terminate.

The court further found that it was seriously arguable that BNZ had not acted reasonably in deciding to terminate its services to Gloriavale and granted the injunction. In reaching this view, the judge, in reliance on Targa, asked whether BNZ was procedurally fair and reasonable and whether its decision was substantively reasonable. The judgment does not expressly state what standard of reasonableness is used but it has been said that it appears 'reasonableness simpliciter' rather than the higher threshold required by the default rule (or even the expanded default rule).[87] The court considered that there were at least three relevant factors to whether BNZ's substantive decision was reasonable: (i) whether it was managing a 'real risk to its banking operation' (ii) whether termination of a banking relationship is reasonable when there were no other banking services available to Gloriavale; and (iii) whether banking is an essential service, importing public law obligations on BNZ.[88] BNZ sought to appeal the interlocutory decision and in declining leave to appeal, the court noted "I accept BNZ's submission that this proceeding raises issues of public interest, is important to the parties, and has precedential value on a bank's contractual powers to terminate customers' accounts…I consider this reinforces the need for a substantive decision in this case, not an appeal on an interlocutory decision".[89]

In 2024, the substantive decision of Bank of New Zealand v The Christian Church Community Trust & Ors[90] overturned the position of the NZ HC in the interim injunction application, and confirmed that BNZ had an express right to terminate and that it was not necessary to decide whether the common law 'default rule' or 'expanded default rule' in Braganza[91] applied for implied terms in New

[86] See analysis in Peart (2023).

[87] See Peart (2023).

[88] Christian Church Community Trust v Bank of New Zealand [2023] NZHC 2523 [65], [72], [75].

[89] Christian Church Community Trust v Bank of New Zealand [2023] NZHC 2523 [31].

[90] Bank of New Zealand v The Christian Church Community Trust & Ors [2024] NZCA 645

[91] Braganza v BP Shipping Ltd [2015] 1 WLR 1661.

Zealand.[92] The Court noted that "there is a substantial body of overseas authority to the effect that a discretionary contractual power conferred on one party may be subject to implied limits broadly analogous to the limits that apply to the exercise of public powers. These authorities do not speak with one voice: the law is developing and remains unsettled".[93] It was further noted "some overseas authorities suggest that a term should be implied into every contract that confers a discretionary power on one party to the effect that the power must not be exercised dishonestly, in bad faith, or capriciously or arbitrarily".[94] In the circumstances of the case, even if such an implied term existed, it had not been breached. Ultimately, it was not necessary for the court to decide if the approach in Braganza should be adopted in New Zealand and the case law remains unsettled.

5 An Area Ripe for Legislative Intervention?

Given the tension that exists for financial institutions between contractual obligations to customers and their AML/CTF obligations, this may be an area ripe for legislative intervention. As Edelman J commented in Mineralogy Pty Ltd v Sino Iron Pty Ltd (No 6),[95] "private parties cannot contract for themselves in mandatory terms to have power over areas regulated in public law by legislation". Certainly, AUSTRAC has felt the need to publicly comment on de-banking and has indicated that "AUSTRAC expects banks and all regulated businesses to adopt a case by case approach to managing ML/TF risks".[96] Ultimately, in the UK, legislative intervention was considered necessary to provide some requirements for de-banking.

In June 2023, the Australian government agreed with a recommendation in relation to de-banking.[97] Recommendation 2 was "[t]hat all banks implement five related measures to improve transparency and fairness in relation to de-banking". These measures would apply to all instances of de-banking and included: (1) that banks document reasons for de-banking a customer; (2) that banks provide a customer with reasons for being de-banked; (3) that banks ensure a de-banked customer who is an individual or small business has access to their Internal Dispute Resolution procedures; (4) that banks provide a minimum of 30 days' notice before closing existing core banking services of a customer. This account closure notice should also inform the customer that they may access the bank's Internal Dispute

---

[92] MinterEllissonRuddWatts (2024).

[93] Bank of New Zealand v The Christian Church Community Trust & Ors [2024] NZCA 645 [11].

[94] Bank of New Zealand v The Christian Church Community Trust & Ors [2024] NZCA 645 [12].

[95] Mineralogy Pty Ltd v Sino Iron Pty Ltd (No 6) (2015) 329 ALR 1; [2015] FCA 825; BC201507863

[96] AUSTRAC (2021b).

[97] Australian Government, (2023); Senate Select Committee on Australia as a Technology and Financial Centre (2021), Recommendation 2.

Resolution procedures; and (5) that banks self-certify adherence to measures 1–4.[98] In June 2023, AUSTRAC also issued guidance in relation to de-banking, commenting on excessive de-banking.[99]

While the above measures may improve experiences for those customers faced with de-banking, the proposed measure is not a legal change and the requirement for banks to 'self-certify' does not provide clarity in terms of the clear tension between obligations on financial institutions with respect to the 'tipping-off' provisions, nor do such measures compel banks to act reasonably. These suggested, non-binding measures do not overcome the difficulties with the current system. For example, a bank may be unable to provide wholesome reasons to a customer and may be bound by the tipping-off provisions. Such non-binding measures do not ensure that banks will act reasonably or in good faith—if that is the standard to be expected.

6 Implied Contractual Terms in Australia?

The case law examined in this chapter has shown that the interpretation of de-banking clauses in some instances has been influenced to date by a consideration of whether there is an implied term of good faith or Braganza reasonableness (or some other standard of reasonableness) in contractual relationships between bank and customer. The implication of such terms in Australian contract law generally remains unclear and yet to be finally determined.

The concept of good faith in Australian contract law remains unsettled,[100] and the High Court has not made any comprehensive statement on the matter.[101] In Renard Constructions,[102] the court in obiter discussed an implied duty of good faith. Since that decision, Baron writes (in the NSW context) that "Renard Constructions has become the basis upon which an obligation to act in good faith is to be implied, not only in relation to construction contracts but (possibly) all commercial contracts".[103] In ASIC v Australia and New Zealand Banking Corporation Ltd (No 3)[104] it was observed by Allsop CJ that the relationship between a bank and its customer is contractual but also said to be "founded on trust and good faith in a commercial

[98] Australian Government, (2023). Council of Financial Regulators (2022) made four recommendations in relation to de-banking (1) data collection, (2) transparency and fairness measures, (3) guidance by specified banks and (4) capability uplift.

[99] AUSTRAC (2023). Also see AUSTRAC (2025b).

[100] See, for example, Whelan v Cigarette & Gift Warehouse Pty Ltd [2017] FCA 1534; Greenbot Pty Ltd v Clean Energy Regulator [2025] FCA 369.

[101] Fielder (2021), p. 324.

[102] Renard Constructions (ME) Pty Ltd v Minister for Public Works (1992) 26 NSWLR 23.

[103] Baron (2002).

[104] ASIC v Australia and New Zealand Banking Corporation Ltd (No 3) [2020] FCA 1421 [13] per Allsop CJ.

sense",[105] and "[r]eliance by customers on the integrity and good faith of their bank is at the heart of social and commercial life in this country".[106]

In Esso Australia Resources Pty Ltd v Southern Pacific Petroleum NL,[107] the Victorian Court of Appeal rejected an obligation of good faith generally, stating that, "[t]he modern law of contract has developed on the premise of achieving certainty in commerce. If good faith is not readily capable of definition then that certainty is undermined. It might be that a duty of good faith is no more than a duty to act reasonably in performance and enforcement, a long established duty".[108]

Baron described the emergence of an obligation to act 'in good faith' (in the context of construction contracts) as an example of judicial law-making. Chief Justice Gleeson has recently remarked that:[109]

> for a number of reasons, some to do with the work of legislatures, some to do with judicial law making, and some to do with the temper and spirit of the times, we can no longer say that, in all but exceptional cases, the rights and liabilities of parties to a written contract can be discovered by reading the contract.

An example of judicial law making is the emergence of an obligation to act 'in good faith' — both in the performance of obligations under, and the exercise of rights in relation to, a contract.[110]

Interestingly, in Whelan v Cigarette & Gift Warehouse Pty Ltd,[111] Collier J commented that a duty of good faith "may be more readily implied as a matter of fact in circumstances involving a significant disparity of power between the parties".[112]

Like any implied duty of good faith, the relevance of reasonableness in Australian case law remains unclear, and whether the Braganza duty applies to Australian contract law is yet to be judicially determined.

As Fielder observes in relation to the interaction between good faith and reasonableness:

> Some courts have factored reasonableness into the duty of good faith and others have referred to both 'good faith' and 'reasonableness' as separate (but equal) standards. Despite the lack of clarity as to how 'reasonableness' interacts with the duty of good faith, the authorities generally indicate that the duty does not subject the exercise of a contractual power to a test of objective reasonableness alone. That said, reasonableness has more often than not been factored into the assessment of good faith and it is not uncommon for the courts to concurrently assess, effectively as one cause of action, whether a power was exercised 'in good faith' and 'reasonably'.[113]

---

105 ASIC v Australia and New Zealand Banking Corporation Ltd (No 3) [2020] FCA 1421 [13].

106 ASIC v Australia and New Zealand Banking Corporation Ltd (No 3) [2020] FCA 1421 [13].

107 Esso Australia Resources Pty Ltd v Southern Pacific Petroleum NL [2005] VSCA 228.

108 Esso Australia Resources Pty Ltd v Southern Pacific Petroleum NL [2005] VSCA 228 [3].

109 Gleeson (1995), p. 428.

110 Baron (2002).

111 Whelan v Cigarette & Gift Warehouse Pty Ltd [2017] FCA 1534.

112 Whelan v Cigarette & Gift Warehouse Pty Ltd [2017] FCA 1534 [226].

113 Fielder (2021).

In light of the continuing uncertainty and state of 'flux' concerning the implication of terms in commercial contracts, the de-banking cases and the interpretation of contractual terms between bank and client are likely to be without certainty. It can probably be said, however, that there is every likelihood that a judicial consideration of de-banking will consider to some degree, the extent to which a financial institution has acted in good faith and reasonably and certainly s 235 (at present) requires a bank to have acted in good faith to be absolved from liability in a proceeding. Whether such terms assume a greater prominence in de-banking cases as compared with contract law generally remains to be seen, but certainly, financial institutions in Australia have long been considered as having a 'privileged place in society which carries social responsibilities'[114] and a corporate social responsibility. It is possible that financial institutions will be taken to have a greater responsibility to act reasonably or in good faith than ordinary contracting parties. Certainly, the reference to such implied terms has been overt in some of the case law to date but the question remains—will there be an implied duty of good faith/Braganza reasonableness implied in cases of de-banking in Australia?

7 Concluding Remarks

De-banking is essentially a contract law issue that will be influenced by general approaches to commerciality, contract law, and contract law legal principles. This occurs within the overlaying AML/CTF regulatory context and financial services regulation. Ultimately, where banks are to largely self-regulate de-banking without very specific legislative guidance, there will be considerable uncertainty for all parties. Such an approach has significant commercial and legal consequences for financial institutions and potential human rights and financial implications for customers, given the importance of banking relationships. Further, customers who have been de-banked face a potential lack of any legal redress in circumstances where a bank need not prove any wrongdoing before de-banking. There is a clear tension between the interaction of AML/CTF legislation and obligations that are imposed on financial institutions for a public purpose (that is, minimising money laundering and counter-terrorism financing) and the contractual and commercial principles and relationship between customer and bank. With de-banking often occurring within the prism of attempted or purported compliance with AML/CTF legislation, perhaps it is time for more specific legislative intervention, as is occurring in the UK. Ultimately, financial institutions and customers may find themselves between a rock and a hard place. What is clear is that this is an emerging issue that will not easily resolve and will likely face further judicial consideration in the near future.

[114] Joint Committee on Corporations and Financial Services (2004), especially chapter 17 (Community service obligations: Public expectations of financial service providers).

References

Asher J (2025) Fraud markers, de-banking and financial crime: a legal analysis of counter-fraud practices in the UK and beyond. Routledge

AUSTRAC (2021a) 2020–21 annual report. https://www.transparency.gov.au/publications/attorney-general-s/australian-transaction-reports-and-analysis-centre-austrac/australian-transaction-reports-and-analysis-centre-annual-report-2020-21/our-performance/strengthen

AUSTRAC (2021b) AUSTRAC statement 2021: de-banking. https://www.austrac.gov.au/news-and-media/media-release/austrac-statement-2021-de-banking

AUSTRAC (2023) New guidance released on debanking. https://www.austrac.gov.au/new-guidance-released-debanking

AUSTRAC (2025a) List of enforcement actions taken. https://www.austrac.gov.au/lists-enforcement-actions-taken

AUSTRAC (2025b) Financial services for customers that financial institutions assess to be higher risk. https://www.austrac.gov.au/business/core-guidance/financial-services-customers-financial-institutions-assess-be-higher-risk

Australian Government (2023) Government response: potential policy responses to de-banking in Australia. https://treasury.gov.au/sites/default/files/2023-06/p2023-404377-gr.pdf

Australian Government (2024) Overview of the AML/CTF Amendment Act. https://www.homeaffairs.gov.au/criminal-justice/Pages/overview-of-the-amlctf-amendment-act.aspx

Baron A (2002) 'Good faith' and construction contracts — from small acorns large oaks grow. Aust Bar Rev 22:54–81

Council of Financial Regulators (2022) Potential policy responses to de-banking in Australia. https://www.cfr.gov.au/publications/policy-statements-and-other-reports/2022/potential-policy-responses-to-de-banking-in-australia/

Dahdal A (2024) Immigrants and innovators: financial inclusion and the 'de-banking' of the digital asset industry. Law Innov Technol 16:599–630

De Koker L, Casanovas P (2024) 'De-risking', de-banking and denials of bank services: an over-compliance dilemma? In: Goldbarsht D, de Koker L (eds) Financial crime, law and governance. Ius Gentium: comparative perspectives on law and justice, vol 116. Springer, Cham, pp 45–70. https://doi.org/10.1007/978-3-031-59547-9_3

De Koker L, Goldbarsht D (2024) Towards a global approach to combating financial crime. In: De Koker L, Goldbarsht D (eds) Financial crime, law and governance. Springer, Cham

De Koker L et al (2017) Closure of bank accounts of remittance service providers: global challenges and community perspectives in Australia. Univ Qld Law J 36:119–154

D'Hulster K, Morris N, Jaffer S, De Koker L (2023) The decline of correspondent banking in Pacific Island countries. Pacific Islands Forum report prepared by the World Bank. https://forumsec.org/sites/default/files/2024-05/CBR%20Report_FINAL.pdf

Eversheds Sutherland (2024) New UK legislation for payment service providers designed to prevent de-banking, https://www.eversheds-sutherland.com/en/global/insights/new-legislation-intending-to-reduce-instances-of-debanking

Fielder H (2021) Good faith vs absolute and unfettered discretion in commercial contracts. Aust Bar Rev 50:324

Financial Action Task Force (2015) FATF takes action to tackle de-risking. https://www.fatf-gafi.org/en/publications/Fatfrecommendations/Fatf-action-to-tackle-de-risking.html

Financial Action Task Force (2025) The FATF recommendations. https://www.fatf-gafi.org/en/publications/Fatfrecommendations/Fatf-recommendations.html

Fujii-Rajani R (2017) Money remitters left out in the cold: blanket de-risking policies, counterterrorism and government intervention in New Zealand. Auckland Univ Law Rev 23:204–235

Gleeson (1995) Individualised justice – the holy grail. Aust Law J 69:421–433

Herbert Smith Freehills (2023) High Court refuses customer's interim mandatory injunction application to unfreeze bank account. https://www.lexology.com/library/detail.aspx?g=700b00c7-5082-4cef-9586-2174875a8b2d
Johnson et al. (2024) De-banking in the Asia-Pacific Region, Academy of excellence in financial crime investigation and compliance white paper series no. 1.2024; Griffith University. https://www.griffith.edu.au/__data/assets/pdf_file/0029/2008667/De-Banking-White-Paper_FINAL_PUBLISHED.pdf
Joint Committee on Corporations and Financial Services (2004) Money matters in the bush: inquiry into the level of banking and financial services in rural, regional and remote areas of Australia. Parliament of Australia, Canberra
MinterEllisonRuddWatts (2024) BNZ v Gloriavale judgment informs "debanking" decisions. https://www.minterellison.co.nz/insights/bnz-v-gloriavale-judgment-informs-debanking-decisions
Nicholson R, Wilcock A (2022) Corporate criminal liability: a guide for boards and senior management. https://www.allens.com.au/insights-news/insights/2022/07/Corporate-criminal-liability-in-Australia
Parasol M (2022) Avoiding the wholesome de-banking of cryptocurrency exchanges in Australia. Univ New South Wales Law J 45(4):1623
Peart E (2023) De-banking: a tale of two cases. New Zealand Law J 317
Scott A (2025) De-banking/de-risking: issues for the 119th congress. https://www.congress.gov/crs-product/IF12886
Senate Select Committee on Australia as a Technology and Financial Centre (2021) Final report, Parliament of Australia, https://parlinfo.aph.gov.au/parlInfo/download/committees/reportsen/024747/toc_pdf/Finalreport.pdf;fileType=application%2Fpdf
Shaw B (2024) De-banking: the legal issues BLB 39(10):159
Whyte J (2024) Debanked: the economic and social consequences of anti-money laundering regulation' IEA Discussion Paper No. 125. https://iea.org.uk/publications/debanked-the-economic-and-social-consequences-of-anti-money-laundering-regulation/

Legislation

Anti-Money Laundering and Counter-Terrorism Financing Amendment Act 2024
Anti-Money Laundering and Counter-Terrorism Financing Rules Instrument 2007
Anti-Money Laundering and Counter-Terrorism Financing Act 2006
Anti-Money Laundering and Countering Financing of Terrorism Act 2009 (NZ AML/CFT Act)
Payment Services (Amendment) Regulations 2024
Payment Services Regulations 2017

Case Law

ASIC v Australia and New Zealand Banking Corporation Ltd (No 3) [2020] FCA 1421
Braganza v BP Shipping Ltd [2015] 1 WLR 1661
Esso Australia Resources Pty Ltd v Southern Pacific Petroleum NL [2005] VSCA 228
E-Trans International Finance Ltd v Kiwibank Ltd [2016] 3 NZLR 241
Flynn v Westpac Banking Group [2022] ACAT 21
Greenbot Pty Ltd v Clean Energy Regulator [2025] FCA 369
Harvey v Santander UK plc [2023] EWHC 2947 (KB)

Human Appeal International Australia v Beyond Bank Australia Ltd (No 2) 415 ALR 134; [2023] NSWSC 1161; Human Appeal International Australia v Beyond Bank Australia Ltd (No 3) [2023] NSWSC 1622
Marundrury v Commonwealth Bank of Australia (No 3) [2023] FCA 807 (13 July 2023)
Mineralogy Pty Ltd v Sino Iron Pty Ltd (No 6), (2015) 329 ALR 1; [2015] FCA 825; BC201507863
N v The Royal Bank of Scotland plc [2019] EWHC 1770
Renard Constructions (ME) Pty Ltd v Minister for Public Works (1992) 26 NSWLR 234
Shah & Anor v HSBC Private Bank (UK) Ltd [2012] EWHC 1283 (QB)
Targa Capital Limited v Westpac New Zealand Limited [2023] NZHC 230
The Christian Church Community Trust v Bank of New Zealand [2023] NZHC 2523 (Gloriavale)
Uzbekov v Revolut Limited [2024] EWHC 98 (KB)
Whelan v Cigarette & Gift Warehouse Pty Ltd [2017] FCA 1534

Megan Styles is a barrister with the Victorian Bar with a particular interest in anti-corruption, AML/CTF regulation and corporate offending. Megan is currently undertaking her PhD on proceeds of crime with Monash University. She was previously employed as a Principal Litigation Lawyer with the Australian Federal Police Criminal Asset Confiscation Taskforce. This research was undertaken in the author's capacity as a PhD candidate with Monash University.

Challenging Risk: The Case of Maples Corporate Services v CIMA

Derwent Coshott

Abstract The risk-based approach is at the core of the international AML/CTF regime. It requires governments to adopt regulations taking account of the money laundering and terrorist financing risks within their particular jurisdictions and, similarly, tailor enforcement of those regulations to the ML/TF risks facing individual businesses therein. Yet under the risk-based approach, businesses are responsible for determining what risks they face, and how best to mitigate them; with regulators retaining the power to oversee such decisions and, most importantly, question them. This leads to a tension in which businesses must decide what are their own levels of risk, but are subject to such being second-guessed. This issue has notably arisen in the Cayman Islands decision of *Maples Corporate Services Ltd and MaplesFS Ltd v Cayman Islands Monetary Authority*, in which the Maples entities successfully challenged the Cayman Islands Monetary Authority's assessment that they had failed to meet their obligations with respect to Customer Due Diligence. This was on that basis that Maples was permitted to exercise its own judgment in making risk assessments of customers, and their transactions, and in deciding the appropriate CDD measures to be deployed. The judgment, and what it represents, is an important case study which calls into question the differing roles held by businesses and regulators under the risk-based approach. Accordingly, this chapter examines the decision, and its reasoning, to determine what lessons it can teach. The chapter argues that the challenges raised by the case are inherent to the risk-based approach, but that it is still superior to more prescriptive methods. As such, in order for the risk-based approach to be properly implemented, the decision in *Maples* militates in favour of greater guidance from regulators, and cooperation between them and businesses, elsewise we can expect to see more of the like.

D. Coshott (✉)
University of Sydney Law School, Financial Integrity Hub (FIH), Camperdown, NSW, Australia
e-mail: derwent.coshott@sydney.edu.au

D. Goldbarsht et al. (eds.), *Combating Financial Crime*, Ius Gentium: Comparative Perspectives on Law and Justice 131,
https://doi.org/10.1007/978-3-032-06858-3_11

1 Introduction

At the heart of the international anti-money laundering and counter-terrorism financing (AML/CTF) regime is the risk-based approach. As the opening sentence of R.1—Assessing risks and applying a risk-based approach, of the Financial Action Task Force (FATF) Recommendations states:

> Countries should identify, assess, and understand the money laundering and terrorist financing risks for the country, and should take action, including designating an authority or mechanism to coordinate actions to assess risks, and apply resources, aimed at ensuring the risks are mitigated effectively.[1]

However, it did not always represent the international norm that it does today. Prior to the 2010s, the international AML/CTF regime was instead characterised by a rules-based approach in which AML/CTF measures had "to be precisely indicated and spelt out in … regulation".[2] As Costanzo states:

> The objective [of the rules-based approach] is to cover all possible circumstances and limit as much as possible the room for interpretation (which is often associated with uncertainty) and the need for covered entities and persons to exercise discretion in order to identify which behaviour should be put in place in a particular circumstance that is not fully and specifically envisaged in the law.[3]

Yet, in the AML/CTF context, in which criminals are ever vigilant for new ways to evade the law, this came with clear problems:

> Obviously, not everything can be regulated and, therefore, new rules are added over time to take account of the experience in implementation as well as of the evolving interpretation of existing provisions. For these reasons, in rule-based systems the rulebook tends to grow in size and complexity, in a continuous search for clarity and completeness. New provisions and changes to the existing provisions have to be introduced through the appropriate procedures, depending on the type of regulatory means. This can bring an element of rigidity in rule-based systems which can also translate into delayed updates to the rulebook.[4]

As such, in a rules-based system's quest for completeness, there are sacrifices: adaptability, responsiveness, and simplicity chief amongst them. Criminals can act faster than new rules are written; and the more rules that are created, the more complex the system becomes and, concomitantly, the more difficult it becomes to comply with.

These issues necessitated the adoption of the risk-based approach by the FATF in the late 2000s, which was ultimately codified in the 2012 update to the Recommendations. Its purpose was to avoid the problems of the rules-based approach by adopting a more context sensitive one. Under a risk-based approach, obligations could instead be spelled out at a high-level with their specific

---

[1] FATF (2012–2025), p. 10.

[2] Costanzo (2013), p. 350.

[3] Costanzo (2013), p. 350.

[4] Costanzo (2013), p. 350.

application "determined by the obliged parties themselves in light of concrete circumstances and the inherent risks".[5] As Costanzo characterises the differences between the two different approaches, the rules-based approach operates *ex ante*, with subjects clearly being instructed in advance of what to do; whereas the risk-based approach operates *ex post* with the appropriate measures being determined by subjects "based on the factual circumstances and the appreciation of risks".[6]

However, for all the problems that the risk-based approach was intended to solve, new ones emerged; central to which was the question, if appropriate measures were to be determined by subjects (i.e., regulated businesses), what happens if a regulator disagrees with such determinations? This was the issue that came before the Grand Court of the Cayman Islands in *Maples Corporate Services Ltd and MaplesFS Ltd v Cayman Islands Monetary Authority* ("*Maples v CIMA*").[7] The matter arose out of a series of inspections conducted by the Cayman Islands Monetary Authority (CIMA) in 2020 of Maples Corporate Services Ltd ("MCSL") and MaplesFS Ltd ("MFS") to assess their compliance with the Cayman Islands' Anti-Money Laundering Regulations ("AMLR"). These inspections resulted in findings by CIMA that MCSL and MFS were in breach of various obligations under r. 12 AMLR relating to customer due diligence (CDD).

In 2021, MCSL and MFS sought judicial review of these findings, challenging them before the Grand Court of the Cayman Islands. In a judgment handed down in 2023, Kawaley J found in favour of MCSL and MFS: that while CIMA was of the view that MCSL and MFS were not carrying out proper CDD, both entities, in the judge's view, clearly had.

The fact that MCSL and MFS had been successful was noteworthy in and of itself. As part of the Maples Group, each entity was explicitly associated with the Panama and Paradise papers.[8] Furthermore, at the time of CIMA's inspections, and the judgment, the Cayman Islands was still listed on the FATF's 'Jurisdictions under Increased Monitoring' or 'grey list'.

However, what particularly resulted in the decision being labelled as a "landmark"[9] case was that it was based on the court's interpretation of what the risk-based approach required. It was not something which could be mandated by a regulatory authority such as CIMA; rather, it required businesses determining for themselves what level of risk a particular customer or transaction posed, and acting accordingly. As such, the judgments of businesses, having conducted appropriate risk assessments, and acting in accordance with an AML/CTF and Counter-Proliferation Financing (CPF) plan formulated according to those assessments, could not be second-guessed by a regulatory authority that might take quite a different view of a business' relations with its customers.

[5] Costanzo (2013), p. 352.

[6] Costanzo (2013), p. 352–353.

[7] GC 20 of 2021.

[8] Marriage and Thompson (10 November 2017).

[9] Whittaker (19 April 2023).

The purpose of this chapter is, therefore, to examine the decision in *Maples v CIMA*; and explain why the view that the court took of both the risk-based approach, and the role of regulators in assessing compliance with AML/CTF/CPF requirements, is so important. It will elucidate the key lessons that can be learned from what has been termed a "technical judgment";[10] and, using the case as a critical lens through which to analyse the issues surrounding the risk-based approach, what it has to teach other jurisdictions about the risk-based approach in practice. It will argue that the inherent tension arising from the risk-based approach—in which businesses are instructed to make their own judgments, but which are always open to being second guessed by regulators—will, invariably, lead to further cases of the like. However, this chapter will also argue that such is an unavoidable consequence of the risk-based approach which, nevertheless, does not outweigh its benefits. Accordingly, the challenge going forward will be how to best manage these tensions; and, it is suggested, that the approach taken by Kawaley J in the decision represents the correct means of doing so.

2 The Facts

In late 2020, CIMA issued two reports against MCSL and MFS; described in the judgment as the 2020 MCSL Final Report and the 2020 MFS Final Report.[11] As noted above, in these reports CIMA found that MCSL and MFS had breached various obligations under r. 12 AMLR relating to CDD. The relevant parts of r. 12 AMLR at time were as follows:

> Obligation to identify customer
> 12. (1) A person carrying out relevant financial business shall — …
> (b) verify that a person purporting to act on behalf of a customer is properly authorised and identify and verify the identity of the person; …
> (d) understand and obtain information on, the purpose and intended nature of a business relationship; and
> (e) conduct ongoing due diligence on a business relationship including — (i) scrutinising transactions undertaken throughout the course of the business relationship to ensure that transactions being conducted are consistent with the person's knowledge of the customer, the customer's business and risk profile, including where necessary, the customer's source of funds; …[12]

Dealing with each sub-regulation in turn, CIMA alleged the following:

- Regulation 12(1)(b) AMLR: the obligation to verify persons acting on behalf of a customer extends to all representatives that a Financial Services Provider (FSP)

[10] Cayman News (19 April 2023).
[11] GC 20 of 2021, par 4.
[12] GC 20 of 2021, par 57.

has "within its ability to be aware of (e.g. through documents it maintains at the registered office)".[13]

- Regulation 12(1)(d) AMLR: the obligation to understand and obtain information on the nature and purpose of a business relationship requires the FSP to understand the client's entire business, as well as seeking independent verification as to whatever a client has told the FSP with respect to that business.[14]
- Regulation 12(1)(e) AMLR: the obligation to scrutinise transactions "clearly requires that the FSP scrutinises not simply transactions it undertakes but also those its client undertakes with third parties, to ensure that they are consistent with its understanding of the nature and purpose of the client's underlying business".[15]

In response, MCSL and MFS argued:

- Under r. 12(1)(b) AMLR, the regulation only "requires the FSP to verify persons acting on behalf of their customer in relation to the customer's transactions with the FSP";[16]
- Under r. 12(1)(d) AMLR, that the obligation of an FSP "is primarily to understand the nature of the business relationship with their own client and that in appropriate cases reliance can be placed on the client's own indication of the nature of the underlying business";[17] and,
- Under r. 12(1)(e) AMLR, "the Regulation, properly construed, only requires FSPs to scrutinise transactions it has some involvement in as part of the services it provides to its customer. It imposes no obligation to scrutinise transactions the customer undertakes with third parties".[18]

In other words, the dispute between CIMA and the Maples entities was as to the scope of CDD that needed to be carried out under the relevant sub-regulations of r. 12 AMLR. The issue to be decided was, did they require a broader monitoring of the customer (and its activities) beyond those transactions which simply, and directly, involved MCSL and MFS?

The reason for such divergent views rested in the kinds of services that the Maples entities provided: as Trust and Corporate Service Providers (TCSP), MCSL and MFS provided registered office services for companies and trusts; as well as, in more limited cases, directors, company secretaries and trustees for them.[19] This, in CIMA's view, gave the Maples entities a great deal of access to information about their clients' businesses and dealings. In turn, CIMA argued that r. 12 AMLR

[13] GC 20 of 2021, par 13.
[14] GC 20 of 2021, par 11.
[15] GC 20 of 2021, par 16.
[16] GC 20 of 2021, par 13.
[17] GC 20 of 2021, par 11.
[18] GC 20 of 2021, par 15.
[19] GC 20 of 2021, par 20.

required MCSL and MFS to collect and utilise this information as part of carrying out appropriate CDD.

Consequently, the dispute between the parties was, foremost, a matter of statutory interpretation. If the view MCSL and MFS took of r. 12 was accurate there would likely be no breach of the AMLR. The key, therefore, was what the relevant sub-regulations required. To this end, it was necessary to construe r. 12 in light of the objects and purpose of the AMLR to determine whether CIMA, or the Maples entities, were correct.

3 The Legislative Context

The Cayman Islands' AML/CTF/CPF regime is, by-and-large, shaped by its international obligations; specifically, those contained within the FATF Recommendations.

Although it is likely that readers of this chapter will already be familiar with both the FATF and the Recommendations, briefly put, the FATF is the leading international AML/CTF/CPF body. In its own words, "[i]t sets international standards that aim to prevent these activities [being money laundering, terrorist financing and proliferation financing] and the harm they cause to society".[20] Those international standards are the FATF Recommendations which, by the FATF's own reckoning, have been adopted by over 200 jurisdictions worldwide.[21] Further, the Recommendations are not simply just recommendations. They are regarded as binding on those over 200 jurisdictions,[22] with their compliance regularly assessed through Mutual Evaluations: a form of peer review in which delegations will carry out an evaluation of a jurisdiction's compliance with, and implementation of, the Recommendations.[23]

The effect of an unsatisfactory Mutual Evaluation can be further follow-up reports or, more seriously, being placed on the grey list, as the Cayman Islands was at the time of CIMA's findings against the Maples entities; or, even more seriously, being placed on the 'black list', officially known as 'High-Risk Jurisdictions subject to a Call for Action'.[24] Being placed on either of these lists has serious reputational and financial consequences, with enhanced scrutiny needing to be performed on dealings with individuals and businesses from countries on the black list;[25] and, in some cases, those on the grey list.[26]

---

[20] FATF (2025a).

[21] FATF (2025b).

[22] De Koker (2013), p. 171.

[23] FATF (2025c).

[24] FATF (2025d).

[25] De Koker and Goldbarsht (2024), p. 253–256.

[26] De Koker, Howell and Morris (2023).

This explains why, in an affidavit given by Mr Rohan Bromfield, the Head of the Fiduciary Services Division of CIMA, and CIMA's authorised deponent in the court proceedings, the following was stated:

> The entire regulatory framework for AML/CFT/PF in the Cayman Islands is derived from, and is meant to be consistent with the international framework established to combat money laundering, terrorism financing and proliferation financing. The Authority views the maintenance of the jurisdiction's position as a premier international financial centre as being inextricably linked with its level of success in meeting the international standards set for fighting financial crime, its cooperation with international regulatory authorities, and in ensuring that the Cayman Islands plays its part in limiting the opportunities for 'regulatory arbitrage' by criminals, whilst at the same time promoting a level playing field for legitimate business.[27]

With regard to that international framework (i.e., the Recommendations), of particular relevance to the proceedings were R.1—Assessing risks and applying a risk-based approach, and R.10—Customer due diligence.

As noted above, R.1, and the risk-based approach it outlines, lays at the heart of the Recommendations, and thus the international AML/CTF/CPF regime. Recommendation 1 explicitly requires countries to make informed assessments about the levels of risk they face in particular industries and businesses, and to allocate legislative, regulatory and law enforcement resources accordingly. Consequently, the effect of R.1, and the risk-based approach itself, is that a country should neither approach risks with too light or too heavy a touch based on a prescriptive (rules-based) formula; rather, a country must make informed assessments of what risks it faces, and from these decide (as guided by the Recommendations) how best to address them.

Importantly, the last sentence of R.1 explicitly requires countries themselves to mandate that businesses take the same approach: "Countries should require financial institutions and designated non-financial businesses and professions (DNFBPs) to identify, assess and take effective action to mitigate their money laundering, terrorist financing and proliferation financing risks".[28]

Recommendation 10, therefore, outlines how countries (and, by extension, their regulated businesses) should apply the risk-based approach with respect to CDD. Thus, R.10 requires that CDD measures be taken:

> When establishing business relationships;
> Carrying out wire transfers or transactions that exceed a designated threshold;
> Where there is a suspicion of ML/TF; and/or,
> There is reason to doubt the veracity or accuracy of previously provided identification information.[29]

The measures articulated under R.10 include, almost verbatim, what is also required under r. 12 AMLR:

[27] GC 20 of 2021, par 32.

[28] FATF (2012–2025), p. 10.

[29] FATF (2012–2025), p. 14.

> Identifying the customer and verifying that customer's identity using reliable, independent source documents, data or information.
>
> Identifying the beneficial owner, and taking reasonable measures to verify the identity of the beneficial owner, such that the financial institution is satisfied that it knows who the beneficial owner is. For legal persons and arrangements this should include financial institutions understanding the ownership and control structure of the customer.
>
> Understanding and, as appropriate, obtaining information on the purpose and intended nature of the business relationship.
>
> Conducting ongoing due diligence on the business relationship and scrutiny of transactions undertaken throughout the course of that relationship to ensure that the transactions being conducted are consistent with the institution's knowledge of the customer, their business and risk profile, including, where necessary, the source of funds.[30]

But the nature and extent of these measures must be informed by the risk-based approach: "Financial institutions [and DNFBPs under R.22] should be required to apply each of the CDD measures under (a) to (d) above, but should determine the extent of such measures using a risk-based approach (RBA)".[31]

Thus, as the Cayman Islands AML/CTF/CPF regime was intended to implement and, therefore, reflect what was required by the FATF Recommendations, the question before Kawaley J in *Maples v CIMA* was what did the Recommendations, and the risk-based approach it mandates, require in these circumstances? More broadly, what can his answer to this question tell us about what the risk-based approach means, in practice, for other countries who, similarly, have sought to implement the FATF Recommendations?

4 The Judgment

4.1 The Risk-Based Approach

Under the risk-based approach, risk assessments can be made on three different levels: nation/country (or jurisdiction), business sector, and individual business within a sector (what is often referred to as the institutional level). Naturally, the three are not mutually exclusive: individual businesses collectively make up business sectors, which themselves collectively constitute a significant part of a country's economy. With respect to the national/country level, as noted above, at the time of CIMA's assessment of MCSL and MFS, and the decision in *Maples v CIMA* itself, the Cayman Islands was on the FATF grey list for its failures to adequately comply with the Recommendations. Following its being placed on the grey list, the Cayman Islands carried out a National Risk Assessment in 2015 ("2015 NRA") in which individual business sectors were evaluated for their level of ML/TF/PF risk.

[30] FATF (2012–2025), p. 14–15.

[31] FATF (2012–2025), p. 15.

With respect to the TCSP sector, of which the Maples Group is a leading player, the 2015 NRA stated the following:

> Trust and Corporate Service Providers were assessed to be the most vulnerable to ML, with a score of 0.57. While this sector is supervised for AML/CFT purposes by CIMA, its vulnerability arises, due to the complexity of its international financial transactions. Trust and Corporate Service Providers are typically engaged in international investments and structured finance activities, and the high value funds and asset transfers (both locally and abroad) add to the vulnerability.[32]

This was reflected in the 2019 Mutual Evaluation of the Cayman Islands,[33] and in CIMA's own analysis of the TCSP sector, in which it was given a risk-rating of 'Medium High':

> The risks associated with the products and services offered by TCSPs are impacted by the potential for opacity. TCSPs are used in sophisticated cross-border commercial transactions such as tax, financing and private asset structures that are established for purposes of preserving and managing private wealth. … Providing registered office services or business address facilities is considered higher risk where the TCSP is not providing other services to the client (i.e. no other business relationship). This service allows the entity to maintain a physical footprint in the country but can distance itself from the assets and activities controlled by the beneficial owner.[34]

Each of the above—the 2015 NRA, the 2019 Mutual Evaluation, and CIMA's Sector-Specific Risk Assessment—were relied on by CIMA to support its view of the Maples entities' non-compliance with the AMLR: i.e., the TCSP sector posed a reasonably high risk of ML/TF/PF where a specific TCSP provided the exact kind of services that MCSL and MFS did.

The level of assessed risk regarding the TCSP sector is what led CIMA to then determine that MCSL and MFS were not doing enough with respect to CDD. This is what Kawaley J referred to as the 'visibility' argument: the idea that if a TCSP has access to information because of a service it provides, then that information must be subject to CDD requirements.[35] As CIMA put it:

> … part of MCSL's activities is the keeping of the minutes. The minutes of a company can be a potential treasure trove of evidence regarding the activities of a client. No other service provider is likely to have that information within the jurisdiction. It could provide extremely useful information to the TCSP, the Authority, or law enforcement in the event of an investigation, as to whether the client is continuing … [to] conduct its business in accordance with the nature and purpose previously disclosed.[36]

This was also noted to be consistent with the FATF's Guidance for TCSPs.[37] However, any requirement to collect information on clients, and scrutinise their transactions, is, nevertheless, subject to the risk-based approach. As Mr Bromfield

[32] CFATF (2017), p. 15. See also, GC 20 of 2021, pars 38 and 41.

[33] CFATF and GAFIC (2019), par 25.

[34] CIMA (2020), par 43. See also, GC 20 of 2021, par 39.

[35] GC 20 of 2021, par 43.

[36] GC 20 of 2021, par 43.

[37] GC 20 of 2021, par 43.

for CIMA stated, 'what is adopted will depend on the risk assessment, the nature and circumstances of the FSP, and the client in the relationship.'[38] As he went on to state:

> The measures put in place would depend on the nature of the business, and the risk rating applied. A TCSP which provides directors for example, would expect to have information as to the authorised signatories, since they would have had to be authorised by the directors. The directors in those circumstances would be required to satisfy themselves as to the identity of the person being authorised. If the directors delegate the power, then they should ensure that the person delegated is satisfied. As a producer of fiduciary services, MFS very often provides directors for entities within the structure, who would therefore be in a position to ensure that persons authorised to act on behalf of the company are properly verified. … A TCSP which acts as corporate secretary, which is a service provided by MCSL, would also be in a position to ascertain information regarding the account signatories if this is included in the minutes. If the signatory changes, the TCSP is expected to know who the new signatory is, and where the accounts are kept. For example, what if the company inexplicably sets up accounts in high risk countries? Even the payment of the annual fees may be an opportunity to ascertain whether the signatories have changed, and if so, what is the identity of the new signatory?[39]

Yet the Maples entities did not necessarily provide these kinds of services in the ubiquitous way that CIMA argued in favour of. For example, MCSL's predominant business was providing registered office services.[40] Why then should a blanket approach be applied to all of its dealings with customers? If the nature of the services provided would not necessarily bring certain kinds of information into a business's hands, why should it be required to separately collect that information?

For Kawaley J this was a significant gap in CIMA's reasoning regarding the services actually provided by the Maples entities as it pertained to the application of the risk-based approach. As he stated, it was a 'counterintuitive' argument put by CIMA that a regulatory regime, purpose-built to implement the FATF Recommendations, should adopt an approach that appeared to ignore the specific circumstances of a business.[41] As Kawaley J stated:

> … the Regulations appear on their face to impose duties which are intended to be shaped, to some extent at least, by the circumstances of the commercial context. And CIMA's Guidance Notes … appear to acknowledge both explicitly and implicitly, that what the AMLRs mean in an operative sense is very much shaped by the context in which the relevant FSP conducts its business. Indeed, giving a wooden, mechanistic interpretation to the AMLRs so that each service provider is required to adopt the same 'cookie cutter' approach would seem to be the antithesis of the risk-based assessment principles which lie at the heart of the FATF and AMLRs regimes.[42]

The explicit drawing of the line between the FATF Recommendations and the AMLR is key. As noted above, risk can be assessed at the three different levels of

[38] GC 20 of 2021, par 44.

[39] GC 20 of 2021, par 45.

[40] GC 20 of 2021, par 46.

[41] GC 20 of 2021, par 46.

[42] GC 20 of 2021, par 62.

nation, sector, and institution/business. Inherent to the idea that risk is context-specific though, is that the information sought from and/or about the customer (and any transactions it engages in) must be directed by the nature of the risk inherent to the specific situation.[43] It should not, therefore, be applied in a blanket way, and at the wrong level of analysis: i.e., when assessing an individual business for compliance, applying a sector-level risk assessment cannot be determinative.[44] As noted above, R.1 requires businesses to "identify, assess and take effective action to mitigate" their ML/TF/PF risks.[45] Accordingly, a large degree of trust is placed in their hands; otherwise, the risk-based approach, with its underlying rationale of allowing *ex post* decision-making following high-level objectives, becomes meaningless.

4.2 What the Risk-Based Approach Requires

At this stage, it may be obvious why CIMA was ultimately unsuccessful: it had applied r. 12 AMLR in a dogmatic way, and at the wrong level of analysis (i.e., at the business sector instead of the individual institution/business concerned). But understanding the wrong way a law is applied does not necessarily lead to doing something the right way: i.e., institutional compliance. The Maples entities may have been correct with respect to CIMA misconstruing what was required under r. 12 AMLR, without necessarily complying with its CDD and transaction monitoring requirements. This is where the real importance, and significance, of the decision in *Maples v CIMA* rests with respect to the broader implications of the risk-based approach.

If not necessarily inherent to the idea, or purpose, of the risk-based approach is, nevertheless, its effect of turning businesses into kinds of quasi-police investigators with respect to ML/TF/PF.[46] By this it is meant that businesses are given the discretion to determine what are, and what are not, risky customers and transactions. The counterpoint is that of adopting a rules-based, prescriptive approach: i.e., having a set of technical rules which must be rigidly complied with and that leave no room for businesses to exercise individual judgment. As noted above, this is what characterised the international AML/CTF regime before its failings were recognised and the risk-based approach was adopted.[47] It is, however, still present in some of the Recommendations: e.g., the USD/EU 15,000 reporting threshold.[48]

The failings of a prescriptive approach are obvious and well-documented: technically precise rules lead to technical compliance: the so-called regulatory arbitrage

---

[43] De Koker and Goldbarsht (2024), p. 247; Southworth and Levi (2024), p. 111–112.

[44] GC 20 of 2021, par 46. See also, Goldbarsht and de Koker (2024), p. 6.

[45] FATF (2012–2025), p. 10.

[46] Goldbarsht and de Koker (2024), p. 6.

[47] Goldbarsht and de Koker (2024), p. 2.

[48] As well as in the lower threshold for gambling transactions: FATF (2012–2023), p. 14.

noted above.[49] To avoid a transaction reporting threshold, for example, one may simply engage in transactions of amounts less than that threshold.[50] The benefits of the risk-based approach are, therefore, similarly obvious by way of juxtaposition: rules become more like standards that must be adhered to, but permit flexibility based on individual circumstances. The analogy is that if one were looking at a map, a technical rule would outline a precise route to get to your destination, whereas a standard would provide you with a number of options based on the typography of the land. It is up to you to select the best route based on your own individual circumstances. The analogy is not precise, but broadly illustrative of what the risk-based approach entails. There will be national and sector level risks—the typography—and while these will inform what route an institution/business may take to compliance, it is free to exercise a choice as to its route; so long as it choses one that is not manifestly unreasonable.

The discretion afforded by the risk-based approach also necessarily entails a degree of trust being placed in businesses; with the concomitant effect that this should not be second-guessed by regulators unless, as noted above, a manifestly unreasonable route to compliance is taken. Generally, examples of the latter are many and usually take the form of businesses not even carrying out adequate risk assessments, which follow through to their AML/CTF programs and specific measures being inadequate.[51] If a business does not properly understand the risks it faces, then it cannot be said to have properly exercised the discretion that the risk-based approach affords it when carrying out its obligations under a country's AML/CTF/CPF regime.

Much rarer then, are examples of a regulator pursuing a business which does properly carry out a risk assessment, formulates an AML/CTF/CPF program based on this assessment, and acts in accordance with that program. If the risk assessment is sound—in the sense that it properly considers the country and sector specific risks, as well as any relevant guidance issued by the FATF or the country's Financial Intelligence Unit (FIU)—and its AML/CTF/CPF program is formulated in accordance with that and the relevant regulatory regime, what room is there for a regulator to question its efficacy?

This is the question, and the tension, at the heart of the risk-based approach as it applied *Maples v CIMA* itself. On the one hand, the purpose of an AML/CTF/CPF regime is to set out a legal framework to address ML/TF/PF risks, and to empower governmental bodies to assess whether businesses are complying with this

[49] For an in-depth discussion of the concept see, Coendet (2021), p. 159. See also, De Koker and Casanovas (2024).

[50] Note, in the absence of the standards-based offence of structuring.

[51] For example, in Australia see: Chief Executive Officer of Australian Transaction Reports and Analysis Centre v TAB Ltd (No 3) [2017] FCA 1296; Chief Executive Officer of Australian Transaction Reports and Analysis Centre v Commonwealth Bank of Australia Ltd [2018] FCA 930; Chief Executive Officer of Australian Transaction Reports and Analysis Centre v Westpac Banking Corp [2020] FCA 1538; Chief Executive Officer of the Australian Transaction Reports and Analysis Centre v Crown Melbourne Limited [2023] FCA 782.

framework. On the other hand, discretion is, and has to be, given to businesses in complying with that legal regime. Thus, the question for the court, in light of the legislative intention underpinning the AMLR to implement the risk-based approach, was what was required to be done by the Maples entities under r. 12 AMLR? More broadly, given r. 12's mirroring of the R.10, what can the court's answer tell us about how the risk-based approach should work in practice?

4.2.1 Regulation 12(1)(b) AMLR

With respect to r. 12(1)(b) AMLR, Kawaley J held that '[t]he scheme of the Regulations is to create general obligations, expressed with varying degrees of specificity, leaving the scope of the obligations to be flexibly measured applying the overarching risk-based approach on a case by case basis.'[52] But what does 'flexibly measured' mean? Kawaley J delineated between a "regulatory ideal" and "how regulatory provisions are [actually] construed".[53] The 'ideal, as reflected in the FATF Recommendations, its related documents, the CIMA Guidance Notes, and implicitly in the AMLRs themselves, is that heightened scrutiny is required in relation to high-risk clients and/or transactions and less scrutiny in low-risks situations.'[54] As such, "there is very arguably no general obligation to analyse all documents held on behalf of a client to see whether authorised signatories are mentioned and, if so, to verify them".[55]

However, while this appears to be correct—in the sense that there cannot be any general requirement—it is unclear how the regulatory ideal is different from the regulatory reality. As Kawaley J expresses it, the ideal is adopting a risk-based approach; but the reality is also that. The key to understanding the difference may be in the following statement, which is contained within the same paragraph of the judgment as that above: "CIMA rightly identifies verification of authorised signatories as an important monitoring tool. This general consideration cannot alter the broad (but necessarily limited) parameters of a specific statutory provision".[56] In other words, CIMA's view of what r. 12 AMLR requires represents an ideal world in which all information is gathered by businesses and provided to FIUs. As discussed above, CIMA deposed that "[t]he minutes of a company can be a potential treasure trove of evidence regarding the activities of a client. No other service provider is likely to have that information within the jurisdiction".[57] Such would "provide extremely useful information to [regulators and] law enforcement in the event

[52] GC 20 of 2021, par 106.

[53] GC 20 of 2021, par 106.

[54] GC 20 of 2021, par 106.

[55] GC 20 of 2021, par 106.

[56] GC 20 of 2021, par 106.

[57] GC 20 of 2021, par 43.

of an investigation".[58] This is reflexively self-evident: FIUs would, in an ideal world, want access to all information about clients and their transactions. Superficially, this would be in the self-interest of the FIU, but what about the costs to a business? Compliance is not cheap, and hits smaller businesses particularly hard.[59] As such, implementation of the risk-based approach—the effective recruitment of private businesses as de facto ML/TF/PF investigators—has had to be carefully managed by governments so as to not impose an overbearing regulatory burden on affected businesses.[60] AML/CTF/CPF is important, and believed by jurisdictions to be necessary to ensure the integrity of their financial systems; but it should not be implemented at the cost of making the conduct of business prohibitively costly.[61] Accordingly, the drafting and implementation of an AML/CTF/CPF regulatory regime should balance the compliance cost to businesses against the risk actually posed by the services that they provide: i.e., the regulatory reality. This is an inherent part of the risk-based approach that all countries must face and manage.

4.2.2 Regulation 12(1)(d) AMLR

Considerations surrounding real-world compliance costs are also reflected in the view Kawaley J took of r. 12(1)(d) AMLR:

> CDD obligations are intended to be fulfilled, in my judgment, applying a risk-based approach, expending more resources where risks seem higher and less resources where risks seem lower. Adopting [a] "one size fits all approach" would … be endorsing a regulatory approach akin to building castles in the sand.[62]

For those unfamiliar with the saying, it represents the idea of creating something that is not built to last. In the case of AML/CTF/CPF regulation, it would mean creating an unsustainable regime. However, this cannot mean unsustainable in the sense that it would not function. Such a prescriptive regime could function and, indeed historical has under the rules-based approach; but it would be prohibitively costly for businesses (for the reasons stated above), and also for FIUs (whether they realise it or not). As Kawaley J goes on to state with respect to r. 12(1)(d) AMLR: "Independently verifying and documenting the nature and purpose of the business relationship for well-known commercial brands setting up vehicles to conduct entirely familiar forms of business would be an obvious waste of resources that

[58] GC 20 of 2021, par 43.

[59] See, for example, a 2021 report by AML Experts, Initialism, and Arctic Intelligence stated that "The development of an AML/CTF Program [for PFPs/DNFBPs] will be from $10,000 and maintenance [will be] from $2500—depending on the size nature and complexity of the business.": AML Experts, Initialism, and Arctic Intelligence (9 November AML Experts, Initialism, Arctic Intelligence 2021), p. 6.

[60] See, Australian Government (30 January 2025) pp. 6–7.

[61] For example, in the context of AML/CTF compliance costs and financial inclusion, see: Stanley and Buckley (2016).

[62] GC 20 of 2021, par 91.

could be more effectively deployed elsewhere".[63] This is about costs; however, it appears to be not just directed towards businesses themselves, but the wider efficacy of an AML/CTF/CPF regime. It is, for example, well-known that over-reporting can be just as much of a problem for FIUs and law enforcement as under-reporting. Too little information, and FIUs cannot properly do their jobs; but too much information, and analysis becomes an exercise akin to panhandling for gold.[64] FIUs possess limited resources to properly evaluate reports made by businesses. As such, if businesses, seemingly paranoid about what is or is not suspicious, make large volumes of so-called junk reports, then this places a heavy cost burden on FIUs.[65] Indeed, in some jurisdictions, this has led to reforms to guide businesses in being more discerning regarding the kinds of reports they make in order to lessen the burden on FIUs.[66]

This is one of the risks that needs to be managed as part of the risk-based approach; and, as such, it should not be one that is actively encouraged by FIUs as part of their own enforcement of an AML/CTF/CPF regime. This explains why, as Kawaley J went on to remark:

> To construe Regulation 12 (1) [(d)] as excluding 'in every case' an obligation to substantiate the purpose of business would clearly be inconsistent with the manifest purpose of the legislative scheme in its wider local and international policy context. Somewhat less clearly, construing the relevant sub-paragraph as requiring such substantiation 'in every case' would also be inconsistent with the purpose and wider legislative context of the relevant provision.[67]

In other words, despite CIMA's desire for more information from the Maples entities, there are good public policy reasons as to why both CIMA and the Maples entities should be constrained from, respectively, receiving and supplying that information. The risk-based approach is contextual, and grounded in real-world considerations that must always be kept in mind

4.2.3 Regulation 12(1)(e) AMLR

Finally, with respect to r. 12(1)(e) AMLR, Kawaley J held that the requirement to scrutinise transactions undertaken throughout the course of the business relation ship "... will undoubtedly apply to a far lesser extent in the case of the more passive service provider than for a more transactionally active one".[68] The point, as before, is application of the risk-based approach:

---

[63] GC 20 of 2021, par 91.

[64] Chaikin (2009).

[65] In the Australian banking context, see Frost (9 November 2020).

[66] Vedrenne (13 September 2023).

[67] GC 20 of 2021, par 92.

[68] GC 20 of 2021, par 122.

> How to monitor transactions and be alert to any unusual business trends is a very context-specific question to which there are no black or white answers. Front and centre must be, of course, the risk-based approach; so that with some clients next to nothing might be required on the part of a bare registered office provider as regards low risk clients, and more would be required as the risk rating increases.[69]

Kawaley J goes on to suggest some examples of what might be required in low-risk versus high-risk situations; but this only serves to reinforce the main point about risk and its context-dependent application.

What is most important though, is what Kawaley J goes on to conclude regarding r. 12(1)(e): "It is ultimately for FSPs who understand their business to develop bespoke CDD solutions for their peculiar business relationships and for the Authority and other designated statutory regulators to stress-test those solutions applying a suitably flexible-yet firm approach".[70] This reiterates what was stated above regarding how the risk-based approach should be applied by businesses and, most importantly, what the job of FIUs and regulators should be regarding its application. Returning to the map analogy, FIUs and regulators are there to examine whether, given the typography of the ML/TF/PF landscape (the country/jurisdiction and business sector risks, which are largely determined by the FIU), a specific business has selected an acceptable route to AML/CTF/CPF compliance. The role of FIUs and regulators is not to mandate—prescribe—that one specific route be taken; especially if that route is not one that properly considers the context-specific issues surrounding compliance costs (for both businesses and FIUs).

5 Conclusions

Kawaley J found in favour of MCSL and MFS: that CIMA's construction of the AMLR was overly prescriptive and broad; and, accordingly, that the Maples entities acted in accordance with the risk-based approach mandated by the AMLR (and, by extension, the Cayman Islands' AML/CTF/CPF regime). However, as important as the result are the reasons behind it. The Cayman Islands' AML/CTF/CPF regime is, like others throughout the world, designed to implement the FATF Recommendations. This includes the risk-based approach. As such, understanding how that is put into practice by the courts—whose role it is to adjudicate on its correct application—is essential.

Maples v CIMA would be an important case for this reason alone, but it is all the more so because it is a rare example of businesses doing what the risk-based approach mandates they should: determining for themselves, based on sound risk assessments of their clients and their businesses, the appropriate level of CDD. This stands in stark contrast to the usual examples of either over-compliance—i.e.,

[69] GC 20 of 2021, par 122.

[70] GC 20 of 2021, par 123.

institutions being overly conservative—or under-compliance, such as those which litter the case law in Australia and overseas. More broadly, the decision in *Maples v CIMA* is instructive as to how the risk-based approach should apply more broadly to the application of AML/CTF/CPF legislation that is based on the FATF Recommendations. Determinations of risk are key, and these must be based on an actual consideration of a business' circumstances. The risk-based approach, by its nature, gives business the discretion to make their own decisions in accordance with their own risk assessments (within the boundaries set by the law, and any relevant guidance provided by FIU's, regulators, the FATF and FATF-Style Regional Bodies). This is what legislation implementing the FATF Recommendations must do in order for the risk-based approach to function as intended.

However, for this to be achieved, guidance from a country's FIU, regulators, and law enforcement is essential. This is for two reasons. The first is that it provides the necessary guidance for businesses when determining what level of risk exists in their sectors. This is something which can, in terms of resources, only be provided by governmental/public bodies and is important in keeping the costs of compliance (particularly for smaller businesses) down. The second reason is that, in order for any legal regime to function, there must be certainty regarding it. This is particularly important for a standards-based regime, where there will be an absence of prescriptive rules. Setting out what are the kinds of risks that exist in a given business sector, and disclosing to businesses the criteria that they will be judged against, is essential for businesses to act properly (i.e., to avoid over or under compliance). It is also essential for regulators to do the same and not make adverse findings against businesses that will be susceptible to legal challenges.

Finally, *Maples v CIMA* also shows how, from a litigatory perspective, that the above is all the more important as more businesses come under AML/CTF/CPF obligations. As time goes on, and AML/CTF/CPF regimes mature in countries around the world, more businesses will challenge adverse findings made against them. Regulators will need to be prepared to back up their findings with reference to the AML/CTF/CPF regimes that they are enforcing; and to do so, they will need more than just the text of those laws. As *Maples v CIMA* shows, FIUs, regulators, and law enforcement will need to understand the international frameworks that their local legal regimes are seeking to implement. As statutes are interpreted according to their purposes and objects, understanding the FATF Recommendations will be key to any actions taken by these governmental bodies in terms of making findings legally stick. Likewise, knowledge of the Recommendations will become essential to those advising and representing businesses; both in seeking to comply with their country's AML/CTF/CPF regime, and in challenging regulators when it has been alleged that they have not.

A case like *Maples v CIMA*, therefore, shows one of the emerging challenges to the risk-based approach which is inherent to the policy choices made in taking that approach. It is a challenge that has faced other areas of law which have reference to the surrounding real-world circumstances.[71] But, as in those other areas of law, there are solutions; and *Maples v CIMA* shows the correct approach to tackling the issue. The circumstances must always be considered from a reasonable perspective. There will always be disagreement at the margins, but regulators, like CIMA, will need to determine whether such marginal disagreements are worth the risks of penalties and prosecutions: e.g., such as engendering an environment of over-caution and, thus, over-compliance. To ensure that the risk-based approach does the job it is intended to do, it is suggested here that regulators take a slightly conservative approach: if a business is doing what it should do (in terms of carrying out risk assessments and having properly formulated AML/CTF/CPF plans), and has a view of risk that is something on which reasonable minds could differ, then deference should be given to the business' view. This is commensurate with the idea at the heart of the risk-based approach. If businesses are going to be given the power to make their own judgments, then this should be respected and not second-guessed lightly. This is, perhaps, the most important lesson that comes out of *Maples v CIMA*; and it is one that governmental bodies ignore at their peril.

References

AML Experts, Initialism, Arctic Intelligence (2021) Inquiry into the adequacy and efficacy of Australia's AML/CTF Regime: additional Information, 9 November. https://www.aph.gov.au/DocumentStore.ashx?id=526cd46d-045a-43f9-aa9d-6b91f35eb662. Accessed 14 Feb 2025

Australian Government (2025) Australian Government response to the Senate Legal and Constitutional Affairs Legislation Committee report: Anti-Money Laundering and Counter-Terrorism Financing Amendment Bill 2024 [Provisions], 30 January. https://www.aph.gov.au/DocumentStore.ashx?id=aac35e3a-b557-4914-80fb-4c579fe8b200. Accessed 14 Feb 2025

Cayman News (2023) Maples wins legal battle over CIMA's AML rules. Cayman News Service, 19 April. https://caymannewsservice.com/2023/04/maples-wins-legal-battle-over-cimas-aml-rules/. Accessed 14 Feb 2025

CFATF (2017) Results of the 2015 Cayman Islands national risk assessment relating to money laundering, terrorism financing and proliferation financing. https://amlu.gov.ky/wp-content/uploads/2020/02/Summary-Results-of-the-MLTF-National-Risk-Assessment-NRA.pdf. Accessed 14 February 2025

CFATF and GAFIC (2019) Anti-money laundering and counter-terrorist financing measures Cayman Islands Mutual Evaluation Report. https://www.fatf-gafi.org/content/dam/fatf-gafi/fsrb-mer/CFATF-Cayman-Islands-Mutual-Evaluation.pdf. Accessed 14 Feb 2025

Chaikin D (2009) How effective are suspicious transaction reporting systems? J Money Laundering Control 12(3):238–253

Chief Executive Officer of Australian Transaction Reports and Analysis Centre v TAB Ltd (No 3) [2017] FCA 1296

Chief Executive Officer of Australian Transaction Reports and Analysis Centre v Commonwealth Bank of Australia Ltd [2018] FCA 930

Chief Executive Officer of Australian Transaction Reports and Analysis Centre v Westpac Banking Corp [2020] FCA 1538

[71] For example, the law of charity, being one the oldest, with reference to determining new charitable purposes according to social and economic changes: Coshott (2020), p. 239–244.

Chief Executive Officer of the Australian Transaction Reports and Analysis Centre v Crown Melbourne Limited [2023] FCA 782
CIMA (2020) Combined 2019 sectoral risk ratings. https://www.cima.ky/combined-2019-sectoral-risk-ratings. Accessed 14 Feb 2025
Coendet T (2021) The concept of regulatory arbitrage. In: Mathis K, Tor A (eds) Law and economics of regulation, economic analysis of law in European legal scholarship 11. Springer, Cham
Coshott D (2020) To benefit another: a theory of the express trust. Law Q Rev 136(April):221–244
Costanzo P (2013) The risk- based approach to anti- money laundering and counter- terrorist financing in international and EU standards: what it is, what it entails. In: Unger B, van der Linde D (eds) Research handbook on money laundering. Edward Elgar Publishing, Cheltenham
De Koker L (2013) The 2012 revised FATF Recommendations: assessing and mitigating mobile money integrity risks within the new standards. Washington J Law Technol 8:165–196
De Koker L, Casanovas P (2024) De-risking, de-banking and denials of bank services: an over-compliance dilemma? In: De Koker L, Goldbarsht D (eds) Financial crime, law and governance, Ius Gentium: comparative perspectives on law and justice. Springer, Cham, pp 45–70
De Koker L, Goldbarsht D (2024) FATF's risk-based approach: has the pendulum swung too far? In: Goldbarsht D, De Koker L (eds) Financial crime and the law: identifying and mitigating risks, Ius Gentium: comparative perspectives on law and justice 115. Springer, Cham, pp 247–262
De Koker L, Howell J, Morris N (2023) Economic consequences of greylisting by the Financial Action Task Force. Risks 11:81–112
FATF (2012–2025) International standards on combating money laundering and the financing of terrorism & proliferation. www.fatf-gafi.org/en/publications/Fatfrecommendations/Fatf-recommendations.html. Accessed 14 Feb 2025
FATF (2025a) Home page. Financial Action Task Force. https://www.fatf-gafi.org/en/home.html. Accessed 14 Feb 2025
FATF (2025b) Countries. Financial Action Task Force. https://www.fatf-gafi.org/en/countries.html. Accessed 14 Feb 2025
FATF (2025c) Mutual evaluations. Financial Action Task Force. https://www.fatf-gafi.org/en/topics/mutual-evaluations.html. Accessed 14 Feb 2025
FATF (2025d) "Black and grey" lists. Financial Action Task Force. https://www.fatf-gafi.org/en/countries/black-and-grey-lists.html. Accessed 14 Feb 2025
Frost J (2020) Banks bury AUSTRAC in junk reports, 9 November. Financial Review. https://www.afr.com/companies/financial-services/banks-bury-austrac-in-junk-reports-20201109-p56cu0. Accessed 14 Feb 2025
Goldbarsht D, de Koker L (2024) Financial crime and the law: identifying and mitigating risks. In: Goldbarsht D, De Koker L (eds) Financial crime and the law: identifying and mitigating risks, Ius Gentium: comparative perspectives on law and justice 115. Springer, Cham, pp 1–14
Maples Corporate Services Ltd and MaplesFS Ltd v Cayman Islands Monetary Authority GC 20 of 2021
Marriage M, Thompson B (2017) 'Offshore magic circle' law firms fear paradise papers fall-out, 10 November. Financial Times. https://www.ft.com/content/8aff482c-c4a3-11e7-b2bb-322b2cb39656. Accessed 14 Feb 2025
Southworth R, Levi M (2024) Application of the risk-based approach (RBA) for financial crime risk management by banks. In: Goldbarsht D, De Koker L (eds) Financial crime and the law: identifying and mitigating risks, Ius Gentium: comparative perspectives on law and justice 115. Springer, Cham, pp 101–122
Stanley RL, Buckley RP (2016) Protecting the west, excluding the rest: the impact of the AML/CTF regime on financial inclusion in the Pacific and potential responses. Melbourne J Int Law 17:83
Vedrenne G (2023) After Years of Turmoil, Germany Seeks to Reinvigorate, Modernize FIU, 13 September. ACAMS MONEYLAUNDERING.COM. https://www.moneylaundering.com/

news/after-years-of-turmoil-germany-seeks-to-reinvigorate-modernize. Accessed 14 Feb 2025-fiu/
Whittaker J (2023) Maples wins court battle over 'onerous' anti-money laundering rules, 19 April. Cayman Compass https://www.caymancompass.com/2023/04/19/maples-wins-court-battle-over-onerous-anti-money-laundering-rules/. Accessed 14 Feb 2025

Derwent Coshott is a Senior Lecturer at the University of Sydney Law School, and a Research Fellow at the Financial Integrity Hub (FIH). He is an expert in the fields of AML/CTF, trusts, property and contract law. His scholarship has appeared in leading international journals, and he has written extensively on the use of trusts in offshore jurisdictions. He is a sought-after speaker on AML/CTF and trust law issues, appearing regularly at conferences and industry events, and regularly engages with businesses to assist and educate them on AML/CTF, property and contract matters.

Intended and Unintended Consequences of the Combating of Financial Crime: A Research Agenda

Louis de Koker, Doron Goldbarsht, and Jamie Ferrill

Abstract While the intended outcomes of the financial crime control measures of the Financial Action Task Force (FATF) and especially how to ensure that they are attained effectively and efficiently remain an important research area, it is clear that the FATF-related measures do lead to unintended negative consequences. This chapter considers some of the important questions that arise in relation to unintended consequences, especially in view of the FATF's program to address unintended consequences. In light of its 2025 revision to its standards and the adoption of new guidance to support financial inclusion this chapter gives specific attention to questions relating to financial inclusion and exclusion to illuminate the paradox that has been discussed throughout this collection.

1 Introduction

In 1989 at a summit in Paris, the G7 and the then Commission of the European Communities convened the Financial Action Task Force (FATF) from summit participants and other countries, and stated: [1]

[1] G7 (1989), para 53. For an overview of the FATF's mandate, structure and recommendations, see Goldbarsht (2022), p. 64, and for FATF history and policy debates, see Moiseienko (2025).

L. de Koker (✉)
La Trobe University and Financial Integrity Hub (FIH), Melbourne, VIC, Australia
e-mail: l.dekoker@latrobe.edu.au

D. Goldbarsht
Macquarie University and Financial Integrity Hub (FIH), Sydney, NSW, Australia
e-mail: doron.goldbarsht@mq.edu.au

J. Ferrill
Charles Sturt University and Financial Integrity Hub (FIH), Canberra, ACT, Australia
e-mail: jferrill@csu.edu.au

D. Goldbarsht et al. (eds.), *Combating Financial Crime*, Ius Gentium: Comparative Perspectives on Law and Justice 131,
https://doi.org/10.1007/978-3-032-06858-3_12

> Its mandate is to assess the results of cooperation already undertaken in order to prevent the utilization of the banking system and financial institutions for the purpose of money laundering, and to consider additional preventive efforts in this field, including the adaptation of the legal and regulatory systems so as to enhance multilateral judicial assistance.

The initial mandate of the FATF was focused on protecting the banking system and financial institutions against money laundering. At that point it was not clearly stated what the crime combating objectives of the task force should be. What were the intended effects of the protection of the banking system and financial institutions against this abuse?

It is unlikely that the drafters of the first set of FATF Recommendations intended dirty money to be forced out of formal financial services into the cash and shadow economies. The first report of the FATF reflected an awareness of the role of cash, especially of currencies that could be spent abroad like the US dollar.[2] They were also aware of informal financial service providers like hawalas.[3] It is therefore likely that they considered risks of displacement of illicit funds into the cash and informal economy. It is, however, not clear what the strategic crime combating objectives of the drafters were. Was displacement intended and, if so, why, or was the assumption perhaps that criminals would stop committing crime if they had difficulty using formal financial services to launder their money?

The objectives of the FATF were debated when the current set of Recommendations was drafted in 2011–2012, two decades after the adoption of the initial set. These debates informed the introduction of the effectiveness criteria and immediate outcomes in the FATF's 2013 Mutual Evaluation Methodology.[4] The effectiveness criteria are aimed at the following high-level outcome:

> Financial systems and the broader economy are protected from the threats of money laundering and the financing of terrorism and proliferation, thereby strengthening financial sector integrity and contributing to safety and security.[5]

While that outcome is laudable, it is not clear how the protection from the threats of money laundering and financing of terrorism and proliferation would practically contribute to safety and security. It would seem that some impact on underlying criminal activity is assumed but it is not clear what that impact would entail and how it would be monitored and measured. The effectiveness framework of the FATF is also questionable as it is not clear how the different immediate outcomes would advance the high-level outcome.[6]

---

[2] Financial Action Task Force on Money Laundering (1990), p. 7

[3] Financial Action Task Force on Money Laundering (1990), p. 8. The term, meaning 'reference' in Urdu and 'transfer' in Arabic, and also known as *hundi*, *fei-ch'ien*, *hui*, and *phoe-kuan*, refers to systems that evolved in India and Southeast Asia and have operated in non-Western societies for centuries: see Goldbarsht (2018), p. 266.

[4] Financial Action Task Force (2013–2023) par 44.

[5] Financial Action Task Force (2013–2023) par 44.

[6] See e.g. De Koker and Turkington (2015), p. 526. For an analysis of the impact of FATF measures on crime and good governance see Morris and De Koker (2025). The analysis could not identify significant correllations.

The focus on protection against threats in the high-level outcome is also noteworthy. In its first guidance on national risk assessment following its adoption of the 2012 revised Recommendations, the FATF defined a "threat" for purposes of the risk-based approach as "a person or group of people, object or activity with the potential to cause harm to, for example, the state, society, the economy, etc."[7] Can financial systems and the broader economy be protected effectively against such threats? Risks to these systems and to the economy can be limited but cannot be eliminated. How does the FATF's call for a proportional risk-based approach square with its high-level objective to protect the financial system and the broader economy against the threats of money laundering and the financing of terrorism and proliferation? Can the full and effective implementation of the FATF standards actually result in such protection, as criminal activity involving cash and unhosted crypto wallets falls outside most of the FATF standards?[8]

The intended outcomes of the FATF require closer research scrutiny. While these outcomes and how to ensure that they are pursued effectively and efficiently, where feasible, remain important research topics, it is clear that the FATF-related measures do lead to unintended negative consequences. These consequences and the impact of the FATF's measures to limit unintended consequences will be an important research area in the coming years. For discussion purposes, this concluding chapter highlights the concept of financial inclusion and exclusion to illuminate the paradox that has been discussed throughout this collection.

2 Unintended Consequences

The first unintended consequences that were identified related to financial exclusion[9] and undue negative impact on Non-Profit Organizations (NPOs).[10]

Unduly conservative customer identification and verification measures excluded many persons in developing countries from regulated financial services.

Financial exclusion was however not confined to individuals. Overly conservative regulatory and enforcement mechanisms excluded informal community-based money and value transfer services too.[11] The FATF's description of NPOs as "particularly vulnerable" to terrorist financing and requiring countries to ensure that they are protected against terrorist financing abuse,[12] hastily adopted after the 9/11 attacks on the US, also informed over-regulation, oppression, and financial

[7] Financial Action Task Force (2013), par 10.

[8] De Koker and Goldbarsht (2022), p. 310.

[9] See e.g. De Koker (2004), Bester et al. (2008), Moiseienko (2025).

[10] Charity and Security Network (2013).

[11] Bester et al. (2008); De Koker, Singh and Capal C (2017).

[12] Financial Action Task Force (2002), SR VIII.

exclusion of NPOs.[13] As Jeanne Nel points out in her chapter, that description was not evidence-based and terrorist financing concerns regarding the NPO sector as a whole remain assumption-driven, elevating a handful of examples to a general trend and threat.[14] Increasingly, concerns were being raised that FATF standards, especially the terrorist financing measures, were being abused by some autocratic regimes to oppress political opposition. After the adoption of the FATF's mandatory risk-based approach in 2012, regulated institutions began to engage in large-scale de-risking, defined by the FATF as "the phenomenon of financial institutions terminating or restricting business relationships with clients or categories of clients to avoid, rather than manage, risk in line with the FATF's risk-based approach".[15] This impacted on a range of businesses, including FinTechs, and hastened a decline in correspondent banking relationships that endangered the linkages of small island states to the international financial system.[16]

The FATF took some steps to address these concerns, for example: by adopting financial inclusion guidance in 2011;[17] by issuing statements advising against de-risking;[18] and by retracting the general description of NPOs as "particularly vulnerable" to terrorist financing abuse, and by supporting a more proportional approach to NPOs through guidance and a revision of the FATF standards.[19] While laudable, the impact of these measures remained limited. As a result, the FATF launched a deeper investigation into unintended consequences. Unfortunately only a high-level synopsis of their analysis was published but it identified issues and informed further work focused on (1) de-risking; (2) financial exclusion; (3) undue targeting of NPOs; and (4) curtailment of human rights (with a focus on due process and procedural rights).[20] The FATF's subsequent actions to address these unintended consequences, especially their implementation and success, provide rich ground for further impactful research.

While the FATF's improved messaging on NPOs, its 2023 amendments to Recommendation 8 on NPOs[21] and its 2023 Best Practices Paper on Combating the Abuse of Non-Profit Organisations[22] are welcomed, researchers will need to help monitor whether they are leading to improved results for the NPO sector. Are countries and regulated institutions responding appropriately and, if not, why not?

---

[13] Hayes (2012), Charity and Security Network (2013); Nel (2025).

[14] See Nel (2025).

[15] Financial Action Task Force (2014).

[16] D'Hulster et al. (2023).

[17] Financial Action Task Force (2011).

[18] E.g. Financial Action Task Force (2014).

[19] See e.g. Financial Action Task Force (2015), para 7; Financial Action Task Force (2016). See Nel (2025).

[20] Financial Action Task Force (2021).

[21] Global NPO Coalition on FATF (2023).

[22] Financial Action Task Force (2023).

In June 2025, the FATF adopted new procedures to ensure that anti-money laundering and counter-terrorist financing (AML/CTF) measures do not impede the positive work of civil society. Concerns about negative country practices may be raised during mutual evaluation and other assessment processes to enable assessors to consider and address any NPO-related unintended consequences of misapplication of FATF standards in the assessment.[23] This is a positive step as concerns were often only raised after the reports were published and that did not enable the FATF to address the concerns appropriately. How will the new processes work in practice, and will they have the desired effect, especially on autocratic regimes that may have been abusing FATF standards to suppress civil society?

A particularly important set of research questions for the future relate to financial exclusion risk, including the impact of the FATF's 2025 amendments relating to payments and value transfers.

3 Financial Inclusion to Mitigate Financial Exclusion Integrity Risks

The FATF's recognition of the importance of financial inclusion informed regulatory frameworks globally that enabled the development of digital financial and related services, reducing the number of financially excluded individuals from 2.5 billion in 2011 to 1.3 billion in 2025, with 79% of the global adult population now owning a bank or mobile money account.[24] Reducing financial exclusion levels further is important for the FATF, as its ministers recognised in 2012 that financial exclusion can represent a real risk to achieving effective implementation of the FATF standards.[25] The priorities of the Mexican presidency of the FATF under Elisa de Anda Madrazo (2024–2026) therefore included the promotion of the proportional, risk-based implementation of the Standards, particularly those that can contribute to advance financial inclusion.[26]

3.1 *Revisions to the Standards in 2025*

This work under the Mexican presidency resulted in a February 2025 amendment to the FATF's Recommendation 1 aimed at promoting the full implementation of the risk-based approach by encouraging AML/CTF measures that are proportionate to

[23] Financial Action Task Force (2025b).

[24] Klapper et al. (2025), p. xxi; World Bank Group (2025).

[25] Financial Action Task Force (2012).

[26] Financial Action Task Force (2024a).

both higher- and lower-risk situations.[27] While the FATF standards, since 2012, have required countries and regulated institutions to employ enhanced due diligence measures where higher risks are identified, it allowed countries to choose whether they would allow simplified measures where the risks were assessed as lower. Many countries opted not to permit simplified due diligence in these cases,[28] leading regulated institutions to implement overdesigned, disproportionate risk and compliance measures.

Recommendation 1 and its interpretive note were therefore amended to require countries to identify lower risks[29] and to allow and encourage simplified measures in those cases.[30] Furthermore, the FATF replaced "commensurate" in Recommendation 1 and its interpretive note with "proportionate", emphasising the need for proportionate risk measures or actions that appropriately corresponds to the level of identified risk and effectively mitigates the risks. In its financial inclusion guidance, it further introduced as best practice a "least burdensome" test where different control measures are available:[31]

> As a best practice, where there are two or more measures that would both effectively mitigate ML/TF risks, the least burdensome option, having regard to financial inclusion, would typically be the most appropriate option.

Measures therefore not only need to be proportionate to effectively mitigate the risk, but the impact of selected measures should also be considered to ensure that the appropriate options are selected.

The FATF also adjusted its language relating to low-risk exemptions. Since 2003[32] the FATF standards allowed countries to exempt particular types of regulated institutions from some AML/CTF/CPF due diligence requirements provided there was "a proven low risk" of ML/TF. "Proven" was viewed as a higher bar that required more than an appropriate risk assessment. Many countries, therefore, refrained from applying the exemption.[33] During the 2025 revisions of the interpretative note to Recommendation 1, the FATF replaced "proven low risk" with "assessed low risk",[34] clarifying that a low risk assessment, for example in a national risk assessment, would suffice to allow for low-risk institutions to be exempted in whole or in part from the full AML/CTF/CPF compliance burden.

Since 2003 the FATF has pointed to non-face-to-face business relationships as potentially higher risk.[35] In its 2020 digital identity guidance, however FATF noted

---

[27] See in general Kerse et al. (2025), Financial Action Task Force (2025a).

[28] Celik (2021).

[29] Financial Action Task Force (2012–2025), INR 1.2.

[30] Financial Action Task Force (2012–2025), Rec 1.

[31] Financial Action Task Force (2025a), p. 34.

[32] Financial Action Task Force (2003), p. 14.

[33] Celik (2021).

[34] Financial Action Task Force (2012–2025), INR 1.2, INR 1.4 and INR1.8.

[35] E.g. Financial Action Task Force (2003), Rec 8 that required measures to ensure that financial institutions have policies and procedures in place to address any specific risks associated with non-

that non-face-to-face customer identification and transactions that utilise reliable, independent digital ID systems with appropriate risk mitigation measures, may present a standard and even a lower level of risk.[36] In 2025 this approach was incorporated into the Standards and non-face-to-face transactions will now only be viewed as a potentially higher risk if "appropriate risk mitigation measures" are not in place.[37] This will allow for appropriate use of FinTechs to advance financial inclusion and limit the integrity risks of financial exclusion in many developing economies, especially in relation to populations in remote or underserved areas where in-person interactions may be impractical or too costly.

These 2025 amendments need to be read within the context of broader work of the FATF. In 2024, for example, after many years of requests for a FATF definition of risk, it issued new national money laundering risk guidance with the following statement: "Risk occurs when a threat successfully takes advantage of a vulnerability to produce a consequence".[38] This formulation of the materialisation of risk puts the focus more strongly on consequences of a threat event than FATF's earlier standard description that risk "can be seen as a function of three factors: threat, vulnerability and consequence".[39] A focus on the likelihood of a risk event and its likely consequences in combination with risk tolerance may increase the ability to identify lower risks in future ML/TF/PF risk assessments.[40]

These amendments raise important research questions. How will countries and institutions respond to the new risk concepts to identify lower risks? Will we see adoption of simplified measures in such cases and what will they entail? Will these measures prove effective or will they allow criminal abuse? Will these amendments help to bring compliance costs under control and increase the effectiveness and efficiency of AML/CTF measures? Will we see a decline in overcompliance by countries and institutions?

These questions range beyond financial inclusion but they were linked to the unintended consequences workstream in relation to financial inclusion. This work also resulted in revised financial inclusion guidance in 2025 that will provide a rich seam of work for researchers.

face-to-face business relationships or transactions.

[36] Financial Action Task Force (2020), para 3

[37] Financial Action Task Force (2012–2025), INR 10.15.

[38] Financial Action Task Force (2024b), p. 9; Financial Action Task Force (2025d), p. 9.

[39] Financial Action Task Force (2013), para 10

[40] See e.g. Financial Action Task Force (2025), para 74: "Clarity about the country's AML/CFT priorities and risk tolerance is important to inform appropriate and granular risk assessments. With limited resources a focus on more likely and more significant ML/TF risks with more severe consequences may mean that less likely or less significant ML/TF instances or those with more minor consequences may be tolerated in order to focus the AML/CFT system on the priorities set by the country."

3.2 Revised Financial Inclusion Guidance

The 2025 updated financial inclusion guidance of the FATF positions financial inclusion in the context of financial exclusion risk to achieving effective implementation of the FATF standards:

> Financial exclusion not only harms individuals and businesses, but can also represent a real risk to achieving effective implementation of FATF Standards by driving financial activity into unregulated channels. The risks of financial exclusion on these grounds are mitigated through financial inclusion measures that increase reliance on regulated, registered or licensed financial services, ultimately strengthening the integrity of the financial system.[41]

Importantly, the FATF's positioning of financial inclusion as a risk mitigation measure should be viewed through the lens of a new definition of financial inclusion that was adopted in the guidance. The new definition broadens the focus to active use of regulated services:[42]

> In general terms, financial inclusion refers to both access to and active use of an adequate suite of regulated, appropriate, safe, convenient and affordable financial services by individuals (including households) and entities that would benefit from such services.

The FATF's previous definition was focused on access to financial services only, for example the holding a bank account. Research showed, however, that newly included persons often continued to engage in informal and cash transactions.[43] In many cases new bank accounts remained dormant or under-utilised. Given that these users continue to transact in cash and engage informal financial services the financial exclusion risk to the FATF's objectives were not mitigated. The new "active use" element of the definition responds to these concerns and aligns financial inclusion and financial integrity policy objectives more appropriately.[44]

Through its guidance the FATF has therefore positioned "financial exclusion as an important money laundering (ML)/terrorist financing (TF) risk" and access to and active usage of regulated financial services as an important risk mitigation measure. How this will unfold in countries around the world and in relation to forcibly displaced and other vulnerable persons as well as small businesses and NPOs will be important to monitor. Will countries and institutions adopt appropriate measures? If not, why not? What are appropriate measures that will align financial inclusion and financial integrity policy objectives? How will the new risk assessments inform policies to support digital financial services while also ensuring that these remain safe from criminal abuse?

The relationship between these measures and payment and value transfers will be especially important to study in view of the FATF's adoption of revisions to its payment transparency standards in 2025.

---

[41] Financial Action Task Force (2025a), para 25.

[42] Financial Action Task Force (2025a), para 22.

[43] De Koker and Jentzsch (2013).

[44] Financial Action Task Force (2025a), para 22; De Koker (2018), pp. 250.

4 Financial Inclusion and New Payment Transparency Standards

In June 2025, at the same plenary meeting where the FATF adopted its revised financial inclusion guidance, the FATF also adopted a revised Recommendation 16 on payment transparency with measures that may create financial exclusion risk. This FATF standard, also known as the "travel rule", was initially adopted after the 9/11 attacks on the USA to ensure that minimum payment originator and beneficiary information accompanies the payment message, and is available to those facilitating the payment and to law enforcement.

Payment technologies and business models developed significantly since 2001 when the standard was first adopted. In addition, the G20 launched an ambitious project to enhance cross-border payments.[45] These developments necessitated a revision of Recommendation 16. In addition, the FATF also wanted to enhance transparency by requiring more information about the originator and the beneficiary of the payments to be available to the key AML/CTF stakeholders in the payment and value transfer system.

The revised Recommendation 16 requires financial institutions to include enhanced and verified originator information and enhanced beneficiary information in cross-border and domestic payments and value transfers and related messages by the end of 2030. The standard information required is: the name of originator and beneficiary; the account number of originator and beneficiary where used, or unique transaction reference number; and the address or, in the absence of standardised postal address information for the originator, the country and town name (or the nearest alternative) for the originator and the country and town name (or the nearest alternative) for the beneficiary. If the originator is an individual, the date of birth of the originator, or, if full information is not available, the year of birth is also required. If the originator or beneficiary is a legal person, the following information is required, where it exists: the connected business identifier code (BIC), or the Legal Entity Identifier (LEI), or the unique official identifier of that entity.

This information should be structured, to the extent possible, in accordance with international standards such as ISO 20022.

The originator and beneficiary information requirements that were originally proposed were adjusted after concerns were raised that the many people do not have standardised postal address information or full birth information, and that the collection and exchange of full birth information may give rise to privacy and data risks. The requirements remain complex and the FATF undertook to issue non-binding guidance to prevent exclusionary measures, especially where people lack documents or data to verify the relevant information.[46] The impact of these requirements will however need to be monitored closely to ensure that financial exclusion risks are limited.

[45] Financial Stability Board (2024).

[46] Financial Action Task Force (2025c), para 15.

The FATF allows countries to require simplified information for certain transactions such as cross-border payments and value transfers below a *de minimis* threshold that may not exceed USD/EUR 1000. In principle, the *de minimis* threshold can play an important role in ensuring that simplified data requirements for lower-value payments support financial inclusion. Country adoption of a such a threshold is, however, optional. The FATF furthermore requires countries to minimise thresholds where they are adopted. Different countries may therefore have different thresholds below USD/EUR 1000. This has informed a complex, fragmented global regulatory landscape that large banks find difficult to navigate. As a result, these banks do not implement the *de minimis* threshold but prefer to require full (non-simplified) data. This problem was acknowledged by the FATF, but it was decided to rather address it in non-binding guidance.[47] Whether that will result in improved use of the *de minimis* exemption will need to be studied.

The revised Recommendation 16 imposes simpler information requirements on card-based payments for service and goods but applies the standard requirements on electronic payments—or instant or "fast" payments—for such goods and services.

In many developing countries, instant payments are widely used for payments for goods and services. In India, for example, they account for 60% of the transactions in India's UPI system. As this technology continues to evolve, instant payments are likely to become even more widespread and integral to everyday financial transactions in many regions. They hold significant potential to innovate the payments landscape, particularly benefiting customers in developing and emerging countries.

The new Recommendation 16's more onerous obligations for fast payments for goods and services puts this innovation at risk. Other concerns arise too. In practice, there is a growing convergence between card-based payments and instant payments. Treating card-based payments and fast payments for goods and service differently creates a risk of market distortion and gives rise to competition concerns.

In a 2025 explanatory note,[48] the FATF recognised the fast pace of evolution in the payment sector, and the feedback received on the increasingly important role of instant payments. They committed themselves to conducting further work on the risks and controls applicable to different payment mechanisms for goods or services. Future work on this topic, according to the FATF, will reflect "the evolving risk landscape, the effectiveness of AML/CTF and fraud controls in different channels, and the goal of promoting responsible innovation, a level playing field, and safe and inclusive payments".[49]

[47] Financial Action Task Force (2025c), para 34.

[48] Financial Action Task Force (2025c).

[49] Financial Action Task Force (2025c), para 32.

5 Transparency and Accountability: Up to a Point

The phrase *"coalition of the willing"* has increasingly come to describe an informal grouping of states that coordinate to pursue shared objectives outside formal treaty frameworks.[50] While the phrase gained prominence during the post-9/11 invasion of Iraq, it has broader application in global governance. It is submitted that the FATF is a striking example of such a grouping. It is a coalition of like-minded states seeking to combat money laundering, terrorist financing, and proliferation threats. Unlike traditional legal regimes grounded in sovereign equality and the consistent treatment of like cases, the FATF does not operate on such assumptions. Its authority stems not from universally accepted legal norms but from the perceived justness and urgency of the objectives it pursues. The FATF's 2019 mandate declares that:[51]

> "1. We – the Ministers of the FATF – reaffirm the role of the FATF as the global standard-setter for combatting money laundering, terrorist financing and the financing of proliferation of weapons of mass destruction (WMD).
> 2. We commit to step up our fight against these significant threats to global security and the integrity of the international financial system. Criminals exploit the financial system to move illegally obtained proceeds, and this can undermine and destabilise economies. Terrorists exploit vulnerabilities in the financial system to raise and move funds that then are used to support and facilitate attacks against our citizens. State and non-state actors and take advantage of lax laws or weak oversight in some countries to channel funding to the development of WMD.
> 3. The FATF is at the centre of the effort to take decisive, co-ordinated and effective action against these threats. **The objective of the FATF is to protect the integrity of the financial system, and enhance its transparency, which contribute towards global security."** (Emphasis added).

These claims inform the normative influence and economic enforcement of compliance with its non binding standards.

However, this regime of "soft law" raises serious challenges. As discussed in the first chapter of this book, it remains unclear how the FATF's effectiveness and that of its standards is to be measured,[52] and whether our measures of "effectiveness" are themselves effective to attain the FATF's stated objectives.[53] The FATF's global influence generally stems from the threat of economic or reputational consequences of non-compliance rather the appreciation of the crime combating impact of its standards. As Australia's Attorney-General recently acknowledged:[54]

> Australia is now one of only five jurisdictions out of more than 200 that do not regulate tranche-two entities - lawyers, accountants, trust and company service providers, real estate agents and dealers in precious metals and stones.

[50] Benvenisti (2006), p. 1.

[51] Financial Action Task Force (2019b), para 1–3.

[52] Goldbarsht et al. (2025).

[53] Goldbarsht et al. (2025).

[54] Dreyfus (2024).

> This is placing Australia at risk of being 'grey-listed' by the Financial Action Task Force (FATF), which could result in significant harm to our economy.

While the Australian government action to broaden the scope of its AML/CTF obligation was in part informed by greylisting concerns, it is not clear whether this concern was well-founded. No country has yet attained full compliance with the FATF standards and Australia's general level of compliance with the standards may have been sufficient to ensure that it did not meet the triggers for greylisting.[55]

The FATF regime's legitimacy is conditional and arguably limited. Despite its success in promoting compliance, its procedures often lack transparency, broad participation, reasoned decision-making, and avenues for appeal or independent review. These shortcomings would be unacceptable in most domestic legal systems, where comparable decisions are typically subject to robust judicial oversight. Moreover, these structural flaws give rise to significant unintended consequences. The emphasis on rapid compliance and external validation may lead to superficial legal reforms that prioritise appearance over substance, and to the neglect of context-specific challenges. States may implement technical rules without genuine commitment, simply to avoid greylisting, thereby weakening both local legal coherence and broader financial governance goals.

The FATF has adopted internal decision-making processes that contribute to its perceived legitimacy, most notably its reliance on consensus among member states.[56] This consensus-based model is intended to reflect the sovereign equality of its members and to promote cooperation through mutual agreement rather than coercion.[57] In theory, this approach ensures that no member, regardless of its geopolitical influence, can unilaterally impose its will on others. However, in pratice, effective substantive rather than full consensus often suffices, as determined by the FATF president chairing the FATF plenary meeting. Furthermore, consensus does not equate to equal negotiating power. Smaller or less powerful states may collaborate to block initiatives, but they do so at the risk of alienating more influential members. Should a powerful state find its priorities consistently frustrated, it may threaten to withdraw or disengage from the process altogether. Such an outcome would pose an existential risk to the FATF. The regime's influence depends not merely on formal agreement but on the sustained participation of major economies. Without their involvement, the FATF could lose relevance, highlighting the fragile balance between collective decision-making and power politics that underpins the regime.[58]

To sustain long-term compliance and avoid these unintended consequences, the AML/CTF regime must do more than provide compelling evidence that compliance with its standards is achieving crime combating outcomes; it must also be procedurally and substantively legitimate. If the regime's powers remain unchecked, if

[55] De Koker (2024), p. 2.

[56] Financial Action Task Force (1992), p. 18.

[57] Steinberg (2002), p. 339.

[58] Goldbarsht and Harris (2022), p. 542.

transparency and accountability extend only "up to a point", states may begin to reconsider the costs and benefits of cooperation, threatening the very foundations of the system.

Further research is therefore needed to explore mechanisms for enhancing the legitimacy of the AML/CTF regime. This includes assessing procedural safeguards, improving transparency in decision-making, and establishing accountability frameworks that are consistent with the principles of international rule of law and domestic administrative law. Without such reforms, the regime's long-term effectiveness may ultimately prove unsustainable.

6 Geopolitics and the Limits of FATF's Authority

While the FATF is formally presented as a neutral, technical body responsible for setting global standards on AML/CTF/CPF, its operations reveal a complex interplay of geopolitics. As noted above, FATF's consensus-based decision-making framework, although intended to promote cooperation and inclusivity, allows political considerations to influence outcomes, including the processes of grey- and blacklisting jurisdictions.[59] For instance, the Democratic People's Republic of Korea (DPRK) has been on the FATF blacklist since 2011. Yet major FATF members such as China and Russia have continued to maintain robust strategic and economic ties with the regime, including illicit oil transfers, infrastructure projects, and energy deals.[60]

The suspension of Russia's FATF membership in 2023 following its full-scale invasion of Ukraine further illustrates the body's limitations. Although Russia was excluded from participation, the FATF failed to achieve consensus for Russia's grey- or blacklisting, despite extensive trade with already blacklisted jurisdictions and credible allegations of state sponsorship of terrorism[61, 62] China received a relatively favourable technical compliance rating in its Mutual Evaluation Report, despite longstanding concerns over opacity in its financial system and the role of state-owned enterprises in enabling illicit financial flows and its reported linkages with sanctions and blacklisting breaches by the DPRK and Iran.[63] Close attention will also be given the next FATF evaluation of the USA as the second Trump administration weakened compliance with the FATF standards, for example, in relation to beneficial ownership transparency of US companies.

[59] De Koker, Howell and Morris (2023).

[60] Nguyen (2023).

[61] Sulayman (2025). The European Commission is considering adding Russia to its AML/CTF higher-risk third country grey list. Reuters (2025).

[62] Reuters (2025).

[63] FATF (2019a).

The FATF's legitimacy as an impartial enforcer of global financial integrity norms is increasingly questioned,[64] and these questions may become more urgent as geopolitical alignments change.

Further research is needed to evaluate the extent to which political alliances and strategic rivalries undermine the FATF's credibility and efficacy. Two key research questions warrant exploration: To what degree do geopolitical interests shape FATF listing decisions and their enforcement? And how can the FATF strengthen its normative authority in a multipolar world where major powers are increasingly willing to circumvent global standards?

7 Conclusion

The FATF's 2025 commitment to addressing the "evolving risk landscape" and promoting "responsible innovation" in payment systems embodies the central challenge examined throughout this volume: the perpetual tension between adaptation and unintended consequences in financial crime control. While such commitments signal regulatory awareness of technological change, they also highlight the reactive nature of a system that consistently finds itself responding to innovations rather than anticipating their implications. That is, the greater the ambition to create comprehensive, coordinated systems of prevention and detection, the more pronounced become the unintended consequences that undermine the very objectives these systems seek to achieve.

From privacy-preserving data analytics in Australian AML systems to the constitutional tensions within Canada's AML regime, from the de-banking of "risky" customers to the displacement effects of coordinated terrorist financing measures, the chapters in this collection reveal how technical solutions often create new vulnerabilities while failing to address fundamental tensions between security imperatives and democratic rights. The FATF itself exemplifies this contradiction: positioned as a technical standard-setting body, it operates within an inherently political environment where consultation processes, while ostensibly inclusive, are dominated by industry voices and captured regulatory interests, while geopolitical considerations shape both agenda and implementation.

The chapters demonstrate that financial crime control cannot be understood merely as a technical challenge requiring technical solutions. Instead, it must be recognised as a complex governance challenge that sits at the intersection of security, rights, development, and democracy. The unintended consequences examined throughout these chapters are not just unfortunate side effects of well-intentioned policies; they are predictable outcomes of systems that tend to prioritise coordination and control over accountability and proportionality.

[64] For FATF legitimacy and bias concerns, see Littrell (2024).

Moving forward, the financial crime control community must confront these paradoxes directly. This requires acknowledging the limitations of current approaches while developing new frameworks that can balance security imperatives with democratic values. It requires recognising that global coordination cannot come at the expense of local accountability and inclusion, and that technical solutions cannot substitute for political solutions to fundamentally political problems.

References

Benvenisti E (2006) Coalitions of the willing and the evolution of informal international law. Tel Aviv University Legal Working Paper Series 31

Bester H, Chamberlain D, De Koker L, Hougaard C, Short R, Smith A, Walker R (2008) Implementing FATF standards in developing countries and financial inclusion: findings and guidelines. The FIRST Initiative, World Bank. https://www.findevgateway.org/sites/default/files/publications/files/mfg-en-paper-implementing-fatf-standards-in-developing-countries-and-financial-inclusion-findings-and-guidelines-feb-2008.pdf

Celik K (2021) Impact of the FATF recommendations and their implementation on financial inclusion: insights from mutual evaluations and national risk assessments. EFI Insight-Finance. World Bank, Washington, DC. https://documents1.worldbank.org/curated/en/597781637558061429/pdf/Impact-of-the-FATF-Recommendations-and-their-Implementation-on-Financial-Inclusion-Insights-from-Mutual-Evaluations-and-National-Risk-Assessments.pdf

Charity and Security Network (2013) The Financial Action Task Force and human rights. https://charityandsecurity.org/issue-briefs/fatf_human_rights

D'Hulster K, Morris N, Jaffer S, De Koker L (2023) The decline of correspondent banking in Pacific Island countries: state of knowledge and what can be done to fix the problems countries, Pacific Island Forum/World Bank, Suva. https://forumsec.org/sites/default/files/2024-05/CBR%20Report_FINAL.pdf. Accessed 25 July 2025

De Koker L (2004) Client identification and money laundering control: perspectives on the Financial Intelligence Centre Act 38 of 2001. J South Afr Law/Tydskrif vir die Suid-Afrikaanse Reg 4:715–746

De Koker L, Singh S, Capal C (2017) Closure of bank accounts of remittance service providers: global challenges and community perspectives in Australia. Univ Queensl Law J 36(1):119–154

De Koker L (2018) Editorial: ML/FT risk and financial inclusion of the poor: increase the focus on actual usage of formal financial services. J Money Laundering Control 21(3):250–252

De Koker L (2024) Submission 15 to the Senate Legal and Constitutional Affairs Committee: Tranche 2. https://www.aph.gov.au/DocumentStore.ashx?id=d61f7a90-1214-41b0-bf41-5d8894d3068b&subId=768058. Accessed 25 July 2025

De Koker L, Goldbarsht D (2022) Financial technologies and financial crime: key developments and areas for future research. In: Goldbarsht D, De Koker L (eds) Financial technology and the law. Law, governance and technology series, vol 47. Springer, Cham, pp 303–320. https://doi.org/10.1007/978-3-030-88036-1_13

De Koker L, Jentzsch N (2013) Financial inclusion and financial integrity: aligned incentives? World Dev 44:267–280

De Koker L, Turkington M (2015) Anti-money laundering and the effectiveness question. In: Rider BAK (ed) Research handbook on international financial crime. Edward Elgar, Cheltenham, pp 520–531

De Koker L, Howell J, Morris N (2023) Economic consequences of greylisting by the Financial Action Task Force. Risks 11:81. https://doi.org/10.3390/risks11050081

Dreyfus M (2024) https://www.markdreyfus.com/media/media-releases/boosting-australia-s-anti-money-laundering-and-counter-terrorism-financing-regime-mark-dreyfus-kc-mp/. Accessed 2 Aug 2025

Financial Action Task Force (1992) Annual report 1991–1992. FATF, Paris. https://www.fatf-gafi.org/content/dam/fatf-gafi/annual-reports/1991%201992%20ENG.pdf. Accessed 25 July 2025

Financial Action Task Force (2002) Annual report (2001–2002). FATF, Paris, https://www.fatf-gafi.org/content/dam/fatf-gafi/annual-reports/2001%202002%20ENG.pdf. Accessed 25 July 2025

Financial Action Task Force (2003) The Forty Recommendations. FATF, Paris, https://www.fatf-gafi.org/content/dam/fatf-gafi/recommendations/FATF%20Recommendations%202003.pdf. Accessed 25 July 2025

Financial Action Task Force (2011) Anti-money laundering and terrorist financing measures and financial inclusion. FATF, Paris, https://www.sbs.gob.pe/Portals/5/jer/guiasinf_bp/files/020-AML-CFT%20and%20Financial%20Inclusion%20-%202011.pdf. Accessed 25 July 2025

Financial Action Task Force (2012) Ministers renew the mandate of the Financial Action Task Force until 2020: declaration of the ministers and representatives of the Financial Action Task Force. FATF, Paris. https://www.fatf-gafi.org/en/publications/Fatfgeneral/Ministersrenewthemandateofthefinancialactiontaskforceuntil2020.html. Accessed 25 July 2025

Financial Action Task Force (2012–2025) International standards on combating money laundering and the financing of terrorism & proliferation. FATF, Paris. https://www.fatf-gafi.org/en/publications/Fatfrecommendations/Fatf-recommendations.html. Accessed 25 July 2025

Financial Action Task Force (2013) FATF guidance: national money laundering and terrorist financing risk assessment. https://www.fatf-gafi.org/content/dam/fatf-gafi/reports/National_ML_TF_Risk_Assessment.pdf.coredownload.inline.pdf. Accessed 25 July 2025

Financial Action Task Force (2013–2023) Methodology for assessing compliance with the FATF recommendations and the effectiveness of AML/CFT systems. FATF, Paris. http://www.fatf-gafi.org/publications/mutualevaluations/documents/fatf-methodology.html. Accessed 25 July 2025

Financial Action Task Force (2014) FATF clarifies risk-based approach: case-by-case, not wholesale de-risking. FATF, Paris. https://www.fatf-gafi.org/en/publications/Fatfgeneral/Rba-and-de-risking.html. Accessed 25 July 2025

Financial Action Task Force (2015) Best practices: combating the abuse of non-profit organisations (Recommendation 8). FATF, Paris. https://www.fatf-gafi.org/content/dam/fatf-gafi/guidance/BPP-combating-abuse-non-profit-organisations.pdf. Accessed 25 July 2025

Financial Action Task Force (2016) Outcomes of the plenary meeting of the FATF, Busan Korea, 22–24 June 2016. FATF, Paris. https://www.fatf-gafi.org/en/publications/Fatfgeneral/Plenary-outcomes-june-2016.html. Accessed 25 July 2025

Financial Action Task Force (2019a) Anti-money laundering and counter-terrorist financing measures – People's Republic of China, fourth round mutual evaluation report. FATF, Paris. http://www.fatf-gafi.org/publications/mutualevaluations/documents/mer-china-2019.html. Accessed 25 July 2025

Financial Action Task Force (2019b) Mandate of the Financial Action Task Force. FATF, Paris, https://www.fatf-gafi.org/en/the-fatf/mandate-of-the-fatf.html. Accessed 25 July 2025

Financial Action Task Force (2020) Guidance on digital identity. FATF, Paris. https://www.fatf-gafi.org/publications/documents/digital-identity-guidance.html. Accessed 25 July 2025

Financial Action Task Force (2021) High-level synopsis of the stocktake of the unintended consequences of the FATF standards. FATF, Paris. https://www.fatf-gafi.org/content/dam/fatf-gafi/reports/Unintended-Consequences.pdf. Accessed 25 July 2025

Financial Action Task Force (2023) Best practices paper: combating the terrorist financing abuse of non-profit organisation. FATF, Paris. https://www.fatf-gafi.org/en/publications/Financialinclusionandnpoissues/Bpp-combating-abuse-npo.html. Accessed 25 July 2025

Financial Action Task Force (2024a) Objectives for the FATF during the Mexican presidency (2024–2026). FATF, Paris. https://www.fatf-gafi.org/en/the-fatf/fatf-presidency/Mexican-priorities-2024-2026.html. Accessed 25 July 2025

Financial Action Task Force (2024b) Money laundering national risk assessment guidance. FATF, Paris. https://www.fatf-gafi.org/en/publications/Methodsandtrends/Money-Laundering-National-Risk-AssessmentGuidance.html. Accessed 25 July 2025

Financial Action Task Force (2025a) Guidance on financial inclusion and anti-money laundering and terrorist financing measures. FATF, Paris. https://www.fatf-gafi.org/content/fatf-gafi/en/publications/Financialinclusionandnpoissues/guidancefinancial-inclusion-aml-tf-measures.html. Accessed 25 July 2025

Financial Action Task Force (2025b) Outcomes joint FATF-MONEYVAL Plenary, 12–13 June 2025. FATF, Paris. https://www.fatf-gafi.org/en/publications/Fatfgeneral/outcomes-FATF-MONEYVAL-plenary-june-2025.html. Accessed 25 July 2025

Financial Action Task Force (2025c) Explanatory note for revised R.16. FATF, Paris. https://www.fatf-gafi.org/content/dam/fatf-gafi/recommendations/Explanatory%20note%20for%20revised%20R.16.pdf.coredownload.pdf. Accessed 25 July 2025

Financial Action Task Force (2025d) Money laundering national risk assessment guidance (updated August 2025). FATF, Paris. https://www.fatf-gafi.org/content/dam/fatf-gafi/publications/Money%20Laundering%20National%20Risk%20Assessment%20Guidance.pdf.coredownload.inline.pdf. Accessed 10 October 2025

Financial Action Task Force on Money Laundering (1990) Report, FATF, Paris, https://www.fatf-gafi.org/content/dam/fatf-gafi/annual-reports/1990%20ENG.pdf. Accessed 25 July 2025

Financial Stability Board (2024) G20 roadmap for enhancing cross-border payments: consolidated progress report for 2024. https://www.fsb.org/2024/10/g20-roadmap-for-enhancing-cross-border-payments-consolidated-progress-report-for-2024/. Accessed 25 July 2025

G7 (1989) Economic declaration. https://g7g20-documents.org/database/document/1989-g7-france-leaders-leaders-language-economic-declaration. Accessed 25 July 2025

Global NPO Coalition on FATF (2023) FATF Plenary approves revision of Recommendation 8 and Best Practices Paper. https://fatfplatform.org/news/plenary-approves-revision-of-recommendation-8-and-new-best-practices. Accessed 25 July 2025

Goldbarsht D (2018) Shedding light on shadow banking: the money or value transfer service regime in Australia and its origins. J Crim Law 82(3):264–276

Goldbarsht D (2022) Global counter-terrorist financing and soft law: multi-lateral security governance. Edward Elgar, Cheltenham

Goldbarsht D, Harris H (2022) Check the balance: is the doctrine of separation of powers sufficient in the context of intergovernmental organisations? A case study of Australia's AML/CTF financing framework. Fed Law Rev 50(4):527–557. https://doi.org/10.1177/0067205X221126558

Goldbarsht D, De Koker L, Ferril J (2025) The illusory truth effect and financial integrity objectives and consequences. In: Goldbarsht D, De Koker L, Ferril J (eds) Combating financial crime: intended and unintended consequences. Springer, Cham

Hayes B (2012) Counter-terrorism, 'policy laundering' and the FATF: legalising surveillance, regulating civil society, Transnational Institute/Statewatch. https://www.statewatch.org/media/documents/analyses/no-171-fafp-report.pdf

Kerse M, Jeník I, De Koker L (2025) FATF supports inclusion with recent revisions. CGAP. https://www.cgap.org/blog/fatf-supports-inclusion-with-recent-revisions. Accessed 25 July 2025

Klapper L, Singer D, Starita L, Norris A (2025) The global findex database 2025: connectivity and financial inclusion in the digital economy. World Bank, Washington, DC. https://doi.org/10.1596/978-1-4648-2204-9. Accessed 25 July

Littrell C (2024) Economic and demographic biases in FATF mutual evaluation results. In: Goldbarsht D, de Koker L (eds) Financial crime and the law. Ius Gentium: comparative perspectives on law and justice, vol 115. Springer, Cham, pp 191–224. https://doi.org/10.1007/978-3-031-59543-1_8

Moiseienko A (2025) Doing business with criminals: between exclusion and surveillance. Cambridge University Press, Cambridge. https://doi.org/10.1017/9781009609845

Morris N, de Koker L (2025) The impact of the Financial Action Task Force (FATF) standards and focus: from effectiveness to effect. In: Goldbarsht D, de Koker L, Ferrill J (eds) The financial war on crime and terrorism: opportunities and challenges. Springer, Cham

Nel J (2025) Charities, non-profit organisation and the FATF: testing the evidence base and proportionality of risk-based counter-terrorist-financing regulation. In: Goldbarsht D, De Koker L, Ferril J (eds) Combating financial crime: intended and unintended consequences. Springer, Cham

Nguyen T (2023) The challenges of dark ships to the safety and security of commercial shipping and the way forward. Asia-Pac J Ocean Law Policy 8(2):310–328

Reuters (2025) EU considers adding Russia to money laundering 'grey' list (6 June). https://www.reuters.com/markets/emerging/eu-considers-adding-russia-money-laundering-grey-list-ft-reports-2025-06-06/. Accessed 25 July 2025

Steinberg RH (2002) In the shadow of law or power? Consensus-based bargaining and outcomes in the GATT/WTO. Int Organ 56(2):339–374

Sulayman Y (2025) Re-evaluating human rights in global counter-terrorism financing: a case for preliminary judicial moderation. In: Goldbarsht D, De Koker L, Ferril J (eds) Combating financial crime: intended and unintended consequences. Springer, Cham

World Bank Group (2025) Financial inclusion is a key enabler to reducing poverty and boosting prosperity. https://www.worldbank.org/en/topic/financialinclusion/overview. Accessed 25 July 2025

Louis de Koker is a professor of law at La Trobe Law School (Australia), an advisory board member of the Financial Integrity Hub (FIH) and an extraordinary professor in the Department of Commercial and Labour Law of the University of the Western Cape (South Africa). A significant part of his financial crime research focuses on managing the relationship between financial inclusion and anti-money laundering and counter terrorist financing objectives. He has undertaken various university research engagements with the bodies such as the World Bank and the Asian Development Bank and has worked closely with the World Bank-housed Consultative Group to Assist the Poor (CGAP). This work extended to a range of developing countries including Ghana, Indonesia, Kenya, Kyrgyzstan, Malaysia, Namibia, Nigeria, Uganda, the Ukraine and Palau. His research has been cited in publications and research papers of international bodies such as the World Bank, the IMF, the Basel Committee on Banking Supervision, and the International Labour Organization. Louis has held visiting positions at a range of institutions including the Institute for Advanced Legal Studies (London) SOAS (London); Wolfson College (Oxford), the University of Florida (US) and the Autonomous University of Barcelona.

Doron Goldbarsht LLB LLM (HUJI) PHD (UNSW) is an Associate Professor at Macquarie Law School, the Director of the Financial Integrity Hub (FIH) and the Academic Head of the Graduate Certificate in Financial Integrity Law. With over 20 years of expertise in anti-money laundering and counterterrorist financing, he has co-edited several books on financial crime and compliance, including Financial Crime and the Law: Identifying and Mitigating Risks (Springer 2024) and Financial Technology and the Law: Combating Financial Crime (Springer, 2022). Certified as a lawyer in both Israel and Australia, Doron also provides expert opinions to government and private sector in litigation, advising on financial crime and regulatory matters.

Dr Jamie Ferrill is a Senior Lecturer at the Australian Graduate School of Policing and Security, Charles Sturt University and a research fellow with the Financial Integrity Hub (FIH). Before transitioning to academia, she gained nearly a decade of experience in law enforcement, serving with the Canadian federal government. Jamie's research addresses threats to national and economic security, with a particular interest in the intersection of financial crime with border governance frameworks, international cooperation, and organizational effectiveness. Jamie has been a visiting fellow at the Academy of International Affairs NRW and the Border Policy Research Institute, and she is a fellow of the Financial Integrity Hub and the Institute of Intergovernmental Relations at Queen's University. Her latest book is titled Dirty Money: Financial Crime in Canada (McGill-Queen's University Press).

MIX
Papier aus verantwortungsvollen Quellen
Paper from responsible sources
FSC® C105338

If you have any concerns about our products,
you can contact us on
ProductSafety@springernature.com

In case Publisher is established outside the EU,
the EU authorized representative is:
Springer Nature Customer Service Center GmbH
Europaplatz 3, 69115 Heidelberg, Germany

Printed by Libri Plureos GmbH
in Hamburg, Germany